The Holy Trinity Decryption

The Hidden Autobiography of Sir Francis Bacon

Jacob Roberts

SLEWFOOT Publishing, January 2020

Acknowledgements

As with any book, there are several people who I need to thank who helped me complete this project. First among them is my wife Audrey. Without her patience, encouragement and (at times I'm sure feigned-) interest, I wouldn't have been able to put in the time to complete this book. I'm eternally grateful for having her in my life.

As you will see as you read this book, I need give a big thanks to my friend and fellow researcher Chris Donah. From the moment that I shared my initial discoveries with him, he provided unhesitating encouragement. He used my "character counts" to generate his own results using completely different methods that independently verified the messages of the cipher texts I discovered. He was also one of the Oak Island researchers who were studying the plaque of Shakespeare's Funerary Monument in Holy Trinity Church in Stratford-upon-Avon, along with Corjan Mol and Christopher Morford. Their work in this area drew my close attention to the plaque in the first place and motivated me to use a new approach.

Along those lines, I want to thank the same group of researchers - Chris Donah, Christopher Morford, Corjan Mol and Erin King Helton, for welcoming me into the fold. I'm honored to be sharing my ideas with people of your caliber.

Lastly, thanks to one of my editors who wishes to remain nameless, but cleverly wanted to rename me "Jacobus." Thanks!

.

Fig. 1 *Si tabula daretur digna animum mallem.* - "If one could but paint his mind."
- Nicholas Hilliard's inscription on portrait miniature of 18-year-old Francis Bacon.

To the Reader, Greeting.

What my Lord the Right Honourable Viscount St. Albans valued most, that he should be dear to seats of learning and to men of letters, that (I believe) he has secured; since these tokens of love and memorials of sorrow prove how much his loss grieves their heart. And indeed with no stinted hand have the Muses bestowed on him this emblem (for very many poems, and the best too, I withhold from publication); but since he himself delighted not in quantity, no great quantity have I put forth. Moreover let it suffice to have laid, as it were, these foundations in the name of the present age; this fabric (I think) every age will embellish and enlarge; but to what age it is given to put the last touch, that is known to God only and the fates.

W. Rawley, S.T.D., *Manes Verulamiani*

Introduction

    The contents of this book are controversial. Many of the messages that appear within the cipher texts appearing in these pages are not only unconventional in terms of accepted history, but some of them sound crazy. Many of them seem completely impossible, and completely unbelievable. All that can be said is, this whole experience has forced me to remove those two words from my vocabulary. As crazy as the messages appear, please suspend your disbelief until you have looked at the evidence in this book. In spite of the fact that some of them run contrary to accepted history, they actually make sense in multiple ways.

    I know that many people have aligned themselves within camps of theorists regarding the Shakespeare / Bacon conundrum, and the information here-in may resonate with a few of them, while others simply will reject it as it does not support their current views. A very few might praise my efforts, while in other circles I could be vilified. I go into this venture fully accepting all criticisms, especially those that are warranted.

    I never intended to find something this, large, for a lack of a better term. It seems just *too big* for a Hobbit living a quiet life in the Shire. Friends of mine who were involved in research for the hit *History Channel* television show *The Curse of Oak Island*, had begun to study the plaque of Shakespeare's Funerary Monument in Holy Trinity Church as a possible clue to the Oak Island mystery. Having recently taken-up steganography and cryptography as a hobby, I thought perhaps I could apply some of those techniques to the plaque to see if it could generate results. To my shock, it did indeed generate results.

    As I said, it seemed too big, too daunting, for an amateur researcher such as myself. I also understood that, if I were to truly dig into this puzzle, I would need to focus a great deal of time and attention to detail above and beyond what I'm accustomed. Enter Shakespeare's strumpet Fortune, in the form of the COVID pandemic of 2020. Suddenly, quarantined and working from home, I had the time to focus on the puzzle of the plaque. When I began to unravel its mystery, I realized the information was too important, regardless of any backlash, to keep to myself. So now what started as a mental exercise that I imagined would end in frustration and failure, has become this book.

    With most of the first draft already written, I sit here today writing this introduction and arranging my draft in a readable form, nearly 404 years to the day after the date that appears at the bottom right of the plaque itself,

April 23, 1616. This very date would be one of the keys to unraveling the encrypted message.

I attribute this puzzle as the main reason I was able to weather the unprecedented situation presented by the reaction to the COVID-19 virus. While I greatly appreciate the patience of my wife with my new-found obsession, and her smiles and nods of feigned interest in my announcements of each new discovery, I realize she's wise beyond her years. It kept me occupied and prevented me from driving her nuts during our whole sequestering experience.

So what *were* the discoveries? As I list them off, please understand I do so with a caveat - these were the messages I discovered, using standard decryption methods explained in later chapters. I make no claim that this is definitive proof of *anything*. I'm afraid that short of as-of-yet-undiscovered manuscripts in the handwriting of the individual named by the ciphers, with his explicit signature in his handwriting, clearly stating all of the messages in these ciphers, scholars will always cast doubt. My hope is to have contributed something new and unique in this field of research. Also, now that I've had time to digest the messages and see them repeated in other sources, I fully believe they are true and accurate. On with the claims.

First and foremost, the plaque contains not just a cipher, but *several* ciphers. Secondly, the ideas concerning the methodology of how to decode its messages proved true. They worked. Thirdly, and astonishingly, none other than Sir Francis Bacon not only took credit for the messages, he names himself a Brother of the Rosi Crosse, and also takes credit for the works of William Shakespeare. At one point, Bacon reveals the truth regarding the relationship between Elizabeth I, Edward deVere, and Robert Devereux, 2nd Earl of Essex. Lastly and most shockingly, he reveals the answer surrounding his own "royal birth." And it's not the answer any of us expected. It's actually an answer many are going to dislike.

One eminent researcher in this field, when one of my friends "floated the idea" of part of this discovery on an online social media group, responded with, "this easily can be dismissed." I hope that after careful review of this work, he at least acknowledges, even if he still dismisses the idea, that perhaps it can't be dismissed quite so *easily*.

One person in my circle stated that it was impossible that Bacon had done all of these things, and impossible to encode the message the way I claim. I told him that he had misspoken himself. What he really meant was, *he* never could have accomplished such a task (meaning my friend). I pointed out that *I* certainly couldn't have done it either. But of one thing I'm certain - Francis Bacon did accomplish such a thing. The plaque exists, and its messages can be deciphered and read.

I was a recent guest on a popular podcast, and fielded some excellent questions from the live audience. One of the best questions came from a young woman who asked, "were ciphers prevalently used during the time of Sir Francis Bacon?" The answer unequivocally is yes. The example I cited in my response was that of the execution of Mary, Queen of Scots. The evidence of her treason appeared in a cipher message she had sent to conspirators who planned to remove Elizabeth I from the throne of England and replace her with their Catholic Queen. The cipher was intercepted and decrypted by Francis Walsingham, and Mary's inferior cipher system sealed her fate (Singh 3).

Another viewer asked, "What was the point of Bacon going through all this effort if he was the only person who could decode it and read it? What was the point?" Though this is a circular question in that it contains the assumption that "he was the only one who could read it," the obvious answer is, he wasn't. In an interesting example related by the "Father of the NSA" William Friedman, he discusses an anecdote about a doctor who was a contemporary of Francis Bacon. The doctor used Bacon's Bi-literal Cipher in a drawing of a castle. The cipher appeared as shaded and unshaded stones, and the message stated:

> My business is to write prescriptions
> And then to see my doses taken;
> But now I find I spend my time
> Endeavoring to out-Bacon Bacon. (Fieldman 31)

So plainly others had the ability to use his cipher systems. As you'll see, he also left behind instructions to allow the truth to eventually come out.

In Manly Palmer Hall's magazine *Horizons*, the prolific writer, philosopher, lecturer, Rosicrucian adept and 33rd degree Mason has this to say:

> All ciphers are legible to those for whom they are intended but for the rest they are meaningless. Imagine a man placing in his writings a code to be discovered by persons unknown in some future age. This required a combination of elements. Certain traces must be left, as it were, a tail hanging out, to stimulate curiosity. On the other hand, this curiosity must not lead to an easy discovery, for like all human inquiry, it must be perfected by diligence. Clues must lead to other clues and especially there must be blind clues, leads that lead to nowhere. Still, there needs to be hope or the decipherer becomes discouraged. There must also be quality to the message by which the mind, having solved part, would proceed with the rest. How should such a method be devised? To a man of Bacon's mind the answer is obvious – copy nature. Nature itself is a mass of clues, indications, and

intimations leading through long and devious complications to the light of truth. If a cipher is set up, patterned upon natural law, whoever solves the cipher solves the mystery of his own existence; one is the symbol of the other. The cipher is Bacon's method, the missing key to his reformation of the world.

I do not mean that the cipher conceals the secret; rather the cipher itself is the secret. It shows how nature unfolds toward cause, and how the arts and sciences are in fact themselves ciphers concealing a hidden meaning under circumstances and appearances.

The key to the cipher is therefore the inductive method by which all riddles in nature may be resolved. Bacon wrote the key in his epitaph, "Let all compounds be dissolved." The cipher is the compound; the master key to a master mind. The true reading of the hidden message depends upon a patient weighing of evidence and a constant elimination of long treasured nonessentials. The end of the code is the knowledge of hidden causes. It is a larger riddle concealed in a smaller one. All answers when discovered become insufficient and demand larger answers. Even when the mind reaches Bacon himself, the end is not attained. Bacon is chancellor of Parnassus, a High Priest in the Temple of the Muses, but behind him is the greater universal pattern represented by the god Apollo, the principle of light. (Hall 47)

Unfortunately, I found this article after I had completed my first round of decryptions. The passage perfectly describes the experience throughout the whole process of discovery. My assumption that deciphering the messages required Bacon's favored inductive reasoning was a fortuitous one – I got lucky. And when Hall states that "even when the mind reaches Bacon himself, the end is not attained," he isn't kidding.

The messages within the cipher texts encrypted within the plaque of Shakespeare's Funerary Monument have led me to Renaissance maps, astronomers, and the writings announcing the presence of the Order of the Rosy Cross. The rabbit hole leads, in twists and turns, to some of the most famous names in history, revealing royal secrets that could have destroyed monarchies. It's led to the unraveling of the secrets of some of Bacon's shocking aliases and pseudonyms.

Orthodox history states that Sir Francis Bacon was the youngest son of Sir Nicholas Bacon, Lord Keeper of the Great Seal for Queen Elizabeth I.

Accordingly, his mother Lady Ann Bacon was a close confidant and friend of the queen as well. Francis was raised and educated by Ann with his older brother Anthony. He went to college at an early age, studied law, and when he was 16 he was sent to France by the queen herself as a part of the entourage of Ambassador Sir Amias Paulet. He returned to England in February when Sir Nicholas Bacon died, and strangely, Francis was left out of his will. The story then goes that Francis takes up residence at Gray's Inn to practice law, and in the meantime tries to appeal to the queen through his maternal uncle for a better station, appeals that appear to go unfulfilled.

Again, the exoteric story of Francis Bacon states that he sat for seats of parliament at different times, but never advanced under the reign of Queen Elizabeth I. He advised her on occasion, and in the aftermath of the Essex Rebellion, she order Francis to lead the prosecution. After the succession of James VI to the throne as James I, Bacon is knighted, and serves as Attorney General and High Lord Chancellor. At one point, Francis ruled as Regent in James' absence for a month. His career ended with "his fall from grace" when his enemies charged him with accepting bribes, so he stepped down, pursued science and writing until his death in April of 1626.

Those are the "facts" of the known history of Sir Francis Bacon. As you'll see, there is far more to the man than what we think we know. As for another spoiler, just as many researchers have often suspected, Sir Francis Bacon did not die in 1626.

His seemingly ignored petitions to Elizabeth I, along with veiled references to Bacon's secret royal birth, gave rise to what is known as "the Prince Tudor Theory." As one of the main theories of the alternative authorship of Shakespeare's works, it states that Francis Bacon was the secret child of Queen Elizabeth, and he wrote the works attributed to William Shakespeare. Alternatively, the "Oxfordian Theory" of authorship makes the same claim regarding Edward deVere, 17th Earl of Oxford. Other candidates for authorship include Robert Devereux, 2nd Earl of Essex and Sir Philip Sidney. As you're going to see, according to the cipher texts these theories "all got it wrong," but they didn't "get it all wrong."

With a build-up like that, I believe the procedures used, the messages found, and the way in which the messages have revealed themselves, will satisfy you as a reader, and will hold up under scrutiny. I'm sure I've made errors. But I hope that a typo, an addition error or misplaced letter won't be enough to cause the reader to dismiss the whole of the messages.

When I stated earlier that I accepted all criticisms, I meant it. I've included full descriptions of the methods I used specifically to that end - so my work can be verified or repudiated. Perhaps it can be expanded and extended. I know that some people, making such a discovery might be unwilling to share not only their methods, but also the discovery itself. I understand this feeling all too well. After completing all of this work with such a level of difficulty, there could be a tendency to want to keep it to oneself instead of sharing it. "After all,' the thought might go, "if others want to know what the message is, they should have to find it themselves the way I did. Why do all of the work for them?"

The answer is simple - this information is so important, it shouldn't be kept secret. While we're on the topic of secrecy, it's very important to state the following in response to another question I've received: Since I was able to decrypt this message from the plaque of Shakespeare's Memorial in Trinity Church at Stratford-upon-Avon, and I'm an amateur, then how am I possibly the first person to do it?

I'm not.

Others certainly have done so, and probably in a better form than what you are about to read. Afterall, a long history of "Bacon as Shakespeare" researchers precedes me. Doing a quick internet search, anyone can find a list of names of researchers who have also found evidence supporting the theory, such as James Wilmot, William Henry Smith, Constance Mary Fearon Pott, and of course Ignatius Donnelly. But when it comes to this specific plaque, I'm certain others have followed the same or similar (more precise) methods and read the same messages. However, they obviously felt they couldn't openly divulge the information. A clue of why, appears in Manly P. Hall's *The Secret Teachings of All Ages*, in a section about the Bacon / Shakespeare question:

> For some reason not apparent to the uninitiated there has been a continued and consistent effort to prevent the unraveling of the Baconian skein. Whatever the power may be which continually blocks the efforts of the investigators, it is as unremitting now as it was immediately following Bacon's death, and those attempting to solve the enigma still feel the weight of its resentment...
>
> The forging of Shakspere's handwriting; the foisting of fraudulent portraits and death masks upon a gullible public; the fabrication of spurious biographies; the mutilation of books and documents; the destruction or rendering illegible of tablets and inscriptions containing cryptographic messages, have all compounded the difficulties attendant upon the solution of the Bacon-Shakespeare-Rosicrucian riddle. (Hall 550)

Hall also makes a point to state that the reason for the centuries of secrecy surrounding this topic is not "apparent to the uninitiated." This indicates that

6

those who are "initiated" may be aware why this veil of secrecy exists. This is not to say that this is the result of some conspiracy among members of a secret society. That is not what is meant at all. What this means is, I'm not the first person to discover this cipher encrypted within the plaque of Shakespeare's Memorial at Trinity Church at Stratford upon Avon. I'm certain many have decrypted it before me. I just think they may have believed that they were under certain obligations to their brethren to keep this as a protected secret. Additionally, there is a passage in the publications of the Rosy Cross that if anyone were to learn their secrets, that they were to not reveal them to others, but to express them in their art, literature or music in a veiled form.

Multiple examples appear in literature, such as works by Alexander Dumas, Sir Walter Scott, Samuel Clemens, and Edgar Allen Poe. Examples appear in the artwork of Nicholas Poussin, and they all reveal hints and themes alluding to these secrets about Francis Bacon. There seems to be a tradition and belief that this truth needs to be kept secret.

I question such a belief and respectfully disagree. This information and these secrets that glorify Sir Francis Bacon are not secrets that anyone should be obliged to keep quiet in this modern age. If anything, it's important to venerate this genius and shaper of the modern world. In addition, I'm under no obligations to anyone other than the assertion from Mr. William Rawley in his collection of "eulogies" of Bacon, *Manes Verulamiani*, that someone in some future time would continue to reveal Bacon's true achievements when he states, "Moreover, let it suffice to have laid, as it were, these foundations in the name of the present age; this fabric (I think) every age will embellish and enlarge; but to what age it is given to put the last touch, that is known to God only and the fates."

Since the verses, or "eulogies," of *Manes Verulamiani* continuously hint and joke about Bacon's writings and how he was "greater than the nine muses," they lay plenty of foundation regarding Bacon's true accomplishments. Additionally, verse IX, titled "A Threnody of the Death of the Most Illustrious and Renowned Personage, Sir Francis Bacon, Baron Verulam," refers to him as "the precious gem of concealed literature."

This term "concealed literature" describes exactly what we have here - a message concealed within another piece of writing, as well as Bacon concealed as the true writer behind the name of Shakespeare. This term is also the meaning of "occult literature," which most people misinterpret as "books about magic" or "alchemy." While such concealed literature does exist about these topics, I'm focused here on the plaque and related areas. Combining all of the work already done on Bacon and Shakespeare, the "foundation" laid by the contributors of verses to *Manes Verulamiani*, and this work, I hope to "embellish and enlarge this fabric" here in this modern age.

In this spirit, I'm sharing with everyone not only the messages encrypted within the plaque, but also the methods used to uncover them. In this way, others can do the same, improve upon the methods, and hopefully correct any errors, extending our knowledge.

The time has come to shed light on this topic. This book is not intended to be any kind of definitive treatise on this "riddle." But I hope it will be a beginning, a starting point, beyond those who have attempted the same, but were unclear regarding their methods.

Any critics who read this book, might point out that I am ill-equipped to accomplish this task. And they are correct.

I do not nor have I ever belonged to any fraternities or secret societies where I could have learned these cipher systems at work here on the plaque. I do not have a command of multiple languages that I have found encrypted within it, but it's obvious to everyone that the person who created it, Sir Francis Bacon, certainly did have such knowledge. Some of the ciphers remain unsolved even at this time, as I would need to have enough of a command of Latin, Greek and Hebrew to pick out more than what I've been able to identify.

Again, because of this I am publishing not only everything I have found, but also the methodology used in making the discovery. I encourage anyone who wishes to replicate the process to check my accuracy, to do so. I encourage anyone with a background in Latin, Greek, Hebrew, or any other languages used by the designer of the plaque, to pour over the results to see if they can identify any other words or phrases that remain hidden to me. Also, each "key" or cipher text contains more than one message beyond what I've presented. There is still much to discover.

Hopefully, I will succeed in clearly and concisely explaining the process I used, and the messages it yielded.

A word on the genius of Sir Francis Bacon. The complexity in planning and executing the cipher on the plaque boggled my mind when I stumbled over the first discoveries. Now that I've neared the completion of my work, baffled or boggled doesn't begin to explain what I think of all of this. Researchers today refer to Bacon as a true polymath, but that term neither embodies an idea to describe him, nor the true depth and breadth of his mind. Others described him as the "Hercules of Philosophy," and the writers of the verses compiled in *Manes Verulamiani* referred to him as a "demi-god." I used to view such high praise as hyperbole. Now, I'm not so sure. At any rate, he was an intellectual giant beyond comparison.

Lastly, I've been an English teacher for 30 years, so I know all too well the blasphemy I'm committing by taking a side on a debate that has covered centuries. But the truth will be brought to the light, in the manner the spear-shaking Greek gods (AA) intended.

Not Entombed, but Encrypted

My career as an English teacher has not only involved the close study of the works of William Shakespeare, but also led to my primary area of research, symbolism. This led me to emblems and symbols of Freemasonry and the Fraternity of the Rosy Crosse, and to the works of Manly Palmer Hall and Paul Foster Case. And now, my attempts at decryption and steganography have led me to tackle the inscribed plaque on Shakespeare's Funerary Monument in Trinity Church at Stratford-upon-Avon. If you're bothering to read this book then you may already be familiar with the plaque. However, if we're going to analyze it, we need to first deal with the surface text of the verse itself, and its features indicating that a cipher exists.

Looking at the physical characters on it made it obvious that we were dealing with a transposition cipher (with a combination of literal and numerical ciphers) for reasons I'll explain later. But the surface text, states:

IVDICIO PYLIVM, GENIO SOCRATEM, ARTE MARONEM, TERRA TEGIT, POPVLVS MÆRET, OLYMPVS HABET

STAY PASSENGER, WHY GOEST THOV BY SO FAST,
READ IF THOV CANST, WHOM ENVIOVS DEATH HATH PLAST
  WITH IN THIS MONVMENT SHAKSPEARE: WITH WHOME,
  QVICK NATVRE DIDE: WHOSE NAME, DOTH DECK Y^S TOMBE,
  FAR MORE, THEN COST: SIEH ALL, Y^T HE HATH WRITT,
LEAVES LIVING ART, BVT PAGE, TO SERVE HIS WITT.
        OBIIT AÑO DO^I 1616
        ÆTATIS · 53 DIE 23 AP^R.

First of all, we need to understand this message as it appears. Much has been said and written regarding the monument as a whole, and many have commented upon the (forgive the pun) cryptic nature of this message. But if we understand what it says, we'll quickly realize that this plaque seems to be naming someone other than William Shakespeare. It does contain the name of the actor "Shakspere" to whom people have attributed the plays and poems of William Shakespeare.

The first two lines in Latin venerates him as having the judgment of King Pylius, the genius of Socrates, and the art of the poet Virgil, whose last name was Maro. I've always found this to be odd, as the comparison to another poet like Virgil makes sense, but why a famous king / judge / advisor, and the father of philosophy? By the end of this process, I understood clearly why this would be: these attributions make far more sense when we consider they actually refer to Sir Francis Bacon. Lawyer / judge / advisor, philosopher / father of the scientific method, and writer, they all fit. They fit even better when we consider the theory that Bacon was responsible for the creation of the works attributed to Shakespeare. And yes, the encrypted message on the plaque repeatedly makes that astounding statement.

The second line in Latin has been translated as "the earth buries him, the people mourn him, Olympus possesses him," stating he belongs on Mount Olympus as one of the Greek gods. Since Bacon has been called "the Hercules of Philosophy" and was referred to as a "Demi-god," this would also make sense.

The first words of the third line begins with "Stay passenger, why goest by so fast?" It's been said that this is referring to anyone "passing by" as "passenger." I disagree. I've noted a similar phrase in a completely different place, unassociated with William Shakespeare in any traditional sense. It appeared in a eulogy verse for Sir Francis Bacon, in the collection published by William Rawley as *Manes Verulamiani*, numbered as "VII," in which one of the writers states to Bacon "but your fame adheres not to sculptured columns, nor is read on the tomb (with) "Stay, traveller, your steps"..."

I believe that both of these examples refer directly to the members of the Rosicrucians and similar orders. It's well-known that Francis Bacon used the ship The Argo, and its sailors the Argonauts, as a symbol for the Rosicrucians as searchers for knowledge and truth, their version of the Golden Fleece. Referring to them as "passengers" or "travelers" seems appropriate. At any rate, anyone passing in front of the plaque is not only admonished to "stay," but the next line urges a challenge, "Read if thou canst."

This is the next clue indicating that the plaque contains a code encrypted within the text itself, and that cipher contains the name of the person commemorated by this monument, or as it states, "whom envious death hast placed within this monument Shakspeare." And again, we need to look at what this line actually states - it explicitly states that Shakspeare *IS* the monument. This is why the colon appears *after* the name - if it were trying to imply that Shakspeare was *in* the monument, the colon would appear between the words "monument" and "Shakspeare." So the message becomes, if we can, we need to read *whose* name appears in this "monument Shakspeare."

The next clue would be the strange spellings and characters. Characters are conjoined or ligatured in one area, yet not in another, etc. But a couple of features are immediately noticeable as mentioned earlier, which is the spelling of both "writ" and "wit" are both spelled with two T's, or what could be called a "double Tau." The letters are the initials of the number Thirty Three, which is the cipher signature for "Bacon" in Simple Cipher. (I go into such cipher signatures in detail in the next chapter). This is used as a signal to the members of Bacon's group, as the Triple Tau is also a symbol of Francis Bacon, the Brothers of the Rosi Crosse and Freemasons. Some argue that the people who composed the message had an imperfect understanding of usage and punctuation, or that the rules had not been fully developed during that time period. This is mostly untrue. The person who appears to be the creator and planner of this plaque, Sir Francis Bacon, not only had a masterful command of multiple languages, it's been argued that he was responsible (as Shakespeare) for the creation of modern English itself.

The rest of the poem is awkwardly phrased, which is also a clue to the presence of a Baconian, alphanumeric or transposition cipher. For the cipher to work, the number of characters needs to be precise, and the correct characters need to appear in the perfect order in the correct positions on the plaque. An algorithmic key needs to be used to count the characters and rearrange them. Logically, this explains the purpose of the odd spellings, awkward phrasing and especially the conjoined letters as they are intended to be counted as one character and moved together. All of these things are necessary for the message to be properly decrypted.

Additionally, the plaque refers to the monument as a "TOMBE," which it obviously is not. Most historians interpret this to mean that the monument was originally intended as a tomb. Again, I respectfully disagree. This error is again, a purposeful clue as to the nature of the plaque itself. Ciphers, codes and steganography use errors as clues and often use word play. Another word for "tomb" is "crypt." So, instead of someone's body being entombed, someone's name has been *encrypted*.

Lastly, it concludes with the date of Shakespere's death and his age, April 23, 1616, age 53. While conventional scholars might howl in disagreement, his age is wrong. Scholars agree that the actor was actually 52 when he died. Because of this discrepancy, they have interpreted this to mean that he "was in his 53rd year of age." This type of "mistake" however is common in steganographic messages, and as you'll see, necessary. Additionally, it's no less important that the number 53 previously has been noted by researchers as a link between Bacon and Shakespeare. A clue I've discovered explains one meaning of this enigmatic number as "the source of Bacon," as the Simple and Kaye Cipher value of the word "sow." An additional meaning will be explained in its proper place as it would spoil the coming discoveries.

Therefore, this obvious "mistake" is not only another clue that a cipher exists, but an indication of the nature of the cipher itself. When studying steganography and ciphers, the code maker usually will make some type of glaring error that will be obvious to anyone else who understands such signposts - a wrongly numbered page in a Folio or manuscript (ending in 53) for example, or misspellings and punctuation errors. In this case, the wrong age. It also plays the dual role of later providing a needed "3" in a specific position, where a "2" would not work. While "Aetatis" can *also* mean "at the stage of life," disagreeing about this detail as its conventionally interpreted is of the least concern. Considering the claims to come, it's a small matter really.

When deciding to see if the cipher of the plaque of Shakespeare's monument could be cracked, I honestly didn't expect to find this information. If anything, I thought I would find at best a phonetically spelled bawdy joke, or worse, gibberish, or at worst, a cipher that I wouldn't be able to understand.

Inspired and encouraged by some of my friends who were attempting to identify clues to help them in their own research, I dove in. As mentioned, they were attempting to find a connection to the "Oak Island mystery," as they had both appeared on the hit television series *The Curse of Oak Island*. Many of the researchers associated with the show have long suspected a Shakespearian and/or a Baconian connection. Since I had just begun to attempt to teach myself to decipher cryptic works using steganographic methods to find if hidden messages truly existed in such places, I decided to just give it a try. Nothing really could have prepared me for the result. With few expectations for success, I certainly didn't expect this much success.

Although multiple cipher signatures of Sir Francis Bacon appear within the text of the inscribed plaque of Shakespeare's Funerary Monument in Trinity Church at Stratford-upon-Avon, to immediately say that this means that Bacon wrote all of Shakespeare's works is a bit of a leap *over* logic. However, he not only leaves his signature on the plaque in *multiple ways*, in the cipher he claims to have used the name of Shakespeare. Together with several references from his peers in Rawley's publication of *Manes Verulamiani*, it all suggests that he was the main writer of the works attributed to William Shakespeare.

Much has been written about the ciphers and examples of Bacon's name appearing throughout the First Folio, so there isn't a need to review them here. Instead, this story began with the aforementioned-pamphlet called *Manes Verulamiani*, by Sir William Rawley. In this booklet whose title means "Shades (Ghosts) of Verulam," Sir Francis Bacon's contemporary men of letters eulogized their fallen friend.

Honestly, I would hardly call them eulogies. Full of high praise, backhanded compliments and outright insults, (including multiple not-so-veiled references to his poetry, plays, musicianship and Royal pedigree), the entirety reads like the period's version of a celebrity roast! If one imagines them actually reading aloud with him present, or as I imagine it happened, he sitting and reading it on holiday in the colonies, the result is hilarious. Reading it, I couldn't help thinking that it not only added evidence to his responsibility for Shakespeare's works and that his contemporaries knew it, but also to the theory that others have proposed: he had experienced what is called a "philosophical death." In other words, the he "retired" the identity of Sir Francis Bacon, and went on to live elsewhere under a different name. As mentioned, many others have also speculated he lived out the rest of his life in the colonies that he had helped to create. The cipher messages confirm this was the case.

While evidence of these latter theories appears encoded within the plaque, they also provide interesting background information and some context for what follows.

Also, a few words about the type of ciphers employed on the plaque. The discerning reader will need to understand the nature of codes, ciphers and steganography in general, as well as how a combination of all these things plays a role in the hidden messages of the plaque on Shakespeare's Funerary Monument.

Though today most people assume that steganography refers to data hidden within digital images or video, the concept is actually quite old. Based upon the Greek words "steganos" meaning concealed, and "-graphia" meaning writing, the art of concealing messages is an ancient one. The trick is to hide a message in such a way that the average passerby doesn't know it exists. The average person looks at the message and they see a painting, a personal letter, book, play script, or in this case, a verse on a plaque.

In terms of hidden messages, Bacon took an interest in steganography at an early age as a superior method to substitution ciphers, in that anyone who looks at a substitution cipher can tell that it contains a hidden message. Steganography appears as a "normal" message requiring a close examination and study of the image or text to discover what is secretly written.

The messages hidden within the text of the plaque on Shakespeare's Funerary Monument were encrypted by Francis Bacon. As you will see, he signed his work. Multiple times. There can be no question that he was responsible for it, and he unequivocally wanted everyone looking for his message to understand that.

The message encoded or enciphered in the plaque makes use of multiple forms of cryptography which is why I use both terms, encoded and enciphered. We often use these words interchangeably, though they do have slightly different meanings.

While Bacon used steganography to hide the existence of a message, he also used cryptography to hide the meaning of the message. When a steganographic message exists in a text, the person leaving the message will leave clues in the forms of purposeful "mistakes" as I stated earlier. It bears repeating. Most people view these as spelling errors, typos, or random marks. These are usually signs that will lead to the "key" that unlocks the code which is exactly the way it works on the plaque.

In an online interview, one viewer asked me if ciphers were used in Bacon's time, or if it was a common thing back then. The answer is a resounding yes. In my answer, I cited one of the most famous examples from his own time. The execution of Mary Queen of Scots resulted directly from the decryption of a cipher intercepted by Queen Elizabeth I's chief code breaker. As Bacon was a spymaster himself, he is known to have used multiple forms of cipher systems.

Bacon used (now known) ciphers in his encryption scheme, namely his Biliteral Cipher, Simple Cipher, Reverse Cipher and Kaye Cipher, which are explained in detail in the coming chapters. He also used a substitution cipher between the Simple and Reverse ciphers (an Atbash Cipher), and made use of phonetic messages, acrostics, anagrams and acrostic anagrams in English, Latin and Hebrew. I was able to use techniques I had only read about in Manly P. Hall's *The Secret Teachings of All Ages* in order to unlock the messages.

My curiosity was piqued as I read the chapters regarding Rosicrucianism, chapter "XXXVIII Bacon, Shakspere, and the Rosicrucians," and chapter "XXXIX The Crytogram as a Factor in Symbolic Philosophy." After a brief mention of the "Athbash Cipher" as a substitution cipher (this will be explained at a later time), he discusses "numerical ciphers" and states:

> Authors sometimes based their cryptograms upon the numerical value of their own names; for example, Sir Francis Bacon repeatedly used the cryptic number 33 – the numerical equivalent of his name. Numerical ciphers often involve the pagination of a book. Imperfect pagination, though generally attributed to carelessness, often conceals important secrets. The mispaginations found in the 1623 Folio of "Shakspeare" and the consistent recurrence of similar errors in various volumes printed about the same period have occasioned considerable thought among scholars and cryptogrammatists. In Baconian cryptograms, all page numbers ending in 89 seem to have a special significance... Several volumes published by Bacon show similar errors, page 89 being often involved.
>
> There are also numerical ciphers from which the cryptic message may be extracted by counting every tenth word, every twentieth word, or every fiftieth word. In some cases the count is irregular. The first important word may be found by counting 100, the second by counting 90, the third by counting 80, and so on until the count of 10 is reached.

The count then returns to 100 and the process is repeated.
(Hall 561 – 562)

The idea of using an algorithmic key to decipher messages and using presumed "errors" as clues seemed to apply here for reasons already discussed and will become clearer.

As implied earlier, Bacon left the "keys" that unlock the message right on the plaque itself, and one of them appears as a "mistake."

When I talk about this project, one of the questions I hear most often is, "why? Why would he (or anyone) go through all of that effort to hide a message? And why leave the keys that unravel it in plain sight?" These are excellent questions.

After you read this book, I hope you will agree with my belief that he wanted the truth to be protected and preserved until such a time that it would be safe to reveal it. He desired to preserve the story of his life so that others would know at some future date, who Francis Bacon really was, and everything he had accomplished and created. He left the keys there so eventually these secrets would be unlocked, and the truth would be told. In his day and in the centuries after his death, the secret would have challenged and upset the social order of Europe.

Lastly, though details regarding the processes used to decrypt the cipher appear in the next chapter, a few general statements about this process as a whole need to be made. The first thing needing mention is, this process was a major learning curve. Also, it wasn't until most of the transpositions of the "Keys" had been completed, that I understood how to truly decrypt them. That was when I discovered each Key contains multiple messages. While learning the deciphering process through my understanding of Bacon's cipher systems, plenty of trial and error was required. A message "not tying out" using the "cipher signature checking system" I found, required starting all over again at the beginning. If I tried to make assumptions regarding what the message was "going to be," I was wrong. I would then start over and by just following the process, a completely unexpected, but contextually consistent, message would appear, fleshing out the story in more detail.

While I used tried-and-true decoding / deciphering methods, because they involve the use of anagrams, some will want to argue that letters were subjectively selected. Charges of subjectivity are always the case with anagrams, and you will see I followed a standard procedure to maintain as much objectivity as possible. Believe me, if I could have avoided their use, I would have done so. However, I couldn't ignore what kept appearing. Through more research, I later learned that transposition ciphers are well-known to produce "acrostic anagrams" of the type produced by the plaque. So, I followed the clues and the messages where they led me. By developing a standard operating procedure, this was objectively accomplished. While the first two keys were a true learning experience, it wasn't until I unlocked what I call Key 38 or the Double Tau Key, that I began to understand how the cipher system really worked. I think that this progression was intended by Bacon, and also comes through in the narrative.

Lastly, remember each section or "key" permutation actually contains at least two (overlapping) messages, beneath and beyond the surface acrostic and phonetic messages. *Yes, it really is THAT complex.* Only by continuing this work and using these methods, can we fully decode the entire messages. Perhaps you can take this work using the following techniques, and implementing your own ideas, see if you can detect additional messages, and add to the fabric of our understanding of this fascinating character of Sir Francis Bacon.

- Jake Roberts

Chapter 1 - Overview, Process and Order of Discoveries

Before jumping into the bulk of the encoded messages, it's important to cover a brief overview of the actual processes used to decrypt the ciphers. In case the reader is unfamiliar with the numerical ciphers that Bacon used in his works, the following information will be invaluable in understanding the process and the logic employed in unraveling these secrets.

While performing spy craft for Queen Elizabeth I, Bacon employed a number of ciphers and his most famous one, the Biliteral Cipher, he created as a teenager. A forerunner of binary code used by computers today, it's one of the most well-known cipher systems. The short version of the explanation - he believed the best way to keep a code hidden was to make it appear as if it didn't exist, by embedding the message within a mundane letter, essay (or even a play). He would use two subtly different fonts or type-faces. The letters were placed in groups of five characters, and the combinations of the two different fonts within each group of five would indicate the actual letter of the cipher message. People who understood that the code was based upon two subtly different fonts within the piece of writing would use the key to transpose the real message.

The bulk of this writing does not concern the Biliteral Cipher. Attempting to identify subtle differences in the characters as they appear on the plaque at first seemed impossible. The apparent complexity of the fonts used in the surface message make such a deciphering seem completely implausible. However, after nearly completing this work of unraveling the other codes, I realized that the solution must be far simpler than it appears. As it turns out, it actually was simpler. A biliteral interpretation of the plaque appears in the following chapter. Though it was the last one discovered and unraveled, it's presented first among my findings, since in comparison to the other messages, the contents of the Biliteral Cipher though interesting, are relatively unremarkable. (Considering the complexity of the typeface, I have to entertain the possibility that it contains more than one Biliteral Cipher, separate from the one I uncovered). The bulk of the messages however appear in the transposition ciphers. These other cipher texts appear in Bacon's form of gematria, assigning numbers to the letters of the alphabet in the same manner the Cabbalists would do with the Hebrew alphabet.

Bacon used and/or created three such alphanumeric ciphers of this type called the Simple Cipher, the Reverse Cipher and the Kaye Cipher. (Two others, Elizabethan Short Cipher and Fourfold Cipher are not discussed in this work). The Simple Cipher assigned number 1 to A, 2 to B, and so on to 24 and Z. The Reverse Cipher is the same, only in reverse order (it's not just a clever name) - 24=A and 1=Z. In Kaye Cipher, the numbering system begins with the letter K at 10, continues to Z as 24 just like Simple Cipher, includes ampersand (&) as 25 and "et" as 26, and continues with A as 27 until we reach "I" at 35. Also, unlike our modern English alphabet with its 26 letters, the Elizabethan English alphabet had only 24, with "I" being used as "J" and "V" in place of "U." These tables 1-1, 1-2. and 1-3, illustrate the numerical values of the alphabet in these three systems:

Simple Cipher Table 1-1

A	B	C	D	E	F	G	H	I	K	L	M
1	2	3	4	5	6	7	8	9	10	11	12
N	O	P	Q	R	S	T	V	W	X	Y	Z
13	14	15	16	17	18	19	20	21	22	23	24

Reverse Cipher Table 1-2

A	B	C	D	E	F	G	H	I	K	L	M
24	23	22	21	20	19	18	17	16	15	14	13
N	O	P	Q	R	S	T	V	W	X	Y	Z
12	11	10	9	8	7	6	5	4	3	2	1

Kaye Cipher Table 1-3

A	B	C	D	E	F	G	H	I	K	L	M
27	28	29	30	31	32	33	34	35	10	11	12
N	O	P	Q	R	S	T	V	W	X	Y	Z

13	14	15	16	17	18	19	20	21	22	23	24

One of the features of these ciphers allows people to represent words or names as numbers, known as "cipher signatures." For example, by adding the values of each letter of Francis Bacon in the Simple Cipher, his name equals 100. Francis = 67, and Bacon = 33 (a two to one, or octave relationship). There are plenty of sources of lists of Francis Bacon's cipher signatures, along with that of The Rosicrucian Order. Though the messages I deciphered indicate additional examples, Table 1-4 shows common numerical signatures that appear:

Cipher Signature Table 1-4

Name	Simple	Reverse	Kaye
Shakespeare	103	172	259
Francis	67	108	171
Bacon	33	92	111
Francis Bacon	100	200	282
Fra Rosi Crosse	157	168	287

And so, these numbers become significant when they appear in a manner that is obvious and intentional as a cipher signature. The symbolic nature of the context where they're found makes them unmistakable. Context is everything, otherwise it can be written off as coincidence. Additionally, you'll see signatures can appear in other forms.

This numerical substitution system is the "language" of these ciphers. One way it's used, is to provide a "key" to the transposition, producing a number to create an algorithm to rearrange the letters in such a way that it reveals a part (or all) of the underlying message. This happens when a word is "highlighted" or "pointed out" within the language of a text, or a group of characters is likewise "singled out." By calculating the values of such words by adding the values of the letters in them, we can discover the "key" being used that can algorithmically unlock the cipher text. Lastly, one element of the cipher system at work on the plaque was not revealed until much later in the process.

I learned how these three cipher systems *work together*. Most of the research others have done regarding Bacon's Ciphers, only identifies cipher signatures using each cipher individually, and that's that. But they were intended to be used together in a much more complex cipher system. We know that using the Simple Cipher with a group of letters can produce a cipher signature that has a meaning in Reverse or Kaye. Reverse or Kaye Ciphers can produce signatures from Simple, etc. However, this is not the only way they are used in conjunction with one another.

Another substitution cipher possibility happens through the uses of these alphanumeric ciphers, as a form of an *Athbash Cipher*. Letters in Simple Cipher can be substituted for their numerical counterparts in Reverse Cipher, and vice versa. A "Y" equals 22 in Simple Cipher and can become a "B" because "B" holds that value in Reverse Cipher. Likewise, an "I" can become a "Q," an "L" can become "O" and an "N" becomes "M" and so on. Though it complicates the deciphering process, it became obvious that this method provided the creator of the cipher with greater flexibility while encoding his message. Though this may sound incredible, you'll see for yourself - this method consistently produced results that were recurrent and contextual. Additionally, it wasn't until later I discovered the precedent for such a substitution system among the Talmudists, the Jewish scholars studying Kabbalah, upon which the Rosicrucians based much of their symbolism and work.

In a publication by the National Security Agency (NSA) called *Sources in Cryptologie History Number 3,* titled "The Friedman Legacy: A Tribute to William and Elizabeth Friedman," several lectures from William Friedman (the father of the NSA) discuss the history of codes and ciphers. Friedman was also associated for a time with the Riverbank Laboratories, a research group who investigated secret messages Francis Bacon encrypted in various texts. As such, references to Francis Bacon abound in this publication of his lectures. However in this section, Friedman discusses the Athbash Cipher and the mystery of the name "Sheshakh" in the Bible. He states:

> But then it was discovered that if you write the twenty two letters of the Hebrew alphabet in two rows, - eleven in one row and eleven in another, [as in figure 11], you set up a substitution alphabet whereby you can replace letters by those standing opposite them. For example, "shin" is represented by "beth" or vice versa, so that "Sheshakh" translates "Babel," which is the old name of Babylon. (Friedman 19)

Given the heavy influence of the Kabbalah on the Fraternity of the Rosicrucians, this revelation speaks volumes. If those who studied the Talmud were using such a technique as a cipher, we have a precedent that would have influenced Bacon to do the same between the Simple and Reverse Ciphers. The discovery of the relationship of Bacon's substitution system between these two ciphers before ever encountering the Friedman information just adds more credibility and validity to its presence. However, he is not the only source confirming its legitimacy.

Additionally, another example of this procedure comes to us through Freemasonry. In an article titled "The Stone Which the Builders Refused" by Bro. Gregory H. Peters, the author mentions this practice as the "Athbash

Cipher." He writes, "The Athbash Cipher of Hebrew notariqon is a simple substitution cipher that takes the Hebrew alphabet and splits it in half and reverses it, substituting the corresponding letters… essentially reversing the entire alphabet" (1). Francis Bacon used this exact technique in the cipher messages on the plaque. He used the 24 letters of the Elizabethan alphabet, split it in half and reversed it, and substituted between these letters throughout the message. The following table illustrates the system:

A	B	C	D	E	F	G	H	I	K	L	M
Z	Y	X	W	V	T	S	R	Q	P	O	N

For future reference, whenever I use the term or idea of the "substitution system" or substituting between "Simple and Reverse Ciphers," I'm referring to this Atbash cipher system as used by Bacon.

Two other forms of ciphers are also at work within the transpositions these methods produced and are explained below. Decoding the plaque requires rearranging the letters in a systematic manner, in an algorithm, using the "keys" provided on the plaque itself. When viewing the rearrangement of letters, the messages appeared in four forms - 1) complete or phonetically spelled words in English, Latin or Hebrew; 2) acrostics; 3) anagrams; and 4) lastly, acrostic anagrams.

To further complicate things, as previously mentioned the messages appear in a mixture of English, Latin and Hebrew. This turned out to be a blessing in disguise. Though I don't speak Latin or Hebrew, discerning use of online translators and college databases was extremely helpful and provided another level of objectivity. Since the words weren't understood until after they had been looked up, I couldn't engage in a form of confirmation bias – looking only for what I wanted to see. Instead, I translated the Latin words I could identify, and groups of consonants I suspected were Hebrew. It turned out that the translations fit the context. When you see such translations throughout this narrative, that is how they happened and how they were recorded.

Also as stated above, the two other cipher forms that appear are acrostics and anagrams. Both forms have a time-honored history as legitimate forms of cipher systems. Acrostics appear in an arrangement of letters where words appear upwards, downwards or in a geometric pattern in letters next to one another. Once they are seen they become obvious. Anagrams are more problematic, as they open the cryptanalyst to claims of subjectivity, and therefore criticism.

As earlier stated, I had tried to avoid utilizing anagrams for that reason. However, they began appearing throughout the arrangements of letters with irritating frequency. I would note an obvious, correctly spelled word, and next to it, an obvious anagram, that when taken together formulated an intelligible context. In the end, I had to accept that it was intentional, and after learning that acrostic anagrams should be expected in this type of cipher, it all made sense. As such, through working with the anagrams I was able to work out their "rules," and I was amazed.

Anagrams and Avoiding Subjectivity

The anagrams needed to be approached in a logical manner. First, I would pick out any obvious words that needed no rearrangements of letters. Next, I would identify all of the letters that were juxtaposed with one another that could form a word. Next came the words that could be formed with some of the letters that were side-by-side along with other letters nearby, only one or two spaces away. (As you will see, I was able to refine this process further with the later keys, by creating a table of the remaining letters and placing them on their original lines, but left-justified). Lastly, I would look at all the unused letters to form any possible constructions that fit the context, whatever it may be. These sometimes provided a missing "I," "a" or "the" that filled in a meaningful sentence, but often they were simply "useless" letters. I couldn't imagine that with the complexity of the cipher's construction (and that of the plaque itself), that the left-over letters were "just there."

On a hunch, after picking out the first set of anagrams and exhausting any other possible constructions, I added together the values of the leftover letters using the Simple, Reverse and Kaye ciphers. The totals were cipher signatures of Francis Bacon. Amazement and excitement are words that fail to describe what I felt. A healthy dose of fear was mixed in there as well - what if it was merely a coincidence? I proceeded on to the next arrangement of letters to test the method. It worked a second time. Encouraged, I continued through the first "key" that I used, and it worked consistently, every time. If it had worked only once, it would have been a coincidence. But the fact that it consistently yielded results, proved to me that it was *a part of the coding and decoding process.* As amazing as this process is, in and of itself, most of the time the cipher signatures fit the contexts of the messages I was checking. For example, if the message referred Francis Bacon's brother or the Rosi Crosse, one of the signatures would be a number for "Frater."

So, like a child "checking their work" on a math assignment, the cipher had a system in place to "check the work" to see if the correct message had been discovered. The Biliteral Cipher message in the next chapter also seems to allude to this system.

This step-by-step approach is best understood in this list of procedures:

1. Identify all obvious "markers" of Bacon and the RC (letter combinations such as AA, TTT, RC, etc..
2. Identify acrostic messages that could provide context.

3. Identify obvious words and (acrostic) anagrams that also provide a context.
4. Identify any other words in anagram / acrostic anagram form that fit the context. Repeat until all possibilities are exhausted.
5. Remove every letter used up to this point.
6. Place remaining letters in a table, left justified (and removing empty rows.
7. Repeat the process until all possibilities are exhausted.
8. Add the values of any leftover letters in Simple, Reverse and Kaye Ciphers. If they equal the signatures associated with Francis Bacon and the Rosy Cross, the decryption is successful.

Lastly and most importantly, the messages I found for the most part correlated with each other perfectly. The same themes and messages repeated amongst the different permutations the "keys" produced. They all repeated the same contexts. And one of the most significant of the discoveries was so unexpected, explicit, *and controversial,* that it has to be the main reason for the coded messages in the first place.

Now, the above are the decoding "rules" discovered within the cipher. Before continuing, some of the concerns you still may have as the reader need to be addressed, the same concerns I experienced before I embarked on this journey - are these methods legitimate and viable? I mentioned some of the criticisms that have been used in the past. One of which was, "*No one* could possibly have done something so difficult and complex, particularly in that time period."

First, this argument is a combination of a pair of logical fallacies called "the bare assertion" and "hypothesis contrary to fact." A bare assertion happens when a person makes a statement as a surety without any support of facts, data or logic. The person simply makes a statement as a truism, whether factual or not. *Hypothesis contrary to fact* is a fallacy of logic where a person floats a theory that either is simply untrue, or more likely, makes a statement that has never happened in reality, and uses it as an argument. The statement that such a cipher would be impossible to create is on its face a false one. Hundreds of examples are known to exist.

Another example of a criticism I've heard is called the Infinite Monkey theorem, when someone makes the statement that, "if you give a million monkeys each a typewriter and they start banging the keys, eventually one of them will write the works of William Shakespeare." Again, hypothesis contrary to fact. This situation has never happened, and it never will - no one will ever be able to test it out. Complete fallacy of logic.

Additionally, it's a false analogy. This idea originally was created as a metaphor attributed to mathematician Emile Borel to explain a real mathematical principle. Unfortunately, people often mistakenly attempt to use it as a rhetorical argument against people who claim to have "deciphered a code" that others have never seen. By misapplying the statement, they not only reveal simplistic thinking and that they do not understand the statement as a metaphor, they commit the afore-mentioned logical fallacy of false analogy.

Lastly, I based these methods on the cipher systems known to be used by Francis Bacon, and tried and true decryption techniques. They are based upon the alphabet and mathematics. These things are fixed. I then used logic, inductive (favored by Bacon) and deductive reasoning, and looked for any messages within the text itself for indications or directions on how to proceed. That's it. With no preconceived agenda or idea that I was setting out to "prove," I followed the procedures as outlined to see if these methods could produce results. They did.

If I had conducted this experiment and it simply produced random words (which surely would happen), I would have acceded that I had failed to find a cipher. The one message I had hoped for, failed to appear (the Prince Tudor theory). If I had any other presumptive hope, it was that some clue would appear connecting Shakespeare and Bacon to the Oak Island mystery. Such a connection would have gone a long way in helping my friends in their research. However as you will see, nothing that explicit appeared until the end, because I had discounted its existence. Thinking the messages had nothing to do with Nova Scotia caused me to completely miss an entire set of messages. Such is the nature of cognitive biases.

In the end, I knew the information wasn't just random. The messages repeat in each "Key" used. They're consistent. And I was completely unprepared for the most surprising part of the message.

Before moving on to the actual decoding process and the initial results at this point, I'll interject a discovery I made midway into the process, as it deals with the plaque as it stands. As other researchers have done before, the plaque as it appears contains interesting correlations. The work of Petter Amundsen and my friends Chris Morford and Chris Donah come to mind. So, I thought I would do something quite simple that had never occurred to me (or to anyone else as far as I could tell). I counted all the characters on the plaque. In this process, though people have attempted to arrive at an accurate count, I believe that my count is accurate since I adhered to the rules of logic, and the accepted rules of the alphabet as it has evolved over time. I knew there had to be a transposition cipher hidden within this verse, so the conjoined or ligatured characters would count as one character. For example, the Latin Æ has always been used as a single vowel letter, and so I used this convention throughout this process. As you'll see, it worked in multiple ways. Also, I include a chapter at the end of this book that deals with hidden Bacon signatures revealed by the cipher texts of the plaque. They all involve Francis Bacon's true identity, and will produce results just like those contained in this chapter.

Character Count Signatures

I counted the characters to see if numbers of known cipher signatures appeared in correlation with symbolic or meaningful characters on the plaque, such as A, F, G, H, I, O, *T* and V. Though I'll explain the symbolism of these letters in more depth later, I think it's important to look at a brief explanation here. "A" represents Apollo and Athena as well as light and shadow, as well as the "Apis blanco and Apis negro." As you'll see, one of the predominant symbols and "Keys" for the RC is the bee, which in Latin is "apis." And "F" of course stands for Francis, as well as in the substitution system can be "T" or the Tau. The letter "G" is obvious as its value in Kaye Cipher is 33, the signature for "Bacon" in Simple. "T" and "H" represent the Tau and double Tau, and "I" is simply the first-person pronoun. In fact, the words "I" and "ME" figure prominently in terms of providing meaning at this level of deciphering the plaque's many messages. Lastly, V and O also figure as RC keys as you'll see in chapter 3. The letter V not only represents the name Verulam, but it is the counterpart to the "A" symbolism and is possibly represented by the Freemasonry square and compass. Additionally, I contend that the "E's" as they appear on the plaque are intended as a Triple Tau symbol, and due to the substitution system at work in Bacon's version of the Atbash cipher, can be thought to reinforce the idea of "V" as one of the symbolic characters on the plaque.

Name	Simple	Reverse	Kaye
Shakespeare	103	172	259
Francis	67	108	171
Bacon	33	92	111
Francis Bacon	100	200	282
Fra Rosi Crosse	157	168	287
Baron Verulam	133	167	237

I numbered each character on the plaque, and again conjoined or ligatured characters count as one. When completed, "I" in the upper left was "1," ending at "P" in the lower right as "305." Again to be clear, I was looking for correlations between the number of the character as I counted it, and significant Cipher Signatures. As you will see in Plate 7, there were far too many correlations to be mere coincidence. I've again included in Table 1-4 that appeared earlier in this writing for convenience sake.

Figure 1-1

Figure 1 - 2

Before I explain the correlations, I need to share a recent discovery as a form of how this system works. I looked at the first characters on the first three lines – "I" which is number 1, "T" which is 38, and "S" is number 72. These letters form an acrostic spelling "ITS." Their sum of their number places is 111, "Bacon" in Kaye. The message is, "IT'S Bacon." See Figure 1-1.

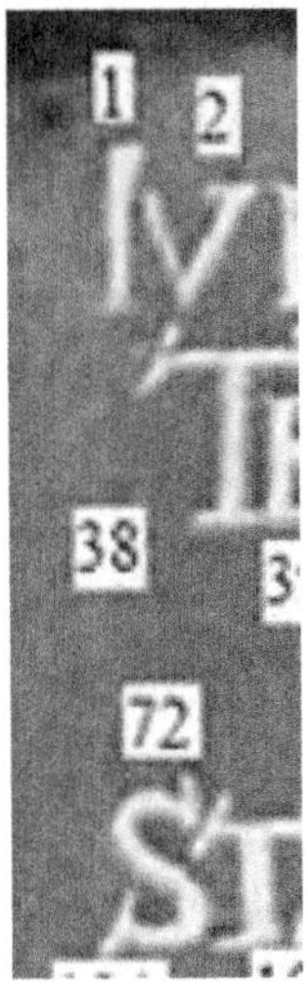

In this way, my "count system" produces multiple messages. So using the above numbers, I looked at the characters on Shakespeare's Funerary Monument plaque that corresponded with each one. I performed this with the forward or "regular" count, as well as the backward count. I then compared the character corresponding with the signature to our symbolic or meaningful characters to see if any meaningful information could be gained.

Right away there were several that appeared to be significant and carry meaning. The easiest way to analyze these correlations is to identify where on the plaque a large number of them appear and follow the chart. The complete count can again be seen in Plate 7.

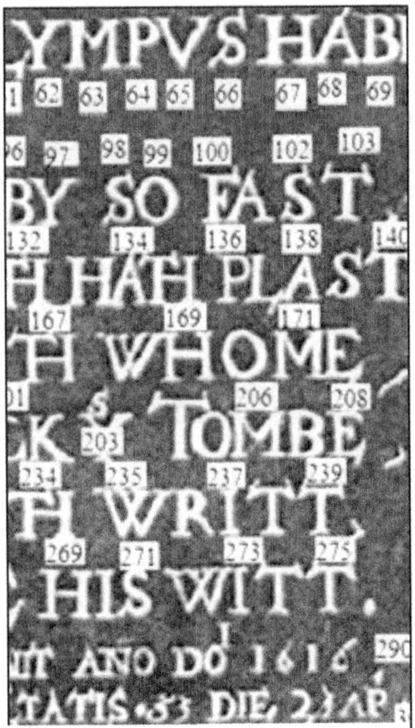

Beginning with the signatures for Shakespeare, character number 103 is "T" or Tau, which has carried a great deal of significance throughout this cipher, and to the Rosi Crosse and Freemasons as discussed previously, meaning "truth." Character number 172 is the "E" in "WHOME," and while this letter carries no significance on its own other than being the Reverse value of "V," it suddenly does when taken with its neighbor, character 171 which is "Francis" in Kaye Cipher, the letter "M." The 171st and 172nd characters spell "ME," and represent Francis and Shakespeare, respectively, making the implications obvious. Lastly, the Kaye cipher signature of Shakespeare, 259, is the letter "A" in "PAGE" (appropriately) on the last line. As discussed elsewhere, the letter "A" represents Bacon's reverence for Apollo and Athena, as well as representing light and shadow.

Moving on to Francis, the Simple signature of 67 points to the 67th character on the plaque on the second line as the "H" of "HABET." The letter H is the first letter of the Latin word Hierusalem, meaning Jerusalem, and an integral part of the Triple Tau symbol, and represents the Double Tau as two T's joined at the stem. This also represents the initials of the number Thirty-Three, the Simple Cipher signature for "Bacon." The Reverse value for Francis, the 108th character is the first person pronoun as the letter "I" in "IF," therefore stating "I, Francis." As stated in the previous paragraph, the Kaye Value of the 171st character is the letter "M" spelling the word "ME" associated with the names "Francis" and "Shakespeare."

The cipher signatures for "Bacon," 33, 92 and 111 are probably most well-known within the Bacon / Shakespeare community. Character 33 is the letter "R," which at first glance appears irrelevant. However, when we consider the substitution function between Simple and Reverse ciphers as an integral part of the cipher system, the "R" can be read as "H" which we now know represents the double Tau symbol. "Coincidentally" the 92nd character is "T" or the Tau. Also, it's value in Simple Cipher is 19, which is "F" in Reverse, for "Francis." The 111th character is "O" which as you will see in a later chapter, is claimed to be one of the "Keys" of the RC, representing light. I will explain this fully in the results of the Biliteral Cipher interpretation. Also, taken together the 92nd letter "T" (value 19) and the 111th letter "O" (value 14) added together in Simple Cipher are 33, "Bacon" in Simple.

The full name "Francis Bacon" produces the signatures of 100, 200 and 282 in the three ciphers. Character 100 is on the third line, and is the "F" in "FAST," for Francis. Character 200 is the letter "E" in "DECK," which in the substitution system can be read as "V" for Verulam. Character 282 is the letter "N" in "ANO" in the lower right corner of the plaque. Again, though this seems to be a "miss," by substituting "M" in its place, we see another of the "RC Keys" discussed in a later chapter, regarding a "hand-sign" used by the RC.

"Fra. Rosi Crosse" produces the sums of 157, 168 and 287 in Simple, Reverse and Kaye Ciphers, respectively. Character 157 is the first "A" in "SHAKSPEARE" appropriately enough. The 168th character coincides with the previous letter, as it's "W" in "WHOME" for "William." Character 287 is the first "1" in the date 1616, which again can be read as "A."

The last entry in the above table are the signatures for Bacon's title granted to him by King James I, Baron Verulam, which are 133, 167 and 237. Most people often recognize 133 and 167 as "double Bacon signatures," however they more accurately represent "Baron Verulam." The 133rd character on the plaque is the "H" in "HATh," representing the double Tau. Character 167 is the conjoined Th symbol, again a double Tau. The 237th letter is "I" in "WRITT," identifying himself in two ways as, "I, Baron Verulam" and "I – TT" with the remaining letters in the word.

I became curious at this point, that since 305 is an odd number, I wanted to see which character was at its mathematical "center." I went to character 153. This character was actually a pair of conjoined letters "ME" before the conjoined "NT" at the end of the word "MONUMENT" before "SHAKSPEARE," and can be seen here in Figure 1-2a:

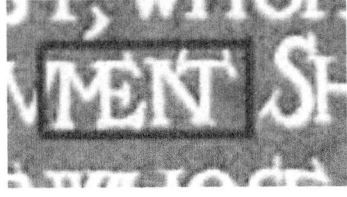

Figure 1-2a

There is so much to remark upon regarding this number and correlating word of "ME," yet I hesitate to fully disclose it here. Rest assured, the number of 153 carries a special significance to Bacon. I will devote one section at the end of the book to this enigmatic number. But for now the following should suffice.

Many writers and researchers have often puzzled over these characters, wondering why among all of the others on the plaque, these were chosen to be joined. The fact that they are "mathematically" at the "center" of the message relative to the other characters is an indication that we need to closely look at them. The obvious thing that everyone notices immediately is that the word "ME" appears. First of all, the number 153 is actually the total of the words "I, Sir Francis Bacon" in Simple Cipher. I (9) + Sir (44) Francis (67) + Bacon (33) = 153. ME = 153. It's also the Simple Cipher signature of "Francis Verulam," and the signature for various versions of his true identity. Also, having experienced the way the cipher plays around with the subjective and objective cases of pronouns, I decided to see what cipher might appear as "NT." In Simple Cipher, N's value is 13, and T's value is 19 and their sum is 32. Since only Kaye Cipher has numbers over 24, looking at Kaye provides the letter with the value of 32 as "F," which of course stands for Francis in this context.

The juxtaposition is telling. These clues point to the message, Me F. Shakspeare. *I, Francis, am Shakspeare?* If you'll recall earlier, the interaction of the cipher signatures 171 and 172 of Shakespeare and Francis in the count of the characters. Also, as noted elsewhere, the word "ME" totals 33 in Reverse Cipher, which is the Simple Cipher signature for "Bacon." Here at the numerical "heart" of the plaque, Francis Bacon shows us who is at the "center" of all this work.

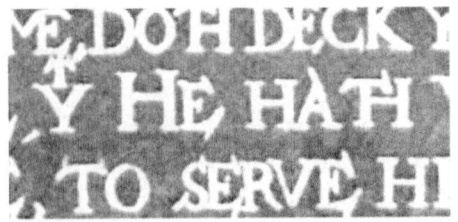

Figure 1-3.

One more astonishing cipher signature presented itself. Since the beginning of our work on the plaque, friend and fellow researcher Chris Donah drew my attention to the oversized "H" in the word "HE" near the end of line 7 of the verse. He pointed out to me the way it seems to "standout" in a way that draws attention to itself. He reasoned that in some way it must be important. During our most recent collaboration meeting, I noted that it is the 231st character on the plaque. That's when I did a quick calculation and realized that 231 is the total of 33 times 7. It's as if Bacon were multiplying "G" from Simple Cipher times "G" from the Kaye Cipher. It's also the Reverse Cipher signature of "Sir Francis Bacon" as well as two versions of his true identity. As earlier stated, and according to the cipher in a later chapter, one of Bacon's devices representing the Double Tau of the initials of the number thirty-three is the H, representing two T's joined by their stems.

Within the context of the "surface" plaintext message of the plaque, we're being instructed to "Sieh all that He (Bacon)" has written, including the cipher on the plaque itself.

In reference to looking for more Cipher Signatures, I could have stopped there. I needed no more convincing. Still, I thought it might be interesting to do a reverse count of the entire plaque and analyze any correlations in a similar manner. Afterall, both Simple and Reverse Ciphers were used in the cipher system, so why not a count of the characters of the plaque in reverse order? The results were also impressive, and an image of the backward count appears as Plate 8.

Character Count Table 1-4

Name	Simple	Reverse	Kaye
Shakespeare	103	172	259
Francis	67	108	171
Bacon	33	92	111
Francis Bacon	100	200	282
Fra Rosi Crosse	157	168	287
Baron Verulam	133	167	237

For the sake of clarity and convenience, I've again included the signature table in this section as I look at the "reverse count" of the characters on the plaque. Additionally, I will simply follow the same procedure I used for the signatures in the forward count.

Starting with the three signatures of "Shakespeare" of 103, 172 and 259, each of the corresponding characters are significant. The 103rd character of the backward count is actually the "S" and "Y," where the "S" is a superscript above the "Y" used as the word "this." I believe the S represents "Shakespeare" as the "speare-shaker" in terms of "light." The Y shape suggests light shining downward in the manner of Apollo and Athena shining knowledge downward in the form of insight. Additionally, the letter Y is considered a predecessor of the Tau or "T." (In a similar manner, the T above the Y meaning "that," would represent the same idea in the form of "Truth" in the form of the Tau). Also, since "S" can be read as "G" using the substitution cipher, we have the signature of Bacon behind the disguise of "S," or Shakespeare. Character 172 appears as the "A" in "HATh" on the fourth line. 259 appears as the last "T" in "TEGIT."

The "Francis" signatures of 67, 108 and 171 unsurprisingly all contain symbolic significance. The 67th character working in reverse from the last character of "P" is the last "T" of "WRITT." Character number 108 is the double Tau symbol of the conjoined T-H at the end of "DOTh", and 171 is the conjoined double Tau at the end of "HATh" on the fourth line.

Next, the "Bacon" signatures of 33, 92 and 111 continue the trend. The 33rd is the letter "I" in "WITT," providing the double message of "I, Bacon" and "I TT" with characters 68 and 69. Character 92 is the "R" in "MORE" of the lower left corner, and as before, subbing an H for the R provides us with the double Tau symbol. Character 111 is the conjoined M-E at the end of the word "NAMe," providing the message, "Me, Bacon." Looking at the way these characters seem "condensed" with no space between ME, the comma that follows the first letter in "DOTH" drew my attention. On either side of the character directly below it, the Y and T signifying the word "THAT," we see extra space. These "errors" led me to the conclusion that they should be read steganographically together as, ME F B, after substituting F for T and B for Y.

In this backward count, the signatures for his full name, 100, 200 and 282, point to the characters "M" in "TOMBE," "A" in "READ" in the fourth line, and the "T" in "SOCRATEM," respectively. Each of these letters are significant for the reasons previously discussed, and I would like to remind the reader that a more thorough explanation of "M" is forth coming.

Next, the signatures for "Fra. Rosi Crosse" of 157, 168 and 287 of course provide a further study in the trend. 157 is another "M," this time beginning the word "MONVMeNt." The 168th character in this reverse count is the "A" in "PLAST." Lastly, character number 287 is the over-sized "S" of "SOCRATEM," again conversely representing "Shakespeare" and the "hidden G" of "Bacon."

133, 167 and 237 of "Baron Verulam" point to still more letters confirming the intent. 133 is the "Q" of "QUICK" and can be read as "I" due to the substitution cipher between Simple and Reverse Ciphers. The 167th character is the "S" in "PLAST" containing the same meaning as above, G. Lastly, 237 is the "B" in "HABET." While it's possible this could represent the name "Bacon," I think that if taken with the letter "E" beside it, we can read it as "B V," or the initials of "Baron Verulam." Taken together, B and E total 7, the number of the letter G in Simple Cipher, and as such, a Bacon signature. Additionally, they are the phonetic spelling of "BEE," a highly venerated symbol of Rosicrucianism and Freemasonry.

In a related surface analysis, ten of the commas appear to actually be shaped as the number 7 (G). There are also ten of the double Tau conjoined Th symbols. (For the remainder of the narrative, I refer to the conjoined Th symbol as a "double Tau" even though one of the cipher texts states that Bacon was using it as a "Triple Tau" to represent himself, since the H is a double Tau in itself. However as you'll see, Bacon used it as T, TT, Th and TTT (in reference to himself) as it suited his needs). Both can be understood to be signatures of 33, so both state Bacon's name "times ten."

And so, the plaque is telling us, "Read if thou canst who death has placed within this monument Shakspeare." While just this cursory look at the plaque produces multiple cipher signatures, after reading the rest of this book, everyone will be able to see the name encoded within that monument is Francis Bacon. However before moving forward, let's address the symbolism of many of the relevant letters of the alphabet as they are used within the ciphers to come.

Though the process of numbering each character has produced a dizzying number of correlations between significant letters and cipher signatures related to Francis Bacon, I've chosen to leave out some of the signatures that would only confuse the reader at this point. These other correlations are Bacon signatures revealed by the transposition ciphers that follow, and I prefer to introduce them in context of those messages. A complete treatment of all of the character count correlations appears in Chapter 11.

The Symbolic Meaning of Letters and Numbers

Some of the symbolic signposts from the alphabet and mathematics used by Bacon and the Rosicrucian Fraternity require more explanation. The main letters from the alphabet would be A, V, O, T, H, M and G. As I mention elsewhere, the letter "A" has been used by Bacon in headpieces and frontispieces of his written works, and they can also be found in Shakespeare's folios. In addition to representing Apollo and Athena, it is also a symbol of light and shadow. Yet another associated meaning is the "Apis Blanco" and the "Apis Noir," represented by the light "A" and the dark "A" in Baconian headpieces and frontispieces, and *apis* of course being Latin for "bee." Both the letters A and M can represent the shape of this animal. As you will see in the cipher texts to come, these groups honored "bees" as a powerful symbol by placing their hands in an "M" position in paintings. Additionally, calculating the Simple Cipher signature for "bee," B (2) + E (5) + E (5), totals 12, the value of the letter "M" in Simple. The corresponding letters for the numerals 1 and 2 also phonetically spell "a bee." While bees can represent the muses (M) who had turned themselves into bees in mythology, they can also represent the "buzzing" that reportedly occurs when initiates experience a surge of kundalini energy rising up their spine and activating their pineal gland, making it vibrate. This vibration creates a powerful buzzing sound, akin to electric sparks and swarm of bees during this stage of the enlightenment process. While the bee is venerated for a variety of other reasons, among which is the alchemy of taking the base materials of pollen and transmuting them into golden honey, all of these reasons should suffice for our purposes here.

As a pictograph, the letter A also appears as rays of light shining and spreading downward, and likewise the way a shadow can be cast. Related to the A symbolism is V, which is the same shape inverted. In this way, we can see the Hermetic dictum of the unification of opposites of the male blade and female chalice in the Freemason square and compass, as above so below. Additionally. the "O" would be how that light or shadow would appear if viewed from above, as a circle. The "O" and "T" often appear together, as their total in Simple Cipher is 33, the signature for "Bacon" in Simple.

The "T" or Tau, and the "H" are among the most complex examples of letter / number symbolism in the RC tradition. First of all, the number of "T" in Simple (and "F" in Reverse) is 19. Bacon frequently refers to himself as the Tau and Triple Tau, for multiple reasons. The letters TT stand for the initials of the number 33, which we know is the signature for Bacon. However, considering the RC veneration of knowledge and mathematics, when we consider prime numbers more secrets are revealed. For example, the 19th prime number is the number 67, which is the Simple Cipher signature for "Francis." In this way, the "T" can represent his first name. Therefore, another meaning of the Triple Tau emerges – the first Tau represents "Francis," and the double Tau represents 33, which is "Bacon." Therefore, this much venerated symbol symbolically states his name, "Francis Bacon." Additionally, the value of "TTT" in the Fourfold Cipher (not discussed here) is 67 in that system. So in that way the Triple Tau equates to "Francis." There is a relationship between the Triple Tau and the letter G as well.

Since the initials of Triple Tau are the same as Thirty-three, we recognize both as the Simple Cipher signature of "Bacon." When we consider the values in Reverse Cipher an interesting relationship reveals itself. The value of TTT in Reverse Cipher is 18. The character with the value of 18 in Reverse is the letter G. Therefore the Triple Tau is the equivalent of the letter G, whose value in Kaye Cipher is again, 33. Likewise we need to consider the letter "H."

The use of the "H" as a symbol of the double Tau is well known, particularly in relation to the Royal Arch degree of Freemasonry and its Triple Tau, representing the Temple of Hierusalem, the Latin spelling of Jerusalem. As such, an "H" is formed by the joining of two Taus at their stems. Also, we know that the value of "H" in Simple Cipher is 8, and the eighth prime number is 19, the number of "T" in Simple. Lastly, the letter "H" appears on the Coat of Arms of the Dauphin of France, which as you will soon see is also highly significant.

Also the importance of specific numbers, especially prime numbers cannot be stressed enough, and how they appear in the plaque. First of all, all of the standard signatures or values in Simple, Reverse and Kaye Ciphers for "Francis, Bacon, Francis Bacon," as well as "Fra. Rosi Crosse" each communicate the associated name. Some of these signatures themselves are prime numbers which also communicate Rosicrucian keys.

As already demonstrated, the Simple Cipher signature for "Francis," 67, is the 19th prime number and therefore can be equated with the letter "T" or "Tau." As you'll see, in the cipher texts Bacon frequently refers to himself as the Tau, double Tau and Triple Tau. This is also related to the RC marker in the word "See." Number 137 is the 33rd prime number and as such becomes a signature for "Bacon" as its value in Simple, 33. The number 193 is the 44th prime, the number of what is called "Bacon's Secret Signature" thoroughly explained at a later time. It also contains a phonetic anagram of "See Tau" in 19 (T) and 3 (C). Likewise, the 67th prime number is appropriately enough 331, which can be read as "Bacon A," or "Light on Bacon, or See Bacon." However, one prime number deserves final attention.

A couple of numbers kept appearing and repeating in my research and Chris Donah's as well, and we couldn't understand their meaning. They didn't seem to match any known Bacon signatures. They were 198 and the other was 231 (as you'll see later, both of these numbers are cipher values of his true identity). I then realized the number 198 represents the Triple Tau, as 19 = T and 8 = H. Chris pointed out that the digits of 231 are the first three letters of the name Bacon. Then I realized that 231 is not only the Reverse Cipher value of *"Sir* Francis Bacon," it's also the product of the factors of 7 times 33, or the letter G in Simple and Kaye as stated earlier. That's when I tried the same function with 198, and discovered that it's the product of 6 times 33, or F times Bacon (G in Kaye). The 198th character in the forward count on the plaque is the double Tau symbol of the ligatured T and H. The 231st is an "E," which of course we can read as "V." In the backward count, the 198th character is the letter "I" as first-person pronoun, and the 231st is a "Y." This letter can be read as "B" or *bee* via a substitution, is also visually in the shape of a bee, and is a known predecessor of the Tau symbol. Chris also brought to my attention what I'll now call "only one" of Bacon's "secret signatures."

This "secret signature" is the number 44 and can be calculated in three different yet valid ways. The first is through the double Tau, in that the initials of TT represent the words "Thirty Three," the signature for "Bacon" in Simple. The Tau is the 22nd letter of the Hebrew alphabet, and therefore the double Tau equals 44. Another way to calculate the secret signature is the use of the substitution cipher between Simple and Reverse Ciphers. In this method, 33 can be represented as CC in Simple. In Reverse Cipher C is 22, so CC would again equal 44. Lastly, if we note the signature in Reverse of Francis Bacon as 200, this can be presented by the Roman Numeral CC. Again through the same protocol as above, we have 44. Just as importantly, as stated above the last letter of the Hebrew alphabet is Tav, and its Kabbalistic Gematria value is 400. However, its "small gematria" value is 4, so in this way, TT again becomes 44. This isn't the only way that this number is the "secret signature of Sir Francis Bacon, however. One more tantalizing, arguably most important, reason Bacon used 44 as his "secret" signature, isn't because it's the Reverse Cipher value of the word "pig," but because it's the Simple Cipher value of "REX."

So, these are a few of the ways that Francis Bacon created a system for math and the alphabet to interact.

Just like the cipher signatures we've already observed, prime numbers provide multiple correlations with these same significant letters, as well as producing more messages regarding who was responsible for creating the plaque (as if more evidence were necessary). Since there are a total of 305 total characters on the plaque, only primes 2 through 293 actually can appear. This provides a total of 62 (or read, FB) opportunities for correlations to occur. An image of these correlations appears in Plate 9. As you'll note in Plate 8, multiple correlations between the primes and the list of significant characters appear. In fact in the forward count, all but three are significant, and the ones that are not, are all examples of the letter "D." In Simple Cipher, they total 12, the same as the word "BEE," 2 + 5 + 5. In Reverse, their total sum is 63 (21 x 3), the same as the signature of the word "BEE" in Reverse, 23 + 20 + 20. The total in Kaye Cipher for 3 x D (30) is 90. The word "BEE" in Kaye is 28 + 31 + 31, 90.

Maybe it's a coincidence.

When I checked for correlations with the backward count which can be seen in Plate 9, an interesting phenomenon appeared. Two of the D's from the regular or forward count were the same as the backward count, the D in "READ if thou canst," and the D in "DECK this tombe." In addition to another D, this count includes a W, the substitution counterpart of letter D. So since checking the sums had produced interesting results in the forward count, I did the same for the backward count.

The sum in Simple Cipher of 4 + 4 + 4 + 21 is 33, the signature for "Bacon" in Simple. The sum in Reverse of 21 + 21 + 21 + 4 is 67, the signature for "Francis" in Simple. In Kaye the sum of 30 + 30 + 30 + 21 is 111, the signature for "Bacon" in Kaye.

Lastly, the letters D and W can represent the number 4, due to their positions in Simple and Reverse Ciphers. The 4th prime number is 7, which we read as the letter G, a known Bacon signature as its value is 33 in Kaye Cipher.

In terms of the odds of the 62 (FB) prime numbers landing on one of the 7 (G) significant letters, considering the multiple possibilities and combinations amid the 610 characters (forward and backward), I'm sure that the number of hits can be considered unsurprising. It's unnecessary to count the number of instances each of our special characters appear on the plaque out of the 305 characters, and then calculate the odds of how many of the 62 would coincide. The real question at hand is this – what are the odds of the letters that were *not* correlations, three D's in the forward count and three D's in the backward count with one instance of W (the D Atbash substitute), adding up to the RC key of "BEE" in all three ciphers in the first instance, and the three most commonly known cipher signatures for Francis Bacon in the second? The value of the 4th prime representing Bacon is also significant, as well as the fact that the number of "misses," six D's and a W, is the number 7, or G. All of these things taken as a whole defy coincidence.

In summary, all of the accumulated evidence by identifying correlations between the regular (forward) and backward counts of the symbolically significant characters on the plaque, and known cipher signatures of Francis Bacon, indicates that my method of counting the characters is the correct one. Additionally, every example presented shows design. The plaque was designed to demonstrate the use of Baconian ciphers and symbols and in a very true sense, teach the reader of them how to use them.

The Keys

Many more signatures await (and clear messages), but first the cipher needs to be unlocked. To this end, we need the key, or in this case the *keys.* And as stated, all of the features of the characters on the plaque of Shakespeare's Funerary Monument indicated the obvious use of a transposition cipher.

A key to such a transposition cipher as mentioned, often appears as a word or letter that can be translated into a number using Bacon's cipher systems. This "key" is then used as an algorithm by counting the letters or words of a given text, and as the key number is reached, that letter or word is written down. The count continues until the key is reached again, and that letter or word is recorded, and so on, continuing until all of the characters have been recorded. In this way, the key / algorithm rearranges the letters of the original text in a new order. The following example will help to illustrate this idea before moving on to the examples on the plaque itself.

The key is a number that allows the cryptanalyst to create the algorithm that rearranges the letters in a way that reveals the message of the transposition cipher. To complicate the matter, often multiple keys are required to decode the entire message: Sometimes an obvious answer will present itself, while other times the key is far more subtle. For example, one of the very first hidden messages I attempted to decode was a pamphlet by Manly Palmer Hall titled, "The Occult Anatomy of Man." In this work, the author often uses the word "key" in the context of a passage, and with a certain view or understanding of the sentence, the reader can "see" the keys. This word would appear on pages with typos, wrong page numbers or misspellings that when joined with a line using a ruler or compass, will point at (or bracket) a word or phrase. Such are the subtle tricks a cryptographer uses when concealing a message using steganography.

In the case of my reading of Rawley's *Manes Verulamiani*, I couldn't help but notice a "list" of descriptors in the stilted language of the text which appeared to me to be "keys" of a hidden message. When I tested out my theory to my surprise, it worked in a rudimentary way. Here is the text from passage number VII mentioned earlier:

VII

To The Same

Some there are though dead live in marble, and trust all their duration to long lasting columns; others shine in bronze, or are beheld in yellow gold, and deceiving themselves think they deceive the fates. Another division of men surviving in a numerous offspring, like Niobe irreverent, despise the mighty gods; but your fame adheres not to sculptured columns, nor is read on the tomb (with) "Stay, traveller, your steps"; if any progeny recalls their sire, not of the body is it, but born, so to speak, of the brain, as Minerva from Jove's: first your virtue provides you with an ever-lasting monument, your books another not soon to collapse, a third your nobility; let the fates now celebrate their triumphs, who having nothing yours, Francis, but your corpse. Your mind and good report, the better parts survive; you have nothing of so little value as to ransom the vile body withal.
-- T. Vincent, Trinity College.

After listing ways others have been memorialized, this writer mentions a curious reference that sounds much like the Shakespeare memorial plaque, replacing the word "PASSENGER" with "traveller." (This combined with all of the other references to his greatness as a poet in the other eulogies, makes the "Bacon as Shakespeare" hypothesis seem more like an inside joke that the writers knew). He states that his memorial cannot be read on a plaque, but is "of the brain." He then provides a list of three things in parallelism that will provide Bacon with his monument - his virtue, his books and his nobility. I read this to mean that in order to see what "T. Vincent" has to say, these three words needed to be used as keys. So reducing them by adding the digits to a lower numerical value allowed them to be used to reorder the letters in the text:

Table 1-6

Virtue	(90) = 9
Books	(58) = 13
Nobility	(100) = 10

I first noted the number of the eulogy was the Roman Numeral VII which as we know is the number of the letter "G" in Simple Cipher. I also noted that the sum of the reductions of the words as "keys" equaled 32, the number of the letter "F" in Kaye Cipher. Therefore, we could claim that the verse number itself, along with the total of the key words' values becomes the cipher signature, F. Bacon. This is just one way you will see how the ciphers interact.

Having located these possible Key values, I then needed to use these numbers to rearrange the letters. I accomplished this by counting the characters in the original message. First, I counted every ninth letter, and wrote them down in a row. When I arrived at the end of the message, I started over again at the beginning, creating an algorithm that rearranged the letters. I continued this process until all of the letters had been rearranged. I then followed this same process with the new arrangement with the second, and then third keys, respectively. After applying these numbers to rearrange the letters, one part of the message read (with Latin separated by the brackets), *ehy [libeete]see...ughhegothfoot bihly lilsad tthvweshit.* In the phonetic message, "Bihly lilsad" probably refers to William Rawley. This can easily be read phonetically (with English translation of the Latin in brackets) as:
eh, why? Libe e te [because of you we drink] Ugh. He go the foot (euphemism? Or, see later interpretation). Billy's a little sad. T (Tau) [As] Though we shit."

As they drink libations to Bacon, Rawley is sad as if the rest of them are worthless? So, after following this process, even after it has been transcribed from original sources, the cipher can still be interpreted in a meaningful way that fits the context. Except that it seems to make light of Bacon's death.

"Billy, he's a lil' sad" doesn't sound very sincere to me, but instead sounds like an inside joke intended for Bacon himself.

I also want to point out that the above example is a modern translation. I'm sure that the original Latin version would produce clearer results.

As I've already mentioned however, substitutions can be made across the Simple and Reverse ciphers. This could be the case in Eulogy Verse #7 as interpreted above. Before employing this substitution system, the message *could* be interpreted as, "*eh, why? Libe e te [because of you we drink] Ugh. He go the foot (euphemism?). Billy's a little sad. T (Tau) [As} Though we shit."*

However, after using this method, suddenly a joke about Bacon appears that is in keeping with the humor employed by that writer: *ehy libeete]see...ughhegothfoot bihly lilsadtthvweshit,* becomes-

"Eh, B. Because of you we drink (We drink to you). See… ugh. He "frtoot." Billy a lilsad, T (read as "Francis" as per earlier explanation). fed U shit." Or other fun alternative endings, "T Few! (h)E shit," or "Ffew! U shit," OR "G few! U shit!"

The last rendering is my personal favorite. Since we know the letter "G" is the number 33 in Kaye Cipher, the number of "Bacon" in Simple, here we have the writer of the eulogy writing directly to Bacon to "bust his chops" so to speak. If true and accurate, it's comforting to see that intellectual men at the birth of the Renaissance really hadn't matured beyond the age of 11 years old in terms of their love of low brow humor. Additionally, given what I've since learned from the later cipher texts the algorithms produce, I suspect the potty humor is simply there as a distraction for the "profane" such as myself. Another careful, more thorough treatment of the letters from Verse VII, especially in the original Latin version, could possibly yield a more profound or important message. Another experiment the reader might enjoy is counting the words instead of the letters to see what messages might appear.

So even though multiple examples abound throughout that text, I use this one to illustrate what occurred to me regarding "keys" when I approached the plaque for the first time. Since all of the clues indicate a cipher exists encoded within the plaque, the key *must* appear on the plaque itself.

The Plaque and the Keys

With that in mind, I approached it with new eyes. Having a key that could symbolically be translated into a number was necessary, to then create an algorithm to rearrange the letters of the surface message, revealing the cipher text.

As I looked at it even more closely, I became fully convinced that every feature of it indicated a transposttion cipher at work. Letters combined - T's and H's, N and T, the words THE and ME, etc. This is exactly what the creators of the plaque would need to do in order to create the correct "count" for a working algorithm and produce results. They would need to combine letters in certain areas to have the correct number of total characters along with their placement, according to the count of the "key" being employed. Then, I saw what I had seen every time I had looked at the image, but this time I thought there could be a special significance - the numbers in the lower right hand corner (image 1-3):

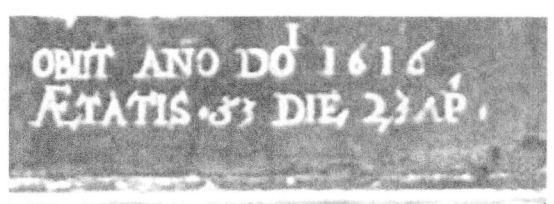

Image 1-3

The year 1616. Could it really be that simple? 16+16 equals 32, the number of eulogies in *Manes Verulamiani.* Shakespeare's age, incorrectly listed as 53? April 23rd? There would only be one way to find out.

I developed the strategy that I would use the number 32, as the symbolism of it had a form of elegance about it. In addition to the 32 eulogies in *Manes*, 32 is a number associated with the Sephiroth and the Paths connecting them in the Kabbalistic Tree of Life symbol. (Incidentally, there is a 33rd unseen part of the Tree of Life, so the name "F. Bacon" can represent the same Tree of Life). In Kaye Cipher 32 is the number of the letter "F" for Francis and in the Athbash substitution system was "T" or Tau, while the Simple Cipher signature for Bacon is 33. Since 32 is one less, perhaps it represented the loss of Shakespeare? Doubtful, but enough other evidence made me willing to give it a try. If 32 yielded any positive results indicating a cipher, I would continue with the process using the other numbers as well, unless a new key appeared in the text. Additionally, the "mistake" here needs to be clearly stressed.

As said, obvious mistakes such as typos, misspellings or wrong paginations are used as clues that a text contains a cipher. The plaque lists Shakespeare's age at the time of his death as 53, but by most accounts he was 52. Scholars have offered explanations for this apparent error as previously mentioned, however I suspected it purposely had been done. Continuing, since the 4 digits of 16 and 16 were added together, I used the same protocol in dealing with the other digits as well: 53 would be reduced to 8, justifying the "change in age" along with repeating the "H" symbolism, and 23 to 5. I also reasoned that if 5 yielded no results then I would include April, raising the number to 9. Mind you, this was only if the first algorithm worked.

Also, I truly was learning how this cipher system worked on the plaque as I went along. As you're going to see in the chapters immediately following, I had little idea what I was doing other than seeing if Bacon's ciphers could be applied to the plaque. In the beginning of the process, I naively thought (read *foolishly* if you like) that after using the second and third keys, that they would just spell out the clear messages: *"Hi! My name is Francis Bacon and I wrote all of the works attributed to William*

Shakespeare. Oh, and I'm the illegitimate son of the Queen..." If only it had been that easy.

So at this stage of writing, since I know how all of this has turned out, I would like to explain the process of the discoveries, before presenting them. The sequence of the discoveries in some examples will be different from the order in which I made them. I've made these adjustments in organization for clarity and readability.

To that end, the different transpositions produced by the above algorithms are labeled as Key 32, Key 8 and Key 5. Key 5 was also reinforced within the messages of other keys. I used these "keys" to transpose the characters in different permutations. As previously stated, by counting each character on the plaque according to the Key, an algorithm was created that reordered all the letters in a new configuration.

Though I've already explained the process, I go into detail how this process actually works in each chapter. But the results of what I came to call "Key 32" produced several distinct messages (though I missed the most profound messages at first). In fact, multiple messages appeared, and then using "Key 8" also produced even more explicit messages. One of the messages was a clue to another key, so when I ran into an impasse with "Key 5," I moved on to the new Key, 38. After I had deciphered all of the messages from Keys 32 and 8, and created the new Key 38, I discovered the clue that allowed me to use Key 5, also providing stunning results.

I discovered Key 38, as you will see in a later chapter, because of a message that stated "EYE THE T⊣." Many people who have studied the plaque consider this to be a ligatured Th, which we all now know is a double Tau symbol, representative of Bacon. As "T" is 19 in Simple Cipher, I reasoned that the prominence of the T⊣ character was also intended as a Key of 38, by doubling the value of "T," 19. I'll more completely explain that process in the chapter revealing the results of that specific key.

Again, the answers did not arrive in a linear fashion. Key 5 revealed its message only after I used the new Key 38 and I found a clue that allowed Key 5 to work. Again, for the purposes of clarity and ease of presenting the messages, I will presenting all of the findings within each Key, as opposed to the order in which I made each of the discoveries. And so, I will be presenting the keys in the following order - Keys 32, 8, 5, and then 38, and its own Key 5. After the preliminary findings, I then give a full analysis of each key in their own respective chapters.

Only as I went through the process did I actually learn how the whole cipher system worked. Key 8 taught me how to use Key 38. Key 38 taught me how to use Key 5 in both Keys 38 and 8. And so the process was anything but linear. Like I said, my original thought to rearrange the characters three times using the numbers 32, 8 and 5 to create the transposition, and then at the end of that tedious process, the secret message would be laid bare. That did not pan out.

I had been unprepared to find that each Key generated its own set of messages. Each chapter presents the original findings, but then the deeper analysis of the phonetic, acrostic and anagram messages, appears respectively. As such, the findings of Key 32 seem in a word, "clunky." In retrospect, I was still learning the processes and at first glance, the Key 32 results seem unimpressive. However, I had missed the majority of messages at that early stage. Therefore, some added insights are provided at the end of the book on Key 32 with all of the things I missed. As I became more adept at the process, things fell into order particularly in Keys 5, 38 and Key 5 of 38. But first, the true count of the characters needs a brief explanation.

The Count

Moving on to another original concern as I began to "use the keys" to create the transpositions, another variable needed to be contended with - when counting the characters on the plaque, what constitutes a true "character?" I knew that the conjoined or "ligatured" letters should be counted as only one character, assuming the purpose of their existence was to create the correct count and positioning of letters. However, the characters that had letters above them puzzled me (see Image 1-4).

Image 1-4

Since the Y with the S above it represents the whole word "THIS" and the Y with the T is the whole word "THAT," I treated each of them as a single character. For the sake of consistency in procedures, I used the same approach with the "I" above the "O" in the misspelled "DIO." I assumed that the fact that the letters seemed to be out of order (the "I" appears to the right of the "O") again was an indication of a transposition cipher at work.

Instead of walking you through each step at this stage to heighten the excitement, I'll just confess that the first attempt didn't work. I began counting at the first letter in the upper left, the capital "I" of JUDICIO, and on the third or fourth pass through the entire inscription, the algorithm terminated by ending on the very last character. I ended where I had started, on the very first letter.

That was when I decided that since the "I" in DIO was not forming a whole word with the "O" under it, "I" needed to be included as its own letter in the count. It seemed logical. And, it worked.

By identifying the number of characters (not letters) as being 305, all of the keys generated a rearrangement of the letters, except for Key 5 of course. Since the number of total characters was evenly divisible by 5, this meant that the characters wouldn't be rearranged after just the first pass, as the count would terminate on the last character on the plaque, "P." Luckily as I will later demonstrate, hints within the Keys themselves provided the answers of how to proceed.

The following chapters contain the messages from the ciphers. Since we just ended on a note that the number of characters is divisible by five, the Biliteral Cipher is presented first, though it was the last to be discovered.

Chapter 2 - The Biliteral Cipher and the "RC Keys"

Though the previous chapter explained the nature of the transposition ciphers of the plaque and Bacon's Simple, Reverse and Kaye Cipher systems, the character count finishing the last chapter would be a good segue to Bacon's biliteral cipher. This will give you an idea of the multiple ways information can be encrypted.

Much has been written about Bacon's biliteral cipher, but in case the reader is unfamiliar with it, a brief description will suffice. He created it as a teenager during his time in France with the English ambassador. This cipher uses two different type faces or fonts, and groups of five characters each represent one letter of the alphabet. To decipher it, the text of the original message is put into groups of five characters (again, the count of 305 characters on the plaque is a good indication of the presence of a biliteral message as it's evenly divisible by 5). Then each character of the text must be studied in order to identify the two different typefaces being used. The main typeface is labelled "a" and the second is labeled "b." The combination of "a's" and "b's" indicates what letter of the alphabet is represented by each group of five characters. The combinations and their corresponding letters of the alphabet appear in Table 2-1.

Table 2 - 1

A	aaaaa	N	abbaa
B	aaaab	O	abbab
C	aaaba	P	abbba
D	aaabb	Q	abbbb
E	aabaa	R	baaaa
F	aabab	S	baaab
G	aabba	T	baaba
H	aabbb	V	baabb
I	abaaa	W	babaa
K	abaab	X	babab
L	ababa	Y	babba
M	ababb	Z	babbb

The typeface of the characters that is used on the plaque appears so complicated, that at first glance it seems identifying any distinguishing characteristics would be impossible. However, as stated earlier and as was the case with the other ciphers, the solution was simpler than I originally thought.

Either the overly ornate typeface was a ruse designed to hide its simplicity, or more than one biliteral cipher exists that focuses on another "difference" between the typefaces that I couldn't detect. Perhaps another aspect of the font could be separated into two categories in a different way than the following one I found. It probably was intended to distract the would-be decoder from the simplicity of the differences between the two types of characters. The multiple differences between the characters themselves compound the effect. Some are thick and bold while others are spidery and thin. Some have ornate flourishing serifs and others have none. It wasn't until ignored all of these differences that I was able to see what similarities would constitute an "a" character, and what would make a "b" character.

The answer was symmetry. Straight lines forming some of the characters maintained their thickness and proportions throughout, where as others contained variations. An example of one of these "variations" in thickness happens to be the very first character on the plaque, the "I" of JUDICIO:

Image 2-1.

As you can see, the top of the "I" is thick, the character seems to curve as it tapers down toward its base. By way of contrast, the lines comprising the next character "V" run straight and true in terms of thickness. The "D" seems to bulge on the right and seems to be tilted ever so slightly as well. The following "I" again is straight with no variations in thickness. The "C" seems to be tilted to the right as if it's italicized. I reasoned that characters that were symmetrical without any variations in thickness could be labeled as "a" characters, and those with any aberrations would be "b" characters. As such, the first five characters on the plaque can be read as "babab" representing the letter "X." This was disconcerting, since words generally do not begin with the letter "X." However, it was likely that it too may have been intended to discourage those who may not be up to the challenge, and I continued. This turned out to be the correct course of action. I had correctly identified the first letter, and successfully discovered a cipher text.

I also need to make a caveat here. This treatment of the characters very well could contain a couple of errors as the typeface makes it difficult to be definitive. What follows is my first inclination for each group of letters without any attention paid to any possible messages that might appear. I double and triple checked each character, but again, make no claims of absolute certainty. I simply recorded each letter on its own merit, and this was the result.

To simplify the process, Table 2-2 arranges all the characters from the plaque in groups of five characters. Conjoined or ligatured characters again count as one character. The "TH" character is represented here by "Th" and other linked characters employ the same method. The "a" characters appear as normal, and the "b" characters are italicized:

Table 2-2

IVDIC	IOPYL	IVMGE	NIOSO	CRATE	MARTE	MARON	EMTER	RATEG	ITPOP
babab	ababa	ababa	aaaaa	abaaa	abbaa	baaaa	aaaba	abaab	aabaa
X	P	L	A	I	N	R	C	K	E
VLVSM	ÆRETO	LYMPV	SHABE	TSTAY	PASSE	NGERW	HYGOE	STThOV	BYSOF
babba	babbb	aaaba	babaa	aaaaa	ababa	baaba	Aabaa	baaaa	aabba
Y	Z	C	W	A	L	T	E	R	G
ASTRE	ADIFTh	OVCAN	STWHO	MENVI	OVSDE	AThHATh	PLAST	WIThIN	ThISMO
aaaaa	aaaaa	aabaa	babab	ababa	aabaa	baaba	aaaba	aaaaa	aabba
A	A	E	X	L	E	T	C	A	G
NVMeNtS	HAKSP	EAREW	IThWHO	MEQVI	CKNAT	VREDI	DEWHO	SENAMe	DOThDE
abaab	aabaa	babba	aaaaa	babba	aaaba	ababa	abbab	baaba	aaabb
K	E	Y	A	B	C	L	O	T	D
CKYSTO	MBEFA	RMORE	TheNCOS	TSIEH	ALLYTH	EHAThW	RITTL	EAVES	LIVIN
abaaa	abaaa	aaaaa	aaaaa	aaaba	ababa	baaaa	babab	baaab	abaaa
I	I	A	A	C	L	V	X	S	I
GARTB	VTPAG	ETOSE	RVEHI	SWITT	OBIIT	AÑODO	11616	ÆTATI	S53DI
babaa	ababb	aaaab	baaaa	aaaaa	abaaa	baaab	aaaaa	aaaaa	abaaa
V	M	B	R	A	I	S	A	A	I
E23AP									
aabba									
G									

The letters that appear within the biliteral cipher appear as follows - XPLAINRCKEYZCWALTERGAAEXLETCAGKEYABCLOTDIIAACL VXSIVMBRAISAAIG.

In the first edition of this book, I had only just begun work on the biliteral cipher. Though the work was still preliminary, it was included as it was a solid decryption, but needed refinement. In the rush to publish, that preliminary lacked revision and therefore contained errors. The "bare-eye" interpretation of the subtle differences between the type-faces revealed the limitations of that method. The changes appearing in this decryption are the result of magnification, character by character, from beginning to end. While the majority of the decryption was correct, the refinements and revisions suddenly produced a far clearer message. As stated in the first edition, the opening phrase, "XPLAIN RC KEYZ" or *explain Rosi Crosse keys*, was encouraging as it presented the possibility of more keys to the transposition cipher being revealed. In truth, the cipher text points to a name and letters as symbols and "keys" of the RC. Also, while preparing the Second Edition, the errors discovered in the next set of characters had perplexed me during the first writing so much, I then wrote "I could have made a deciphering error." I did, and now those errors are corrected.

The next letter of "C" is used here as the phonetic, telling the reader to "see" the name that follows – "Walter." This was a shock, as the only Walter as a contemporary of Bacon coming to mind is Sir Walter Raleigh. The "Bacon" signature G follows "Walter" and then "AA" appear, making the first part of the message "XPLAIN RC KEYS – C WALTER G AA." While confusing at first, it requires a bit of inductive reasoning. Letters like this appearing after a clearly written name usually indicate a cipher message of some kind, so I wondered if it could be the last name of "Walter." Looking at the values of these letters in Simple Cipher provides 7 for G, and 1 and 1 for AA. Since the AA (or 1 and 1) appear as separate letters, this indicates a special function, beyond simple addition or multiplication. So, I reasoned that it indicated 7 squared, or 7 to the power (AA) of 2. This obviously produces a factorization of 49, the value of "Ralegh" in Simple Cipher (a common spelling at the time). Therefore, the first part of the message of Bacon's biliteral cipher states, "XPLAIN RC KEYS – C WALTER RALEGH," or if the Keys of the Rosi Crosse are to be explained, we need to take a closer look at Sir Walter Raleigh. The message however continues.

The next series of letters contains two distinct messages – one completes the above thought about Raleigh, and the other provides a hint in understanding the decryption process of the plaque. The next sequence of letters can be read as "EX LET CAG KEY ABC LOT." The Latin word "ex" means, "out of." Of course, "CAG" can be read as a phonetic spelling of "cage." This makes perfect sense in terms of events in orthodox history, as Sir Walter Raleigh spent a large amount of time jailed in the Tower of London. The message therefore becomes, "See Walter Ralegh let out of cage." The last part of the message states who was the "key" in that taking place.

The letters "KEY ABC LOT," again require using Simple Cipher. The letters ABC can be read as 123, the value of the name "James" in Kaye Cipher. The value of the letter L O and T totals 44, "Rex" in Simple Cipher. "To explain the RC keys, see Walter Ralegh let out of his cage. King James was key." While a very odd message, it appears to make sense considering another recent discovery within the upcoming cipher texts. However, these letters also can be understood another way.

These same letters, "KEY ABC LOT," also indicates a hint regarding the decryption process of the messages in the plaque. The word "lot" means "the whole amount, or quantity that is involved or implied." The letters ABC simply indicate the alphabet. Therefore, the key to understanding the cipher texts is the entire quantity of alphabets involved or implied. This indicates that in order to unravel the messages, all of "Bacon's alphabets" or ciphers are required – Simple, Reverse, Kaye, Fourfold and Short Ciphers. The last set of letters provides the instructions to use inductive reasoning.

The next letters in the sequence are DIIAA, where DII is Latin for "blessed," as a veneration of the letters that follow, AA, again representing Athena and Apollo, and Light and Shadow. It also can be a veneration of Bees for reasons already discussed in addition to the combined value of the pair of A's being 2, or the letter B (bee). Seeing the Latin words that follow, the first meaning appears that one intention of the "C" is to stand alone as a cipher signature. Letter C is 100 as a Roman numeral, and "Francis Bacon" in Simple Cipher. Also stated earlier, in several other parts of the cipher texts, the letter "C" simply means *see*. This also seems appropriate considering the following.

The Latin phrase "LVX SI VMBRA" follows, meaning "light if shadow." It finishes with IS AA, and I G. It therefore states, "See light if shadow, is AA. I, Bacon." As many other writers have pointed out in the past, Bacon's headpieces and Frontispieces to his writings (and Shakespeare's writings) often contained the light "A" and shaded "A" symbol. This statement seems to explain that this symbol represents the Rosicrucian concept of providing light amid shadow. When things are "in the dark," unclear or unknown, we are to use knowledge, reason and science to "illuminate" or shed light on the subject, and to bring light where there had been ignorance.

This represents Bacon's favored inductive reasoning in his scientific method. He believed that a part of the answer to what we are trying to discover is partly in our hypothesis or contained in what we already know. As the earlier quote from Manly P. Hall's *Horizon* article indicated, this type of reasoning is the "key" to decrypting Baconian ciphers, and in the above message, Bacon instructs us to do the same. This message encourages us to use what we know about Bacon's cipher systems, and apply them to what we haven't yet discovered, the cipher texts. The cipher text is the truth that is hidden within the shadow of the plaintext of the surface message, and we're called upon to bring it into the light.

In summary, Bacon wished to "explain the Rosi Crosse keys," and the philosophical meaning of "AA." Having decoded several transposition ciphers of the plaque, I can say that this message makes sense given the need to understand Bacon's other ciphers in order to continue the process. We are also instructed to "see Walter Ralegh" to understand the "RC," the true meaning of which remains to be seen.

Since the general message of the Biliteral Cipher states, "The RC Keys explained: See Walter, the AA and Bacon Keys See Light if shadow," it seems to be pointing out letters as symbols of light, as well as telling the cryptographer to use inductive reasoning to solve the cipher, and understand the role of "Walter." "Use what you know about the RC and Bacon keys and their meanings, and his ciphers and his signatures, to discover the hidden message." This is one way he points the reader of the cipher text in the direction of the Keys on the plaque - 32, 8, 5 and 38.

So, on to the first transposition, Key 32.

Chapter 3 - Key 32

So my thought of applying the three keys in sequence to arrive at the "grand revelation" had been completely wrong. But as a process, I initially looked over the results each time to see if any signatures or Rosicrucian sign-posts appeared. Therefore, in presenting the discoveries of Key 32, the superficial discoveries are discussed first, before delving into the more complex messages.

Also a caution to the reader: this first rendition of the character arrangement is only one step in the process. This chapter serves as a bit of a primer of sorts. The more definitive, explicit cipher messages appear later in a more explicit manner. Also, after applying the next set of keys, and another rearrangement of the characters, more explicit signposts and messages appear. However, this algorithm does produce messages and cipher signatures in significant ways that can be used to provide context for messages within other transmutations. They also serve as a confirmation of the process. If a phonetic reading provided a logical and explicit reading, I did my best to spell it out in a way that hopefully makes objective sense. In other words, in this chapter discussion of Key 32, please reserve judgement as the explicit decryptions will appear elsewhere. And so, here are the results from the algorithm produced by "Key 32."

Again, to use Key 32 I counted the characters on the plaque, reached the 32nd character, then recorded that letter. I counted to the 32nd letter after that, and recorded it beside the first, and so on. As I reached the end of the plaque (being sure to include the "I" over the "O" in the count), I began over again at the top of the plaque. When starting at the beginning of the plaque, I created a new row on the algorithm table. That was when the algorithm clicked into place, and every character on the plaque was rearranged in a new order. Every 32nd letter was counted and recorded, until the algorithm had arranged every character out of the original message into what I called "Key 32." The results appear below in rows of nine and ten letters. The special character that appears to be a conjoined T H (the double

Tau) is recorded as "T⊣" and the compound letters representing THIS and THAT appear as Ys and Yt, respectively:

1	A	P	B	S	P	E	E	V	6	
2	E	T	S	O	T⊣	I	B	T	S	3
3	E	Y	O	O	K	O	S	T	I	
4	M	G	A	F	W	Q	O	I	H	E
5	R	O	T	V	H	W	S	A	D	
6	I	T	Y	D	S	M	Ys	W	V	D
7	M	E	E	E	NT	D	C	N	N	
8	Y	R	T	E	L	H	C	A	E	5
9	T	Æ	G	O	V	D	THE	V	T	
10	O	E	T	T	⊣	⊣	D	E	O	I
11	R	S	H	W	O	R	R	L	I	
12	C	M	B	A	H	W	O	Yt	E	A
13	O	L	R	S	S	T	M	E	O	
14	D	N	H	O	A	R	ME	L	A	Æ
15	O	P	G	A	T⊣	N	A	A	T	
16	I	R	V	Y	D	E	N	H	T	1
17	N	P	E	V	I	C	E	L	W	A
18	M	M	V	V	S	S	I	B	1	
19	G	I	S	T⊣	I	V	M	T	I	2
20	T	L	T⊣	I	A	H	T	R	O	
21	V	E	P	E	T	E	T	R	E	I
22	A	T	S	N	S	E	O	G	O	

23	L	A	A	A	A	O	K	T⊣	R	3
24	E	R	O	M	ME	I	N	I	A	
25	P	R	S	R	P	W	E	H	S	S
26	A	M	Y	H	N	E	E	I	I	
27	I	T	E	S	A	I	T⊣	H	T	T
28	C	V	W	T	M	V	O	S	B	
29	I	E	A	F	H	E	D	L	G	T
30	S	V	E	N	I	A	R	V	T	
31	V	O	S	S	E	A	A	A	P	6
32	I	O	N	G	N	K	F	E	I	P

At first the result revealed nothing of significance until a closer look revealed a few Bacon / Rosicrucian signposts, indicating I might have something. However, far more appears here than at first glance as will be seen in a later chapter. At this point in the narrative, I'll stick with what I was able to see at the time as I began to pour over the results. Many of these examples carry a significance due to juxtaposition and other context clues.

First, note the three sets of "Double Taus" at the center of Line 10 (or two Triple Taus), followed by "DEO," Latin for God. Line 19, the number of "T," contains multiple signatures. It reads "G (Bacon) IS T⊣ (Fr. or TT as in 33) I (V+M=32) I B." Another message also appears, but it will presented at a later time. Line 23 contains two (three) sets of double "A's" all in a row - AAAA. (The value of the beginning letter L in Simple Cipher is 11, which also can be read as "AA," therefore 3 sets of AA). AA we know is a known Bacon and Rosicrucian signature, representative of Apollo and Athena, the Speare-shakers. Coincidentally the double Tau symbol, T⊣ appears, which I have already explained as a cipher signature. Just as significantly, the line ends with "R3." 3 = C in Simple Cipher, so the line ends with a signature of the Rosi. Crosse. Additionally, as this process continues to unfold, you will see the appearance of several significant symbols, numbers or phrases indicates the presence of a cipher, and that we should continue on with the process with the current set of letters. Now, let's look at just one message Key 32 contains.

Let's look at the first noticeable message which appears in the upper left corner of our grid of letters. Starting with "A," we can transcribe the following letters:

AEEMRIMYTORC. These letters can be arranged into the following sentence, with no substitutions, composed of Latin and English:

A EEM RI MY TO RC. The letter A can be read as Latin for "away." According to the Notre Dame database accessed via Lexilogos dictionary website, eem is Latin for the following - "go, walk; march, advance; pass; flow; pass (time); ride; be in the middle." According to the same translation website, "ri" means "thing; event, business; fact; cause; property; [res familiaris => property]."

Though the Latin "ME" can mean "I," I have seen word play in the cipher text of the English objective case personal pronoun "ME" being used in the subjective case in place of "I" and "my." It's only reasonable that either explanation works.

Combining the meanings of these Latin words to the rest of the statement, MY, TO, and RC, a logical translation of this message becomes, "advance my property to the Rosi Crosse."

The next noteworthy acrostic appears in the second and third columns of Lines 2 - 7:

Table 3-1

2	E	T	S
3	E	Y	O
4	M	G	A
5	R	O	T
6	I	T	Y
7	M	E	E

By subbing "F" for "T" and "B" for "Y" in rows 2 and 3, we have the initials of Francis Bacon and while this seems an arbitrary inclusion of random letters, I include them due to the juxtaposition of the following. Continuing downward, we see two more Bacon signatures in the form of "G" as already explained, and OT. O = 14, and T = 19, the sum of which is again, 33. The message continues with the just mentioned "T" phonetically spelling the letter T. If we treat the "E's" separately, by adding them to the "Y" above, we have 5+5+23, which again is 33. Then we can continue from the bottom upward in the third column, EY TAOS - eye Taus. As you will see (and this same message repeats itself), this message carries a double meaning. First it's a pun on the words "eye" and "I," whereby Bacon identifies the double Tau as a signature of his name (the message appears more explicitly in the next chapter explaining Key 8). The word "eye" also implies the word "see" and the Tau is a symbol of "Truth," or the message "See the Truth." The other meaning is to draw our attention to the Taus on the plaque, and the full importance of this is explained in the next chapter. As is always the case with the complexity of this cipher, an additional acrostic appears in the same group of characters.

Reading in the opposite direction starting at the "T" in Line 6, we can read the words "TO SEE" because by substituting S for G in Line 4, "SY" becomes a phonetic for "see." Next of course we see the "T" in Line 2 as the symbolic Tau. To its right we read downward, after subbing B for the Y in row 6, "SO A T BEE." This means that, in order to "see" or understand the letter "T," we need to understand the message, "just as A can represent a bee, SO too can T." In this way, we are to understand the complexity of the interrelation between the shapes of the letters and the insect as pictograms. Perhaps an A represents the insect as it crawls, and T is the bee with wings splayed in flight.

Another noteworthy signpost was a square of letters beneath the above-mentioned Line 23:

Table 2-3

24	E	R	O
25	P	R	S
26	A	M	Y

I first noticed the acrostic word EROS meaning *"love,"* but then I realized the word ROSY also appeared. Following the square in a clockwise manner, we see MAP. Was the RC making maps? By substituting a K for P using the substitution system, we also see the word "MAKER." Therefore, the message appears as "ROSY MAP MAKER." Though this was very odd in the early stages, it becomes highly significant in a later chapter, when we see the name of said "Rosy map maker" as an acrostic anagram in the same area. This acrostic is also like an interesting acrostic signpost in another transposition to come.

In summation, all of these superficial observations of signposts, signatures and acrostics indicated a successful transposition of the characters. Given these indications, a closer look reveals even more information. While what follows seems a bit rudimentary, far more explicit, and even shocking, messages await in the following chapters.

Phonetics

One of the layers of messages appear as "phonetics" within the transmuted letter arrangement. While these phonetically spelled messages seem to be mostly superficial in nature, it's important to include them here to not only demonstrate one way in which the messages appear, but also to yield as much information as possible. It also serves as a bit of a primer for understanding the more "robust" and explicit decrypting process to come in future chapters. So, please understand that this stage of decryption is not intended to represent the whole process to come. Also, this section shows how multiple meanings appear within the same sets of letters, so that a more complex message is sent with the fewest possible letters. To begin, Line 1 seems to be another message designed to discourage any of the "profane" if they take a cursory look:

1	A	P	B	S	P	E	E	V	6

Substitutions of "Y" for "B" and "G" for "S" provide a play on Bacon's name with "A PYG PEE," reminiscent of the famous "hang-hog" reference from *The Merry Wives of Windsor*. By subbing the last two characters, the letter "F" is spelled out as EF. Likewise, subbing a K for a P we can see, "A

PYG KEE EF," also meaning the letters "A" and "F" are Bacon Keys. After all, other researchers have noted references to the words *hog, pig and sow* as a reference to "Bacon." Another interpretation would be "APYS KEE EF," a phonetic spelling of "apis," Latin for "bee." As you've seen, bees are mentioned in the other keys and ciphers as being important to the Rosicrucian Order. Perhaps that's why Line 2 contains signatures and a message, since it is the value of the letter "B."

And here Line 2 provides the first of several cipher signatures:

2	E	T	S	O	T⊣	I	B	T	S	3

It begins with the Latin word ET meaning "and," therefore it begins with *And so.* The double Tau follows which we recognize now as a Bacon signature. So, along with pigs, bees, and the letters A and F, his double Tau (Triple Tau) is also a one of his "keys." The rest of the line phonetically reads, *"I be T's 3, I be Triple Tau,"* or *"I am double Tau. See?"* With substitutions between Simple and Reverse Ciphers, the end of the line can be phonetically read as, *"I be F. G. (Bacon)."* The number 3 also becomes "C" which can spell the message, *"I be F. Bacon. See?"* Lastly, this last section can be read as *"I be F. S. 3,"* which at this point is meaningless, but becomes extremely meaningful considering the cipher texts to come. We also already know "C" which is the Roman numeral for 100, the Simple Cipher signature for "Francis Bacon."

Line 3 can be read in conjunction with Line 2 as it continues from the letter "C" read phonetically as "see..."

3	E	Y	O	O	K	O	S	T	I

Substituting "B" for "Y" provides the word *BOOK.* By subbing an "L" in place of the next "O," an obvious anagram for the word *LIST* appears. Using the C at the end of Line 2 with E at the beginning of Line 3, the message therefore reads, *"See book list."* As other ciphers to come explicitly state that Bacon wrote the works attributed to Shakespeare, this line possibly refers to the Rosicrucian clues and signatures in the First Folio, specifically in the titles in the Catalogue of plays. For example, *Richard III* provides "RC" when subbing C for III as its value is 3 in Simple Cipher. With *Love's Labour's Lost*, adding the values of the initial letters LLL in Simple Cipher gives us 33. Adding the initials of *The Merry Wives of Windsor* total 85, "Frater" in Simple. I suspect that many of the titles of the First Folio with such a cipher signature in the title will contain cipher texts within them as well. By collectively looking at all these ciphers as a whole, we can see the depth and breadth of Bacon's work, as well as that of the Rosicrucian Fraternity.

For the next message, the "I" from the previous line is used again, combining with the first letter of Line 4 to form the word *"I'm."*

4	M	G	A	F	W	Q	O	I	H	E

Again, Bacon announces himself with a "G" as a signature. Immediately following two other initials appear which Bacon has already established as representing his signature or keys, A and F. The "A" symbolism is now obvious and familiar. The letter "F" is obvious as Francis, and is also interchangeable with "T" or the Tau of truth. Also when A and F are added together the sum is "7" or again, the equivalent of "G" in Simple Cipher. Therefore a series of "signatures" leads to the rest of the line, working in conjunction with Line 5 to provide more phonetic messages:

4				W	Q	O	I	H	E
5	R	O	T	V	H	W	S	A	D

With substitutions between Simple and Reverse, "Q" becomes "I" and "O" becomes "L," resulting in *WILI*. The "tongue in cheek" message appears, *"Willy, he rot."* The rest of the line could be read phonetically as, *"how sad."* However, this is not the only interpretation that fits. With one substitution, the last letter of Line 4 becomes V. The "H" represents the Double Tau. If we view the "W" in Line 5 as having the value of 4 in Reverse Cipher, then we can read the text as *"I HV (who) ROTE H4."* This can be understood to be a statement from Bacon that he wrote H4, or *Henry IV,* the famous "Shakespearian" three-part history. When we see the other messages in later chapters, the relevance of these plays will be clear.

If we consider the original reading of the end of Line 5 as *"how sad,"* we can read an interesting message in Lines 6 - 8:

6	I	T	Y	D	S	M	Ys	W	V	D
7	M	E	E	E	NT	D	C	N	N	
8	Y	R	T	E	L	H	C	A	E	5

By subbing "B" for "Y" and "W" for "D" in Line 6, we can read, *"how sad it b, WS."* Subbing "N" for "M" can suggest that it's a null. Substituting one "W" for the "D" in the middle of Line 7 and subbing an "R" for the "H" directly below in Line 8, produces the following phonetic message, *"this wud meeen W cn nyr tel. RC."* Or in proper English, *"How sad it be, WS, this would mean W can never tell. RC."* The line ends with A E 5, and since E is 5 in Simple Cipher, we see, "A 55." The number 55 is actually a cipher signature for "Francis Bacon" in Elizabethan Short Cipher. In this way, Bacon and his fraternity convey the message that the actor, William Shakspere, can never tell the secret that Bacon wrote the literary works bearing the name *William Shakespeare.*

Before jumping into the cipher clues in the remainder of Line 8 and throughout Line 9, the signatures that are so prevalent in Line 7 need mentioning, with "7" being the letter "G" in Simple Cipher:

7	M	E	E	E	Nt	D	C	N	N

First of all, it's important to note that many of the lines within the multiple ciphers are "self-aware" in the sense of their location. Since the number 7 is the letter G in Simple Cipher, the line begins with what appears to be a long, drawn out version of the word "MEEE," as Bacon Identifies himself with Line 7 as a whole. The NT of Line 7 is the conjoined letter beside the "mathematical center" of the plaque and as we know from previous experience, equals 32, or "F" in Kaye. The remaining letters, D C N N total 33 in Simple Cipher, the signature of "Bacon" in Simple. And so, Line 7, the number of the letter G in Simple Cipher, we see the message, "*ME. F. BACON,*" in addition to the phonetic messages already discussed. To round out the message and to make sure we understand Bacon is the messenger, adding these four letters in Reverse produces a total of 67, "Francis" in Simple. Adding the Kaye Cipher values produces the sum of 85, "Frater" in Reverse. The cipher signatures do not end there however.

By adding all the Simple Cipher values of these letters, (including N and T for the conjoined letters), the sum is 92, the signature for "Bacon" in Reverse. The Reverse Cipher values, (removing the T from the conjoined letters to symbolize the hiding of "Truth"), the sum is 152 the number of this character on the plaque according to the forward count, the signature of Bacon's true (previously unknown) last name, and "William" in Kaye Cipher.

The phonetic message continues to provide clues in how to decode other areas of the cipher in the remainder of Line 8 through Line 9 and into 10:

8							C	A	E	5
9	T	Æ	G	O	V	D	THE	V	T	
10	O	E	T	T	T⊣	T⊣	D	E	O	I

The next rearrangement of the letters in Key 32 hypothetically requires the use of the number 8 as the next key, and then the number 5 as the final key. Here in the eighth "pass" of Key 32, is a direct reference to "CAE 5." The words Kaye and Key are interchangeable in reference to the Kaye Cipher, so it's only fitting that we would encounter a phonetic spelling of Kaye as "CAE," meaning "key." So, this can be read as a clue that Key 5 will need to be used to reorganize the letters of what will be Key 8.

The next line is line 9, a number with a special occult (read, esoteric or hidden) importance. Nine is the number symbolic of man's lower nature and impulses. Manly Hall states that the digit is a pictogram of the soul descending downward into the material or corporeal world. And the point of human existence is to raise oneself and one's awareness above the physical, by pursuing intellectual and spiritual achievements. Line 9 begins and ends with "T" or the Tau symbol, and contains the whole conjoined word "THE," indicating it may contain a part of a whole phrase.

The phonetic reading gives more clues regarding solving the cipher. But at first glance when read as a whole, we see the Tau as a signpost, and we can read the letters Æ G O as *"EGO"*, the Latin word for "I" or "self." Additionally, since this is Line 9, that number's letter in Simple Cipher is "I," indicating the word EGO "knows" its location within this arrangement of letters. Also, an interpretation of this line along with the first two letters of Line 10, becomes TÆ GOVD THE V TO E, or *"tie good the V to E."* I've encountered this language in other ciphers in the past, and this specific message repeats in the cipher. I had suspected it indicated how to align two alphabets as a substitution cipher, and my working hypothesis had been to substitute between the Simple and Reverse Ciphers, as this seems to "tie" E to V, "good." It was one of the clues leading to the understanding that this substitution or Athbash cipher existed between Simple and Reverse Cipher, which will be corroborated throughout the rest of this book. So, this line is another clue in decoding the plaque and unlocking more of its secrets.

Another hint of the Rosi Crosse appears directly beneath it on the table in Line 10. It contains three "double Taus," or two "Triple Taus," in the form of T T T⊣ T⊣, followed by the word DEO, Latin for God. The O and E at the beginning of the line creates symmetry with the last letters of Deo at the end of the line, with the Taus in between them, and adding the O and E together arrives at the sum of 19, the Simple Cipher number of the Tau. As the line ends with the words, *"DEO I,"* this could imply that the initiation process, if the "T" teachings are followed correctly can produce what is known within esoteric circles as "the God-man." Back to Line 10.

So, for the Rosicrucians and like-minded societies like Freemasonry, 10 represents the first step of initiation. Perhaps this line represents the first step through the initiation process and instruction represented by the Tau on the way to God, or even becoming a "God-man." Additionally, there are several correlations between this line and the surface of the plaque in its original form as Bacon employs the conjoined Th / double Tau symbol ten times, and the Tau appears in multiple forms on this, the tenth line of the algorithm.

An additional acrostic appears here in this section as well. The four squares at the beginning of the two lines 10 and 11 contain an anagram of the word ROSE, with the first letter of line 9 being a T, or Tau cross. To the

9	T	Æ	G
10	O	E	T
11	R	S	H
12	C	M	B

right of ROSE are the letters T and H, which actually represent the Triple Tau symbol. Above them is the Letter G, which in this juxtaposition can represent a Bacon signature. The first two squares of lines 11 and 12 are the letters RC, being an actual signature of the Rosicrucians.

It could also be meant as an acrostic message, "TO RC ET SH," as if dedicating the plaque "to" the Rosicrucian Brotherhood and "SH," which could be "Shakespeare."

Moving on, using the letter "I" from the end of Line 10, we can read a phonetic message in Line 11, which can actually be read as AA for context:

11	R	S	H	W	O	R	R	L	I

Again, Bacon announces his presence with a signature. Using the "I" at the end of Line 10 and subbing "G" for "S" we see the message, *"I R G."* Transposing it to proper English we have, *"I am Bacon,"* followed by the "H" as a double Tau. The rest of the line requires borrowing the first letter of the next line, which is a "C" on Line 12. This is significant. The number twelve in esoteric terms is the number of the "completed man." As stated earlier, 9 is also a significant number. There are three "steps of initiation" and the letter "C" equals the number 3 in Simple Cipher. After completing the three steps of initiation, the candidate becomes an actualized man.

Substituting "D" for the "W" at the center of the line and "O" for "L" at the right (continuing to use the C from the beginning of the next line), a phonetic anagram appears using all of the letters in the sequence: *R DO CROI*, which in French appears, *"du croix,"* or *"are of the cross."*

Line 12 again repeats a theme that appears elsewhere in the cipher system amid the transposition of letters according to the other keys. Once again, Bacon employs the letter "C" as a Roman numeral to provide his cipher signature of 100. The message from Line 12 continues into Line 13:

12	C	M	B	A	H	W	O	Yt	E	A
13	O	L	R	S	S	T	M	E	O	

By using the substitution system supplied by the Simple and Reverse Ciphers, we replace H, W and O with R, D, and L, respectively. The message appears, *"C M BARD. L Yt E A -"* at which time the message continues into Line 13. With a substitution of an "H" for the "R" we are given another Double Tau symbol. Adding the values of S S and T produces 55, again the signature of "Francis Bacon" in Short Cipher. Adding the first part of the message provides *"OL H 55 MEO."* The phonetic reading of the message becomes, *"[C] Francis Bacon am Bard. All that [Latin E A] from the ol' H(TT). 55 (Francis Bacon) [Latin MEO] I."*

Line 14 at first was difficult to understand due to substitutions and the use of an anagram:

14	D	N	H	O	A	R	ME	L	A	Æ

Subbing W for D and R for H, provides the characters of W-N-R-O-A-R- Me-L-A- Æ. The letters can be rearranged into the

58

following phonetic and read in reference to the previous message in which Bacon took credit for all the work attributed to "the Bard," *RAWLÆ NO AR ME*. The message correctly rendered becomes, *"Rawley know are me,"* or *"Rawley knows it was me."*

Line 15 appears to be a signature line, providing a sign-post that anyone using these methods to decode the message is on the right track:

15	O	P	G	A	T⌐	N	A	A	T

As no discernable message appears either as a phonetic message or anagram, I tested the values of the letters of the line, and found something in Reverse Cipher. It seemed to be a collection of RC and Bacon signposts. When adding their totals in Simple Cipher the values totaled the words "I, Francis Bacon" in Simple. In Reverse Cipher the sum of the characters is 135 which is no known cipher signature. On a hunch, I used the precedent of including the word "I" like in the Simple example. By subtracting 16 I arrived at 119, again not a common signature. It wasn't until I considered Bacon's known history as a spy and as having spent two years with the English Ambassador in France, that I realized 119 is the signature of the name "Francois" in Reverse! In Kaye they totaled 161, the Kaye Cipher signatures of both "St. Albans" and "Fraters." Wondering what significance the line number had concerning the signatures, I realized 15 is the value of the letter K in Reverse Cipher, the name of the cipher that didn't require the addition of the word "I." Little did I know that this row of characters would lead me on to yet another discovery which will need to wait for another time.

Line 18 contains an interesting message along with signatures:

18	M	M	V	V	S	S	I	B	1

First of all, 18 is the value of the letter "G" in Reverse Cipher. Line 18 is also a multiple of 9, and reduces *to* 9, the number of Muses in Greek Mythology. The word "muse" appears phonetically *twice*, (e.i. 2 x 9 = 18) as *"MMVVSS,"* or an anagram for *"MVS MVS."* With the letters at the end of the line, we can rearrange their order to read the phonetic message, *"I B A MVS,"* or even *"MVS I B one."* In either of these arrangements, the leftover letters are the "extra muse," *MVS*. Their numerical equivalents in Simple Cipher, 12, 20 and 18 total 50. Though not a common cipher signature per se, you will see later that it is an extremely important cipher signature, possibly the *most* important one in all of the ciphers. Also, the number 50 is a meaningful value. As the number of Argonauts in search of the Golden Fleece, the symbolic significance in reference to Bacon and the Fraternity of the Rosi Crosse is unmistakable. As a Roman numeral it appears as "L," it can represent "Light" and is representative of the Freemason's square. In this way it is interchangeable with the Tau in the shape of the drafter's square. Lastly, you will later see that it is the signature of an unknown name of Francis Bacon.

As one would begin to expect from the number value of the Tau in Simple Cipher, Line 19 contains easily discernable signatures:

| 19 | G | I | S | T⊣ | I | V | M | T | I | 2 |

The first message we see of course is, *"G IS TT."* Subbing "E" for "V" we see, *"I EM T"* or *"I am Tau,"* and it ends with *"I, B."* In Simple Cipher, letters G-I-S-T⊣-I counting the Tau twice, totals 81, "Francois" in Simple. The remainder of the characters, V-M-T-I-2, in Simple total 62. While not on the list of cipher signatures per se, the numbers can represent the letters F and B in Simple Cipher, the initials of Francis Bacon. To illustrate the values of the entire line in Simple, Reverse, and Kaye Ciphers, note Table 3-2:

Table 3-2

Simple	7	9	18	38	9	20	12	19	9	2	143
	G	I	S	T⊣	I	V	M	T	I	2	SUM
Reverse	18	16	7	12	16	5	13	6	16	2	111
Kaye	33	35	18	19	35	20	12	19	35	2	228

Special characters provide a level of flexibility within cipher features in the later signatures. The double Tau can be counted as either one T value or two. Numbers such as the "2" in the above Line 19 can either be counted as the letter it represents and it's counterpart in the substitution protocol when calculating the Reverse signature value, or it can retain its original value. Added all together in Simple Cipher, if we use the value of 38 for the double Tau, the sum is 143, the cipher signature for "Frater" in Kaye Cipher. In Reverse Cipher the total is 111, "Bacon" in Kaye. The Kaye Cipher total uses the single value of 19 for the double Tau, totaling 228 which is the cipher signature of multiple secret identities of Francis Bacon that cannot be discussed at this time, as they haven't been explained yet. However, it will suffice that 22 is the number of the Tav in the Hebrew alphabet, and 8 is the letter H in Simple Cipher, making the number 228 represent the Triple Tau.

I decided to check for other signatures using the Reverse Cipher. I logically thought I would work from right to left due to the symmetry - from left to right, the line ends with the characters of *"I B."* Likewise, from right to left the line ends with *"I G,"* with G as the signature for Bacon. In Reverse Cipher, the characters 2-I-T-M-V-I-T⊣-S, ending before the *"I G,"* total 92 (using the Reverse value for 2 as 23 and 6 for the double Tau), the signature for "Bacon" in Reverse. Adding 16, the value for "I" in Reverse, the sum totals 108, the value of "Francis" in Reverse.

As for phonetics and signatures for now, Lines 20 - 23 are a mystery. What little can be made out seems intriguing, and it contains characters of interest:

20	T	L	T⊣	I	A	H	T	R	O	
21	V	E	P	E	T	E	T	R	E	I
22	A	T	S	N	S	E	O	G	O	
23	L	A	A	A	A	O	K	T⊣	R	3

The last three letters of Line 20 and the first two of Line 21 spell out the word *"TROVE."* The letters in Line 20 leading up to the "T" of trove, T-L-T⊣-I-A-H, when their numerical equivalents in Simple Cipher are totaled, they equal 67, "Francis" in Simple. Subbing a V for E provides the word *"PVT."* The following "E" can be Latin for *"from,"* or when combined with the "T" can be *"ET"* or *"and."* Aside from the strange arrangement of the "E's" in Line 21 the only other notable feature would be the arrangement *"AAAA"* as a symbolic signpost. By subbing an "L" for the first "O" in Line 22, we can make out the phonetic spelling of *"sell."* This could provide a context for the next "substitution" although it doesn't adhere to my rules - by seeing the *AAAA* as one unit of 4, which would be "D" in Simple Cipher. It could then be read as *"SEL GOLD."* The series of characters ends with R3, or the initials *RC.* The letters leading up to the words "Trove, sell gold," T – L - T⊣ - I, total 67 in Simple Cipher, the signature for "Francis" in Simple.

Line 24 is interesting in a variety of ways:

24	E	R	O	M	ME	I	N	I	A

First of all, it's the number of letters in the Elizabethan alphabet, drawing our attention to the relationship between the Simple and Reverse Ciphers. The number reminds us that the alphabet in this sense begins and ends with "A," reminding us of the sigil used by Bacon, AA. In the words of Bacon / Shakespeare scholar Peter Dawkins, in his amazing essay "The Secret Signature" the AA symbol has "an even more profound meaning or additional meaning, one of which is Alpha-Omega, or Creation-Revelation, where the end result is the perfect revelation or image of the beginning... That is to say, the Alpha is Light, the Omega is illumination" (Dawkins 2). Both A and O also symbolize light for reasons already stated. As an interesting illustration of this idea, the sum of the characters in Simple and Reverse Ciphers produce signatures in Reverse and Simple:

Table 3-3

	E	R	O	M	ME	I	N	I	A	SUM
Simple	5	17	14	12	12	9	13	9	1	92
Reverse	20	8	11	13	13	16	12	16	24	133

The numerical equivalents of the characters in Simple Cipher total 92, the ciphcr signature of *Bacon* in Reverse Cipher. If we add the "E" value in "Me" then we have 97, which can be read as "I G" or "I Bacon." The sum of the letter values in Reverse Cipher is 133, the signature for "Baron Verulam" in Simple Cipher,

61

as well as another significant name which will be discussed in the encoded messages to follow. If we add the Reverse "E" value in the "Me" character we have the sum 153, which has already been explained. The Kaye Cipher value is 227, the 49th prime number, and 49 is 7 times 7, an idea we have seen in other areas of the cipher texts. It's also the Simple Cipher signature of his true name which hasn't appeared yet. However, it wasn't until much later in this process that I learned how to use Bacon's *Four-fold Cipher*. When calculating the value of "Sir Francis Bacon" using that cipher system, the total is 227. (A full explanation of this cipher system appears in a later chapter).

Interestingly, it's also possible to read words within these leftover letters. The line ends with the Latin word *INIA*, meaning "*belong to; be involved in.*" *ME* appears at the center, and to the left two possibilities present themselves. The first could be an obvious anagram for *ROME,* or *MORE reversed.* The next could be the phonetic spelling of Rome as *ROM,* with the Latin word *E,* meaning "from." I made note of it for my more detailed analysis to follow.

Another interesting correlation to previous research appeared in Line 25 as well:

25	P	R	S	R	P	W	E	H	S	S

The symmetry of the first five letters P R S R P immediately catches attention. Presuming a purpose, I reasoned that it could be a clue. Because of the symmetry I checked their value in Reverse Cipher and PRS totaled 25. The rest of the line can be read with substitutions for the last three characters as, *WE R GG.* As for signatures, using Simple Cipher values, the first *PRS* totals 50, the number of the Argonauts, and therefore the Rosicrucian Order, along with another signature to be revealed in a later chapter. Next, *SR* total 32 and WEH total 33, leaving the *GG* as being self-evident at this point.

The number 25 reminded me of an interesting question friend and fellow Oak Island researcher Erin Helton had asked our group. Her research had led her to Renaissance images of two historical figures, Manuel de Moura y Corte Real, and his father Cristobal de Moura. They both had been depicted with a key with its "bit and wards" cut in the shape of the number 25, and she wondered if there could be a cipher connection. It does.

The number 25 represents the letters "AA" in Bacon's Fourfold Cipher. Also, since 25 can be seen as 2 + 5, the number 7 or G, as well as "BE," a phonetic spelling of "bee." This powerful symbol to Bacon and the RC, makes it appropriate that other interesting signatures appear at the same time. The first four letters total 67, Francis in Simple. The remainder of the letters total 85, Frater in Reverse. The total is also 152 in Simple, the signature for "William" as well as another historical name that will become relevant. The lead-up to this total is interesting as has already been noted, however even more so when taken on a step-by-step basis. Adding P (15) + R (17) is 32, the letter F in Kaye Cipher. Adding S (18) to 32 if 50, the number of Argonauts as well as an until now unknown signature of Bacon. Adding the letter R (17) we have 67, "Francis" in Simple Cipher. Next we add P (15), W (21) and E (5) to arrive at 108, "Francis" in Reverse. To this, we add the remaining characters of H (8), S (18) and S (18), and we arrive at a total of 152, "William" in Kaye cipher, as well as the other unknown cipher signature. In the line that spells "be" there were five cipher signatures of Bacon.

Line 26 contained a very curious phrase that only made true sense after I had decrypted later keys:

26	A	M	Y	H	N	E	E	I	I

I first noticed the arrangement of the pair of "I's" like pillars at the end of the line. The next obvious word that jumps out is MY, the letter H (double Tau, or conjoined TH?) and the phonetic spelling, NEE. If we assume that the word MY is actually associated with NEE, then this leaves us with *AH*, and I remembered a reference in a different area of my research in Hebrew. A quick search showed AH as Hebrew for "brother," spelled " אח. " Initially, this seemed to reference a vow to the Brethren of the RC, but in light of later discoveries, these references will make even more sense in a more complete context.

Line 27 was far more puzzling than the last, and was another that would benefit from context from the later keys:

27	I	T	E	S	A	I	T⊣	H	T	T

The obvious feature of this line is the prevalence of the double Tau symbol at the end in the form of T⊣ H and TT. And in actuality, all eight letters are meaningful in and of themselves. As this symbol can represent the number 33, I noted the relationship with the line number as well. If we view 33 as 3x3, then the three examples of the double Tau can be seen as 9 times 3, which equals the line number 27. The fact that there also are a total of 7 Tau total, multiplying the value of 19 times 7 produces 133, "Baron Verulam" in Simple. The remaining characters, I (9), E (5), S (18) and A (1), total 33 plus the letter I, stating "I Bacon." Taken at face value with the Tau symbols removed, the anagram of "I ESAIH," "ESAH" or "ESA" appears as a phonetic message of "I Esau." Why Bacon would reference himself as such, *"I, F, ESA. I T⊣,"* or *"I Francis am Esau - I Bacon,"* made no sense in reference to his brother Anthony Bacon, at least not at this time. In fact it wasn't until the later keys were unlocked that a return to this line made sense of it. The phonetic SAITH precedes two double Tau symbols, following the Latin *"E"* meaning *"from."* This can be seen as "From it sayeth H TT." Not knowing the antecedent of *"IT,"* I looked at alternative readings. Subbing an F for T and a V for E, it can render, *"IF V SAITH (double Tau double Tau)."* It could also be read as *"I*

Tau" or with a substitution, *"I, F."* Again, nothing definitive, but excellent signposts.

Line 28 contained nothing noteworthy, but Line 29, with multiple substitutions between Simple and Reverse contains another message about authorship:

29	I	E	A	F	H	E	D	L	G	T

For the first time in the entire plaque's coded message, it was necessary to substitute every letter in the line, with the one unsurprising exception of "A." The letters then appear as the anagram, Q V A T R V W O S F. Rearranged, the letters spell *"QVARTO WVS F,"* possibly attributing the writing of the Quarto to Francis.

Lines 30 and 31 contain a signature and a message to the profane, such as this author:

30	S	V	E	N	I	A	R	V	T	
31	V	O	S	S	E	A	A	A	P	6

The first part of Line 30 appears to have a phonetic signature that states, *"Seven I are,"* which at this point we could read as Bacon claiming the letter "G" as a cipher signature (Kaye value). Subbing E for V, the remainder of the line with Line 31 reads as, *"ET VOS SE A P. F AA."* Translated from the Latin we have, *"And you had a pee. F AA."* If we sub the K for the P, it could also again be naming A A as a "Kaye" or key, meaning *"And you have a key, F = AA."*

Line 32, the value of F in Kaye Cipher, simply appears to contain another message along the same "main vein," so to speak:

I	O	N	G	N	K	F	E	I	P

With substitutions of an M for N, P for K, T for F and V for E, the phonetic anagram states, "IM GON P TV. I P," or *"I'm going pee too. I P."* It could also be a pun as it seems the Hebrew translation of the letter "P" is often "F."

A Fun Digression

On that particular note, one thing that may have perplexed you as the reader is the use of the term "pee." While *"piss"* was known to be in early usage in Latin, early French and English in various forms, conventional wisdom contends that the word "pee" wasn't recorded as being used in reference to urination until the 1800's. However, a well-known precedent exists in the play *12th Night* which conventional wisdom also claims was written by the actor named William Shakspere. *(As a fun aside: 12 x 56 (night) = 672 - 6 - 7 - 2 = F, "G" and B in Simple Cipher, or Francis (67) B (2). It could also be interpreted as a few other signatures).*

The hilarious scene, Act II Scene 5, involves a prudish steward named Malvolio, who has been fooled by three pranksters that the Lady he serves (and watches over) has written a letter to a lover. The trio (and the audience) overhears him as he confirms her handwriting aloud, and the joke becomes obvious. He states:

> *"By my life, this is my lady's hand. These be her very C's, her U's and her T's, and thus makes she her great P's..."*

Picture the trio overhearing this prudish man spell out the vulgar word and the volume of the woman's urination, while displaying their stifled laughter to the audience, and you can imagine the added hilarity of the scene. Even if one were to discount the use of the word "and" in place of the letter "N," the word *cut* was also used as vulgar slang for vagina. Naughty bathroom humor stands the test of time.

In Summary

While this section involved some speculation, the signposts shone through. While it's unfair to expect fully clear explicit messages so early on in the decryption process, the Key 32 rearrangement of the characters appears to yield a large amount of information. What at first glance appears to be a random collection of noise, yields messages in the form of acrostics, phonetic spellings and anagrams, all of which are time-honored forms of cipher systems. Also, it's important to remember that we are still early in this process and other transpositions await. Yet I maintain that by employing the cipher systems known to be used by Sir Francis Bacon and his contemporaries, produces not only some clear messages, but multiple well-known cipher signatures specifically known to be used by him. The messages range from cryptic hints and clues regarding decrypting the rest of the message, from possible Biblical allusions to low-brow references to bathroom humor. Taken all together, the typical sign-posts all indicate that the initial steps taken to decipher the code were correct, and the original plan should continue.

While I had been hoping for better results with the next key's rearrangement of letters, nothing could have prepared me for the messages that appeared.

(AUTHOR'S NOTE: Little did I know back when I originally wrote this chapter, that Key 32 held far more complex, profound and controversial messages. While preparing this book for print, more messages were discovered in the Key 32 transposition of the characters from the plaque. Though the following chapters are surprising enough in terms of the uncovered cipher texts, the acrostic anagram messages of this key are so provocative and controversial, another chapter covering them is included at the end of the book, before the final chapter and appendices. Though people often preface extraordinary information with the phrase, "you're not going to believe this," sadly I think that people truly will not believe the revelations of Key 3)].

Chapter 4 - Key 8

Following the original plan, 8 was used as a key to rearrange the letters in the table created by Key 32. The number 8 is also "H" in Simple Cipher and is also representative of the double Tau symbol. One specific "H" on the plaque actually carries a special significance. You might recall the "forward count" of the characters from Chapter 1, and how my friend and fellow researcher Chris Donah had commented on the H of the word HE in the seventh line of the plaque was larger than all of the others. That character was the 231st character on the plaque, which you will remember is 33 multiplied by 7. Also, the symbol used by Bacon on the plaque, the conjoined Th represented as "T⊣" in this writing was yet another hint. And so, not only did the mistaken age of Shakespeare indicate this would be an important key in the cipher, but the letter H also pointed to 8.

So, the number 8 created an algorithm rearranging the letters from Key 32 in the same manner as the original arrangement. And not so coincidentally, each pass of Key 32 produced two rows of 19 (T) characters. This I believed represented H (8) as the double Tau, since a double Tau would be two times nineteen. Each conjoined letter from the plaque is displayed in the same manner as the table above. Font size may vary due to the limited space. The number at the left indicates the number of the "pass" I made of the table. For example, after I counted out the 8th letters from the chart the first time, as I returned to the top of the table, I counted that as the beginning of the "second pass," and so on. Each pass is numbered in the table below, again organized in two rows of 19 characters, the double Tau.

Here is the result:

Table 4-1: Key 8

1	V	B	K	F	O	I	V	C	H	O	T	R	I	Yt	T	Λ	G	R	I
	L	S	I	T⊣	E	I	G	K	ME	R	M	I	T	O	E	N	S	I	I

2	E	I	O	A	R	D	W	D	L	G	E	I	L	O	S	O	P	0	T
	E	S	T⊣	L	V	E	O	O	M	S	A	I	H	V	H	E	O	6	E
3	E	T⊣	O	G	E	A	Ys	Nt	E	Æ	O	O	R	W	S	H	O	T	H
	C	V	S	T	O	R	E	A	O	R	S	I	T⊣	M	F	V	V	P	E
4	P	O	Y	M	H	S	M	E	T	T	T	E	R	H	R	N	Æ	A	N
	I	V	I	2	R	T	S	A	R	P	S	E	I	T	A	S	T	A	K
5	S	S	E	I	I	W	S	E	R	5	V	D	O	A	L	D	A	A	E
	V	M	G	I	T	E	N	A	E	A	H	E	A	W	E	T	V	A	N
6	B	T	3	T	O	H	D	E	Y	E	THE	T⊣	W	B	O	O	L	N	D
	E	M	1	T	H	T	S	A	3	I	E	N	S	V	I	G	R	A	G
7	P	E	S	S	Q	V	Y	M	N	A	D	T⊣	H	M	A	E	ME	T⊣	Y
	P	A	B	M	A	E	T	L	R	N	W	H	E	C	B	L	A	E	N
8	A	6	T	O	W	T	T	D	N	C	V	T	S	C	E	M	R	A	V
N	W	I	V	I	P	A	O	T⊣	I	P	Y	T	T	S	D	I	S	O	P

Most of the discoveries that propelled this research forward appeared during the interpretation of "Key 8." Once again, the first step was to identify any features that might indicate that we are still dealing with a cipher. Immediately my eyes were drawn to the Triple Tau nearly at the center of the table, in the middle of line 4. Directly beneath that, they were drawn to the word "EYE" in the middle of line 6.

Focusing on this section, note that directions appear as the phrase, "EYE THE T⊣." Like the acrostic from the previous chapter, the pun was obvious – "I the TT." But it would carry other meanings as well. Eye the Double Tau? Look at the Double Tau? Notice it? The eye is a symbol of reason and understanding – reason out the double Tau? Understand it?

Looking back at the Triple Tau of line 4, the appear after the word "ME," stating ME TTT. IN Fourfold Cipher, the value of TTT is 67, "Francis" in Simple. In fact the three T's were framed by the letter "E" on each side. However, in Simple Cipher TTT totals 57, and adding E and E brings the sum to 67 again, "Francis." The value in Reverse Cipher totaled 58, the value of "Shakespeare" in Short Cipher. Lastly in Kaye Cipher the letters total 119, "Francois" in Reverse Cipher. Additionally, perhaps the juxtaposition of the symbol bookended by the letter "E" supported the planned use of the letter E as a Key in rearranging the letters of the table resulting from Key 8. E = 5. This also coincides with my original theory concerning the keys on the plaque when I added the digits of the date "23." This will be expanded upon later.

Bed-Wetting

So, I went to work trying to apply Key 5 to the Key 8 arrangement, thinking I was well on my way to "decoding the message." Do you remember the scene in the movie *A Christmas Story* where the Peter Billingsley "Ralphy" character locks himself in the bathroom with his Annie Oakley decoder ring? Think that, only my experience wasn't as rewarding as Ralphy's "crumby commercial" for Ovaltine.

The initial thought had been that "EYE THE T⊣" meant skip the Triple Taus at the center. After all, since there were 305 total characters, in order to use the number 5 as a key that would produce a workable algorithm, at least one character would need to be omitted. Initially I believed I had a rousing success on my hands as the algorithm using Key 5 and skipping these characters produced the following letters:

HRKSWOEHEWHOPENVS - I stopped and read the line as, "HARKS! Woe he who opens…" Opens what? The tomb? The memorial? Was it an old superstitious curse? I continued -

HRKSWOEHEWHOPENVSWETSDEEBED3AMMEBLATDRADOO YtMEIDPOET⊣OHRSPRA2

I stopped there as I realized what it said. Without going through the specifics of the actual decrypting, most of it will be obvious to you as well. Substituting out the 2 at the end with a Y from the Reverse Cipher, the message read: *"Harks! Woe he who penus wets dee bed 3 am me blatdr a doo that. Me Id pou thoh ars pray…"*

The letters after this were nonsensical, so I knew the mistake was in the count, or the omission of the Taus strategy.

However, when I began practicing decryption and cipher work, I had run into plenty of examples of low-brow, potty humor, especially when I made a mistake. I took a step back for a moment.

Another interpretation at the end of the line, MEIDPOET⊣ or *Me, I the poet?*

Unsure if it was a dead end, the whole section or table generated by Key 5 of Key 32 merely could be a joke. I think such phonetics exist to distract the "profane" from the actual message, and for a time, I must admit they worked. So was it a test to see if I would continue on to decipher the rest of the message, and if I did, how would I be rewarded? What could be learned?

I stepped back again. I began to look for an acrostic message in the first column of Key 8, since one had been employed in Key 32. This message appears:

VLEEECPISVBEPPAN

If you look at the table of Key 8, you will notice that on line 5, *two* S's appear. I used the cipher system to substitute "K's" for the "P's," resulting in, with only a few substitutions across the Ciphers, BUKKAN in Hebrew is בוככאנ meaning "so here." I used the substitution of "E" for the "V," and "E" is Latin for "from," resulting in "V LEEEC PISS E BUKKAN." Or, *So you leak piss from here.*

This left the same conundrum. Do I waste my time to decode a bunch of jokes about bed-wetting? Do I struggle to solve the problem of Key 5 to get all of the letters into an intelligible order after the Taus? Especially when I had a thought that the *true* main Key had been staring me (and everyone else) in the face? In actuality, the real messages in Key 8 had sat undiscovered on my desk for some time. A part of me thought at the time that perhaps the whole process of using Keys 32 and 8, was simply to generate the message that provided the "real" key. Though this was wrong, it was a fortuitous decision, because it led to what became Key 38, which contained the hints of how to read the cipher. So I followed the clue at the center of the text of Key 8.

"EYE THE T⊣." It had multiple meanings. In the first, Bacon uses the pun of "eye" for "I" and identifies himself as "T T" or Thirty Three. But as stated earlier, the eye is the symbol of reason, of intellect. Reason the double Tau. T = 19 in the Simple Cipher, and doubling the Tau equals 38. And so, at that time a change of direction was in order. That's when I used 38 as a key to again rearrange the characters on the plaque a second time. The discoveries made with Key 38 were nothing short of amazing, which appear in a later chapter.

Other than the previously mentioned message down the left side of Key 8, I failed to identify any other acrostics, or phonetic messages the way they had appeared in Key 32. However, this was when I discovered the anagram system being used by Bacon on the plaque.

I had wanted to avoid using anagrams, however they cropped up with annoying frequency. And as I delved into them, I realized that a methodical system was at work here, so I followed these clues to develop a standard operating procedure that would allow objectivity. This began by trying to identify any complete words forward and backward, then looking for any anagrams that could be completed using letters that were side by side in order to establish a context. After removing these letters, I imagined the remaining letters being left justified, though this isn't conveyed in the tables I included in this section. Next I looked at any anagrams using the remaining very nearby letters, only one or two letters away. After all of these possibilities had been exhausted, I would then try to find any final possible anagrams in the letters that remained. Also, many of the phonetic and acrostic messages provided context of what type of words to look for.

When all of the possibilities were exhausted, there would be only a handful of letters "leftover." This was when I discovered the system used to "check" the work, to make sure the correct letters were used, by calculating the sums of the leftover characters and checking for obvious cipher signatures.

With each successive line, many of which maintained the same "story," theme and context, when I added the numerical values of the leftover letters together using the Simple, Reverse and Kaye Ciphers, the totals would be common cipher signatures of Sir Francis Bacon and Fra. Rosi Crosse. The messages were all unlike anything I could have anticipated which only adds to the legitimacy of the method I employed to avoid subjectivity. As you'll see, none of these specific messages were expected.

Line by Line

I treated each "pass" of the cipher as its own line, and will present them in this manner. Here are the Key 8 arrangement of the characters of Line 1:

1	V	B	K	F	O	I	V	C	H	**O**	**T**	**R**	**I**	*Yt*	T	**A**	**G**	**R**	1
	L	S	I	T⌐	E	I	G	K	ME	R	M	I	T	O	E	N	S	I	I

With a lack of any obvious words in English, I tried to identify words in Latin. At the end of the first row of Line 1, I noticed AGR1, the Latin word for "*land, country.*" Though a number 1 would normally denote a letter "A," one is "I" in Roman numerals, and I had noticed Roman numerals functioning in other areas of the cipher. I also noted the word OTRI, which a Latin dictionary defines as, "*of either one; of whichever of the two.*" Also I had early on decided to use whole words at face value, so the Yt character could keep its meaning as "*that.*"

Exhausting the first row of obvious words, the next step was to move on to the anagrams from the groups of leftover letters:

V	B	K	F	O	*I*	**V**	**C**	**H**			T			

Next I noted that by substituting for each of the letters V, C and H, they became E, X and R, respectively, an anagram for *"REX."* The word "I" seemed obvious.

V	B	K	F	O							T			

With the following remaining letters, no obvious words appeared to use other than "OF," but more context was necessary to see if that word would be needed to complete a contextual idea, or perhaps the letters would be used in a larger word.

Moving on to the second row of Line 1 produced the following:

L	S	I	T⌐	E	I	G	K	ME	R	M	**I**	**T**	**O**	E	N	**S**	**I**	I

71

The only complete word appearing in this row of the arrangement, was the backwards Latin word, "OTI." To get a full sense of the meaning of this three letter word, the Latin database I use lists the meaning as, "*Leisure; spare time; holiday; ease, rest , peace, quiet; tranquility / calm.*" At the end of the row appeared "IS" backwards, and in Latin means "*advance; pass; sail.*" At this point, all obvious words had been selected, and so it's permissible to create any constructions that fit the context from the remaining letters. From the final letters I identified a sizable anagram, demonstrating that the options had been exhausted:

L	S	I	T⊣	E	I	G	K	ME	R	M			E	N			*I*

(Something discovered before the attempted completion of Key 8, was the fact that the conjoined or ligatured characters could be used or counted as either letter that appeared in the construction - in this row, the ligatured letters M and E are being used as an "E"). The L E I G Me R E characters form the Latin word ELIGERE, meaning "*choose.*" Since it is an action verb, looking for a suitable subject for the verb among the remaining letters was provided by settling on one of the leftover "I's."

So far, this creates a word bank of (in the order found) - *AGRI, OTRI, Yt, REX, I, OTI, IS, ELIGERE, I.* The only sentence that could be formed from this mixture of Latin and English truly made no sense, especially in reference to "Shakespeare" and Francis Bacon. So far, I could spell out, "*I REX OTRI AGRI Yt I ELIGERE. OTI IS I.*" This translated as, "*I KING of whichever of the two countries that I choose. I pass in leisure (on holiday).*"

The last step was to study the leftover letters to see if any other words could be formed from them making the message be more complete. The leftover letters were, V B K F O T S I T⊣ M N. The only word that would be "*am*" between *I* and *KING,* and there were the letters V S and M, the anagram for *SVM,* Latin for "am." And so, the final message in Latin is "*I SVM REX OTRI Yt I ELIGERE. OTI IS I,*" or translated, "*I am King of whichever of the two countries I choose. I pass in leisure (on holiday).*"

Assuming I had made a mistake because of the strange message, I checked the remaining letters for an identifiable cipher signature:

Simple	2	10	6	14	19	9	19	13	92
Leftover	B	K	F	O	T	I	T⊣	N	SUM
Reverse	23	15	19	11	6	16	6	12	108
Kaye	28	10	32	14	19	9	19	13	144

One signature would have sufficed for confirmation, but here we have three obvious ones. Simple Cipher produces 92 as the signature for "Bacon" in Reverse Cipher, and the Reverse Cipher completes his name by producing 108, the Reverse Cipher signature for "Francis." With Kaye equaling 144, is interesting because the natural reaction is to see two sets of combined Bacon signatures. The obvious signatures would be 111 as Bacon in Kaye and 33 as Bacon in Simple. The others would be 100 as Francis Bacon in Simple, and 44, which has been called the "secret cipher signature" of Bacon. However the answer is even more obvious than any of these solutions. The letters of the word "Sir" total 44 in Simple Cipher, which when added to 100 for "Francis Bacon," totals 144 or the signature in Simple for "Sir Francis Bacon." Not so coincidentally, it's also the Simple Cipher value of "Rex Francis Bacon."

Though the opening message of Key 8 is very confusing, when taken in consideration with some of the phonetic and acrostic messages I had found in other keys, I worried that the cipher texts may go beyond the "simple question of Bacon / Shakespeare authorship." Was it really Bacon who created the plaque? Who could possibly be the king of two countries? Still assuming I had made a mistake, I hoped that the next two rows of letters of Line 2 would clarify things. They did, but certainly not in a way that simplified the matter:

2	E	I	O	A	R	D	W	D	L	G	E	**I**	**L**	**O**	**S**	O	P	**I**	**T**
	E	**S**	ꓕ	L	V	E	O	O	M	S	A	I	H	V	H	E	O	6	E

First of all, this line was especially challenging as there were two outcomes that can be confirmed by checking them with the cipher signature method. This was the first time a disturbing thought occurred to me – while each key having a single cipher text is amazing, what if there were actually two in each? Additionally, because the information was challenging in terms of common knowledge about Francis Bacon, I had to trust in the methodologies as outlined. Follow the clues. Identify complete words that provide a context, and then continue on. And as I studied the letters, I could only see one complete word, and unfortunately it made sense in the context of the message of Line 1.

Five letters from the end of the first row of Line 2, reading backwards I saw *"SOLI,"* Latin for *"throne."* Directly to its right was an anagram for *"ETSI,"* Latin for *"although."* So, this left me with the following remaining letters:

E	I	O	A	R	D	W	D	L	G	E					O	P		
		ꓕ	**L**	**V**	**E**	**O**	O	**M**	**S**	**A**	**I**	H	**V**	H	E	O	6	E

The next obvious anagram appeared in the second row, *"LOVE."* Just to its right, appropriately enough, the name of the King, *"IAMES,"* with a substitution of an E for the V. The remainder of the letters appear as follows:

E	*I*	*O*	A	R	*D*	W	D	L	G	E			O	P		
	T⊣				O				H	H	E	O	6	E		

First, I saw the words, I and DO in the first row (italicized). In looking for words in the remaining characters, after removing I and DO and left justifying the letters mentally, I noted a word I had seen in the phonetic messages of Key 38. I began to suspect that the messages were more problematic than I had first imagined. I was able to form the word *"ELDER"* using the remaining letters from the top row with no substitutions.

		A		W		**G**				O	P	
	T⊣				O			**H**	**H**	**E**	**O**	**6**	*E*

Then with substitutions (both H's become R's, the 6 becomes F and the ligatured double Tau is T), I saw an opportunity to spell *"FRATER"* which seemed appropriate amid the context of the mentions of the Rosicrucian Order, as the Latin word for "brother." As I began to make sense of the words, I again had a moment where I came to an uncomfortable conclusion. I noted that the last character, *"E"* could be used as the Latin word meaning, "as a result of; out of."

The message of Line 2 of Key 8 then becomes, *"ETSI I ELDER FRATER E LOVE DO SOLI IAMES."* "DO" in this sense is Latin for "surrender." In English, this message is rendered, "Although I'm the older brother, out of love for James, I surrender the throne," or perhaps, "out of love I surrender the throne to James."

I needed to take a breather after that one. At first I thought I had found an actual cryptogram confirming the rumors of Francis Bacon's royal lineage. Did I discover evidence of the Prince Tudor theory? But the message calls Bacon "the elder brother" in reference to James! Stating that this whole situation made me nervous is an understatement. As you will soon see however, the situation was far worse than I originally thought. But first, let's calculate the values of the leftover letters.

They were W G O P O O. Yes. They spell "W go poo." But like all of the other times, it could just be a coincidence...

I calculated the values of the leftover letters in Table 4-1:

74

The obvious cipher signature appears in Kaye Cipher, 111, the Kaye cipher signature for the name "Bacon." At first I thought that the other numbers were irrelevant, as the rule I had set forth for checking the signatures really only requires one obvious signature. However on closer examination, I realized that 85 is the value of "Frater" in Reverse Cipher. 65 is the value of "Frater" in Simple Cipher (as well as the value of St. Alban). Given the values of the leftover characters being two "brothers," I would call this a successful decryption in context of being "the elder brother." But as the reader will recall, this line has another interpretation.

Table 4 - 1

Simple	21	7	14	15	14	14	85
Letters	W	G	O	P	O	O	SUM
Reverse	4	18	11	10	11	11	65
Kaye	21	33	14	15	14	14	111

Given the messages up to this point, I had to consider what they were telling me. I needed to reject my cognitive biases, and logically think through the messages, and take the thought to its logical conclusion, as improbable as it might be.

Line 1 tells us that "I (read as Bacon) have the choice of the thrones of two countries." Line 2 calls James his younger brother. The only way either of these statements could possibly be true, is if they had the same mother. And two thrones? That can only have one meaning - the true parents of Sir Francis Bacon would have to be Mary, Queen of Scots and Francis II of France.

Yes, I understand all the "reasons this can't be true." But I had to logically think through the messages, regardless of any preconceived thoughts and beliefs. This is when I decided to see if the line could be interpreted any other way. Though the signatures confirmed it as a legitimate interpretation, I still wondered if I had gotten it wrong. Could there be another way to read the line? Unfortunately (or fortunately) the answer is "yes."

So, here we go again:

2	E	I	O	A	R	D	W	D	*L*	*G*	*E*	*I*	L	O	S	O	P	I	T
	E	S	T⊣	L	V	E	O	O	M	S	A	I	H	V	H	E	O	6	E

Trying to adhere to my original rules while looking for variations of the original Line 2 interpretation, I had to begin with the first two obvious words from the last decoding attempt, SOLI and ETSI. And then I saw another backwards word with one substitution (in italics). Subbing "O" for the "L" we have the word *EGO*, Latin for "I." At the end (underlined), I also saw "OF" or "TO" (depending on the need) from the "O6." This leaves the following letters:

E	I	O	A	R	D	W	D							O	P		
	T⊣	L	V	E	O	O	M	S	A	I	H	V	H	E			E

Moving on to anagrams that were only a few letters apart, I spotted IVRO, Latin for "swear; or vow obedience to," by substituting "R" in place of the "H." Without any other obvious possibilities, I decided to see what I could make with the remaining letters, considering the context, and the use of inductive reasoning:

E	**I**	O	**A**	**R**	**D**	W	D					O	**P**	
	T⊣	L	**V**	E	O		**M**	S	A	H		E		E

There were a couple of possibilities that needed to be explored. Substituting an H for the R (as it was near the majority of the letters if left-justified), and subbing an "N" for the "M," spells out "*DAUPHIN*."

E	**O**			W	**D**					O		
	T⊣	**L**		**E**	O		**S**	**A**	H		E		E

Substituting "V" in place of "E" and "G" for "S," I was able to spell GAUL, and with two letters from the top row I could spell "DE," Latin meaning "from; of; concerning or with regard to." The "O" can be added to the earlier "TO" as "TOO" and T⊣ and E spell "THE." A sentence can be formed as, "*ETSI EGO ThE DAUPHIN TOO IVRO DE SOLI GAUL,*" or in English, "Although I'm the Dauphin too, I swear obedience (allegiance) concerning the throne of France."

The leftover letters spell out "WOO HEE," and in Simple Cipher they total 67, the Simple Cipher signature for "Francis." The Reverse total is 83, and the Kaye total is 145. Though not obvious ciphers, these numbers seem to repeat in other areas and I couldn't at first reason out the significance. But then considering the context of the message, the number 145 is the Simple Cipher signature of "IAMES STEWART." The number 83 appears in other areas as well and was unclear to me for some time. It's the Simple Cipher sum of the letters of the word "FRATERS." And so the message of the "leftover" letters is, "*Francis, James Stewart, Brothers.*"

This is when I realized that perhaps the other lines of Key 8, as well as the other keys, could have more than one interpretation, but moving forward, only one other alternative reading,was attempted, as you will see later in this chapter. I avoided it as I felt it would compromise the process I had created in the attempt to remain as objective as possible, so I decided to adhere to the original rules.

Moving on to Line 3 of the cipher produced by Key 8, I wondered what controversial information would appear next:

3	E	T⊣	O	G	E	A	Ys	Nt	E	Æ	O	O	R	W	S	H	O	T	H
	C	V	S	T	O	R	*E*	*A*	<u>O</u>	<u>R</u>	<u>S</u>	<u>I</u>	T⊣	M	F	V	V	P	E

The complete Latin words found were ET⊣O, meaning "go; advance," EA, meaning "he, she, it," and ORSI meaning "words; undertakings." The Ys character was used as "this." This left the following letters:

		G	E	A	Ys	*Nt*	*E*	*Æ*	*O*	O	R	<u>W</u>	<u>S</u>	<u>H</u>	<u>O</u>	<u>T</u>	<u>H</u>
C	V	S	T	O	R							T⊣	M	F	V	V	P	E

The first anagram noted was ENt ÆL (in italics) by substitution of "L" for the "O," which is read as the word "entail." Next, by subbing a "G" for "S" and an "R" for "H," we can arrive at the word GROWTH. Lastly, CVSTOR appears on the second row, meaning "try to coin; try to stamp money."

		G	E	A				O	R						
								T⊣	M	F	V	V	P	E

The last word that seemed to make sense in the current context of this line was the word "OVR" created by subbing a "V" for "E." Also an "E" can be used for the Latin word for "from." This makes for the statement, "ETHO EA ENtÆL OUR GROWTH E CVSTOR," or "Go endeavor our growth from trying to coin money." This was a very unusual message in light of the previous lines, but it could be direct instructions to the Fra Rosi Crosse. Following the same procedures as the others, I decided to check the sum of the values of the leftover letters.

The letters that remained were G A T⊣ M F V V P. The sums in Simple, Reverse and Kaye Ciphers are in the table below:

Simple	7	1	19	12	6	20	20	15	− 100
	G	A	T⊣	M	F	V	V	P	SUMS
Reverse	18	24	6	13	19	5	5	10	= 100
Kaye	33	27	19	12	32	20	20	15	= 178

Seeing two out of three ciphers produce 100, "Francis Bacon" in Simple Cipher, was more than enough confirmation regarding the translation, but I couldn't help but notice that the Kaye Cipher total didn't "tie-out" in a manner of speaking. I reasoned that the Kaye Cipher signature of "Francis" was 171. At first I thought that adding 7 which is "G" in Simple would give the correct answer, however this involved "mixing" the values across the different ciphers, so I discounted the idea. But as an experiment, I decided to see what would happen if I subtracted all of the letters that can be used as known symbols of Bacon within this code. They all appeared as correlations in "the count" of the characters of the plaque. So, I subtracted the values of G, A, T⊣ and F from the Kaye Cipher total of 178, and the answer was 111, the Kaye Cipher signature for Bacon. That means the total of the values of these characters were 67, the Simple Cipher signature for "Francis." Since the values are all above 10, the same signature appears as the Simple signature. In Reverse, the remaining characters total 33, "Bacon" in Simple. This made me curious about the other values as well.

To further explain, the values of G, A, T⊣ and F in Simple Cipher logically total the signature of 33 as the result, Bacon in Simple. This meant the remainder totaled 67, Francis in Simple. I checked the results for the values in Reverse, and appropriately enough, the sum of G, A, T⊣ and F was 67, Francis in Simple. The sum of the other characters was 33, Bacon. Finally, it's the signature of "I FRATER" in Kaye Cipher.

Something that I can't impress upon the reader enough - I discovered these signatures as I've recorded them. I had originally recorded the characters at the end of the line, F V V P E, as two words in Greek after substitutions. But when they didn't make sense in context, I was forced to count them as "leftover" letters. And when I did, suddenly multiple signatures appeared. For this group of letters to "behave" in this manner, like so many other things throughout this process, defies coincidence. The discovery of these values and meanings was organic, and I was certainly not expecting this level of sophistication. The only possible explanation is again, it's a purposeful message created specifically to communicate to anyone who understood his cipher systems. The complexity of it all is baffling.

In summary, this line appears to reference a dictate to the brotherhood to expand or advance their efforts in "coining money." Was this the secret behind the rumors of the Rosicrucian Fraternity being involved in alchemy? Were they literally "making money?" Or as historical evidence suggests, were there certain historical figures who were involved in "coining money," but perhaps using base metals to do it? Friend and researcher Daniel Spino has suspected a counterfeiting operation involving a host of characters who are possibly members of Bacon's Rosy Crosse. One of them is none other than Robert Devereux, 2nd Earl of Essex. The value of "Robert Devereux" in Reverse Cipher is 178. Though we'll never know for certain, this plaque has certainly raised plenty of questions.

As you can see, Line 4 will be no different and no less surprising:

4	P	O	**Y**	**M**	H	S	M	E	T	T	T	E	R	H	R	N	Æ	A	N
	I	*V*	*I*	*2*	R	T	S	A	R	P	*S*	*E*	*I*	*T*	*A*	*S*	*T*	*A*	K

The first whole words that are apparent appear on the second row. Beginning on the right in italics we have *"ASTA"* Latin for "spear." Next the underlined letters spell "IT," and then "ES" which is Latin for "is, or be." Next, on the left we see *"BIVI"* backwards with a B in place of its value, 2, Latin for "meeting of two roads; 2 alternatives." And lastly, the word *"MY"* appears at the beginning of the first row.

Next, we move on to the obvious anagrams from the remaining letters:

P	O			H	S	M	E	T	T	T	E	R	H	R	N	Æ	A	N
				R	T	**S**	**A**	**R**	**P**									K

Seeing the word for "spear" suggested that I should look for the other half of the name, which appeared a few letters away from ASTRA in the form of the underlined "SARP." By substituting H for R and K for P, we have *"SHAK,"* forming SHAK-ASTRA, or Shak-spear. Having exhausted the possibilities of letters near one another, from the top row (on either side of the Triple Tau) we have the Latin "OPERAS" meaning "works," and in English "ÆRE" as "are."

The message therefore becomes, "MY OPERAS ÆRE BIVI. IT ES SHAK-ASTA," or completely in English, "My works are two alternatives. It is Shaks-speare," or perhaps "it is two alternatives. My works are Shakespeare." A final alternative with the same meaning for the last sentence would be "Shakespeare are my alternative works."

The remaining letters and their signatures again are complex, and contain the Triple Tau symbol. The leftover letters are M T T T H H N N R T K, and their numerical values total 157 in Simple, the Simple Cipher signature for "Fra. Rosi Crosse." When I checked the total in Reverse, the sum was 118. That's when I remembered that the Line originally contained the phrase, "ME TTT." By removing the Triple Tau as a unit and signature in and of itself, the totals in Simple and Reverse are 100, the signature of "Francis Bacon" in Simple. Considering the above messages, the Kaye total is interesting:

Simple	12	8	8	13	13	17	19	10	100
	M	H	H	N	N	R	T	K	Sums
Reverse	13	17	17	12	12	8	6	15	100
Kaye	12	34	34	13	13	17	19	10	152

The sum of the letters in Simple and Reverse are both 100, as I said "Francis Bacon" in Simple Cipher. The Kaye value of 152 is "William" in Kaye Cipher which is in keeping with the Shakespeare message.

To conclude Line 4, the message shows Bacon claim responsibility / ownership of Shakespeare's works. Additionally, the unused letters total not only the signature of "Francis Bacon," but also "Fra. Rosi Crosse" and "William," confirming the use of all of the other letters used in the anagram.

Line 5 continues on this theme as well:

5	S	**S̲**	**E̲**	**I̲**	I	W	S	E	R	5	V	*D*	*O*	A	L	D	**A̲**	**A̲**	E
	V	M	**G**	**I**	**T**	**E**	N	A	E	A	**H̲**	**E̲**	**A̲**	**W̲**	*E*	*T*	*V*	A	N

As there are many complete words in this line, we'll deal with the top row first. First of all, the bold-underlined "SEI" is Latin for "a fictitious name under the law," which makes sense in relation to Line 4. Next the bold italic word DO in Latin means to "attribute or ascribe" and ALD is Scottish for "old." The "old" refers to the AA signature that follows underlined, as in "Old" Athena and Apollo, the Spear-shakers. In the second row, subbing S for G, forgiving the pun provides "SITE," which in Latin is "positioned or centered on." The underlined letters to the right, substituting D for W provides the word "HEAD." Lastly, we see the Latin words, "E" and "TV" meaning "from" and "you," respectively.

Next, we can form anagrams from many of the remaining letters:

S			I	W	**S̲**	**E̲**	**R̲**	**5̲**	**V̲**					E
V	M				*N*	A	*E*	A					A	N

On the top row, we see the word "I," and next the underlined letters with E in place of the number 5, we have the obvious anagram for "SERVE." As the last step, from the remaining italic letters we can form the Latin word, NEVE, meaning "or not; and not."

All of the words derived from Line 5 are, SEI DO ALD AA SITE HEAD E TV I SERVE NEVE. Although better alternatives probably exist, I placed them in the following order, "*I DO SEI E ALD AA SERVE SITE HEAD NEVE TV.*" In English, he seems to be addressing the actor Shakspere, by saying "I attribute the fictitious name under the law from old Athena and Apollo (the spear-shakers) as figure head, not you." Ouch. Here, Bacon states that he created the name Shakespeare from the symbolism of Athena and Apollo, and not based upon the actor William Shaksper.

Our leftover letters are also interesting. They spell out, *S W A N M A A,* roughly the same message as the cipher - "*the Swan am A A.*" Their values in Simple Cipher equal 67, the Simple signature for "Francis." In Reverse, their sum is 108, the signature for "Francis" in Reverse Cipher. In Kaye, just like in Line 2, the sum is 145, the cipher signature for "James Stewart" in Simple. If we look at the letter M as a symbol of the bee (explained later), the Kaye signature becomes 133, or Baron Verulam in Simple, along with multiple other "secret names" of Bacon.

80

Moving on to Line 6, we have several words appearing without any rearrangement:

6	B	T	3	T	O	H	D	*E*	**Y**	*E*	The	T⊣	W	B	O	O	L	N	***D***
	E	M	1	T	H	T	S	A	<u>**3**</u>	<u>**I**</u>	<u>**E**</u>	<u>**N**</u>	<u>**S**</u>	V	I	G	R	A	G

Due to the context that will be made obvious in a moment, the characters, EYE The T⊣ is a play on words, as well as the first time I encountered the use of the substitution protocol used with the double Tau. In this way, the T⊣ can be read as "*Fr.*" meaning "Brother" or "Francis." And so these first words are read as "I THE Fr." or "I the Brother." Next with the bold italic letters, subbing a W for D the word "WE" appears. Lastly with the bold-underlined characters, replacing 3 with the letter "C" produces the word "CIENS," Latin for "shake."

<u>**B**</u>	T	3	T	O	H	D				**W**	**B**	**O**	**O**	**L**	**N**	
	M	**1**	**T**	**H**	*T*	**S**	**A**				*V*	*I*	*G*	<u>**R**</u>	**A**	<u>**G**</u>

Though the first example isn't an anagram, I treated this separately from the last group due to the many required substitutions. Through the Simple and Reverse substitution system, WBOOLM, becomes WYLLOM, a common pronunciation of "*William*" at the time. Additionally, the Simple Cipher total for WBOOLN is 98, which is also the Simple Cipher signature of "Shake spear" without the final "e," as it is spelled here when translated from Latin. In the bold characters, supplying the A in place of the number 1 an anagram for HASTAM appears, being Latin for "spear." Combining the underlined letter B with the underlined RAG from the end, we see the word "BRAG." Last but not least, the italicized letters on the bottom line with substitutions E for V, and S for G, become the words ET and IS.

Putting the words together into a coherent sentence becomes, "WE BRAG ET I IS The Fr. WYLLOM CIENS-HASTAM." To make things clearer, "*We brag and I am the Brother William Shakespear.*"

The remaining letters actually all appear together, and can be thought of to "spell" T - see TOH (Tau). The sums and cipher equivalents appear here:

Simple	19	3	19	14	8	4	67
Letters	T	3	T	O	H	D	SUMS
Reverse	6	22	6	11	17	21	83
Kaye	19	29	19	14	34	30	145

Here we see again, not just confirmation of the message with the cipher signature of 67, "Francis" in Simple, but the same message as earlier. 83, the sum of the letters of the word "Fraters" and 145, the Simple Cipher signature of "James Stewart."

Therefore, Line 6 (6 is the Simple Cipher of the first letter of Francis) we not only see Bacon claiming to "brag" about being Brother William Shakespeare, by checking our leftover characters, the message of "Francis, James Stewart, Brothers" is repeated.

Like my favorite radio station, "the hits just keep on coming." And here they are in Line 7 (or G):

7	P	E	S	S	Q	V	Y	M	N	A	D	T⊣	H	M	A	E	**Me**	**T⊣**	**Y**

	P	*B*	M	A	E	T	L	R	N	W	**H**	**E**	**C**	**_B_**	**_L_**	**_A_**	**_E_**	**_N_**

Four obvious words can be read without any rearranging of letters. "Me" and "THY" are obvious. Subbing a Y for B at the beginning of the second line gives us "PAY," and in the bold letters to the right subbing R for H and X for C we have "REX," Latin for "king." Lastly in the bold-underlined letters, subbing an M for N and B L A E N becomes "BLAME."

P	E	S	S	Q	V	**Y**	**M**	N	**A**	*D*	T⊣	**H**	*M*	*A*	*E*			
			_M_	**_A_**	**_E_**	**_T_**	L	**_R_**	N	W								

In the bold-only letters, substituting R for H produces the name "MARY." Next the italic bold letters spell "MADE." Lastly, the underlined-bold letters spell out "MATER." The remaining letters are:

P	E	S	S	Q	V		N		T⊣			
						L		N	W			

With no more obvious words, we look for letters that can spell a word that will complete the sentence within the context. "T⊣" and "E" provide a needed "ThE," giving us the statement "MARY MADE ME REX. PAY THY MATER ThE BLAME." Again, we seem to have a message directed to James I from Bacon regarding their family ties.

In checking the correct use of the letters, and in this case, adding them together in order in Simple Cipher provides a jaw dropping series of signatures. The remaining letters are P, S, S, Q, V, N. L, N and W. In Simple Cipher, P + S = 33. Add to this the next two letters S + Q and the sum is 67. Add the values of the next two characters V + N to the previous sum, also 33, and it totals 100. Add the value of the next letter L and we have 111, "Bacon" in Kaye. Add the value for N and the total is 124, "Rosicrucian" in Simple Cipher. Add the last letter W, and we have 145, the Simple Cipher signature of "James Stewart."

This sequence put to rest any question of mere coincidence being at work here. It's important to point out again that this is Line 7, which is the letter G in Simple Cipher.

The Reverse Cipher count is nearly as interesting and just as impossible - P+S+S+Q = 33, "Bacon." Add to that V+N and that total is 50, the number of Argonauts on the Argo. And as the truth is now out, I can now point out 50 is also the signature for "Fr. III" in Simple Cipher (Bacon frequently signed his name with the abbreviated Fr.), and he would have been Francis III of France. We add the rest of the letters L+N+W the total is 80, the cipher signature of "James" in Reverse.

As there are no letters alphabetically before K, the total in Kaye Cipher is the same as Simple.

Given all these statements together, statements that seemingly complement one another, there seems to be only one conclusion to make and many people are not going to like it. In fact, I don't like it. This is going to get messy. At least one cipher text on the plaque states that Sir Francis Bacon was the oldest son of Mary Queen of Scots, and apparently named after his father, Francis II, King of France. This of course would make Bacon the older half-brother of King James I of England, and the rightful heir of both thrones of England and France.

I know. This simply doesn't seem possible. As you will later see, I even go so far as attempting to disprove the notion, by trying my hardest to "re-read" the line by choosing an interpretation in line with the "Elizabeth-as-mother" theory.

Needless to say, if true, this information is truly paradigm shattering. After completing this treatment of the cipher, obviously more corroborating evidence is needed to support or refute such a theory. As it happens, such independent evidence exists.

As hard as it will be to follow an act like that, here is the last, Line 8 of Key 8:

8	A	6	T	O	W	T	T	**D**	**N**	**C**	V	T	S	C	E	M	R	A	V
N	W	I	V	I	P	A	O	T⌐	**I**	**P**	**Y**	**T**	T	S	D	I	S	O	P

This was by far the most challenging of the lines to decipher. First of all, CND in Hebrew - "כנד" translates as "hand." The bold and italicized VT is Latin, meaning "in order to." The last complete word is TYPI meaning "figure; symbol; model; pattern." Next I moved on to the obvious anagrams.

	A	6	T	O	W	T	T						S	C	E	M	R	A	<u>V</u>
<u>N</u>	*W*	<u>I</u>	*V*	I	P	A	O	T⌐					T	S	D	I	S	O	P

The first word in bold with one substitution of H for the R is "SCHEMA," Latin for "form; shape; or figure." The bold-underlined letters spell "NVI," Latin for "nod." Lastly, the bold-italic letters on the second line, subbing E for V is the word "WE."

A	6	T	O	W	T	T										
		I	P	A	*O*	*T⌐*				T	S	D	I	S	O	P

(Remember that the blank spaces should be omitted, and the remaining letters are left-justified). The first of the anagrams from the remaining letters to finish the sentence is APIS, Latin for "bee," a prominent symbol for both the Rosicrucian Order and Freemasons and mentioned earlier. The first bold "A" is used as that article. In bold italics and written backwards is the word "TO" utilizing the double Tau. In bold underlined is the backwards Latin word POSIT, meaning "place or placement."

When all of these words are put in order, we can render the sentence "WE NVI TO APIS, A כנד (CND) POSIT TO SCHEMA TYPI." In common English, this can be read as, "We nod to (honor) bees, with hand placement to pattern that symbol (shape)."

This was the answer to a research question my friends and I had as we were researching Renaissance paintings, and what has been called the "M" hand signal. Many theories have been thrown around, but here was the answer. The "M" hand signal in paintings is meant to symbolize the bee, a well-known Fra. Rosi Crosse and Freemason symbol. And for the record, the letter M is the number 12 in Simple Cipher, and the signature for the word "BEE" in Simple Cipher is also 12 - B (2) + E (5) + E (5) = 12. In Reverse Cipher, BEE = 53, the signature for "Mary" in Simple (M). The total in Kaye Cipher is 90. Interestingly, two of these numbers are the angles of a 3 4 5 triangle, 53 and 90.

Again, to "check the work" and tie out the loose ends, I calculated the values of the unused letters using Simple, Reverse and Kaye ciphers. The unused letters were 6 W T T V T P. After noting the interesting progression of numbers in the previous lines, I decided to take a closer look as I added the values of the remaining letters.

Number 6 can be seen as a symbol of Bacon as 6 equals "F" in Simple and "T" in Reverse as observed in other areas. Adding all of the remaining letters in this sequence in Simple Cipher equals 108, "Francis" in Reverse Cipher. The Reverse Cipher total is 66 which, though not immediately significant, when considering the symbols and signatures used by Bacon, we can identify a purpose. Most people will note that 66 is double 33, Simple Cipher for Bacon. While double Bacon sounds good when ordering a burger, this was the intention here. In Reverse Cipher, 6 = T, so we see the double Tau. Again even in Simple Cipher, the symbol of the

Double Tau as 66 can be read as FF. If the first F is reversed, and they are placed back-to-back, we would have a perfect image of two Taus, or a capital "T" with a smaller cross halfway up its stem, as seen here - Ŧ. (Late edit – I recently learned that Bacon scholar Peter Dawkins notes that Bacon also signed his name as "F. Baconis" which totals 66 in Simple Cipher). Lastly, the total in Kaye Cipher is 145 the cipher signature for "James Stewart" in Simple.

However, I believe that each line contains at least two messages using the method I've outlined. At any rate, one thing is certain - the plaque contains multiple hidden messages.

As I hinted earlier however, I would like to offer one alternative interpretation of Line 7. In light of the anticipated reaction of people who advocate the Prince Tudor theories, who will be quick to bring up a variety of reasons this claim must be false, it will need to be scrutinized in its own chapter. For the time being, out of respect for the work of the many Baconian scholars who have championed Bacon as the son of Elizabeth, I decided to *try to purposefully* decrypt a part of the message to see if I could interpret it in a way that supported the Prince Tudor theories, that Bacon was the secret son of Elizabeth I. The most obvious candidate that I previously mentioned was Line 7:

7	P	E	S	S	Q	V	Y	M	N	A	D	T⊣	H	M	A	E	ME	T⊣	Y
	P	A	B	M	A	E	T	L	R	N	W	H	E	C	B	L	A	E	N

Instead of starting fresh, I'll use relevant words that immediately became apparent last time, and then "cherry pick letters" (near one another or not) to create anagrams that will support the Elizabeth theories. Then we see if any leftover letters "tie-out" as a signature, indicating that we may have a correct decryption. And at first glance I was successful in creating an alternative translation.

The words that I was able to unscramble were: MY MATER QVEEN BESS MAD ATh Me MY REX PLAY.

Additionally, the leftover letters P Y H T⊣ N W L A N, totals 171 in Kaye Cipher, which is the signature cipher for *"Francis"* in Kaye. Simple and Reverse totals produced no known (or hidden) Bacon signatures. So, if we rearrange the words to create the phrase that we want to see to reinforce the Elizabeth-as-mother hypothesis, we've arrived at: MY MATER QVEEN BESS MAD AT⊣ Me MY REX PLAY.

The only way to make sense of this sentence is to read it as, *"My mother Queen Bess mad at me King play,"* or *"My mother Queen Bess mad at my King Play."* Another version could read, "Queen Bess Mad at me. My King mother play."

Could this be in reference to *Richard III? Love's Labor's Lost?* Both plays are "King" plays that Elizabeth watched, and they each contain controversial elements that would apply to her life and reign. Though it couldn't be confirmed, she had apparently once referred to herself as "being King Richard" as she had no heirs either. Additionally, *Richard III* appears on page 173 of the First Folio, which is the cipher signature of the RC, R = 17, and C = 3. Also, Richard obviously begins with "R," and III is the equivalent of "C," so again, we have a symbolic cipher signature of RC. Love's Labor's Lost, with the prominence of the capital "L's," is also a Bacon signature - L = 11. Therefore, LLL = 33, or the Simple Cipher signature for "Bacon."

Though other candidates exist as well, we'll stick to the plaque cipher for now. Though "successful" at first glance, in order to arrive at this meaning for this section of the cryptogram, I had to "break the rules" that I had created for myself when employing anagrams. Instead of identifying words already present first, I simply tried to find Queen Elizabeth's name, or in this case spell out "Queen Bess." In doing so, I also used the letter "B" that was far away from the letters PESSQVY combination. Under the rules I had created for myself at the beginning, in order to prevent myself from making such subjective choices, I should have used the nearby "Y" and substituted "B" according to the Athbash substitution scheme. Doing so would have changed the leftover letters, and with this group of leftovers, no cipher signature appears, making this an incorrect arrangement.

Additionally, why mention Queen Elizabeth I of England in the present tense on a plaque that has a date engraved on it that is fifteen years after her death? This would be highly illogical. Additionally, by most accounts the plaque was put in place by at least 1623. Why reference the unsuccessful Essex's Rebellion, in which the play *Richard III* seemed to play a role? Was Bacon admitting a role in it as well? Again, all highly unlikely.

In all, these questions negate the notion of this "Elizabeth as Mother" interpretation, and it appears to be completely illogical. Perhaps more answers appear in other ciphers on the plaque, or more likely the First Folio, or even the eulogies of the *Manes Verulamiani*. Lastly, while all of the other messages produced known signatures in the leftover characters, this one only produced one, and that one was contrived for the reasons I already mentioned. At any rate, for all of these reasons, and the methodology used in producing the Pro-Elizabeth Theory message, it needs to be dismissed as a viable interpretation.

Messages of Key 8

In summary, the messages coming through in Key 8 are impressive and shocking. While I believe that alternative versions could exist, the methods that used in order to ensure the validity and objectivity of the process have borne fruit. While some messages maintain a common theme of Bacon's "birth parents" and his brother James I, others seem to be only partial disclosures regarding the operation of his fraternity. With hints regarding coining their own money, and signaling to others using the "bee" hand position, Bacon confirms certain suspicions regarding the Rosicrucian Order. While some might point out that the inconsistency of the separate messages would point to a flaw in the deciphering system, I disagree. If anything, any inconsistencies in theme speak to the objectivity of the methods themselves.

The safe-guards against being subjective and simply following the process to where it led, the messages "made sense" in the context of one another. They also make sense within the context of Francis Bacon and the Rosicrucian Order. These facts seem to bear out the efficacy of the decoding system. Little did I know while deciphering Key 8, that following the clues within Keys 5 and 38 would lead to messages that continue to reinforce the main thrust of these cipher texts *from completely different transpositions*.

Putting all of this together, we're able to identify the overall message of Key 8. He begins by declaring, *I REX OF OTRI AGRA I ELIGORE. OTI IS I* or, "I'm king of either of two countries (lands) I choose. I pass on holiday (or rest)." Next he says, *"ETSI ELDER I DO SOLI E LOVE FrATER IAMES,"* or "Although I'm older I surrender the throne out of love for brother James." Putting this alongside line 7 of Key 8, he continues, *"Mary made me king. Pay blame to thy own mother."*

Again, the only way that any of these statements make sense is that Francis Bacon is the older half-brother to King James I of England, meaning that his mother is *actually Mary Queen of Scots, not Elizabeth.*

The fact that the rest of Key 8 claims that Bacon was responsible for the works ascribed to William Shakespeare, explicitly stating that it's a fictitious name, is astounding enough. But to include the message of his Royal lineage, and have it be different than everyone has suspected, is extremely surprising.

The list of reasons to refute this information has a long history. However, much of the "Prince Tudor Theory," a variant of the Oxfordian theory of authorship of Shakespeare's works, is speculative in nature as well. Though I've never read the works of Owen and Gallup, who are credited with much of the work in this area, what I've discovered so far on this plaque isn't made of allusions or hints. Bacon explicitly claims two thrones. He explicitly refers to James as his brother. He calls himself the Dauphin. He makes the statement that "Mary made me first. Blame her."

Overall, more validation will be needed if any of this is to be believed. If I am to make any claims so far, it's that I have decoded messages within the Plaque Shakespeare's Memorial in Trinity Church at

Stratford upon Avon. The messages claim that the works attributed to William Shakespeare, and the plaque itself, to be the work of Francis Bacon. Additionally and more spectacularly, Bacon claims to have had the choice between two thrones of two countries, France and Great Britain. Out of love for James, he abdicated the throne. While these statements seem incredible, it bears repeating this will be discussed further in a later chapter. Also, we need to look at Key 5, to see if any corroborating messages appear by following the process. I think you'll find Key 5 to be... *illuminating*.

Chapter 5 - Key 5 Sheds Light

     The original plan of rearranging the characters on the plaque by first using the number 32 as a key to create an algorithm, and then rearranging those letters using the number 8 as a key, produced results. Since the concept worked, the plan continued to then rearrange the "previously rearranged" letters of Key 8 using the number 5. Having already decoded Key 38 (presented in the next chapter), that key produced 38 rows of 8 letters each or actually, two columns of 19 rows of 8 letters. It replicated the symbolism of the Double Tau, T = 19, H = 8. This appeared to be an indication of how to best interpret the letter arrangement in terms of acrostics and phonetics. Lastly, Key 38 also gave the answer of how to manage the Key 5 rearrangement of letters produced by Key 8.

     This clue in Key 38 explained how to use Key 5. Since there were 305 characters total, in order to set up an algorithm that doesn't terminate using the number 5 as a key, one character would need to be eliminated. One of the phonetic messages of Key 38 states, "*I cut one bamp's T in the TT.*" Combined with the multiple meanings of the statement in the middle of Key 8, "EYE THE T⊣," was the final clue of which character to eliminate from the count. By crossing off the Double Tau at the heart of the Key 8 transposition, number 5 as a key generated the following arrangement:

1	O	O	T	L	I	M	N	I	20	I	5	L	V	E	H	T	T
2	W	I	P	T⊣	O	H	6	G	21	D	T⊣	L	1	A	S	A	S
3	E	W	H	O	R	F	P	S	22	N	M	Y	A	W	L	6	T
4	T	N	V	S	E	T	E	E	23	T	R	I	O	T	S	K	C
5	O	A	I	E	W	N	O	E	24	I	R	T⊣	Me	O	I	R	G
6	O	E	T	E	G	E	Y	T⊣	25	S	E	E	A	E	T⊣	Ys	O

7	Me	B	R	C	N	W	C	E	26	O	S	A	T⊣	P	M	T	H
8	N	P	P	D	V	I	T	A	27	N	R	P	A	S	W	V	D
9	S	G	I	S	O	D	L	I	28	M	N	E	V	3	E	W	N
10	L	M	V	E	E	Æ	S	C	29	T	3	V	G	Q	A	A	P
11	R	S	V	O	M	E	Æ	I	30	E	H	A	T	D	S	A	V
12	A	I	A	I	R	A	E	T	31	T⊣	T	O	F	H	Yt	1	E
13	A	E	B	H	The	O	M	S	32	R	E	E	D	O	S	S	O
14	N	R	S	M	H	T⊣	M	N	33	I	O	O	Nt	R	I	T	O
15	B	A	T	V	M	W	A	Y	34	M	E	H	T	R	I	T	S
16	I	B	V	R	G	I	K	T	35	S	S	S	D	A	G	A	A
17	I	A	L	O	T	V	S	H	36	A	T	Y	B	D	H	I	I
18	E	A	O	H	V	E	I	V	37	P	V	D	E	A	L	E	E
19	Y	E	R	A	2	R	T	K	38	O	N	C	V	I	I	S	P

First and foremost. the first line is an anagram for "LOOMINI," a phonetic spelling of the Latin "lumini," meaning, "light; lamp, torch; eye of a person; life; day, daylight," along with an added "Tau." This seemed a clear confirmation that eliminating the double Tau at the heart of Key 8 was the correct action.

Multiple acrostics and phonetics jumped out while scanning the letters. First of all, in the first column on the left from Line 2 to Line 14, the letters form "WE TOO MeN SL RAAN." Subbing a G for the S and an O for the L, we can then see the phonetic message, "We two men, go reign." This would seem to be a message to James I that since they are both men, Bacon accepts things as they are and James should "go reign."

In the farthest right column, in Lines 1 - 17 we can read, "I G SEE T⊣E A. I C ITS NY TH." Substituting an M for N, and decoding the symbolism of the G and the A, an important message appears. By now we know that the letter G represents "Bacon." We also know that "A" is used by Bacon to represent Athena and Apollo as the "Spear-shakers," and those spears are "light" in the form of knowledge. Also, the letter A can represent rays of light shining downward. So we can read this message as "I Bacon see the light. I see it's my "T⊣"." Here, he's specifically referring to his

Double Tau symbol used on the plaque as the letters TH, but then I noticed the word "SEE" phonetically and correctly spelled in other areas of the key.

Horizontally in Line 4 we read, "V SE TEE" or "You see T," meaning "you see truth," along with two other acrostics with the next two lines:

4	T	N	**V̲**	**S̲**	*E*	T	E	E
5	O	A	**I̲**	*E̲*	*W*	N	O	E
6	O	E	**T̲**	*E̲*	*G*	E	Y	T⊣

Starting clockwise with the bold and underlined **V̲** we can read, "V SEE TI," or "You see T." Counter-clockwise beginning with the bold-italic **W** going upward counter-clockwise we read, "WE SEE G."

Could this message mean "where you see truth, we see God?" Or where "you see the Tau, we see Bacon." Also, another example appears in lines 25 and 26:

25	S	**E**	**E**	**A**	**E**	T⊣	Ys	O
26	O	**S**	**A**	T⊣	P	M	T	H

Line 25 states, "SEE A (light) E T⊣ (Latin for "and"), Ys (this) O." Beginning with the bold **S** in Line 26 and moving clockwise, we read "SEE A T⊣ A." After noting all of the messages to "See the light," I noticed that Line 1 phonetically spelled an anagram for "T LOOMINI," the Latin "lumini" meaning *"light; lamp or torch; eye of a person,"* preceded by the Tau.

This had been the correct path.

Studting Line 1, something else became apparent:

1	O	O	T	L	I	M	N	I

In the anagram just like in the acrostics and phonetic messages, we have a T associated with "light" or "truth." Also, I wondered if the entire columns under each of these letters could actually be rearranged with the letter at the top of the column, to produce yet another arrangement and set of messages. This creates a large problem, however. Due to the substitution ability of the cipher, the O's and L are interchangeable, the M and N are interchangeable, and the I's and O's can be swapped and rearranged, creating multiple ways of spelling the phonetic anagram, LOOMINI. The only letter that isn't included in the word, the Tau, could appear at the beginning or the end of the word.

This may be wrong but by my calculations, that means there are at least 432 different ways to phonetically spell the Latin word for "light" using the letters at the top of the column. Such an idea seemed illogical and implausible considering the way all of the methods had worked up to this point, so that notion was abandoned in preference of looking for any more obvious acrostics and phonetic messages.

Lines 1 - 3 do not disappoint profane eyes with this acrostic, read counter clockwise:

I	M
O	H
R	F

"MIOR" is Latin for "make water; urinate." The "circle" is completed with the letters F and H which of course can be read in two different ways. Using H as a Double Tau, we are given a symbol of the number Thirty Three, "Bacon" in Simple, making the F obvious. Additionally, using the Simple and Reverse Cipher substitution system with T for F creates the Triple Tau, or subbing R for H provides "FR" as Frater or Francis.

In Lines 2 - 4 reading italic bold characters clockwise:

2	W	*I*	P	T⌐	O
3	E	*W*	*H*	*O*	*R*
4	T	*N*	*V*	*S*	*E*

We see the phrase, *"I whoresvn."* Whoreson was a favorite insult used in the plays attributed to Shakespeare, and by applying it to himself, Bacon is stating that he "is the son of a whore." If we consider the messages regarding his "real parents" in the other ciphers, then this can be considered corroboration when we consider how historically Bacon advocated for the death of Mary Queen of Scots for treason. I can't help but notice the word "WE" to the left the I and W, which could imply that he included James I in this descriptor as well.

Though mentioned earlier, Line 4 itself provides another interesting thought:

4	T	N	V	S	E	T	E	E

Subbing M for N, the line begins with a Tau, the word "MVSE" appears followed by the word "TEE." Stating that "TT" is a muse repeats one of the themes of *Manes Verulamiani* of Bacon as Muse.

Line 7 provides an interesting study in phonetics and signatures. As 7 is G in Simple, it's appropriate it begins with the word "ME:"

7	Me	B	R	C	N	W	C	E

The first four characters spell out the phonetic message, "Me B RC," or meaning "I am Rosi Crosse." But another reading provides a now familiar message. "Me BR" is also an abbreviation for "Me (my) brother." Adding the cipher values of the rest of the letters in Simple, Reverse and Kaye in the table below:

Simple	3	13	21	3	5	= 45
	C	N	W	C	E	SUMS
Reverse	22	12	4	22	20	= 80
Kaye	29	13	21	29	31	= 123

The result in each cipher equals the signature of "JAMES." The Simple Cipher signature for "IAMES" is 45, the Reverse is 80, and the Kaye Cipher signature is 123.

Again, an explicit use of a known cipher system used by Francis Bacon indicates that James was his brother.

Another allusion to Bacon's mother appears in Line 15:

15	B	A	T	V	M	W	A	Y

With substitutions of B for Y and D for W, a backwards message reads, "BAD MVTA." The word MVTA is a pun on "mother" and the Roman goddess of silence, "Larunda" who was also called "Muta." This seems to be a message about his bad mother's silence regarding his birthright.

The next apparent "surface" message appears in Line 17:

17	I	A	L	O	T	V	S	H

"I A LOTVS" appears followed immediately by the Double Tau symbol in the form of an H. The rose is said to be the Egyptian or Eastern "lotus" of the Rosicrucians. Sometimes the lotus is associated with the *fleur de lis* associated with the French Royalty, who many claim to be a stylized bee. Bees were also associated with the muses.

Though other lines contain interesting features, they will be saved for the "Line by Line" analysis to follow. Line 23 references "TRIO TS" and then Line 24 provides three different references:

24	I	R	T⊣	Me	O	I	R	G

We see "I R T⊣" as "I am TT." The next characters "MeO" can be a variation of the Latin word meaning "my; belonging to me." By now, the "I R G" is familiar enough to the reader to forego the explanation.

Also, beginning in Line 24, the first letters of Lines 24 - 28 clearly spell out "I SON M" as a vertical acrostic.

The next obvious message appears in Line 32:

32	R	E	E	D	O	S	S	O

"REED" is obviously a phonetic spelling of "read." "OSSO" is old Latin for "bone; kernel; the heartwood of a tree; stone of a fruit." I assumed we are being instructed to read this key, the heart of the message. But this line becomes important when deciphering the section including Lines 14 - 18, O and S, respectively. This is fully explained at that point of the key.

The only clear message in Line 33, an obviously significant number, begins at its center, but then it wasn't until I had decoded the plaque that the first half became clear in its meaning:

33	I	O	O	Nt	R	I	T	O

The Nt character is significant for the reasons I mentioned earlier. It appears beside the mathematical center of the plaque itself and appears at the center of Line 33. The characters added together in Simple Cipher equals 32, which is F in Kaye Cipher, and is also frequently used by Bacon. This was my original thought of the meaning of this line, that he's telling us that "32 (F) are I too." Also, T + O in Simple Cipher totals 33. But then I realized that the first half of the line would be pronounced, "you." The message then becomes, "You 32 (F), are I too (or Bacon)."

To whom was he speaking, I wondered? I then remembered that in my backward counting process of the characters on the plaque's surface, the conjoined Nt character was number 152, the Kaye Cipher signature for

"William" as a possible answer. So I had to assume it hadn't been the intention at all for the Nt character to represent the letter F. Also, 32 is the value of Fr. I, his grandfather, in Simple. In Reverse, 32 is "II," as in "the second," his father.

The last obvious message provides more confirmation to the decryption process with the following from Line 34:

34	M	E	H	T	R	I	T	S

Here, the explicit surface message states, "ME H TRI T'S." Here, Bacon points out that the "H" he conjoined on the plaque with the "T" are "TRI T's" or the Triple Tau. As stated earlier, though I had referred to it throughout this writing as the "double Tau," here Line 34 tells the true story that it is indeed the Triple Tau.

Preliminary Summary

Overall, with only a superficial look at the obvious messages from the acrostics and phonetic messages, as well as explicit surface messages from many of the lines, I was satisfied with the methods I've used and the results they produced. So many repeated messages as confirmation as well as significant cipher signatures cannot possibly be coincidence. The repetition of so many symbols used by Bacon, the Rosicrucian Order and Freemasonry again, also defies coincidence. At this point, the only thing left to do is continue using the same decoding strategy "line-by-line" of Key 5.

Key 5 Line-by-Line: Acrostic Anagrams

I was able to treat Keys 32 and 8 to a "line-by-line" interpretation because of their length. Due to what I learned with Key 38, I knew Key 5 would need to worked with blocks of characters at a time, spanning anywhere between 4 to 9 lines. Another discovery made while working with Key 38 was the process. The reason these new arrangements need to be treated as "blocks" of text is the fact that transposition ciphers are known to produce acrostic anagrams. These anagrams are formed by letters juxtaposed with one another, often in a pattern such as a cross, a letter such as Tau, or even random shapes. Working in this way with Key 5, the first message came through Lines 1 - 8:

94

1	O	O	T	L	I	M	N	I
2	*W*	*I*	*P*	*T⊣*	O	H	6	G
3	E	**W**	**H**	**O**	**R**	F	P	S
4	<u>**T**</u>	N	V	S	**E**	T	E	E
5	<u>**O**</u>	*A*	*I*	E	W	N	O	E
6	O	E	T	E	G	E	Y	T⊣
7	Me	B	R	C	N	W	C	E
8	N	P	P	D	V	I	T	A

Though the discoveries actually came backwards from Line 8 upward, I'll present the findings of Lines 1 - 4 first. The aforementioned "WHORESVN" acrostic appears directly in the middle comprised of characters alongside one another. To its left and downward beginning lines 4 and 5 is the underlined word "**TO**." Above it in Line 2, we have *W I P T⊣*, which with substitutions of D for W, K for P, and Fr. for T⊣, spelling out a backwards "KID" with the Latin abbreviation "Fr." for "brother."

By looking at the remaining letters from Line 1, we have O O T L I N. The first five letters total 67 in Simple. Adding N, we total 80, the signature cipher for "James" in Reverse.

Incorporating the signature into the message, we arrive at, "James, my kid brother." Adding in the italic I and A from Line 5, and he finishes the thought, "I a whoreson too."

Moving on with this section, the majority of the characters in Lines 5 - 8 fall into place:

5				E	W	N	O	E
6	O	<u>E</u>	<u>T</u>	<u>E</u>	G	E	Y	T⊣
7	Me	B	R	<u>C</u>	N	W	C	E
8	N	P	P	D	V	I	T	A

This section begins with an acrostic read counter-clockwise, O Me B, R CETE. *"CETE"* is Latin for "porpoise or dolphin," which in French is *Dauphin,* the name of the heir to the French throne. This whole phrase then can be translated as, "Oh, I Bacon, am Dauphin." I found it as a result of the context of the rest of this section:

5				<u>E</u>	**W**	**N**	**O**	<u>E</u>
6					G	<u>E</u>	<u>Y</u>	<u>T⊣</u>
7					*N*	*W*	*C*	*E*
8	N	P	P	D	<u>V</u>	<u>I</u>	<u>T</u>	<u>A</u>

The bold anagram from the end of Line 5 spells NOW, and the leftover E and E are used with the other underlined letters of Line 6 to create the words, EYE and T⊣E, with only the G remaining. In Line 7 with the remaining italic letters, substituting M for N and D for W,

95

provides the phonetic MDCE. Directly below is the bold underlined Latin word VITA, meaning "life" but also meaning "shunned." Subbing K and K for the P's in Line 8 provides the word NKKD, which in Hebrew would be "נככד" meaning, "grandson." When the remaining letters "didn't tie out at first, one of the remaining G's was used to repeat the name "Bacon" as G is 33 in Kaye Cipher.

The fully completed message is, "Oh, I Bacon are Dauphin." And "NOW EYE G (Bacon) THE VITA MDCE נככד," or in plain English, "*Now I the shunned Medici grandson.*"

Once again, we see another contextual reference reinforcing the storyline presented by the plaque cipher regarding Bacon's parentage. Catherine de Medici as mother to Francis II, would have been any Dauphin's grandmother. Using the word "shunned" provides an important clue, but we need to delve more deeply into this subject in a later chapter.

Now to check the values of the leftover characters for signatures. The following table contains the unused characters:

Table 4-1

				Simple	Reverse	Kaye
O	H	6	G	35	65	113
E	F	P	S	44	56	96
T	E	E		29	46	81
			Totals	108	167	290

The remaining letters in Simple Cipher equal 108, the signature of "Francis" in Reverse. I also realized that the signature number of "Medici" in Reverse Cipher is also 108. Quite interestingly, the Reverse value total is 167, the Reverse Cipher signature for "Baron Verulam." However, considering the subject matter of the messages, I noted that the Simple Cipher value of the name "Stewart" is 100. Therefore, 167 is also the cipher signature for "Francis Stewart." The Kaye total was very confusing, but after writing one of the final chapters it became a part of a mind-blowing discovery.

Using inductive reasoning, and taking the new information regarding Francis' true identity, creates a series of cipher signatures of that hidden (true) name. One of them logically would be "Francois III," the Kaye Cipher signature of which is 290! Then something else became obvious. The Simple Cipher signature of "Francois III" is 108, and the signature in Reverse is 167. The cipher signature checking system in this section which explicitly states that Bacon was the "shunned Medici grandson," all three totals of the leftover letters are the three cipher signatures of the name "Francois III."

It seemed logical to look for other possibilities that also included the values of "G" instead of using it as a part of the message. This gives us values of 115 in Simple, 185 in Reverse and 323 in Kaye. That led to the discovery that 115 could be read as "Frater Fr. III" or "I F. Stewart" in Simple Cipher, since Fr. And F. were common ways he abbreviated his name on correspondence. The number 185 in Reverse is "Francois" in Kaye Cipher. Number 323 is the Kaye Cipher signature of "Francis Stewart." All of this indicates that Bacon's "secret yet true" identity plays a major role in his cipher signature system. This will be validated time and again throughout this process.

The next section appears in Lines 9 - 13 and is no less stunning. The first obviously apparent whole words appear in bold:

9	S	G	I	**S**	**O**	**D**	**L**	**I**
10	L	M	V	E	E	Æ	S	C
11	R	*S*	V	O	M	E	Æ	I
12	A	*I*	A	I	R	A	E	T
13	A	E	B	H	**The**	O	M	S

With one substitution of G for S, the top line produces GODLI. In Lines 11 and 12 we have the italic IS or Latin SI, depending on what the context dictates. Lastly, as is often the case with the complete words from the plaque, the word THE will be used from Line 13. The next table contains our first obvious anagrams in acrostic form: After substituting the Q for I and the N for M in the bold-underlined letters, the first acrostic anagram appears in bold underlined letters in Lines 9 and 10, providing the word QVEEN. On the right in Lines 10 and 11 in bold-italic, the letters of SIC, Latin for "so, or thus," appear in an acrostic. Directly underneath QVEEN in italics and underlined, we see the word OVR.

9	S	G	**I**					
10	L	**M**	**V**	**E**	**E**	Æ	*S*	C
11	*R*		*V*	*O*	M	E	Æ	*I*
12	A		A	I	**R**	**A**	**E**	**T**
13	A	E	B	H		O	**M**	S

Appearing in the lower right in underlined-bold, the acrostic anagram of MATER.

Lastly, we will look the remaining letters to identify any remaining words:

9	S	G					
10	L					Æ	
11					**M**	E	Æ
12	A		**A**	_I_			
13	A	E	**B**	**H**		O		S

An anagram appears at the lower center of the arrangement in a partial acrostic and the nearby M. Subbing a Y for B and an R for H, we spell MARY.

As has been the case in other areas of the cipher, I scoured the remaining letters for any other anagrams or words. The first obvious one is the underlined word "I" in the lower center. Then I noted the word angling up from the lower right of the table, with SÆÆ as "SEE." I then wrote out the remaining letters in the order they appear in the table - S G L E A A E O. Looking at the available letters, I realized I could spell a name that I thought had appeared in another part of the cipher. Subbing a V for an E produces ESAV, an allusion to the Bible story of Jacob in which the older twin brother Esau is cheated out of his birthright and as a result never becomes King. Since Jacob is a form of the name James the allusion becomes obvious considering the cipher texts. The remaining letters (G L A O) with their values and signatures appear in the following table:

Table 5-2

Simple	7	11	1	14	= 33
	G	L	A	O	SUM
Reverse	18	14	24	11	= 67
Kaye	33	11	27	14	= 85

As you can plainly see, Simple and Reverse produce the cipher signatures for "Bacon" and "Francis," respectively. 85 is the signature for "Frater" in Reverse Cipher, and "Francis II" in Simple. Like in many other examples of left over letters, these form an anagram as well. Subbing O for L, it spells "GO A O," which represents "Alpha" and "Omega," which appear in other forms throughout the transpositions.

This confirms the following message in this section of the encoded cipher of Key 5 as: *"SEE, The GODLI QVEEN MARY IS OUR MOTHER. SIC, I ESAV."*

The "SIC" demonstrates that this message is intended to be read with the sections around it, as "thus" would be used in conjunction with an explanation. By putting them together in plain English, we see Francis Bacon stating, "I was the Dauphin but now I'm the shunned Medici grandson. See, the Godly Queen Mary is our mother. Thus, I'm Esau." Using the term "Godly" would be an obvious allusion to the Catholicism of Mary, Queen of Scots. Bacon referring to himself as Esau alludes to his displacement as the rightful heir to *both* thrones.

The next six lines continue along the same vein, and at this point I began to think that Key 5, as the "deepest layer" of this cipher, was the true and most important message on the plaque. This section was very challenging. But remembering Line 32 of Key 5 – REEDOSSO, this visually implied how Lines 14 – 18 should be read forward and backward. Looking at this section as having two sides, left and right, provided the ability to "REED" lines 14 - 18. This hint helped the discovery of four of the important words here. The next section appears in Lines 14 - 19:

14	*N*	*R*	S	**M**	H	T⊣	M	N
15	*B*	*A*	T	**V**	**M**	**W**	**A**	**Y**
16	I	B	V	R	G	I	K	T
17	**I̲**	**A̲**	L	O	T	V	S	H
18	**E̲**	**A̲**	O	H	V	E	I	V
19	Y	E	R	A	2	R	T	K

Two complete acrostic words appeared along with one acrostic anagram. Along Line 15 and into 14 starting from the right in bold, if we substitute B for the Y and D for W, we arrive at the amusingly appropriate word, BADMVM. Next, moving to the second bold underlined letters in Line 18 and reading in a clockwise manner, by subbing a V for the E we can read AVIA, Latin for "grandmother."

Lastly, bold italic letters in the upper left corner, by substituting M for N and Y for B, we can read the anagram for the name MARY.

The next set of acrostics appear here, along with yet another complete word:

14			**S**		H	T⊣	M	N
15			**T**					
16	I	B	**V**	**R**	G	I	K	*T*
17			L	**O**	*T*	*V*	*S*	*H*
18			**O̲**	**H̲**	**V̲**	**E̲**	I	V
19	Y	**E̲**	**R̲**	**A̲**	2	**R̲**	T	K

At the center of the block of characters, with one substitution of S for G is the Latin word "VRSI." The most popularly known meaning of this word is of course "bear." But it also means to "press hard in attack; threaten by proximity." But seeing that the word crosses the center line of this block of text, I decided to heed the directions of Line 32 and pay attention to words that could be formed on the left and right of this section. That's when I located the acrostic anagram STVRO in the bold letters spanning Lines 14 - 17, Latin meaning "stop, or check." On the right side in Line 17 is the anagram T V S H T in italics. Subbing R for H produces the word TRVST. As the majority of the letters of the next anagram are on Line 19, the "directions" of Line 32 again come into play. The words "overlap" in a very interesting way across the centerline of this section. In the bold and underline acrostic, without substitutions becomes OVERHEAR.

All of the remaining characters appear as follows:

14				H	T⊣	M	N
15							
16	I	B		G	I	K	
17			L				
18						I	V
19	Y			2		T	K

Since this section had been such a challenge, I placed all of the remaining letters in Table 5-3, arranging them together according to the lines on which they appeared. Left-justifying them, we then looked for any other meaningful words that would fit the context:

Table 5-3

H	T⊣	M	N	
I	B	G	I	K
L				
I	*V*			
Y	**2**	**T**	**K**	

Studying the characters, I realized something that opened up a whole host of possibilities. I noticed that the characters on the second line of the table give us a phonetic message by subbing an S for the G, "I be sick." Historically speaking, this is accurate for Francis Bacon. Since all the messages so far did not include a whole line of phonetics like this, should they be used in the actual message in the way that I have been deciphering the others? Did Bacon also use the leftover letters, if kept in the proper order, to reveal more phonetic messages? Had I been missing this the whole time?

After checking for cipher signatures, I realized the purpose - "I be sick" provided more context, and that some of my earlier assumptions were incorrect. The true message is even more shocking. In fact, the leftover letters in table form provided more acrostic anagrams. By reusing letters, the second column provides BVT. The first column with a dogleg right spells, I LIV. The whole context then tells us, "I B SIK, BVT I LIV." On to the core message.

This section so far has produced a word bank of, MARY, AVIA, (what I thought was) BADMVM, STURO, TRVST and OVERHEARD. However, BAD and MVM are on the opposite sides of this section of Key 5, and in accordance with the hint provided in Line 32, need to be read separately. Considering the history of the people allegedly involved here, arranging the words in a manner that might make sense was a simple matter. On a hunch, I decided on the following arrangement - MVM MARY OVERHEARD BAD AVIA STVRO TRUST. So, did Mary overhear that Catherine de Medici didn't trust her? Or did what Mary hear make her stop trusting Catherine?

Looking at our remaining letters to see if any other words could be found to flesh out the message, I used Y 2 as BY, and substituting F for T and E for V (note how these letters form a right triangle in the above table), we have the word FEL, Latin for "gall, or *poison*."

If we take the broad view of this entire section, it paints an amazing picture. At the very center of this block of letters, we immediately see the Latin word VRSI, one definition of which is "threatened by proximity." Following the instructions on Line 32, we simply count that word as a context clue, and use the characters for other words instead within the hidden message. Considering the other context clues, the full message of this section can be read as, "MVM MARY OVERHEARD BAD AVIA (VRSI) I B SIK BY FEL. BVT I LIV." Or, "Mother Mary overheard bad grandmother, threatened by our proximity, that I was sick from poison, but I lived."

This appears to be the obvious reason why this information was buried so deeply within this cipher. Again, I'll be analyzing this message in depth in its own chapter to see if it's even historically feasible. From what I already understand from history, I suspect that it's not only plausible, but probable.

To verify the encoded message, I checked the remaining characters for any cipher signatures, appearing in Table 5-4:

Table 5-4

Simple	8	19	12	13	9	2	7	9	10	9	10	108
	H	T⊣	M	N	I	B	G	I	K	I	K	SUM
Reverse	17	6	13	12	16	23	18	16	15	16	15	167
Kaye	34	19	12	13	35	28	33	35	10	35	10	264

During my analysis of the cipher signatures, I discovered still more information. The signature of "I B G" appears in the center, "I B 33." The line of remaining letters begins with two double Tau symbols, and also symbolically ends with a double Tau - I + K equals 19, the value of T. So therefore, I K I K becomes the equivalent of T T. I also suspected this was a hint to the value of the Kaye cipher signature, which was unfamiliar and therefore "didn't tie-out" in the verification system. It must indicate some form of double cipher signature relating to Bacon in Kaye Cipher.

Up to this point in Key 5, the cipher signatures have had a direct correlation with the content of the message. As you can see the Simple Cipher value's sum is 108, "Francis" in Reverse. However, after reading the message and doing a quick calculation, as mentioned earlier, it is also the value of "*Medici*" in Reverse, and "Francois III" in Simple. The Reverse Cipher values total 167, which we now can read as "Francis Stewart" in Simple, and "Baron Verulam" and "Francois III" in Reverse. But again, the Kaye value was confusing. Since the message is primarily about Francis and Mary, I noted that the signature for Mary Stewart was 231 in Kaye Cipher, which if added to 33, would produce 264. I didn't like this idea of combining a Simple Cipher signature with a Kaye cipher at first. However, I also noted that the Kaye Cipher total was also the sum of "Medici" in Kaye (172) and "Bacon" in Reverse (92). To complicate matters further, it's also the sum of "Bacon" in Kaye (111) and Mary Stewart in Simple (153), which is also "King Bacon" in Reverse (153). Checking other correlations, "Mary Stewart" in Reverse (112) and just "Stewart" in Kaye (152) also equal 264. However, it wasn't until I subtracted "Medici" in Simple (42) that I K I K made sense. The answer was 222 - 111, 111, or "Bacon Bacon" in Kaye – "I Kaye I Kaye." I nearly stopped there. My head had begun to hurt. But then I found the answer – the number 264 is the value of the name and title, "Rex F. Valois-Angouleme" in Reverse Cipher.

The next block of text that I examined were Lines 20 - 25, which also proved to be exceedingly difficult but rewarding. You'll soon see why:

20	**I**	**5**	**L**	**V**	**E**	**H**	**T**	**T**
21	D	T⊣	L	1	A	S	**A**	S
22	N	**M**	Y	A	W	L	6	T
23	T	**R**	I	O	T	S	K	C
24	I	R	T⊣	*Me*	O	I	R	G
25	S	E	E	A	E	T⊣	*Ys*	O

The first obvious acrostic anagram is the now too familiar name "MARY" in bold in Lines 22 and 23. The ligatured bold-italic "Me" was an obvious choice to be used as well as the symbol **Ys** used for "This." The bold-underlined letters in Line 20 along with the adjoining "A" below are an anagram producing, "I FELT HATE" after subbing an E for V, F for T and replacing the 5 with an "E."

20								
21	D	T⊣	L	1	**A**	**S**		S
22	N				**W**	L	**6**	T
23	T		**I**	**O**	**T**	**S**	**K**	C
24	*I*	R	T⊣		O	**I**	**R**	G
25	*S*	*E*	**E**	**A**	**E**	**T⊣**		O

The three bold letters forming the anagram in Lines 21 and 22 can be used as "SAW" or "WAS." At first I noted the acrostic in the lower left corner, spelling "SIRE" clockwise. Unfortunately, it didn't fit with the rest of words that I discovered in an intelligible context nor did it allow me to "tie out" the remaining characters in the signature checking system. I therefore had to reject it for this interpretation, however I suspected it would play a role in an alternative interpretation that remained elusive.

Next to it in bold we see "THE" incorporating the double Tau as the "TH." The large anagram formed by the bold / underlined characters, with a few substitutions forms a word I had suspected would turn up in relation to Mary's name. As acrostics earlier referred to himself and James as "WHORESVN," the letters in this acrostic for the Latin, "PROSTITUTA," by subbing P for K, T for 6, and V for E. This leaves us with the following remaining letters:

20							
21	D	T⊣	L	1			S
22	N				L		T
23	T						C
24	I	R			O		G
25	S	E					O

Putting them together in Table 5-5 in order provides more acrostic anagrams:

Table 5-5

D	T⊣	L	**1**	**S**
N	*L*	T		
T	C			
I	R	*O*	**G**	
S	**E**	**O**		

The bold **1 S** spell AS, while the bold italic letters form the Latin "SOLI" meaning throne, the bold underlined letters form the Latin "NEGO" meaning "deny." One arrangement of all the words in this section can be rendered as, "FELT HATE AS I SAW Ys PROSTITUTA MARY NEGO ME ThE SOLI." In plain English, Bacon relates that he "felt hate as I saw this prostitute Mary deny me the throne."

The remaining characters and the sums of their values in each of the three cipher systems appear in Table 5-6:

Table 5-6

Simple	4	19	11	19	19	3	17	= 92
	D	T⊣	L	T	T	C	R	SUMS
Reverse	21	6	14	6	6	22	8	= 83
Kaye	30	19	11	19	19	29	17	= 144

The total in Simple Cipher is obviously the signature for "Bacon" in Reverse. The total in Reverse is the signature for "Fraters" in Simple. Lastly, the Kaye, we now know is the signature for "Sir (Rex) Francis Bacon" and "Fr. Stuart III" in Simple Cipher. The checking system contains the anagram / phonetic message after substitutions, "C HOW T⊣ TT."

As I had done with other sections of the cipher, I decided to look for any other messages that could be gleaned from the same section of characters using the same methods. Not only did one present itself, but *two more* appeared. Here is the first:

20	**I**	**5**	**L**	**V**	**E**	**H**	**T**	**T**
21	D	T⊣	L	1	A	S	*A*	*S*
22	N	**M**	**Y**	**A**	W	L	6	T
23	T	**R**	I	O	T	S	K	C
24	*I*	*R*	T⊣	**Me**	O	I	R	G
25	*S*	*E*	E	A	E	T⊣	**Ys**	O

Lines 20 and 21 produce, using some of the same main anagrams we see the following appear again - "I FELT HATE" and "AS." Again as the source of that emotion "MARY" appears again. This time the bold-italic acrostic "SIRE," in the lower left corner can be used, along with the conjoined characters "Me" and "Ys" as THIS.

20								
21	D	T⊣	L	1		S		
22	N				W	L	6	T
23	T		I	O	**T**	**S**	**K**	**C**
24			T⊣		**O**	**I**	**R**	**G**
25			E	A	E	T⊣		O

Here, we use the 6 T S K O I R E A E T⊣, by replacing 6 with T and E with V, to create the word "PROSTITVTAE." The remaining characters appear in the following table (5-7):

Table 5-7

D	*T⊣*	**L**	**1**	**S**
N	W	**L**	**T**	
T	I	**O**	**C**	
T⊣	<u>**G**</u>			
<u>**O**</u>				

The biggest word that can be made using the remaining bold characters in the first three rows happens to be "SCOTLAND." We also have "GO" in the bold underlined letters. Additionally, knowing how Francis Bacon often signed his signature with "*Fr.*" a substitution of those letters in place of the italicized T⊣ gives us the initials for "Francis."

Finally, the few remaining characters:

Table 5-8

L	
W	
T	**I**
T⊣	

The W I and double Tau spell "WITH," and with a substitution of O for L, we have the word "TO" without any letters to spare.

This brings our "word bank" to be composed of: I, FELT, HATE, AS, MARY, SIRE, Me, This, PROSTITVTAE, GO, Fr., WITH and TO. These words are easily arranged in the following message, "I FELT HATE AS This PROSTITUTAE MARY SIRE Me WITH Fr. GO TO SCOTLAND."

At this point I was convinced that each section of the characters had overlapping intended cipher messages. Again, using the same methods, an entirely different message appears even when using many of the same exact letter combinations:

20	**I**	5	**L**	**V**	**E**	**H**	**T**	T
21	D	**T⊣**	**L**	1	A	S	**A**	S
22	N	***M***	***Y***	A	W	L	6	T
23	T	R	I	O	T	S	**K**	**C**
24	*I*	R	T⊣	**Me**	O	I	**R**	**G**
25	**S**	**E**	**E**	A	E	T⊣	**Ys**	**O**

Again, using nearly the entire Line 20 (except the 5 and final T), and by adding three characters from Line 21 we have an opposite idea emerge. Subbing R for H, Fr for the T⊣ and O for L, we have "*I LOVE FRATER.*" Bold, italic-underlined "MY" appears in Line 22. The remaining obvious words are I, SEE, Me and again Ys as "THIS." Lastly, in the right corner of Lines 23 – 25, with the bold underline letters we have an anagram for the word SHOCK, by subbing an S for the G and an H for the R. The following table contains the remaining characters in their original positions:

20		5						T
21	D			1	**A**	**S**		S
22	N			A	W	**L**	6	T
23	T	R	I	O	T	**S**		
24		R	T⊣		**O**	**I**		
25				A	E	T⊣		

Words that can be used are the bold "AS" and the bold underlined "SOLI." Assembled in Table 5-9 are the remaining unused letters:

Using every other underlined letter from the fourth line down and subbing an F for the first T, we form "FIT." Using the bold letters we have "NOT." This leaves the following characters:

Table 5-10

5	T	
D	1	S
A	W	6
R		
R	T⊣	
A	E	T⊣

Table 5-9

5	T			
D	1	S		
N	A	W	6	T
T	R	I	O	T
R	T⊣			
A	E	T⊣		

We see the underlined characters create the word "TRADE," and the italicized letters spell "WAS" with A in place of 1. The bolder characters form the word "FATHER" with F for the 6, with the conjoined double Tau as TH, and lastly, though the remaining double Tau could count as a Bacon signature, using the substitution system we have Fr., as the name Francis. This arrangement leaves no leftover characters.

All of the characters have been used to form the following word bank: I LOVE FRATER MY I SEE Me This SHOCK AS SOLI FIT NOT TRADE WAS FATHER Fr.

We've seen in other areas of express love for his brother James. And here not only is this sentiment repeated but he also adds more information. I see the correct word order as, "I LOVE SEE MY FRATER This SOLI. WAS TRADE. I NOT AS FIT - SHOCK - Me FATHER Fr.." Or in plain English the message becomes, "I love seeing my brother on this throne. It was a trade. I'm not as fit for it - shocking (sarcasm) since my father was Francis II."

This confirmed that each block of text had multiple messages as was earlier suspected. Each section was designed to contain over-lapping acrostics anagrams, that when unraveled would leave behind different characters that could be used to flesh out each different part of the messages. Contemplating its construction, to over-use the same word, is mind boggling.

Moving on to the next block of letters in Lines 26 through 32, we again see Bacon's hatred of Mary, surprising considering his reputation for not even feeling hate toward his enemies:

26	**O**	**S**	**A**	T⊣	P	M	T	H
27	**N**	R	P	A	S	W	V	D
28	M	N	E	V	3	E	W	N
29	T	3	V	G	Q	A	A	P
30	**E**	**H**	**A**	**T**	**D**	**S**	**A**	**V**
31	T⊣	*T*	O	F	H	Yt	1	**E**
32	*R*	*E*	*E*	*D*	O	S	S	O

In the upper left corner in bold is an acrostic of "A" and "SON." Line 30 with the E at the end of Line 31 spell out, "SAVED HATE." The italicized and underlined characters in Lines 31 and 32, subbing F for T provides the underlined word "FREED." With all of these removed we move on to the next obvious words:

26				T⊣	P	M	T	H
27			R	P	A	S	W	V	D
28	M	N	E	V	3	**E**	**W**	**N**
29	T	3	V	G	Q	A	**A**	**P**
30								
31	T⊣		*O*	*F*	*H*	**Yt**	1	
32					O	S	S	O

In bold on Line 31 are the obvious choices by subbing R for H in "FOR" and "Yt" as "That." The bold underlined acrostic anagram with substitutions of D for W and K for P spells "NAKED." All of the remaining characters appear in the following table in their current order:

Table 5-11

T⊣	P	**M**	**T**	**H**		
R	**P**	A	**S**	W	V	D
M	N	**E**	V	3		
T	3	V	G	**Q**	A	
T⊣	1					
O	S	S	O			

The obvious word appearing at the top center of the table is "MATER'S." However, the context, though fitting, didn't need this word. The context that had formed due to the word "NAKED" indicated the need for a different construction, and all of the necessary letters were present. Using M T P M N E V Q H S, I substituted N for an M, and I for Q, to spell PVNISHMENT. Removing these characters provides us with the next step to complete the message, which can be seen here in Table 5-12:

Table 5-12

T⊣	P			
R	A	W	V	**D**
3				
T	3	**V**	G	**A**
T⊣	1			
O	S	S	O	

Using the remaining letters to complete the thought, we can form the words with the bold letters as "WAS/SAW," and subbing V for E in the bold underlined letters gives "DEAT⊣." Substituting F for the T in the bold italics (left column) we have "OF."

T⊣	P
R	V
3	
3	
T⊣	1
S	O

The "leftover" letters are very interesting. Subbing E for V, X for 3 and A for 1, we can spell "AXE." Another possibility would have been to substitute E for V, and X for a 3 and spell REX. Other interesting combinations will be discussed when the cipher signatures are calculated to ensure the message "ties out" correctly.

Our word bank in the order of their discovery are: "A SON SAVED HATE FREED FOR Yt NAKED PVNISHMENT WAS(SAW) DEA T⊣ OF."

Putting these in a sensible order, we read the statement, "SAVED HATE FOR PVNISHMENT. SON SAW A NAKED DEATH. FREED OF That."

In the remaining characters, interesting signatures appear: T⊣ P R V 33 T⊣ 1 S O. The first obvious one is the pair of 3's, 33, "Bacon" in Simple. Adding the rest of the values of the other characters equals 123, "James" in Kaye Cipher. Adding the Reverse values of the leftover characters equals 77 (GG) and the signature for both "Sir Bacon" and "Rex Bacon." Or if we "take a P," (-10) we have 67, "Francis" in Simple. Adding the 3's at face value, we have 83, "Fraters" in Simple. If we add the Reverse values of "C" instead, the total is 121, "Roi Francois" in Simple. If we again "take a P," the value is 111, "Bacon" in Kaye.

But then I saw it. Subbing an E for the V gives us "ROSE." If we use the number 1 for the word "ONE" our message becomes complete, "Saved hate for punishment. Son saw a naked death. Freed of that one rose," or "Rose freed of that one."

This leaves us with T⊣ P 3 3 T⊣ as remaining letters. Adding their values from Simple Cipher, minus our 33 signature, the total is 53, "Mary" in Simple Cipher. In Reverse the sum is 22, the Reverse value of "C" and the number of Tav in the Hebrew alphabet. The total in Kaye Cipher, before adding the final double Tau is 92, "Bacon" in Reverse. Adding the value of the Tau and the total is 111, Bacon in Kaye cipher. The message of the signatures seems to be saying "Bacon see Mary," apparently meaning that Francis was present at her execution. And now for the last section of Key 5.

This last block of text contains several messages, but only the most complete are presented. As an interesting aside, Line 33 appropriately enough is a signature. After the word "I," the next 5 letter values total 67 in Simple, the signature for "Francis" in Simple, and the last two character values total 33, "Bacon" in Simple. Line 33 therefore states "I, Francis Bacon." The largest finds appear first:

33	*I*	O	O	Nt	R	I	T	O
34	**M**	**E**	**H**	**T**	**R**	**I**	**T**	**S**
35	S	S	S	D	A	G	A	A
36	A	T	Y	B	D	H	I	I
37	*P*	*V*	D	E	A	L	E	E
38	**O**	**N**	**C**	**V**	**I**	**I**	**S**	**P**

The first words to be apparent were in bold on Line 34 read backwards, "STIR THEM." The word "I" begins Line 33 as previously mentioned. Line 37 begins with a backwards and underlined "VP." And lastly, Line 38 in its entirety after 2 substitutions, E for V and 15 for P, can be read as, "ONCE I IS 15." Removing these characters

allows a second look:

33		O	O	Nt	R	I	T	O
34								
35	S	S	S	***D***	***A***	G	A	A
36	A	T	Y	***B***	D	**H**	I	I
37			**D**	**E**	**A**	**L**	**E**	E
38								

In bold on Lines 36 and 37, by substituting R for H we form the word "LEADER" with the characters directly below in Line 37. Above this in in bold-underlined-italics on Lines 35 and 36 appears an acrostic anagram for "BAD."

This brings our word bank in this latest round to: "I, STIR, THEM, VP, ONCE, I, IS, 15, LEADER and BAD," all apparently referring to himself as a "bad leader."

All of the remaining letters appear on their original lines and left justified in Table 5-13:

Table 5-13

O	O	Nt	R	I	T	O
S	S	S	G	A	A	
T	Y	D	H	I	I	
E						

The first word that made sense in context was the Latin word "ORIGA," meaning "charioteer, driver; or helmsman."

Considering the message seems to be about being a leader, this made perfect sense. Removing these letters and moving the others to the left to fill the spaces results in the following table:

Table 5-14

O	Nt	T	O		
S	S	S	A		
T	Y	D	H	I	I
E					

The underlined characters on the left spell "NOT," using the conjoined "Nt" character as "N." The bold letters spell the Latin word "SATIO" meaning "satisfy."

Again, moving forward with the remaining letters, the next table removes the above used characters:

S	S	I
Y	D	H
E		

With only one substitution of an R for H, all of the letters can be used to spell "DRESSY." And of course we still have an "I" to use as another first person pronoun, leaving no remaining letters.

As we look over all of the words we've accumulated, we can write out the following message:

"ONCE I IS 15, I STIR THEM VP. I BAD LEADER. I NOT SATIO DRESSY ORIGA." Here he tells us that by the time he was 15 years old, he stirred "them" up and was a bad leader. He was satisfied not being a "dressy helmsman," meaning the King steering the country.

Conclusions

After looking at the messages in the phonetics and acrostics, and the messages of Keys 32 and 8, this transposition with Key 5 was extremely successful. First, the main core of the message seems to be information that could never be expected. I had hoped that I would discover a message stating that Sir Francis Bacon oversaw the writing of William Shakespeare's plays. Instead, the message states that Bacon *wrote* the works attributed to the actor "Willom Shakspere." In my wildest dreams, I had hoped to find a

110

message that confirmed the "Prince Tudor" theory. Instead, something totally unexpected appeared. What is recorded on the plaque of Shakespeare's Funerary Monument located in Holy Trinity Church in Stratford-upon-Avon is Sir Francis Bacon's hidden autobiography.

This plaque appears to be the life story, not of the actor people know as William Shakespeare, but Sir Francis Bacon. Additionally, using the same methodology among each of the separate keys, producing repeating ideas, only reinforces the validity of the cipher's message.

The original premise was that Key 5, requiring the deepest level of reorganization of all the characters on the plaque, would contain the clearest and most important message. The main message appears to be about Francis Bacon's real family, James I of England and Mary Queen of Scots. Bacon expresses his hatred for Mary, and how he saved that hatred for her "naked death," an execution whose story nearly everyone knows. Opposite his hatred, he expresses his love of seeing his brother on the throne of England. Lastly, he also provides a possible reason for his departure for France at the age of 16 "from the hand of the Queen." If he revealed his true identity at the age of 15, couldn't that have "stirred-up" some supporters of him to replace Elizabeth I, giving her a very good reason to send him to France under the supervision of one of her most loyal subjects, Sir Amias Paulet? Afterall, he would have been heir to that throne as well. Perhaps Elizabeth I decided he should be their problem, not England's or her own. At this point this is not all idle speculation. All of the messages among the different algorithms produced by the Keys 32, 8 and 5 have all expressed one idea - Francis Bacon was the son of Mary Queen of Scots and Francis II of France. And what we know of Orthodox history seems to align in terms of known events and the timeline, which will later be explained in detail.

Before delving into that possibility, we have another arrangement of characters to analyze. We need to look at Key 38.

Chapter 6 - Key 38 Signs the Work and So Much More

The message of Key 8 was clear - "Eye the TT" symbol. As Bacon states, he used his "TH" symbol to represent the Triple Tau, so looking at his ten T⊣ symbols as a possible key was the next most logical step. Luckily, it not only produces a wealth of information, but it was also the key that provided the clue that helped unlock the message with the previous Key 5.

So, adding the two Tau together, 19 + 19 provided the next key to create the algorithm to again reorganize all the characters on the plaque. Those characters were arranged in two columns of 19 rows, reinforcing the symbolism of the double Tau. Counting every 38th letter, recording it, and counting to the next, and so on, produced the following table of letters:

Key 38

1	T	P	A	V	O	L	R	A	20	S	R	V	H	M	F	I	O
2	M	Y	C	N	H	L	E	3	21	O	Æ	O	T⊣	O	E	L	D
3	E	A	V	O	W	A	S	2	22	I	M	T⊣	A	H	B	S	O
4	N	T	O	M	E	H	O	E	23	N	S	T	E	W	M	E	N
5	O	S	T⊣	S	D	E	T	I	24	E	V	S	D	T⊣	O	V	A
6	R	T	F	I	I	I	E	D	25	G	L	E	S	I	T	A	T
7	A	E	I	T⊣	D	S	G	3	26	M	V	O	V	W	Ys	E	I
8	M	B	D	N	E	T	A	5	27	V	P	G	O	E	K	L	I
9	E	A	A	I	R	S	P	S	28	I	O	Y	I	R	C	T	B

10	T	H	E	T⊣	V	O	T	I	29	L	P	H	V	A	E	T	O	
11	R	S	R	I	T	C	V	T	30	Y	T	W	N	E	D	I	T	
12	A	V	T	W	A	N	B	A	31	P	I	R	E	P	T⊣	R	T	
13	M	P	S	T	N	THE	T	T	32	O	G	E	M	S	O	W	I	
14	E	M	A	S	K	E	R	Æ	33	I	E	G	O	K	D	T⊣	W	
15	T	Y	F	A	C	R	A	6	34	C	T	N	H	A	ME	A	S	
16	A	L	O	L	I	O	G	1	35	I	A	E	W	H	A	H	I	
17	R	O	S	P	V	M	N	6	36	D	R	S	T	S	N	E	H	
18	C	T	Y	T⊣	Q	R	I	1	37	V	R	S	S	Nt	E	H	E	
19	O	E	B	A	E	A	V	I	38	I	E	A	N	ME	S	Yt	V	P

In each pass of the Key, I anticipated the number 33, the numerical cipher signature for Bacon.

This feeling was heightened when I reached pass 32, which can be seen numbered as such in the table above. The letters appeared, OGEMSOWI. I saw the word GEM and remembered this was a term from one of the eulogies in *Manes Verulamiani*, referring to Francis Bacon as the "gem of concealed literature." It also could be a message such as, Oh, gem sow I, as in "I'm a gem from a female pig," as a play on his name. When adding the letters of SOW in Simple Cipher, we total 53 which is the cipher signature for "Mary," effectively calling his mother a pig who was responsible for the creation of "Bacon" in the first place. In other words, "Bacon" came from the "belly of Mary." Also, adding the number values of the letters using the Simple Cipher, they totaled 100, the total of "Francis Bacon" in Simple Cipher. Checking the numbers from the Reverse Cipher, they too equaled 100.

Table 6-1

Simple	14	7	5	12	18	14	21	9	= 100
Text	O	G	E	M	S	O	W	I	
Reverse	11	18	20	13	7	11	4	16	= 100
Kaye	14	33	31	12	18	14	21	35	= 178

This line is a clear cipher signature of Francis Bacon. It doesn't end here, however. I experimented with the cipher system to see if any other interesting results would appear.

The Kaye Cipher resulting total is 178, which is close to a few significant numbers, but for our intents and purposes, close is not close enough. This implied a message beyond the known cipher signatures. The most likely explanation: 178 is the Simple Cipher value of "Dauphin Francois III."

All of this heightened expectations for Line 33. There it was on the 33rd pass - IEGOKDT⊣W. Line 33 states "I" as the first letter or word. Just to make sure we get the message, the next three letters spell EGO, the Latin word for "I" or "self." The number 33 in Simple Cipher together with the word "I" *and* "EGO," we have the obvious message, "I, Bacon." Using the same method as the table above, two more cipher signatures of Bacon appeared on Line 33 in Reverse and Simple Ciphers, respectively:

In Simple Cipher, counting the Double Tau as 38 our total is 108, "Francis" in Reverse Cipher. By counting the "Double Tau" as one T in Reverse Cipher, the number totals 111, which is "Bacon" in Kaye cipher.

Table 6-2

Simple	9	5	7	14	10	4	38	21	= 108
Text	I	E	G	O	K	D	T⊣	W	
Reverse	16	20	18	11	15	21	6	4	= 111
Kaye	35	31	33	14	10	30	19	21	= 193

Reading them in Simple and Reverse Ciphers, his full name, Francis Bacon, appears as yet another cipher signature. The total in Kaye Cipher is 193, the 44th prime number, the number of his "secret cipher signature." It can also represent the Triple Tau as 19 is the letter "T" followed by the number "3," as well as a message to "C the Truth." The final letters of the line, KDT⊣W, at first glance seem to be random "extra" letters. However, seeing the absence of vowels, I converted the English characters into Hebrew as "כדתו." This translated into the phrase, "As his religion."

I don't believe that this meant that he worshipped himself, or this knowledge of the cipher system, as his religion. I believe that the Truth, and the truth about himself, his true identity, had become a religion of sorts.

Having been so preoccupied with lines 32 and 33, I missed two features in line 28 that should have been readily apparent. One of the clues has often appeared in other attempts deciphering texts associated with Rosicrucian topics, and is the Hebrew word, "Oye!" Appearing at different times as "OI, OY" or "OYE," this expression of amazement is used as a way of drawing attention to information nearby. Line 28 also contains the word "I" right before the initials "RC," one of the signatures of Fra Rosi Crosse. Note how the word "OY" is framed by the pair of I's, followed by "RC," a Tau and the letter "B" for Bacon. Through the substitution protocol, "T" can be "F." Bacon appears to be stating, "Oye! I'm RC - FB." Also noted is the number 28 represents the letter B in Kaye Cipher. Next we need to check the "value" of Line 28, as produced by the three Ciphers:

Table 6-3

Line 28	I	O	Y	I	R	C	T	B	Total
Simple	9	14	23	9	17	3	19	2	96
Reverse	16	11	2	16	8	22	6	23	104
Kaye	35	14	23	35	17	29	19	28	200

Along with all of the other signatures, working on this line reveals an astonishing mathematical feature. Kaye Cipher produces the number 200, Francis Bacon as a cipher signature in Reverse. But the realization came from the other two totals, 96 in Simple and 104 in Reverse. Looking at 96 we could interpret it as "I, F," while 104 is the value of "Verulam" in Reverse. Though fairly insignificant in themselves, I noted their sum, because of the simple mathematical principles involved *has to be* 200, the number produced by Kaye Cipher.

Since we have the cipher signature of 200 for "Francis Bacon" in Kaye, it attracted my attention to notice this interesting feature of the Key. Using Key 38 produces 37 lines of 8 characters, and one of 9. Since there are 24 characters in the alphabet, and the Simple and Reverse Ciphers are numbered as they are, if we add the numeral equivalents of Simple and Reverse Cipher of any character, the sum will always equal 25. As stated earlier, since there are 8 characters in each line, the sums of the Simple and Reverse totals *have to* total 200, the signature cipher of "Francis Bacon" in Reverse, as 8 times 25 equals 200.

Table 6-4

Simple	14	7	5	12	18	14	21	9	100
32	O	G	E	M	S	O	W	I	SUM
Reverse	11	18	20	13	7	11	4	16	100
Kaye	14	33	31	12	18	14	21	(I)	143

This is hardly a dismissal of the phenomenon. Francis Bacon created this cipher *specifically* so that each line of characters would repeat his cipher signature in this way.

In summary, in just lines 32 and 33 alone, numbers of esoteric significance for the Rosicrucian Order and the Freemasons, we see multiple cipher signatures of Bacon and the Rosi Crosse. In line 32, the total in Reverse Cipher equals the Simple Cipher total for "Francis Bacon" of 100.

When looking at the total of the Kaye Cipher value 178, another solution presents itself other than it's the signature of "Dauphin Francis III" in Simple. When we subtract the value of 35 of the single letter word "I," the result is 143, the Kaye signature of the word "Frater," conveying the message "I Frater." On one hand this appears to be an explicit announcement of Bacon's membership in a Brotherhood. On the other, especially in light of the signatures in the next line, he could be referencing his younger brother James I of England. Because you will see, Line 33 also tells a story in a series of cipher signatures:

Simple	9	5	7	14	10	4	38	21	108
33	I	E	G	O	K	D	T⊣	W	SUM
Reverse	16	20	18	11	15	21	6	4	111
Kaye	35	31	33	14	10	30	19	21	193*
		66	99	113	123	153	172		(Subtotal)

Table 6-5

As stated previously, the Simple and Reverse Cipher totals produce the complete signature of "Francis Bacon." However, the Kaye Cipher is particularly interesting, when looking at the subtotals as we add the Kaye values of the letters.

Adding the first two characters gives us 66, and then adding the familiar value for "G" we have 99, or a "Triple G" in Kaye. Both values are "missing one" from being a complete "Francis" and "Francis Bacon" in Simple. What was missing each time? They appear when we add the "O" totaling 113, "two more" than "Bacon" in Kaye. Two more *what?* The next two totals of course: 123 is the signature for "James" in Kaye Cipher, and 153 is the signature for "Mary Stewart" in Simple Cipher as it would be spelled in Scotland and England. Adding the Tau produces 172, the Reverse Cipher signature for "Shakespeare." Is Bacon telling us that Mary abdicating the throne to James, and the lack of both of them in his life, allowed Bacon to write the works of Shakespeare? Given the context of so many messages regarding this family relationship, it's probable. Then the secrecy hinted by the final total could be a form of confirmation.

At first I was perplexed at the Kaye value total of 193 as it wasn't a known cipher signature. As an interesting aside, it's the Reverse Cipher value of a name that has appeared in the bilateral cipher – "Walter Raleigh." However, after the interesting subtotals that the characters of the line produced, I thought it odd that the final sum wouldn't also carry a meaning. Perhaps the subtotals were only wishful thinking and confirmation bias? But taking prime numbers into account, 193 is the 44th prime number. Again, my friend Chris had sent me a page from a 19th Century esoteric journal that had made the statement that "44 was a *secret* signature of Bacon" referenced earlier.

If you recall, the first thought is that Tav is the last letter of the Hebrew alphabet, number 22. TT then has a value of 44 and is therefore Bacon's "secret number." But then, it could be a result of the substitution system between the Simple and Reverse Ciphers. The most common cipher signature for Bacon is 33, which can be represented by "CC" or "XX." Therefore it follows that through the substitution system, these letters are also the 22nd letters in Simple and Reverse. Therefore 33 can also be represented by 22 and 22, whose sum obviously is his "secret signature" of 44. So the final total in Kaye of 193 can be read in a way that confirms that his secret family ties led him to secretly write the works of Shakespeare. The final (and the most satisfying) explanation of the secret signature however, is due to his true identity, which itself *was secret*, but 193 allows us to "See Truth."

According to the multiple messages in the cipher texts, Sir Francis Bacon should have been King. This was a state secret of the highest importance. It never occurred to me until very late in this process, yet another important reason Bacon would use 44 as a secret signature. The answer lay in the fact that he should have been King, and the Latin word he used in his cipher texts, "Rex." Rex in Simple Cipher is 44, therefore representing his biggest secret. The Reverse Cipher signature number for "Rex" is 31, which suddenly explains all of the messages throughout the key transpositions stating "I SEE A," or in this sense, "I 31." Another piece that comes together with these numbers, 31 is the 11th prime number, therefore representing the highly meaningful letters "A A." The Kaye Cipher value for "Rex" is 70, the same value of the word "Dauphin" in Simple Cipher.

Lastly, the genius of Lines 28, 32 and 33 still leaves me amazed. The signature of Sir Francis Bacon appears multiple times and clearly comes through as if the spear-shakers themselves were forcing us to see the light.

The more I worked with this cipher system, the more I learned. It wasn't until the very end of the process that I felt I knew how to correctly interpret what I was seeing. When looking at the results of Key 38, it's important to again look at what immediately appears to be obvious. Aside from the previous analysis of the *multiple* Bacon cipher signatures, other features are prominent. For example, in some sections obvious words can easily be read, and in others, words appear phonetically spelled. Some are simple or cryptic statements, while others are clues of how to continue to decipher the code. In others, obvious acrostic messages appear. What follows next is what I would consider a superficial overview of possible messages. And please note, this section contains speculation regarding possible messages, and that's how some of the interpretations here should be viewed.

Phonetics and Acrostics

In Lines 5 and 6, Frances Bacon states his true identity:

5	O	S	T⌐	S	D	E	T	I
6	R	T	F	I	I	I	E	D

The last letter of Line 5 and the first six letters of Line 6 states, "I RT FIII," or "I art Francis III." With the E and D at the end, it could actually be read as "I art Francis Third." So once again, an explicit phonetic repeating the main message of the previous cipher texts.

118

Next, lines 10 - 14 seem to be providing clues of how to continue decoding the cipher:

10	T	H	E	T⊣	V	O	T	I
11	R	S	R	I	T	C	V	T
12	A	V	T	W	A	N	B	A
13	M	P	S	T	N	THE	T	T
14	E	M	A	S	K	E	R	Æ

"VOTI" is a Latin word for "vow." And so the line reads, *"THE double Tau VOTI (vow)."* Line 11 begins with RSR, which *could* be an abbreviation for "Rosicrucians." The rest of the letters from there through line 13 appear as - I T C V T A V T W A N B A M P S T N THE T T.

These lines can be read as, (with one substitution, *"I F. CVT AVT WAN BAMPS T N THE TT,"* or more specifically, *"I (Francis) CUT OUT ONE BAMP'S T iN THE TT (double Tau)."* A "bamp" means "idiot." Also, An acrostic can be read beginning at the same point, and read counter clockwise upward into Line 10, "I F CVT IT OUT," and reading Line 10 forward shows what "IT" is: "THE T⊣." So, I thought at the time that this could be a hint on decrypting the next transposition cipher, which we now know to be correct. I simply skipped one of the Tau's on Line 13, which worked. There are times when calculating the value of the double Tau symbol (T⊣ or Th), that it was only to be counted as a single Tau with a value of 19, or 6, instead of 38 or 12. This could be another additional interpretation, as the concept of "either / or" do not seem to apply to most of these messages. Considering how everything else has worked with this cipher, it's likely all of these meanings are valid. But as I said, after contemplating the next line, the answer became obvious.

Line 14 is very interesting. "Masker" is a word indicating the Key used to encode or *"mask"* the cipher. The hypothesis at the time was the letter E before the word and the Æ after it should be used as the next key, the Key 5 that appeared on the plaque as "23." Other references through the course of attempting to decode the cipher, also had made reference to E and V, one of which stated, "TY GOVD E TO V." Therefore it logically follows that the next step in unlocking any other secrets of the plaque involved using 5 as the next Key with this current arrangement of letters. However, since the number of total characters is divisible by 5 (305) this would mean that any algorithm would end, or begin to repeat the same letters after the first "pass" unless I knew which letter to skip. Of course, the lines above the "masker" line provided the answer.

As I stated, Lines 11 - 13 contained the message, "I cut out one bamp's T, in the TT." When using "E" or 5 as the next Key of the algorithm to rearrange the characters in Key 38, simply skip one of those specific T's. It worked, as evidenced by the next chapter with the Key 5 messages, "E MASKER of TT."

In Lines 14, 15 and 16, an acrostic appears in the center of the text. In the second boxes of lines 14 and 15, we see the word "MY." Right next to this word in lines 15 and 16, we see another message:

14	E	M	A	S	K	E
15	T	Y	F	A	C	R
16	A	L	O	L	I	O

At the center of Line 15, we can read counter-clockwise, "RC A FOLIO." Taken all together, we can read it as "MY RC 1st FOLIO." Another acrostic appears in the first column of lines 16 – 19 as "ARCO," Latin meaning "to keep hidden; protect."

Though at first I saw no context to use to make sense of the next construction, I include it here to only introduce the idea in reference to some of my friends researching connections to the Oak Island mystery and I saw it as nothing but an interesting coincidence. Line 15:

15	T	Y	F	A	C	R	A	6

Beginning with a Tau, the line ends with the number 6. As we know, 6 is F in Simple Cipher and T in Reverse, so the line is framed by these Taus as pillars. Reading the contents within this frame backwards, and with one substitution, again an F for a T, we see *"ARCATY,"* which is not a huge leap, phonetically speaking, to Arcady or Acadia, the original colonial name of Nova Scotia. Bacon was also a key individual in planning the colonization scheme for James I in Newfoundland and Nova Scotia. As you later will see, it's only appropriate that this word appears between these Tau's as "pillars," as the land named here lay far beyond the Pillars of Hercules.

But again, at the time without a context for this place name, framed by Taus, indicating a message about the American colony so the idea was dismissed. As you will see, that had been one of my mistakes. In order to successfully decode this Key, I would be forced to return to this idea.

As for signatures, the characters equal 76 in Simple which can be read as "I Francis" in Simple as we've seen in other places. The sum is 111 in Reverse Cipher, "Bacon" in Kaye and the Kaye total, using the number 6 at face value is 180, "King Francois" in Reverse. If we use the value of "F" in Kaye as 32, the total becomes 206, "King Francis Stewart" in Simple. Another message that seems to be repeated throughout the cipher, going backwards from "6" after substituting F, the message becomes *"F, A RC."*

Another way to read the message backwards would be to view the letters "RC" framed by two pillars on each side, A RC A. With one substitution, "B" for "Y," the initials "F. B." appear. Subbing a "T" for the "6," the message is framed by the Tau on each end. Again, this will be revisited in a later section.

Next, we see Line 16 has a curious arrangement of letters that attracts attention:

16	A	L	O	L	I	O	G	1

First of all it begins with one of the premier Bacon symbols - A, and it ends with the number "1" which we read as A as well. As it's Line 16 which is the letter (word) "I" in Reverse Cipher, it's logical to look for more Bacon signatures. So, this line appears between our pillars of Athena and Apollo (A and 1), the spear-shakers, mimicking line 15 above it with its Taus. Adding the Simple Cipher values of the letters leading up to the number 1 totals 67, "Francis" in Simple. Adding these same letters in Reverse yields a total of 108, "Francis" in Reverse Cipher. The Kaye Cipher value of these letters is 145, "James Steewart" in Simple Cipher.

Using the substitution system between Simple and Reverse Ciphers, L's can become O's. By adding together the values of 4 O's (56) with I (9) and AA, also totals 67, the Simple Cipher value of "Francis," and a G, which equals 33 in Kaye, meaning "Bacon" in Simple Cipher. Reading the 4 O's as 4 L's, produces our secret signature of Bacon, 44, framed by the "A's" and the letters I, G or "I Bacon."

Previously having noticed the letter "O" being used to highlight areas of interest in this Key, and it can be assumed that it's because of the symbolism of the letter itself. Along with being a symbol of light like "A," a circle represents "AIN SOPH" or "the eternal state of being." It represents Creation on the macrocosmic level, and the personal sphere of influence and creation on the microcosmic level of human experience. Additionally, some have speculated that since the value of O is 11 in Reverse Cipher, it could represents Jachin and Boas, the pillers of Solomon's Temple and Freemasonry. (In Simple Cipher, 11 appears as the carpenter's square in the form of the letter "L" which is the Athbash substitution for "O"). If you recall the Bacon cipher signature that appears in line 32 of Key 38, actually was highlighted by O's. Lastly, an "O" appearing with a Tau, would have a total of 33, such as at the center of this next example. I'll be pointing out another example in a moment, but first I want to address lines 17 and 18.

In the first 6 boxes of these two lines, we see an obvious signature of the Rosi Crosse. The word "ROSY" appears in this acrostic:

17	R	O	S
18	C	T	Y

17	R	O	S
18	C	*T*	Y

The Tau provides one example of the cross.

And by continuing clockwise around this same square we see the word spelled out as *"CROS:"*

17	*R*	*O*	*S*
18	*C*	T	Y

Another interesting feature of this acrostic appears when we consider the letters vertically. We have "RC" as a signature of the Rosi Crosse, "OT" which equal 33, and the "S and Y" in the position of the symbol from the plaque used in place of the word "THIS." Curious as why these particular lines contained the Rosicrucian signature, I added 17 and 18, and looked to line 35, only to find a phonetic spelling of Yahweh:

35	I	A	E	W	H	A	H	I

Interestingly, the letters on Line 35 are framed by the letters "I" appearing again as "pillars" and 35 is that value of "I" in Kaye Cipher. This means these characters are also worth a closer look. The letters between the I's total 44 in Simple Cipher, Bacon's secret signature, and checking the Reverse Cipher values totals 106, "King Francis" in Simple. Adding the same framed characters in Kaye Cipher totals 174, the value of "King Francois Stuart III" in Simple.

Going back to the RC signature on Line 17, after the word "I" at the end of the same line, the word OBEY appears phonetically on line 18 as O E B A E, then the Latin word for "forefather or grandfather" AVI, which is also the Hebrew name AVI, meaning *"highest father:"*

19	O	E	B	A	E	*A*	*V*	*I*

This could be a reference to the relationship between the signature on lines 17 and 18 and the name of *"the highest Father"* appearing on line 35 as the name of God. It's also perhaps likely that the speaker is referring to his king, James I. This is hinted at by the context of the next phonetic statement on line 20:

20	S	R	V	H	M	F	I	O

Using the "I" from the end of 19, we can construct, *"I SRV HM"* or even *"I SRV OF HM."* This of course can be read as "I serve him," meaning his King, James I, and also Yahweh.

Line 21 contains the pair of O's I referenced earlier. Aside from light, this could also be a reference to the symbolism of a circle representing perfection, God, Creation and eternity. But here we see it highlighting one of the Bacon signatures previously mentioned with Key 38:

21	O	Æ	O

O's are 14 in Simple Cipher and their sum here is 28. Adding 5 as E, equals 33. This signature also signals the beginning of the statement previously mentioned in lines 21 through 24:

21	O	Æ	O	T⊣	O	E	L	D
22	I	M	T⊣	A	H	B	S	O
23	N	S	T	E	W	M	E	N
24	E	V	S	D	T⊣	O	V	A

Line 21 through 24 can be read as: *"Bacon, ThO ELD IM ThAH B SON STEWMEN EUSD Th OVA."* *"DUES"* can be read as a Latin prefix meaning the number two. So, this section could conceivably be read as, "Bacon, though eldest, I'm the son of Stewart men, thy second egg."

The double Tau is rendered as *"thy"* by substituting a Y in place of the B in the first line. He states he is the older son, indicating that the person to whom he is speaking is the younger due to "your second egg."

Other Early Observations Lines 1 - 19

Having noticed the word OVA in other areas of Key 38 as well, this also led to the discovery of a series of anagrams. In Line 1, we see the word "OVA" reversed in the center of the line. However, the obvious anagram for "valor" also appears, yet without a context such words didn't make sense. Since the only word that appeared in Line 1 that had a precedent was "OVA," I checked the value of the remaining letters, arriving at a sum of 63. Since this is not a signature, it's necessary to continue looking for the rest of a message. Each line is much shorter in Key 38 than in Keys 8 and 32, therefore any messages or signatures could appear across multiple lines. This was when I discovered that, along with Line 2, Line 3 is interesting when "read" with Line 4:

1	T	P	A	V	O	L	R	A
2	M	Y	*C*	N	*H*	L	*E*	3
3	E	A	V	O	W	A	S	2
4	N	T	O	M	E	H	O	E

With a few substitutions in Line 2, "C" becomes "X," and "H" becomes "R." We then have an anagram for REX, and with the opening word, "MY REX," or *"My King."* This leaves N, and as 13, added to the total of 63 from Line 1 totals 76 or "I Francis"

Substituting "V" for "E" at the beginning of Line 3, the text can be seen as, "U [OVA] WAS 2n TO ME," which is read as, "You(r) ova (egg) was 2nd to me." Seeing that Line 1 contained an "R," I decided to adhere to my rule of using as many of the letters in the message as possible and add the letter R to the V to complete the word VR as "your." So, the complete message of Lines 2 - 4 becomes, "Ova, my King. Your ova was 2nd to me!" The only thing left to do would be to make the calculation for the leftover letters in Table 6-6:

Simple	19	15	11	1	3	13	11	8	14	5	= **100**
	T	P	L	A	C	N	L	H	O	E	**Total**
Reverse	6	10	14	24	22	12	14	17	11	20	= **150**

Table 6-6

In Simple Cipher the sum is 100, the Simple Cipher signature for "Francis Bacon." In Reverse the total was 150, which can represent his name as Rex Francois in Reverse. Though not in the table, the value in Kaye Cipher is 204, the Fourfold Cipher value for "Rex Francois III." However, it's important to remember that these are preliminary findings.

Lines 5 and 6 contain another piece of evidence:

5	O	S	T⊣	S	D	E	T	I
6	**R**	**T**	**F**	**I**	**I**	**I**	**E**	**D**

First of all, beginning with the "I" at the end of Line 5, Line 6 (F) phonetically states, "I RT F IIIED," or "I art Francis the Third." The same total of 33 appears when we add the sums of F - I - I - I, 33 meaning that his secret title of F. III has the same value as his name "Bacon." E + D = 9, which is the Simple Cipher for the letter "I" as in again, "I Bacon." In Reverse, F + I + I + I (Francis III) equals 67, Francis in Simple. When we add the E + D Reverse values to 67, it totals 108, "Francis" again but in Reverse Cipher. In Kaye Cipher, F III totals 137, the 33rd prime number. And so Line 6 (read "F") contains multiple signatures for "Francis" and "Bacon" after the phonetic message "I art - ."

When considering the next line, though no clear message appears we do have another cipher signature in the pair of lines 6 and 7, which can represent letter F and G (Bacon) respectively:

6			**F**	**I**	**I**	**I**	**E**	**D**	SUM
7	**A**	**E**	**I**	**T⊣**	**D**	**S**	**G**	**3**	= 108

In Line 7 itself (read "G"), if we use "19" as the value of the double Tau in Simple, totals 66 which is the signature of Fra. Baconi in Simple and represents the double Tau in Reverse Cipher. If we use the value of 38 for the double Tau, that total becomes 85, "Frater" in Reverse. In Reverse Cipher, Line 7 totals 123 (12 for the double Tau), which is "James" in Kaye Cipher.

By including the previous signatures of line 6 above with the letters below, F + I + I + I + E + D, with line 7, A + E + I + T⊣ + D + S + G + 3, we arrive at the sum of 108 in Simple Cipher, which is the cipher signature for "Francis" in Reverse. This is appropriate considering these are Lines 6 and 7, (67 = Francis in Simple) the letters for F and G in Simple Cipher (F. Bacon).

8	M	B	D	N	E	T	A	5

Though not perfect, Line 8 seems to spell out FATE backwards starting with

124

5 (a slant phonetic Vate), and NDBM, which when translated into Hebrew appears as "נידבם" which means *"needed."*

Line 9 presents an anagram that uses all of the letters. Trying multiple combinations of words utilizing the rules as set forth in Chapter 7, none of the remaining letters would result in a cipher signature. The only alternative was to use all of them -

9	E	A	A	I	R	S	P	S

which rearranged to become, *"A PISS EAR."*

At first glance, more pee jokes, but when considered in context, another revelation. Together with line 8 above, the two lines read as, *"FATE NEEDED A PISS EAR."* Within the context of the statements that appear in Key 8, and the references to James I being the second ova, lines 8 and 9 appear to be referencing Francis II of France. Francis II allegedly died of an inner ear infection. The statement of "FATE NEEDED A PISS EAR" follows on the heels of multiple Bacon signatures which follow the words, "HOUSE STEWART." The statement that "Fate needed a piss ear" references Francis II as he died of an inner ear infection. His being struck down because "Fate needed an infected ear," adds to the chain of evidence.

Line 10 is interesting as it too contains more than one message.

10	T	H	E	T⊣	V	O	T	I

My initial interpretation was to read the word "VOTI" as Latin for *"vow."* So, at first it led me to believe that he and the Fra Rosi Crosse made a vow to THE T⊣ of some nature. This could mean that the members made a vow to Bacon, as he is represented by the double Tau. While possibly true, the only solution that seemed to work correctly, especially in conjunction with line 11, is the following solution. The line is pointing out two different cipher signatures for Bacon. THE "T⊣" is one signature, as T T are the initials of the number "33," Bacon in Simple. O T, when added together equal 33 again. So the line reads, *"The T⊣ / O T am I"* or *"I (am) the T⊣, OT."* This solution leaves us with the leftover letter "V" which works in conjunction with line 11, and the message contained within lines 11 - 13.

As you will see, in order to confirm the message, the value of "V" must be added to the remaining letters after removing the message.

11	R	S	R	I	T	C	V	T
12	A	V	T	W	A	N	B	A
13	M	P	S	T	N	THE	T	T

As I stated earlier, this part of the message provides instructions regarding how to use the next Key, which he provides in line 14. The message reads, "I T (F) CVT AVT WAN BAMPS T N the T T," or *"I (Tau or F) cut out one bamp's Tau in the T T."* Again, this is the message that allowed the correct use of the next Key to unlock the next arrangement of letters and the next phase of the message. The sums of the

Simple Cipher values of V R S R is 72, the Simple Cipher signature of "King Bacon," and incidentally the number of degrees of the interior angle of a pentagram, symbolism valued by the RC and Freemasonry.

Line 14 provides the Key in the next arrangement of letters.

14	E	M	A	S	K	E	R	Æ

Obviously, a MASKER is something that "masks or hides" something, in this case the next round of messages. The line begins and ends with the letter "E" indicating that this is the next Key. E is the number 5 in Simple Cipher, and this "masker" appears on line 14, whose digits total 5, all of which confirms my original theory that the keys appeared on the face of the plaque, as the number 5 is also used as a key.

To repeat, given the 305 characters on the plaque that need to be rearranged by the next Key, adjustments must be made in order for the process to work. Since the number is evenly divisible by five, we know the algorithm would terminate after just one pass. Enter lines 11 - 13, which state, "I cut out one bamp's T in the TT." As I stated earlier, Merriam Webster tells us that a "bamp" is an idiotic or ill-mannered person. And so while employing the next Key of 5, I made sure to skip one of the two Ts where they appeared in this configuration (the results appear in the following chapter).

Now, the next section was a real challenge. I had a lot of difficulty in making sense of it, mostly because the thing that jumped out at me was the first word I noticed could be spelled on Line 15 was "ARCATY" written backwards -

15	T	Y	F	A	C	R	A	6

By subbing a "T" for the "F," we can see a phonetic spelling of Arcady, a form of the name Acadia, which is now Nova Scotia. This leaves the "leftover" letters of "T" and "6" which is actually "F." It's important to repeat at this point, that these letters are interchangeable in the cipher substitution system at work on the plaque. T can be F and vice versa, so in a sense this word is framed by a double Tau, one in Simple and the other in Reverse, much like an A in light and an A in shadow.

As you will recall, one of my original reasons for investigating the plaque was to help friends with their research into the Oak Island mystery. For me, this was problematic, because I wanted to protect myself from engaging in confirmation bias where I would "see" or "find" what may not be there. That concept was my primary motivator to make sure that I was using uniform and logical principles in my decoding procedures. So I sought every alternative interpretation I could find, other than the "Oak Island" or Acadia solution. Much of the rest of Key 38 yielded phonetically spelled messages, however lines 15 - 18 yielded no such examples.

Also, I had dismissed the word "ARCATY" as a reference to the Oak Island mystery because of a lack of context for it in the surrounding lines. I found myself at an impasse. All of the other information had been so surprising, that I dismissed an Oak Island interpretation as a whole. I then realized I wasn't following my procedure. What if the word "ARCATY" actually *was* the context I had been looking for? I decided to experiment and entertain the idea that more evidence appears in the lines following it, by actually using ARCATY as such a context. So, using the same procedures and rules I had developed for decoding anagrams and acrostic anagrams, I looked for any that would provide more context for the word ARCATY reference in Lines 15 - 19. This procedure produced the explicit messages that appear in the following section.

Key 38 - Line by Line - Acrostic Anagrams and Oak Island, Nova Scotia

While working on the ciphers of this section, I became completely aware that the Key 38 permutation contained two separate messages in the same letter arrangement. These appear along with the surface line-by-line phonetics and acrostics, and the following acrostic anagrams. The implications were that the other keys also contained at least one more interpretation other than those offered so far. However, in this section due to prospective reader interest, the acrostic anagrams are included which seem to exclusively be about the Oak Island mystery.

For any readers unfamiliar with the Oak Island mystery and the hit show *The Curse of Oak Island* on *HISTORY CHANNEL*, a "Reader's Digest Condensed Version" of the idea is necessary for context. Since the 1790's, rumors have always existed of buried treasure on Oak Island, and searchers have been digging holes ever since. Fortunes have been wasted searching for a fortune, lives have been squandered and even lost. But the tantalizing idea of a buried treasure keeps the hope alive that somewhere, on "an island in the North Atlantic," a vast vault of riches can still be found. The main area that has always drawn the bulk of the attention has earned the name of "The Money Pit," and not because of what is supposed to be at the bottom of it, but because of what has been sunk into it. The two most iconic features of the island are a triangular swamp which has recently been proven to be man-made (dating back at least to the 1600's by scientist Dr. Ian Spooner), and an arrangement of five (most believe six) large, cone-shaped boulders, dubbed "Nolan's Cross."

Named after the man who discovered it, Fred Nolan, Nolan's Cross has become a beloved trope to fans of the show. And to theorists who appear on the show to try to help solve the mystery of the island, incorporating and accounting for the cone-shaped stones is a necessity.

I had become a fan of the show since many of the best theories involve Sir Francis Bacon, Shakespeare and even the Knights Templar, all of which (as you can tell) are areas of interest to me. However, for me watching the show was entertaining for that aspect alone. I never believed that any treasure was still on the island. But then I watched an episode in which appeared my aforementioned friend Chris Donah, explaining his own theory. That season, the team made multiple archaeological discoveries proving that major works had taken place on the island. That was the evidence I needed to begin to believe. After chatting with Chris, I became sucked in, and hence this work on the plaque with its multiple messages.

The realization of dual messages within one Key permutation occurred to me when one feature appearing in the Key 38 results kept appearing, and I could no longer ignore them - the acrostic anagrams. Other Bacon researchers have noted such anagrams appearing within acrostics of texts such as the *First Folio*, so this was not a new phenomenon, but as far as I knew the discovery in these transpositions of the plaque was new.

So in order to maintain objectivity, I followed my procedure in a refined manner. First I would identify the obvious complete words using only letters in juxtaposition which would create the context of the message. After identifying as many words as possible, I would remove these words (the characters in each anagram) from the table. I would then left-justify all of the remaining characters in a new table. I would then identify any other acrostic anagrams of words that contextually made sense, again only from characters juxtaposed with one another. Lastly, I would use any remaining letters if a word could be formed that would complete the thought in the message. Again, to "check the work" I would total the sums of the values of any remaining letters in Simple, Reverse and Kaye ciphers and identify any relevant signatures, as cipher signatures of Bacon or the RC appeared to indicate success.

For the permutation of the plaque characters produced by Key 38, the acrostic anagrams seemed to produce messages exclusively about the Oak Island mystery, which for Oak Island researchers and enthusiasts is highly significant - as again, multiple theories connecting Francis Bacon, Shakespeare and Oak Island have always existed.

By following the above set procedure, clear messages were produced without subjectivity. Just as in earlier sections, I will do my analysis by studying one section at a time. For the purpose of clarity, though the larger constructions that created context were noted first, the words are presented from "top to bottom" to make the process easier to understand. The acrostic anagrams are depicted in the tables by using **bold,** *italic* or underlined characters, and sometimes a combination of these, to differentiate the different anagrams as they appeared.

128

1	T	*P*	*A*	*V*	*O*	L	R	A
2	**M**	**Y**	C̲	N̲	H	L	E	3
3	*E*	A	V̲	O̲	W	A	S	2
4	*N*	*T*	O	M	E	H	O	E
5	*O*	*S*	T⊣	S	D	E	T	I

In the first line is the Latin word "PAVO," meaning "peacock." In the interest of time, and in a gross display of hypocrisy, I'll do what I forbid my students from doing - I'll quote Wikipedia:

According to Mark Chartrand, former executive director of the National Space Institute, Plancius may not have been the first to designate this group of stars as a peacock: "In Greek myth the stars that are now the Peacock were Argos [or Argus], builder of the ship Argo. He was changed by the goddess Juno into a peacock and placed in the sky along with his ship."[6][7] Indeed, the peacock "symboliz[ed] the starry firmament" for the Greeks,[8] and the goddess Hera was believed to drive through the heavens in a chariot drawn by peacocks[9] . (Pavo 2)

This means that Bacon begins this message with a word that symbolizes the stars in the sky associated with Argus, builder of the Argo. With a clear reference to the Argo, and by association Heracles, connections to certain star configurations will become obvious. Also, it's important to note that Bacon referred to the Rosi Crosse members as "Argonauts."

1	T	*P*	*A*	*V*	*O*	L	R	A
2	**M**	**Y**	C̲	N̲	H	L	E	3
3	*E*	A	V̲	O̲	W	A	S	2
4	*N*	*T*	O	M	E	H	O	E
5	*O*	*S*	T⊣	S	D	E	T	I

From there please note the prominent placement of the obvious word "MY," the first-person possessive pronoun of Francis Bacon. To the right of this we see the underlined letters of the anagram C-N-V-O, and subbing E in place of V gives us the word "CONE."

Beneath this to the left in italics, spanning lines 3 - 5, appears the anagram E-N-T-O-S for the word "STONE." The last part of this message is seen in the next table with the previous letters removed:

Here in bold on the right we see a group of letters in what could be interpreted in a *reversed* Chi-Rho Cross, laying on its side. In Lines 1-3 the letters are R A H L E 3 S. As if to reinforce this notion, I've italicized and underlined the two letters under the "arms" of the cross, L and A. Using the substitution protocol L becomes O, and since the image is "reversed," the letters for

1	T				*L̲*	**R**	**A**
2				**H**	**L**	**E**	**3**
3		A			W	*A̲*	**S**	**2**
4			**O**	**M**	**E**	*H*	*O*	**E**
5			**T⊣**	**S**	*D*	*E*	*T*	*I*

Alpha and Omega appear in their correct positions. The juxtaposition of the "O" beside the "L" in Line 1 could be an acknowledgement as a distinction between the two Greek letters Omega and Omicron.

The letters in the acrostic appear as the anagram, R - A - H - L - E - 3 - S, which when we make the obvious substitution of C for 3, we can form the word "HERACLES," the original Greek name for Hercules.

Lastly, the bold acrostic appears at the bottom, O - M - E - T⊣ - S, (and possibly "D" - see below). The first thought was the word "TOMES" as in books (if you recall earlier, I noted the acrostic "MY RC FOLIO" within the section of the cipher referring to ARCATY). Then, another interpretation presented itself.

Using the substitution protocol in Bacon's cipher, S contains the same value as G between Simple and Reverse Ciphers. As G's value in Kaye Cipher is 33, the Simple Cipher signature for "BACON," the letter G is frequently used in the Plaque Cipher as his signpost or signature. We would then have the G symbolic of Bacon being "wrapped" within the word "T⊣OMED," a solid phonetic spelling of "tombed." All of this possibly indicated that Bacon could be entombed in Nova Scotia.

At this stage, we have the words *"MY CONE STONE HERACLES,"* along with either *"TOMES"* or *"TOMED"* wrapped around a "G," symbolizing Bacon entombed within. However, this idea is dismissed as a decryption of these acrostic anagrams because the solution appears to the right in the italicized letters in lines 4 and 5. Substituting a W for the D, spells "I WROTE." However, perhaps both messages were intended.

The plaque contains multiple messages in a contained amount of space. Acrostics appear "over" sections that also use the same letters in phonetic messages, that can then be rearranged in anagrams to create more of the same. It stands to reason and logic that both messages of "tombed" and "tomes" were possibly intended, though I'm skeptical. This treatment only uses the acrostic anagram messages, so I need to go with the context of "TOMES." On to the remaining letters of this section.

130

T	L		
A	W	A	2
E			

In this table of the remaining letters of the "leftovers" from the process we look to see if any final relevant words still exist. The solution actually appears as two words together on each line in the table at left.

By substituting O in place of its counterpart L, the first line spells "TO." By replacing 2 with Y (it's value in Reverse Cipher), the second line spells "A WAY." Lastly the Latin word "E" meaning "From or out of" appears on the final line of the table of remaining characters.

Normally during this process, there will be a handful of leftover letters whose values when totaled will equal a cipher signature in Simple, Reverse and Kaye. In this case there were no leftover letters to calculate. We are left with the message, "PAVO: E MY CONE STONE HERACLES A WAY TO TOMES I WROTE." If we think of the constellation of Pavo as a reference to the Argo and its 50 Argonauts, it makes sense that it would draw our attention to the constellations, and the Argo's strongest hero, Heracles. Additionally, the Fra. Rosi Crosse and Freemasons use the peacock as a symbol as it has the image of "eyes" on each tailfeather. Considering the many messages to "see," this makes sense. This symbolizes the idea to look or pay special attention to this area of the cipher. If we choose to remove the word "PAVO" from the message as it doesn't seem to be a contextual part of it, we can calculate its value and check it for a cipher signature. The sum of the values of the letters in "PAVO" in Simple and Reverse are both 50, the same as Fr. III in Simple and number of Argonauts. Lastly, the value in Kaye is 76. This can be read as "I, Francis" or "Dauphin F." in Simple Cipher.

Since either no leftover letters existed to use the "checking" system of cipher signatures, or we include PAVO as the signature which actually *does* check out, it was time to check the next group of six lines of characters, to see what other messages might appear along this same theme, using the acrostic anagrams:

6	**R**	**T**	**F**	**I**	I	I	E	D
7	**A**	**E**	**I**	T⅃	D	S	G	3
8	*M*	*B*	**D**	<u>N</u>	E	T	A	5
9	*E*	*A*	*A*	<u>I</u>	<u>R</u>	<u>S</u>	<u>P</u>	<u>S</u>
10	*T*	H	E	*T⅃*	*V*	*O*	*T*	*I*
11	*R*	S	R	*I*	*T*	C	V	T

The letters along the length of Line 6 seems to imply the word "ratified," and indeed it appears in the bold letters as the anagram R - T - F - I - A - E - I - D, "RATIFIED." The next anagram produces a phonetic. So all of this, with the theme as set forth in the previous context, pointed toward the italicized letters on the left of the table in Lines 8 - 10 as the anagram M - B - E - A - A - T - R.

Substituting between Simple and Reverse, M becomes N, and for the aforementioned reasons, A becomes O. This gives us the word "BARANET" (as BARONET). On the right, and in the underlined letters the next anagram appears, N - I - R - S - P - S. Substituting between Simple and Reverse H for R, G for S and K for P, we arrive at "KNIGHTS." Lastly beneath the previous, are the italic-bold letters, T⅃ - V - O - I - T. By subbing E for V, L for O, we end with "TITLE." So far we have the words "TITLE KNIGHTS BARONET RATIFIED" using this process. As you can see, this as an explicit connection between the plaque, Francis Bacon, and the colonies in Nova Scotia. Now to see what can be found in the remaining letters:

The anagram of the bold letters was the first obvious word noted: D - E - T - A - H, rearrange into the word "DEATH." Understanding a possible context, the answer lay directly above the first word: T⅃ - I - I. Subbing Fr for T⅃ we have the common abbreviation used by Francis Bacon for his first name, "Fr." Followed up by "II" he obviously is referencing the death of his secret father, Francis II. Lastly, at the bottom of the table in italics is the Latin "SCRVTI," which according to the Notre Dame Latin database means, "trash (pl.), old/broken stuff; job lot; trumpery."

_I_	_I_	E	D	
T⅃	D	S	G	3
D	**E**	**T**	**A**	5
H	E	T	*I*	
S	*R*	*C*	*V*	*T*

The last step is to comb through the few remaining letters to see if any contextually important words can be formed. This leaves us with E - D - D - S - G - 3 - 5 - E - T. By replacing 3 with C and 5 with E, we can spell out "CETE" meaning "dolphin," or as it would be in French, "Dauphin," the title of the first-born Prince of the King of France. Lastly, using the remaining E, we have the Latin word "E" which means "from" or "out of." This provides as a message, *"E Fr. II DEATH CETE SCRVTI,"* or "out of Francis II's death, Dauphin is trash or rubbish." To check the work, we turn to the remaining letters, D - D - S - G. Their respective values among Simple, Reverse and Kaye Ciphers with the totals appear in Table 6-7:

Simple	4	4	18	7	= 33
	D	D	S	G	SUM
Reverse	21	21	7	18	= 67
Kaye	30	30	18	33	= 111

Table 6 - 7

As you can see, the total in Simple Cipher is 33, the signature for "Bacon" in Simple. The Reverse Cipher total is 67, the Simple Cipher signature for "Francis," and the total in Kaye Cipher is 111, the signature for "Bacon" in Kaye. In addition, a phonetic message also appears. The D's equal 4 in Simple, so the phonetic message of the leftover letters becomes "44 is G," meaning 44 is a signature for "Bacon."

Previously, I identified the reference to "ARCATY." Here are the last 7 lines of the first column of letters rearranged with Key 38, where the acrostics MY RC FOLIO, the Latin word ARCO, and ROSY T CROS have been identified. Also, the first three lines contain the previously discussed phonetic message that provide information about the decryption process, but they can be ignored as we study the acrostic anagrams:

12	A	*V*	*T*	W	*A*	*N*	*B*	A
13	M	<u>P</u>	<u>S</u>	T	*N*	<u>THE</u>	T	T
14	E	<u>M</u>	<u>A</u>	*S*	*K*	*E*	*R*	*Æ*
15	T	**Y**	F	A	C	R	A	6
16	*A*	*L*	O	L	I	O	G	1
17	R	*<u>O</u>*	S	P	V	M	N	6
18	C	*<u>T</u>*	*Y*	T⊣	Q	R	I	1
19	O	E	***B***	***A***	E	A	V	I

In line 12 we have the italic word "VT" which is Latin for "to." Usually when an entire word appears such as "THE" it is assumed it's used as a whole. The underlined letters in Lines 13 - 14, P - S - M - A spell out "MAPS." The bold italic letters in Lines 12 and 13, A - N - B - N become the acrostic word "MANY" by subbing M for N and Y for B. The italicized letters in Line 14 S - K - E - R - Æ, by subbing P for K and V for E we can spell "SVPER," Latin for "on / upon; over." Of course, Line 15 spells "ARCATY" backwards by subbing T for F. This is the "obvious" word that is intended to provide the context in this section. Below this on Line 16, the italicized letters spell "LA" backwards. Second column in Lines 17 and 18 contains the italic-underlined letters O - T, which with a substitution of F for T spells "OF." Lastly, the bold italicized letters in Lines 18 and 19 spell "BAY." So far, this section renders a word bank including VT, THE, MAPS, MANY, SVPER, ARCATY, LA, OF, and BAY. This particular collection of words provided me an excellent context for one of the words in the following section. By placing the remaining letters in the following table and moving them to the left to fill the empty spaces, we can see visually what juxtapositions appear thereby creating more acrostics and anagrams.

A	*W*	A				
M	T	T	T			
E						
T	6					
O	**L**	**I**	O	**G**	1	
R	**S**	*P*	**V**	M	N	6
C	*T⊣*	*Q*	<u>R</u>	<u>I</u>	<u>1</u>	
O	E	E	A	<u>V</u>	I	

In the upper left corner in bold italics are the letters A - W - M - E and with a substitution of D for W, we spell "MADE." At the center of the table, the bold letters appear L - I - G - S - V, and by subbing S for G and E for V, we spell "ISLES." Directly beneath this appear the letters P - Q - T⊣ which with a substitution of I for Q we spell "PIT." In the lower right, the underlined characters R - I - 1 -V spell "AVRI" which is Latin for "gold."

All of the words added from this section are then MADE, ISLES, TO, PIT, and AVRI. Narrowing down our available choices, we have only one more table of remaining letters:

A				
T	T	T		
T	6			
O	**O**	1		
R	**M**	N	6	
<u>C</u>				
<u>O</u>	<u>E</u>	E	<u>A</u>	*I*

Table 6-9

The next step is to list all of the words we've accrued in this section to see if we need to use any of the other letters to finish the phrase. So far we have the following words in our bank: VT, THE, MAPS, MANY, SVPER, ARCATY, LA, OF, BAY, MADE, ISLES, TO, PIT, and NOMEN.

In looking at what can be made of the remaining characters in the table, I saw O - O - 1 - R - M - N - 6 - E, which become "ANTEROOM," or two separate words, "ANTE" and "ROOM." The underlined letters C - O - E - A, with a substitution of V for E becomes "CAVO," Latin for "cave." Lastly, the action verb "MADE" requires a subject performing that action, which is supplied by the letter "I."

Putting all of the words together, we can form the message, *"ET AVRI, I MADE PIT ANTE TO ROOM CAVO. ARCATY LA BAY OF THE MANY ISLES SVPER MAPS."* So in complete English, the message states, "I made pit before the cave room in Acadia, La Baye de la Toutes Isles (The Bay of Many Isles) upon (or according to) maps." According to author and Oak Island researcher James McQuiston, La Baye de la Toutes Isles is believed to be the original name of Mahone Bay, Nova Scotia, the location of Oak Island. As you will later see, this will be confirmed using a famous map. The message also contained, "ET AVRI" which means "and gold." I believe these words are intended to be a part of the message in Lines 1 - 5.

Given the implications of the message, it's necessary to "check" the work in terms of the remaining characters in checking for any cipher signatures.

First of all, the initial letter that begins our "leftover" characters is "A" which obviously carries a special significance to Francis Bacon for the reasons already given. Next, we have a Triple Tau. Lastly, if we use the substitution regimen of the number 6 which normally would be the letter F, we have the Double Tau symbol. It's also the source of the Key 38 which created the algorithm that created this reorganization of characters of the plaque.

When looking at the cipher values of the remaining characters, I found cipher signatures in Simple, Reverse and Kaye:

Table 6-8

Simple	1	19	19	19	19	6	83
	A	T	T	T	T	6	**SUM**
Reverse	24	6	6	6	6	19	67
Kaye	27	19	19	19	19	32 (6)	135 (109)

At first glance, the sum of the Simple Cipher values equals the value of the word "FRATERS," Latin for "brothers." The Reverse Cipher sum is obviously "Francis" in Simple Cipher. These two signatures come together in the Kaye total of 135, the signature of "Fr. Francis" in Reverse as a brother of the RC. If we count the number 6 at face value as has been done elsewhere, the sum is then 109 which then can be read as "I Francis Bacon" in Simple.

In my experience with the messages on the plaque, RC signposts and cipher signatures speak to the legitimacy of this rendering of the cipher message. The "A," Triple Tau and Double Tau (a key to the plaque itself) are signposts defying coincidence. Additionally, the cipher signatures of 83, "Fraters" in Simple, 67 which is "Francis" in Simple, and 135 as a combination of them as "Fr. Francis" reinforce the validity.

The messages of Lines 1 - 19 (one Tau) of Key 38, are as follows. By moving two words from Lines 12 - 19 because of a better context, Lines 1 - 5 can render the message, "(PAVO) E MY CONE STONE HERACLES A WAY TO TOMES I WROTE ET AVRI." (For those readers who are unfamiliar with the Oak Island mystery, I fully explain this set of messages in their own appendix of my Oak Island theory as I presented it to their team, and elaborate how they relate to the island itself). Essentially, following the "Nolan's Cross" sky / ground correlations of the Hercules Constellation will lead to books written in the hand of Francis Bacon, confirming his authorship of Shakespeare's words as well as confirming his parentage. As you'll see, Lines 20 - 21 seem to confirm this idea.

Lines 6 - 11 give the messages of "TITLE KNIGHTS BARONET RATIFIED" and *"E Fr. II DEATH CETE SCRVTI,"* confirming a link between the plaque and Nova Scotia, and where Bacon laments his father's death and how it ruined his chances for kingship. Lastly, the message of

Lines 12 - 19 appears to be *"I MADE PIT CAVO ANTE TO ROOM. ARCATY LA BAY OF THE MANY ISLES NOMEN SVPER MAPS."* This section also adds to the value of his "TOMES" by mentioning "gold."

It's important to remind the reader of the acrostics that were found in this section:

14	E	**M**	A	S	K	E	R	Æ
15	T	**Y**	F	A	C	R	A	6
16	**A**	L	**O**	L	I	O	G	1
17	**R**	O	**S**	P	V	M	N	6
18	**C**	T	**Y**	T+	Q	R	I	1
19	**O**	E	B	A	E	A	V	I

They explicitly spell out, *"MY RC FOLIO. ARCO ROSY T CROS."* This message reinforces the message regarding his "TOMES" as the "RC 1st FOLIO guarded (hidden; protected) by the ROSY CROSS."

All of these messages together point to an island in Mahone Bay, Nova Scotia, Canada, where large cone-shaped stones exist, Oak Island. And if one were to understand how to "follow" these clues as a "stone Heracles," they would point the way to the 1st Folio that Bacon wrote as Shakespeare, apparently along with some gold. As I've stated, I included my entire Oak Island theory as another appendix to this book, but we do have 19 more rows of characters to interpret in Lines 20 - 38.

Rows 20 - 38 of Key 38

After completing this section it's now my belief that this set of acrostic anagrams of the Key 38 transposition are specific to Oak Island, Nova Scotia. As a reminder, the messages of Lines 1 - 19 of Key 38 directly identifies Oak Island through the references to Bacon's "Cone Stone Heracles" and "The Bay of the Many Isles." The message "Title Knights Baronet Ratified" establishes a direct link between the plaque and Nova Scotia. As I suspected, the message about Oak Island continued in the second half of Key 38. Not only does it reference Bacon's Thesauri (treasure chamber; repository or vault), but also the danger of "snares."

Beginning with the first six Lines 20 - 25, the next message refers to Royal documents that record Bacon's true lineage:

20	S	R	V	H	M	F	I	O
21	*O*	*Æ*	*O*	*T⊣*	*O*	*E*	*L*	*D*
22	I	M	T⊣	A	H	B	S	O
23	N	S	T	E	W	M	E	N
24	E	V	S	D	T⊣	O	V	A
25	G	L	E	S	I	T	A	T

The first two lines are anagrams unto themselves. Line 20, after substituting E for V and L for O, produces the words "HRM FILES," or "His (Her) Royal Majesty's Files." (As an aside when it comes to these interpretations, the etymologies of the words it produces were researched to ensure that they would all be in usage when the plaque was created. "FILES" was in frequent usage in its current meaning as early as the 1500's, particularly in legal circles, which was Francis Bacon's area of expertise). Line 21 is also an anagram with substitutions of L for every O and W for D, becomes the words "WELL TELL." Together Lines 20 and 21 spell "HRM FILES WELL TELL."

And Lines 22 and 23 are the story these files tell:

22	<u>I</u>	*M*	T⊣	*A*	*H*	**B**	*S*	O
23	<u>N</u>	**S**	**T**	**E**	**W**	M	E	*N*
24	E	V	S	D	T⊣	O	V	A
25	G	L	E	S	I	T	A	T

First of all, it's important to include the overlapping of two acrostics. The bold letters in lines 22 and 23 S - T - E - W - H - A - T⊣ , with a substitution of R for H spell "STEWART." The italic bold letters in Line 22 by subbing R for H and Y for B, spell "MARY." The underlined letters in the first column with a substitution of M for N spell "I'M." The italic letters and the end of both of those lines spell "SON." Putting Lines 20 - 23 together, the message becomes, "HRM FILES WELL TELL I'M MARY STEWART SON." This message explicitly states that Royal documentation records the accurate birth information of Francis Bacon as Mary Stewart's son.

The final lines actually layout the relevance of these files:

23					*M*	E	
24	E	V	S	D	T⊣	*O*	*V*	*A*
25	**G**	**L**	**E**	**S**	**I**	T	A	T

The italic letters in Lines 23 – 24 with a substitution of N for M spells "NOVA" which is Latin for "new." On the bottom line the bold letters with a substitution of S for G spell out "ISLES."

Now to look at the remaining letters:

The italic letters spell "ET," Latin for "and." The bold letters produce "THUS" and the underlined letters spell "DE" meaning "of, or about." And the word "AT" on the bottom row plainly can be seen. All of these words amount to a message in this section stating, "ET THUS HRM FILES AT DE NOVA ISLES WELL TELL I'M MARY STEWART SON." This message seems to be saying that these Royal files are related to, or are on, the aforementioned island referenced in Lines 1 - 19 of Key 38.

E				
E	V	S	D	T⊣
T	A	T		

Table 6-9

By using the Latin word NOVA for new, the message echoes the idea that the "new isles" are in Nova Scotia, as Acadia was renamed in 1621 before the reported appearance of the plaque. With no remaining characters in this section, I moved on to the next 7 lines of the Key 38 permutation of characters:

26	M	V	O	V	W	Ys	E	I
27	V	P	G	O	E	K	L	I
28	I	O	Y	I	R	C	T	B
29	L	P	H	V	A	E	T	O
30	Y	T	W	N	E	D	I	T
31	P	I	R	E	P	T⊣	R	T
32	O	G	E	M	S	O	W	I

Dealing with Lines 26 and 27 first, with substitutions for all four bold letters "M V V P" in the left corner, we spell "KNEE." Continuing to the right, the bold italic letters after substitutions of D for W, V for E and P for K, produce the Latin "DVPLI" meaning "double." Above this, we see the Ys meaning the word "THIS." In Line 28 the italic letters with a substitution of H for R spell "HIC," Latin for "here; in this place." The bold letters on Line 29 form the word "PETRAE" after substitutions of R for H and E for V, a Latin word meaning "rock, boulder; shaped stone as in a building." The italic letters at the beginning of Lines 30 and 31 spell the Latin word "TYPI" which means "ground plan; pattern." To the left of this in the underlined letters, subbing H for R and D for W, we see the word "HIDDEN." Lastly, the bold italic letters in Lines 31 and 32 by substituting K for P and N for M, form the words "K STONE." As Kaye Cipher is also referred to as "K Cipher" and "*Key* Cipher," this obviously should be read as "KEY STONE."

The remaining unused letters are dealt with in Table 6-12:

O	V	E	I	
G	O			
I	O	Y	T	B
L	O			
T				
R	T			
O	G	E	W	I

Table 6 - 12

In the upper left corner, the bold letters spell "GO." Beneath this and to the right, the underlined letters with a substitution of L for O spell the Latin word "OLO," meaning "that; those; that thing." Then we see the italic letters which when we sub O for L we spell "TO." The next set of remaining letters appears in the Table 6-13:

V	E	I		
I	Y	T	B	
R	**T**			
O	**G**	**E**	W	I

Last of all, the bold letters in the lower left corner with a substitution of S for G spell "ROSETI," meaning "garden of roses." This leaves the letters, V - E - I - Y - T - B - W - I. From these we can complete the message by forming three more words. The Latin word "VTI" means "use; make use of." We have the word "BY" and the Latin word "E" meaning "from." This leaves us with no unused characters in this section.

This word bank now appears as follows: KNEE, DVPLI, THIS, HIC, PETRAE, TYPI, HIDDEN, K STONE, GO, OLO, TO, ROSETI, VTI, BY and E. These words tentatively can be used to create the message, "BY VTE TYPI E OLO PETRAE HIC GO TO DVPLI KNEE HIDDEN K STONE. THIS ROSETI." In plain English this can be read as, "By this garden of roses making use of this ground plan of these worked stones in this place, go to the duplicate knee - a hidden key stone." At this point the working hypothesis was the reference to the "garden of roses," refers to the island as a work of the Fra. Rosi Crosse. Additionally, when I asked Oak Island historian and researcher Doug Crowell if a rose garden ever existed on the island, he told me, "there was an iconic rose bush in Smith's Cove that Gilbert Hedden [a previous searcher] decided to protect with a stone and cement wall in the 1930's."

Overall, the message of Lines 26 - 32 appears to validate my theory regarding the use of the cones of Nolan's Cross to identify "the X on the map."

The message of the final six rows of the Key 38 permutation continues within the same context as relevant to Oak Island:

33	I	E	G	O	K	D	T⊣	W	
34	*C*	T	N	H	A	***ME***	*A*	S	
35	*I*	*A*	*E*	W	H	A	H	I	
36	D	R	S	T	S	N	E	H	
37	V	R	S	S	Nt	E	H	E	
38	I	E	A	N	ME	S	Yt	V	P

Beginning with the bold letters in the upper left, substituting V for E and S for G, we spell "ITVS" which is Latin for "going." To the right, the underlined letters spell "PRO" after subbing P for K and R for H, which of course means "forward." Again on the left, the italic letters spell the Latin "CAVI" after a substitution of V for E, which means both "hole, cavity, depression, pit," and "beware, avoid, take precautions." To the right, the bold italic letters spell "MeA," Latin for "my, mine." Moving on, the rest of the letters in this permutation appear in the following table, with the above formations removed. This is purely for clarity purposes and is not yet intended as a "remainders table."

33						D	T⊣	W	
34			N		A			S	
35				W	*H*	*A*	H	I	
36	**D**	**R**	**S**	**T**	*S*	N	E	H	
37	**V**	R	S	S	*Nt*	E	H	E	
38	I	E	A	N	**ME**	S	Yt	V	P

In Lines 36 and 37, the bold letters spell "DVRST," while the underlined letters in 37 and 38 spell "SNARES," both without substitutions. To the right in Lines 35 - 37, the italic letters spell "SHANt" and beneath this we have the word "ME" in bold.

In all, so far the easily identifiable words in the first stage are ITVS, PRO, CAVI, MeA, DVRST, SNARES, SHANt and ME as our word bank.

At this point, having exhausted all of the easily identifiable words, it's time to move on to the "remainders table" below as Table 6 – 14:

Table 6 - 14

D	*T⊣*	W		
N	*A*	*S*		
W	H	*I*		
N	*E*	*H*		
E	H	*E*		
I	S	**Yt**	**V**	**P**

In the left column in bold we see the Latin word "NE" meaning "that not; lest." Beneath this in italic letters appear two words, the first of which is "IS (or Latin SI meaning *if only*)." Directly to the right in the bold underlined characters, by using the "Yt" as "Y," and by substituting E for V and K for P, we form "KEY." Last and certainly not least, the underlined italic letters span much of the table were a real surprise (pleasantly so). These letters form an acrostic anagram that spells the word "THESAURI." This word is Latin for "treasure chamber."

All of the words of the cipher in Lines 33 - 38 are now ITVS, PRO, CAVI, MeA, DVRST, SNARES, SHANt, ME, NE, IS (SI), KEY, and THESAURI. These words can all form the completed message, "Me SHANt DVRST ITVS PRO MeA T⊣ESAVRI. KEY IS CAVI SNARES." Translated into English, this message becomes "I shalt not darest go forward to my treasure chamber. The key is taking precautions against the snares (traps)." In our modern English, the message states not to dare go into his chamber without taking precautions against traps. This could be the additional meaning of the message in the previous section referring to the "garden of roses." Along with the "treasure" of the flower itself, one must avoid the thorns.

All of the leftover letters not used in the message are D - W - N - W - H - H. Their numerical cipher values in Simple, Reverse and Kaye, as well as their sums appear in the table below, followed by an explanation of all three signatures.

Table 6-15

Simple	4	21	13	21	8	8	= 75
	D	W	N	W	H	H	SUM
Reverse	21	4	12	4	17	17	= 75
Kaye	30	21	13	21	34	34	= 153

As has often been the case throughout the plaque ciphers, our first glance reveals nothing obvious. None of "the usual suspects" in terms cipher signatures jump out at us, but again as usual, a closer inspection reveals impressive results. The signature produced by the Simple and Reverse Cipher values actually is a significant signature after all.

Due to the nature of the other messages on the plaque, some uncommon cipher signatures should be present at this point, as mentioned in other chapters. Aside from the Bacon authorship of Shakespeare's works (which is a large enough discovery in and of itself), the predominate message has been regarding Francis Bacon's biological parents, Francis II of

France and Mary Queen of Scots. Also noting aspects of Bacon's personality and sense of humor, I checked the values of not only his family members (including younger, half-brother James), but also Francis III and Fr. III, which is what his name would be if he had become King of France. And as we already know, Fr. had been a frequent way he would sign his first name in his correspondence.

As such, the cipher signature of Fr. III in Reverse Cipher is 75, as is the Reverse Cipher signature of "Stewart." But this is what I like most about the cipher signature in the Simple Cipher values. Before we add the last "8" for H of the Simple values, the total at that point is 67, or "Francis" in Simple Cipher. So it tells us, *"Francis H."* Aside from his use of "H" as a double Tau in other areas of the cipher and therefore meaning "Bacon," it's also comprised of *three straight lines,* I I I. *It's another way of spelling out, Francis III.* It's only fitting that this signature would finish the Key 38 permutation producing these messages, messages that spell out the location of "His Majesty's Files" that would prove his bloodline and birthright. He claims the right to two thrones, one as "Stewart" and the other as "Fr. III." Additionally, friend and fellow Oak Island researcher Chris Donah had pointed out to me that the letter H figures prominently on the coat of arms of the Dauphin of France.

Lastly, Chris had also suggested another signature, "King Bacon." The cipher signature of King Bacon is 153 in Reverse Cipher, the same number that is the Simple Cipher signature of the British and Scottish spelling of "Mary Stewart." Though I'll go into this important number in far more detail, you'll remember that it is the number of the mathematical center of the plaque, the conjoined letters "ME," and the total of the phrase, "I Sir (or Rex) Francis Bacon" in Simple Cipher.

Taken as a whole, the second half of the Key 38 permutation contains the following set of messages:

- "HRM FILES WELL TELL I'M MARY STEWART SON. ET THUS DE NOVA ISLES."
- "BY VTE TYPI E OLO PETRAE HIC GO TO DVPLI KNEE HIDDEN K STONE. THIS ROSETI."
- "Me SHANt DVRST ITVS PRO MeA T⊣ESAVRI. KEY IS CAVI SNARES."

These messages together tell us, apparently in Francis Bacon's own words, that files from the Royal archives will confirm his mother was Mary Queen of Scots, and this is the reason for the work on the "Nova Isles." He continues to state that using the "worked" cone shaped stones as a pattern or map to the knee of Heracles as mentioned in the first 19 lines of Key 38, a hidden keystone can be found. This is an obvious recreation of the Royal Arch degree of Freemasonry involving the discovery of a keystone, the discovery of a chamber and the recovery of lost documents. It is based upon

142

"The Legend of the Three Sojourners" in the book of Enoch, a story about rebuilding the Temple of Solomon. Bacon wrote an allegory called "New Atlantis" promoting this very idea as "The College of the 6 Day's Work." By calling the island "a garden of roses," the message identifies all of this as the work of the Fraternity of the Rosi Crosse. Lastly, the message ends with the warning to make preparations to avoid "snares" or traps, which could be related to the "garden of roses" statement, in that these snares could be thought of as "thorns" amid the roses. When we also take into account the messages in Lines 1 - 19 telling the "passengers" where to go and what to look for, they lead us from the plaque in England to Mahone Bay, Nova Scotia. This becomes even more precise in chapters to come. Once there we only need to find an island with a "cone stone Heracles," and follow the rest of the directions.

All of these messages will be discussed in detail in later chapters and the appendices, detailing my theory regarding Oak Island, Nova Scotia.

153

I first mentioned the importance of the number 153 as a cipher signature for Bacon in Chapter 1, in the section discussing the "counting system" of the characters as they appear on the surface of the plaque. However, due to many of the meanings of the number itself, I decided to wait until after the messages regarding Francis Bacon's biological parents were revealed, before fully exploring the number. Since this last section of Key 38 included the number as a signature, this is an appropriate place to analyze this unique number.

While 153 is not a prime number, it does have multiple unique qualities, particularly as it pertains to the plaque. As I noted in Chapter 1, the 153rd character on the plaque in both the forward and backward count, is the conjoined letters "ME" in the word "MONUMENT." Therefore, the number should logically be relevant to the person responsible for the plaque's construction, whom we now know was Sir Francis Bacon. Reasoning that since the word "I" totals 9 and "Sir Francis Bacon" totals 144 in Simple Cipher, the total 153 actually names the word "ME" at the mathematical center of the plaque means, "I, Sir Francis Bacon." In this way, he reveals who is at the center of the Shakespeare mystery, and whose name is "encrypted" in the monument known as "Shakespeare." However, the significance extends beyond his name.

As previously noted, 153 is the Simple Cipher signature for "Mary Stewart" with the British spelling, as well as the Reverse Cipher signature for "King Bacon." However, it also holds some other significant properties.

First of all, Bible scholars have noted that 153 is the value of the Hebrew phrase, "Ani Elohim," meaning "I am God." The number is also related to the Vesica Pisces symbol, important in both geometry and

Christianity, as well as the brotherhoods of Fra. Rosi Crosse and Freemasonry. Another interesting property of 153 is that it is known in mathematics as a "3-narcissistic number." This means that it is the sum of its digits raised to the power of the number of its digits. In other words, if you add the cubes of 1, 5, and 3, they equal 153: $1 + 125 + 27 = 153$. Also, it's the 17th (read R) of what are called "triangular numbers." This means 153 objects can be arranged to form an equilateral triangle, a shape with special significance to the aforementioned brotherhoods. Being the 17th such number, and 17 being the Simple Cipher value of "R," and a triangle having 3 sides can represent the letter "C." It can therefore represent "RC," or the word "Rosicrucian." Interestingly, the three corners of such an equilateral triangle would be numbered as 1, 137, and 153, and 137 is the 33rd prime number, an already established cipher signature for Bacon. Of course number 1 is the letter "A," which has also been demonstrated to represent Bacon. By association with the other two corners of this equilateral triangle, as well as 153 being the location of the word "ME" at the mathematical center of the plaque, 153 is a Bacon signature in this manner as well. And yet, there is another significance of this number associated with the lore associated with the Fra. Rosi Cosse and Francis Bacon.

This number 153 also is the sum of the "first five factorials." This is expressed in the mathematical expression "$5!=5x4x3x2x1=120$." The sum of 153 is only attained by the final adding of 33, the Simple Cipher signature of "Bacon."

An interesting Biblical correlation involves Mary Magdalene, which in light of the cipher texts and their messages, can be seen as references of her as a prostitute, is significant. In Greek, Mary Magdalene's name has a value of 153 correlating to Mary Queen of Scots, as 153 is the Simple Cipher signature of the British spelling of Mary Stewart. It's also important to remember how Bacon viewed her in terms of the cipher texts, as a prostitute. Though new interpretations of Mary Magdalene exist today in the theories that she was actually the wife of Jesus, it's important to interpret these ideas in light of the original interpretation of the Bible, that she was a "prostitute" and Bacon's references to his mother in the cipher texts. Also, the Simple, Reverse and Kaye Cipher signatures of the word "Mary" are 53, 47 and 79, respectively, all of which are prime numbers. This correlation between Mary Queen of Scots, and Mary Magdalene are extremely interesting. As interesting as this correlation is, the last one captured my imagination. It involved the "Philosopher's Stone."

Evagrius Ponticus was a 4th Century monk and mathematician. He actually wrote a book called "Chapters on Prayer" with 153 chapters and was the first to comment on a specific mathematical property of the number itself. While discussing the "153 fish caught" in the Bible, he also explained that the number 153 is the combination of a "square number (100), a triangular number (38) and a circular number (25)." 100 as a square is obvious, and 153 has already been shown as a triangular number above. 25 is what's called as a "circular number" because its square ends in the same digits as the number itself, 625. I was struck by this combination of shapes as it reminded me of a famous symbol, shown here in Figure 6-1: This geometric symbol represents the philosopher's stone, and since it's

Figure 6-1

comprised of a square, triangle and circle, it can be represented by the number 153.

While it would be fun to claim that this means that Sir Francis Bacon and the Fra. Rosi Crosse possessed the secret of the Philosopher's Stone, and that he had achieved immortality, I prefer a less fanciful interpretation. The word "ME" appears at the mathematical center of the plaque, and due to the presence of countless signatures of Francis Bacon, we know that first person pronoun refers to him. In fact the number of characters on the plaque of 305 is also the cipher signature of his name as "Francois Stuart" in Kaye. The conjoined ME as the 153rd character is one more example of Bacon showing "the Tau," or truth, and the truth about his life. Truth would be the stone upon which a philosopher would ground his or her understanding of reality. I've always believed that Alchemy was actually the pursuit of truth and knowledge, under the guise of "magic." The Philosopher's Stone is merely a symbol of the human brain and skull. This is one of the meanings of the skull in old paintings, and the Michelangelo drawing "Philosopher Holds Skull" comes to mind.

By developing the mind, the philosopher would be able to take the baseness of physical human existence and transmute all experience into intellectual, spiritual and idealized truth, something to be prized above gold. The idea is to take the base gray matter of the brain,and enlighten it with the golden light of truth. According to the website "Universal Freemasonry," the Stone of the Wise Man is "Supreme and unalterable Reason. To find the Absolute in the Infinite, in the Indefinite, and in the Finite, this is the Magnum Opus, the Great Work of the Sages, which Hermes called the Work of the Sun." It goes on to say, "He who possesses the Philosopher's Stone possesses Truth, the greatest of all treasures, and is therefore rich beyond the calculation of man; he is immortal because Reason takes no account of death and he is healed of Ignorance – the most loathsome of all diseases" (Co-Freemasonry).

Considering all of the intricate messages of the plaque, all of the meanings in this one word of two conjoined characters, ME, have the continued purpose that Bacon had in life – the pursuit of truth. The symbolism of the number 153 reveals the geometric shapes of the Philosopher's Stone symbol to emphasize the Truth about "ME," from Francis Bacon. Contained in that one number are two unexpected cipher signatures that reveal his truth, the English spelling of Mary Stewart, and King Bacon, the repeating message of the plaque that "I Sir Francis Bacon" is the son of Mary Queen of Scots and Francis II of France.

Bonus Material – For the Prince Tudor Camp

To finish out this chapter on Key 38, I decided to include a part of the second cipher text that appears in this transposition. While working on a second message, a word or title popped out on the right-hand side of Lines 5 – 7, and then an associated name appeared on the left. Considering the messages regarding Bacon's true parentage, it shouldn't surprise anyone that another message of Key 38 actually contains information about an important aspect of the Prince Tudor theory. Using these two names as a context and looking more closely, a message appears in Lines 1 – 9:

1	T	P	*A*	V	O	L	*R*	A
2	**M**	**Y**	*C*	*N*	*H*	*L*	*E*	3
3	E	A	*V*	*O*	<u>W</u>	<u>A</u>	<u>S</u>	2
4	N	T	O	M	*E*	*H*	*O*	E
5	**O**	S	T⊣	S	*D*	*E*	*T*	I
6	**R**	**T**	F	I	I	I	*E*	D
7	**A**	**E**	**I**	T⊣	D	*<u>S</u>*	G	*<u>3</u>*
8	M	**B**	D	<u>N</u>	<u>E</u>	<u>T</u>	<u>A</u>	<u>5</u>
9	**E**	**A**	A	I	R	S	P	S

On the right in italic characters, subbing S for G and X for 3 in Line 7, and E for 5 on Line 8, spells "ESSEX." On the left in bold, with Z for A, L for O on Line 5 and H for R on Line 6, the letters spell "ELIZABETH." As other letters of the word associated with "Essex" overlap with it and reuse a few letters (as they form the name and title), are indicated by being underlined, and the shared letters will be both underlined and italicized. These underlined letters in Lines 7 and 8 with a substitution of V for E spell "CNATVS," Latin for "child; son." In Lines 1 – 3 in bold italics, subbing Z for A and E for V spells "MY COZEN." The underlined letters in Line 3 spell "WAS." Mentally removing these letters allows us to visualize the juxtaposition of the next construction, spanning Lines 1 – 5 along the right side. As seen in other messages, this name reuses a few of the letters. Subbing R for H, O for L, and B for 2, spells "ROBERT DEVERO" with a phonetic spelling of Devereux.

So far the message reads, "MY COZEN ROBERT DEVERO ESSEX WAS ELIZABETH'S CNATVS." Note that the letters at the beginning of Lines 7 and 8, wrapped by "ELIZABETH" spell "MA." So the message states that the leader of the Essex Rebellion against Queen Elizabeth was her own son. Removing these constructions provides an opportunity to finish the message:

1	T	P	V	O	L	A
2	**3**					
3	**E**	**A**				
4	N	T	O	M		
5	T⊣	S	I			
6	F	*I*	I	I	D	
7	T⊣	*D*				
8	M	*D*				
9	A	**I**	**R**	**S**	**P**	S

Knowing how this story ends made the first word easy to identify. The bold underlined characters in Lines 2 and 3 after subbing X for 3 spell "AXE." The underlined letters in Line 5 spell "T⊣IS" and the italic letters in Lines 6 – 8 spell "DID." The bold letters in Line 9 after substituting K for P spells "RISK."

Removing these letters and left justifying the rest of the letters provides the remaining letters in Table 6 – 16:

Substituting O for L in the bold letters spells "DOOM." To the left of this, "TO" is seen in italics. Using the double Tau Th as H, the underlined letters spell "HIM."

T	P	V	**O**	L	A
N	*T*	*O*	**M**		
F	I	I	**D**		
T⊣					
M					
A	S				

Removing these letters allows the creation of the final remainders table, Table 6 – 17:

T	**P**	V	**A**
N			
F	**I**		
A	**S**		

Table 6 - 17

The bold letters after subbing K for P and G for S spells "TAKING." The letters VF by using both substitutions spells "ET," Latin for "and," leaving the lone article, "A."

The final message here without any leftover letters becomes, "MY COZEN ROBERT DEVERO ESSEX WAS ELIZABETH'S CNATVS ET TAKING THIS RISK DID DOOM HIM TO A AXE."

Deciding to see what else appeared in the rest of the column, some obvious words appear filling the context, however reusing Line 9 is necessary:

9	*E*	A	A	I	R	**S**	**P**	S
10	*T*	*H*	E	T⊣	**V**	**O**	**T**	I
11	R̲	S	**R**	**I**	**T**	**C**	**V**	T
12	A̲	V	T	**W**	A	N	B	A
13	M̲	P̲	S̲	T	N	**The**	T	T
14	E	*M*	**A**	**S**	K	E	R	Æ
15	T	*Y*	F	**A̲**	C	R	**A̲**	6
16	A	L̲	O	L̲	I̲	O̲	G̲	1
17	R	O̲	S	P	V	*M*	N	6
18	C	T̲	Y	T⊣	Q	*R*	*I*	1
19	**O**	**E**	**B**	A	E	A	V	I

The bold letters in Lines 9 – 12 by substituting an E for V and D for W spell "I PROSECVTED" which is in keeping with history. The italic letters in Lines 1 – 2 spell "THE." Below this in Lines 11 – 13, the underlined letters spell "RANKS" after subbing N for M and K for P.

Below this in 14 and 15, the bold letters spell "AS" and the italic letters to its left spell "MY." As usual, the bold conjoined "The" is used whole. The bold underlined letters in Lines 15 and 16 form "ALOGIA," Latin for "folly," without substitutions.

In Lines 16 – 18 the underlined letters spell "LOT." In Lines 17 and 18, the italic letters spell "HIM." Lastly, the bold letters in Line 18 and 19 form "OBEY."

This produces a Word Bank containing I PRSECVTED, THE, RANKS, AS, MY, The, ALOGIA, LOT, HIM, and OBEY.

Removing all of these words allows a closer look at the remainders in Table 6 – 18:

Table 6 - 18

A	A	I	R	S	
T⊣	I				
S	T				
V	T	A	*N*	*B*	A
T	*N*	T	T		
E	*K*	*E*	*R*	Æ	
T	*C*	*R*	6		
A	*O*	*1*			
R	S	P	V̲	N̲	6
C	T⊣	Q̲	1		
A	E̲	A	V̲	*I*	

The bold letters along the left column with substitutions of G for S and E for V spell "GREATEST." The bold italic "NB" spell "MY" after substitutions for both letters, and the bold underlined letters at the bottom of the table spell "QUEEN" with a substitution of E for V. In the interest of space, mentally removing "GREATEST" allows for the next juxtapositions. The block of italic letters at the center of the table actually form three words. The first word is "NECK" and "ARCO" with A for 1, which is Latin for "protect." With F for 6, the remaining three characters can spell "FEAR." The italic bold "I" provides the first-person pronoun for Bacon's message.

148

Adding these to the Word Bank gives us PRSECVTED, THE, RANKS, AS, MY, The, ALOGIA, LOT, HIM, OBEY, GREATEST, MY, QUEEN, NECK, ARCO, FEAR and I. Table 6 – 19 contains the remaining letters:

Table 6 - 19

A	A	I	R	S
T⊣	*I*			
T				
<u>T</u>	A	A		
T	T			
P	6			
<u>T⊣</u>	<u>1</u>			
A	A			

Seeing so many symbolic letters, the "keys" or signposts of the RC, is always encouraging. As such, the letters that do not "seem to fit-in" spell an important contextual word. Substituting K for P provides the word "RISK." Lastly, the italic letters spell "IF" after subbing F for the double Tau. The underlined letters spell "ThAT."

Putting all of the words into an intelligible sentence, the following message is formed:

"I OBEY THE QUEEN PROSECUTED HIM. I FEAR ThAT RISK MY NECK IF ARCO. The LOT RANKS AS MY GREATEST ALOGIA."

In this message, Bacon clearly states that he feared protecting his cousin, Robert Deveraux, Earl of Essex, and had no choice in participating in his prosecution. He saw it as his greatest folly. When calculating the values of the checking system, at first nothing "tied-out." However, after realizing that every value was off by "AA," I realized that the first two A's were from Line 9 which was reused. Removing them produced the correct results. The values of the leftover letters appear in Table 6 – 20:

Table 6 - 20

Simple	19	1	1	19	19	6	1	1	67
	T	A	A	T	T	6	A	A	Sum
Reverse	6	24	24	6	6	19	24	24	133
Kaye	19	27	27	19	19	32	27	27	197

The sum of Simple Cipher is obvious as the signature for "Francis," and the Reverse value represents multiple forms of Bacon's name including "King Stuart, Baron Verulam, King Francis III" all in Simple Cipher. The Kaye value, though not immediately obvious, is the value of "I King Francis III" in Reverse Cipher.

Francis was content to be king in secret, while Robert openly challenged his mother and the influence of Cecil and Raleigh. Additionally, the rivalry between Essex and Raleigh over the favor of Elizabeth is curious. This however is not the only way this section can be read. The name of another son (and his father) appears in this section as well. The above message can be further refined.

Taking another close look at Lines 1 – 9, and using many of the same words, fleshes out the message. This technique of looking over the same sections for additional information was a later discovery in the decryption process, and therefore only appears in a few instances in this book. In this technique, letters can be reused within sets of words that appear together and overlap as acrostic anagrams. For a second time, we look at Lines 1 – 9:

1	T	P	*A*	V	O	L	*R*	A
2	***M***	***Y***	***C***	***N***	H	L	E	3
3	E	A	*V*	*O*	W	A	S	2
4	N	T	O	M	E	H	O	E
5	**O**	**S**	T⊣	S	D	E	T	I
6	***R***	***T***	F	I	I	I	E	D
7	***A***	***E***	**I**	T⊣	D	S	G	3
8	*M*	**B**	D	N	E	T	A	5
9	**E**	**A**	A	I	R	S	P	S

Once again, the message begins with the bold-italic words "MY COZEN" with substitutions of Z for A and E for V. To the right, with one substitution of R for H, the underlined letters spell "EDWARD." Below this in Lines 5 – 9 appears "ELIZABETH'S" in bold, after subbing L for O, H for R and Z for A. Intertwined with her name in italics is the word "MATER" Beside this on the right in underlined letters appear the overlapping words, "SECRETA CNATVS," by subbing C for 3 and E for 5, meaning "secret or hidden son." Also the plural form "cnati" Latin for "sons; children" can also be formed with the nearby "I." This means that so far, the message can be read as "My cozen Elizabeth's secret son / child" and the first name of "Edward." Looking at the entire section again will yield an interesting story.

1	T	P	A	V	O	L	R	A
2	M	Y	C	N	H	L	E	3
3	E	A	V	O	W	A	S	2
4	N	T	O	M	*E*	*H*	O	*E*
5	O	S	T⊣	S	D	*E*	T	I
6	R	T	F	I	I	I	*E*	D
7	A	E	I	T⊣	D	S	G	3
8	M	B	D	N	E	T	A	5
9	E	A	A	I	R	S	P	S

In bold in the columns to the center right from Lines 3 – 5, in the same space as the name "Edward," other words appear that complete the name and this part of the message. the underlined letters spell "WAS, IS" and "OF" after subbing F for T. After their "removal" the italic letters spell the last name "DEVERE" by substituting a V for one of the E's. This name of course appears in the same area and is comprised of many of the same characters as the previous phonetic spelling of "Devereux." Lastly, in Lines 8 and 9 in the same area as "SECRETA CNATVS" is the Latin word for father, "PATER." His name appears again up above, intertwined with deVere's name.

So yet again we'll pour over this same section of the transposition:

1	T	P	A	V	O	L	R	A
2	M	Y	C	N	H	L	E	3
3	E	**_A_**	V	O	W	A	*S*	2
4	**N**	**_T_**	**_O_**	*M*	*E*	*H*	*O*	*E*
5	**O**	**_S_**	T⊣	S	D	E	T	I
6	R	T	F	I	I	I	E	D
7	A	E	I	T⊣	D	S	G	3
8	M	B	D	N	**_E_**	**_T_**	**_A_**	5
9	E	A	A	I	**_R_**	S	**_P_**	S

Spanning most of the width of the table in Lines 3 – 5 appears the acrostic anagram of Edward deVere's "pater." The first and last names share the M at the center of the construction. On the left, the underlined-bold letters spell "THOMAS," using the T⊣ character as "H." The last name appears on the right after substituting Y for 2, V for E and R for H as "SEYMOUR." To the left of the name "Thomas" and sharing its "S" is the word "SON" with the first letters in Lines 4 and 5 in bold . Therefore, this part of the message states "MY COZEN ELIZABETH'S MATER. SECRETA CNATVS IS EDWARD DEVERE. WAS SON OF PATER THOMAS SEYMOUR." As shocking as this may sound, it makes some sense historically speaking. This will be discussed at the end of this chapter, along with the "problematic timeline" this message creates. But first, the message needs to be completed.

1	T	*P*	*A*	_V_	_O_	_L_	*R*	_A_
2	**M**	**Y**	*C*	N	_H_	L	**_E_**	**_3_**
3	E	A	*V*	*O*	_W_	_A_	_S_	2
4	N	T	O	M	E	H	O	E
5	O	S	T⊣	_S_	D	E	T	I
6	R	T	**F**	_I_	I	I	E	D
7	A	E	I	_T⊣_	D	S	G	3
8	M	B	D	N	E	**T**	**A**	5
9	E	A	A	**_I_**	**_R_**	**_S_**	**_P_**	S

Given the context of Francis' obvious claim to the throne, the following set of acrostic anagrams fit in with the information regarding the Virgin Queen's secret sons. Starting in the upper left the word "MY" in bold again plays a role. The italic letters to its right, after subbing an E for V, L for O and D for W, spell "PLACED." In the upper right corner, underlined letters in Lines 1 and 2 spell "ROLE" by substituting E for V and R for H. To the right, the bold italic letters after subbing X for 3 provides "REX." The underlined bold characters intersect with it and subbing C for the 3 and V for E spells "CAUSA," Latin for "plea; case." At the center of Lines 5 – 7, two words appear in a cross on its side. The bold letters a part of the title "F III" earlier identified in the phonetics. The italic letters form the arms of the cross shape with "THIS." Finally in Lines 8 – 9, the bold letters in 8 and the bold-italic and underlined letters spell "AT RISK," after subbing K for P. The words from this word bank form the sentence, "MY ROLE PLACED THIS REX F III CAUSA AT RISK."

Using this enhanced decryption process also complicates the "checking system," though it is still in place. After yielding all of the above messages, we are left with a handful of leftover letters:

T	A
L	
E	
D	
D	
A	S

The letters spell out with no substitutions, "DADS TALE." Since the word was plural, this indicated another father was named. Going back to the message regarding Robert Devereux and applying the same technique of reusing letters, the phrase "WAS ROBERT DUDLEY'S" appears intertwined with the name Elizabeth and "Devero." The letters also spell "LETS ADD A," indicating that it's time to use the signature checking system:

Simple	19	1	11	5	4	4	1	18	63
	T	A	L	E	D	D	A	S	Sums
Reverse	6	24	14	20	21	21	24	7	137
Kaye	19	27	11	31	30	30	27	18	193

The Simple Cipher total was odd at first, but then we can see that it's a reference to the title "F. III" as referenced in the actual message, as it's the value of it in Fourfold Cipher – F (6) + III (57) = 63. The Reverse sum of 137 has been seen elsewhere as the 33rd prime number, and therefore a cipher signature for "Bacon." However, this number *also* refers to the title "F. III" as mentioned in the message, as it totals 137 in Kaye Cipher. Lastly, 193 appears as the 44th prime number, Bacon's "secret signature." Additionally, "Fra. Rosi Crosse" in Fourfold Cipher totals 193.

Given the unused letters produce totals that directly reference "F. III" as it appears in the message itself, confirms a successful decryption.

Full Messages

Using this enhanced decryption technique of identifying multiple acrostic anagrams that reuse certain letters in association with each other, all within the same context, yielded more robust messages. They were uncovered in the following order:

- MY COZEN ROBERT DEVERO ESSEX WAS ELIZABETH'S CNATVS ET TAKING THIS RISK DID DOOM HIM TO A AXE. (Lines 1 – 9)
- I OBEY THE QUEEN PROSECUTED HIM. I FEAR ThAT RISK MY NECK IF ARCO. The LOT RANKS AS MY GREATEST ALOGIA. (Lines 9 – 19)

- MY COZEN ELIZABETH'S MATER. SECRETA CNATVS IS EDWARD DEVERE. WAS SON OF PATER THOMAS SEYMOUR. (Lines 1 – 9)
- MY ROLE PLACED THIS REX F III CAUSA AT RISK. (Lines 1 – 9)

These messages are extremely interesting, considering our modern understanding of that era in history, and the context of the cipher texts so far.

History tells us that Francis Bacon had sent pleas to Elizabeth I through his "uncle," William Cecil, Lord Burghley, for a position at court. History also states that these pleas "failed." However, some historians have observed that the contents of Bacon's letters to the queen remain a mystery. This set of messages seem to indicate that his "causa" was far weightier than merely asking for a position at court, and could have been a petition for the succession of the throne. His role in the intrigue that created the atmosphere precipitating Essex's Rebellion, and his role as prosecution of her son, placed that plea at risk. Bacon ranked the "lot" as his greatest folly.

The message regarding Thomas Seymour and Elizabeth is shocking because he was her stepfather. He was her half-brother's uncle and had married her stepmother Catherine Parr when Elizabeth was 14. In fact, rumors and stories about their relationship were prevalent in their own time. Catherine joined Seymour in playing "tickling games" with their teenage stepdaughter, one time reportedly holding Elizabeth as he cut the dress she wore into shreds. Historians often characterize the relationship between Seymour and Elizabeth as "flirtatious," and one story claims that Catherine sent Elizabeth away at 16 after catching Seymour and her "in an embrace." Considering this happened in 1549, and deVere was born in 1550, it's possible he's the result of this "embrace." However, the timeline appears to be off by at least seven months.

Seymour was beheaded for treason in January of 1549. So even if deVere were conceived during the days leading up to the execution, he would have been born at least seven months before his recorded birthday of April 22, 1550. However given what we now know of Francis Bacon's birth, it's possible that this particular birthdate represents when he went to live with the deVere family. Coincidentally, baby Francis would have been a mere 7 months old when Mary left France with him on her return to Scotland.

Chapter 7 - E MASKER of TT - Key 5 of Key 38

Just like the Keys 8 and 5 permutations of Key 32, Key 5 can also produce a new permutation of the Key 38 arrangement. Again, in order to make the algorithm work, I had to follow the directions provided in Key 38 where it states, "I CVT THE BAMPS T IN THE TT: E MASKER." This allowed the algorithm to create the following permutation. However, the

19	O	E	B	A	E	A	V	I

first attempts didn't work. Finding the directions regarding which line where the count of the algorithm should begin was the key here. Later, it was obvious that more than one hint exists regarding the starting point, but the easiest one to understand appears in Line 19, the number of Tau. Reading this line backwards, I and V can be read as the Roman numerals of 1 and 5. Remember 5 is the key to use next. The number as 1 would mean first. This idea is repeated with the E between the two A's, followed by the word BE and the letter O. "The first line BE O." Therefore, the place to begin first with Key E is Line 14 of Key 38 as O = 14. Running the algorithm using Key 5 on the Key 38 permutation of letters produced the following arrangement:

1	K	Y	A	L	R	M	Y	1	20	T	A	W	D	N	S	E	Me
2	E	R	I	T⊣	I	B	T	N	21	T	L	C	3	W	T	O	S
3	T⊣	L	A	V	V	K	Y	B	22	R	I	I	3	E	A	P	T⊣
4	A	T	I	E	O	O	G	W	23	R	C	T	A	N	A	Æ	C
5	A	A	H	T	V	E	A	V	24	L	G	P	C	R	B	I	M
6	V	M	L	V	2	E	S	T	25	Æ	L	A	N	M	S	A	I
7	I	A	S	D	5	R	H	T	26	V	E	O	I	C	H	O	E

8	I	A	N	S	E	E	F	6	27	I	R	M	I	D	N	S	H
9	I	O	N	T⊣	O	A	V	O	28	R	E	S	I	S	P	R	N
10	O	M	S	E	E	O	E	T	29	E	A	O	E	D	T	E	T⊣
11	W	P	L	I	L	E	W	T	30	M	T	A	S	V	S	V	W
12	P	G	W	O	C	Me	E	S	31	M	The	S	T	R	O	1	V
13	R	H	N	P	O	Y	E	O	32	T	I	A	S	F	O	D	H
14	N	H	T⊣	I	I	E	G	N	33	S	E	D	G	T	O	I	E
15	E	S	E	I	T	V	B	T	34	O	T	V·	Y	D	R	T	S
16	M	R	A	A	O	S	6	O	35	E	T⊣	H	I	A	S	H	Nt
17	E	V	H	O	E	T⊣	O	W	36	E	Yt	A	A	H	A	S	M
18	V	V	S	M	Ys	G	I	R	37	O	E	F	D	D	B	A	I
19	P	T	N	P	T⊣	E	I	K	38	T	O	R	T	A	P	T	T

Rosicrucian Order and Bacon sign-posts appear in the first few lines indicating a successful and correct transposition:

1	K	Y	<u>A</u>	L
2	*E*	*R*	*<u>I</u>*	*T⊣*
3	**T⊣**	L	<u>A</u>	<u>V</u>
4	**A**	T	I	E

This section, using the three characters in the three squares in the upper left corner, we spell "KEY." The rest of Line 1 can read phonetically as "A and O are symbols of light" by subbing O for L. To the right "KEY" in Line 1, beginning with the third letter "<u>A</u>," and then the letter "*<u>I</u>*" below and then the "*R*" to the left, spells the acrostic "AIR." The bold letters in the first column, and both bold letters at the beginning of Line 2, altogether spell "EARTH."

All four of the italic letters of Line 2, with a substitution of "F" for the double Tau we have the backwards word "FIRE." Lastly, the underlined letters, subbing a Q for the I, we have the acrostic anagram for "AQVA." One of the Keys or signposts of the Fra. Rosi Crosse are the classical four elements, AIR, EARTH, FIRE and AQVA (WATER).

All four elements appear around the acrostic anagram starting with the very first letter, "KEY," wrapped around the letter "R" used by three out of four elements. This is only one clue that has led me to believe that the number 17 could produce interesting results as a key for transposition. It's

156

also possible that each of the four elements represent four "keys" of the Rosicrucian Order as represented by the "R." They could also be transposition keys to use to create new arrangements of the characters of the plaque, and produce more cipher texts. At this point, six sets of messages have been identified and deciphered. It's entirely possible then there could be a total of ten ciphertexts, the same number of times the double Tau symbol (T⊣) appears on the plaque. If you are feeling particularly adventurous (or if you need a new full-time hobby), you can check to see if the keys of 17 (R), 27 (AIR), 50 (EARTH, already used as 5), 37 (FIRE) and 38 (AQVA, already used as TT) possibly produce even more results.

For context let's look at a few of the acrostics and obvious messages from a few of the lines of this "E Masker." Aside from the four elements, Line 8 (as H or double Tau) provides an interesting possibility:

8	I	A	N	S	E	E	F	6

A recent area of research mentioned earlier is yet another form of cipher system used by Bacon, called Four-fold Cipher. It utilizes four alphabets one after the other numbered in a similar fashion as his Simple Cipher, however it numbers them consecutively 1 – 96. The purpose of it is to provide separate values for double, triple and quadruple letter patterns. The second repetition of the alphabet represents AA – ZZ for example, and these pairs are numbered 25 – 48, and so on for the triple letters and quadruple letters up to number 96. (As an example of its relevance, the value of the Triple Tau, TTT, is 67, the signature for Francis in Simple). The double pairs of letters with the EE and F6 indicate the fourfold cipher might bare fruit. And so this line can spell, "I am SEE FF" subbing the M for N. Since the letters after the words "I am" should be a possible signature, I looked at each of the values of the letters: S (18), EE (29) and FF (30). Adding these values together we have the message, "I am 77." This number is the Simple Cipher signature of "Sir Bacon" and more importantly "Rex Bacon." Another interpretation would be to read the word "SEE" as a pun on the letter C whose value in Simple (and the four-fold cipher) is 3. Added to 30 as FF, the message then becomes "I am 33."

Since 9 can be seen as the first-person pronoun I in Simple Cipher, that line begins with that very letter for another interesting surface message:

9	I	O	N	T⊣	O	A	V	O

At the end of the line we see the familiar word "OVA" written backward and at the center of the line we see the Bacon signature of 33 in the form of "T⊣ O." Since the word "OVA" is reversed, the "ON" can be read the same way, producing the explicit message "I NO Bacon OVA." This message requires no explanation at this point. Additionally, noting the position of the letter O's on this line reminds us "O's" have been used in other keys to "frame" a message. In this case it seems to be Bacon's "secret" initials on the line correlating to the letter "I" in Simple Cipher. First of all, the value of N and T is 32, the letter "F" in Kaye Cipher. The other letters framed by O's are A and V, the initials of his father's house, Valois-Angoleme. So removing the O's the line reads as "I F. V-A." Moving on to the next notable example continues the theme of Bacon's name.

This block of letters in the first three columns of Lines 6 - 8 provided an interesting acrostic anagram giving me a much-welcomed context:

6	**V**	**M**	*L*
7	*I*	*A*	*S*
8	I	*A*	N

Subbing E for V in the bold letters in Line 6 we see "ME" written backwards. The italics L with all three letters in Line 7 and the A in Line 8 spell "ALIAS." Removing this leaves us with the word "IN" on the last line, all providing the statement, "ME IN ALIAS." It wasn't until later that the realization happened these words also be read in a different order, revealing his alias in a specific part of the world with "ME ALIAS IN…" This was the first indication that this key dealt with some of his aliases, "maskers," including a bombshell regarding his "best alias."

Next in center of lines 10 – 12, the strange message of "SEE LIL COW" appears as an acrostic. Similar acrostics appear in Key 32, and based upon later messages of that key, they seem to reference some of Bacon's

10	O	M	**S**	**E**	**E**	O	E	T
11	W	P	**L**	**I**	**L**	E	W	T
12	P	G	**W**	**O**	**C**	Me	E	S

unknown artwork and cartography. In fact, as indicated by the cipher texts of this transposition, he had aliases as artists which would allow him to gain entrance to the royal courts of Europe and practice spy craft. At this point, this is only speculation, but one founded on very interesting evidence to be discussed in a later chapter involving a specific artist. This artist (a Bacon alias) is the link between several people already discussed within the cipher texts.

Along the right side of rows 11 – 14, another acrostic appears which could also be a part of the actual cipher text:

11	W	P	L	I	L	E	**W**	**T**
12	P	G	W	O	C	**Me**	**E**	**S**
13	R	H	N	P	O	Y	**E**	**O**
14	N	H	T⊣	I	I	E	**G**	**N**

The bold letters plainly spell "Me GONE WEST" with the ligatured "Me" enveloped above and below by the word "EYE." This acrostic (with GONE as an anagram) supports the idea that Sir Francis Bacon underwent a "philosophical death" and lived-on under a new identity, and he lived out that life in the colonies.

Table 7-1

E	T
W	T
E	S
E	O
G	N
B	T
6	O

In this same area along the right columns between Lines 10 – 16, an acrostic regarding Bacon's biological father appears in Table 7-1.

Substituting S for G, F for 6 and 2 for B, and reading upwards in a clockwise manner, we read "SEE WE TT SON TO F2." This message clearly states, "see, we (33) Bacon son to Francis II," once again echoing the main thrust of the messages of the cipher texts on the plaque. An additional message appears when we read the letters at the top "ET" as "and" and sub F for the T below it. Adding a few lines below what is shown here gives us a message along the right column, "And F SON TO WORK" indicating he had to take a job. As you'll see, a famous explorer took him on board as his navigator.

Two acrostic anagrams appear in the form of a cross in Lines 1 – 4 again in Lines 22 – 24, however as they contain information used as context for the actual cipher texts I'll deal with them in the line by line treatment. However two last acrostics appear in the second column in Lines 30 and 31, and 33 – 36.

The first is yet another marker of the Fra. Rosi Crosse:

30	M	T	A	*S*	**V**	**S**	*V*	W
31	M	The	**S**	*T*	**R**	**O**	*I*	V

In bold with a substitution of E for V, we see the counterclockwise word "ROSE." Flanking the rose in italics and read in the same counterclockwise fashion, we see "T1VS" which supplies the "cross" in the form of the word "TAVS."

When the last acrostic was first noted, I assumed it had been placed there to distract "profane eyes". But after closer inspection it can be noted as the intended message. This acrostic appears in Lines 33 – 36 wrapped around a Triple Tau in the form of T and H:

33	S	E	D	G	T	**O**	**I**	E
34	O	T	V	Y	D	**R**	*T*	S
35	E	T⊣	H	I	A	**S**	*H*	Nt
36	E	Yt	A	A	H	**A**	**S**	**M**

On Line 33, beginning with the bold O and reading downward counterclockwise, with one substitution of G for the first S, we have an "ORGASM." In researching the etymology of this word, it existed in this form in both French and modern Latin. The other half of the acrostic is in anagram form, and because of the conjoined Nt character, afforded multiple meanings. First of all, "SENtI" can be read as Latin for, "feel, experience; think, realize, see, understand." This can represent the great pleasure Bacon received from understanding and exploring scientific pursuits. If we read the character as merely N, the word becomes "SENI," meaning "the condition of old age." Could this represent how Bacon viewed his retirement after his philosophical death? In this sense it could truly be his *petit morte*. Lastly, it can be read as a pun on the Latin *scenae* meaning "theater or stage" with the "T" being read as a suffix meaning, "having a, provided with." Again, this would be an expression of how much pleasure it gave him to create the works of Shakespeare. And as can be plainly seen, the Triple Tau is at the center of it.

EMASKER TT Acrostic Anagrams

As impossible as the next set of messages are, they ironically make logical sense. At this point in this text, it's difficult to write off the series of messages regarding Francis Bacon's biological parents. But this next message was difficult to accept. For "Bacon the spy" to divulge his "BEST ALIAS" is one thing. It entirely is another thing when the alias he names is another historical personage, every bit as renowned as Bacon himself. When this happened, I became a bit frightened for the second time while working on this project.

Obviously, the moment the messages about Francis II and Mary Queen of Scots appeared was more than worrisome. This was a direct challenge to a theory I personally favored, and one into which many other, more experienced and prestigious researchers than I, have invested much time, effort and careers. To present information that directly challenges that paradigm is daunting and intimidating. To present the following information is downright foolish. Understand that I am about to knowingly put my reputation on the line and open myself up to far more criticism than the discovery that Francis Bacon was the displaced Dauphin. However, if this is where the clues and the messages are leading, they need to be followed. Also at this point, a clear obligation to the man known as Sir Francis Bacon exists to print his truth, regardless of what names he used, whether it be William Shakespeare, or the one to follow.

This discovery led down another, just as intriguing, rabbit hole. Just like the plausibility of his royal birth needs to be discussed in detail in its own chapter, this section will require its own space for elaboration. This message also led to discoveries of corroborating evidence from completely "separate" and "seemingly unrelated" sources, that will prove to be neither separate nor unrelated at all.

Lastly, this is a presentation of one interpretation of the permutation of characters, while at least one other message in this same arrangement has been noted. This one contains the basis of the overall message. The information here is reinforced by a much closer treatment of Key 32 to come. A full explanation with additional evidence will appear in an upcoming chapter called "Ghosts of Bacon."

First of all, before getting into the message, please note the acrostic

160

1	K	Y	*A*
2	E	R	*I*
3	T⊣	*L*	*A*

anagram in the first three columns of Lines 1 – 3. The upper left spells "KEY" and below this is the word "TO" by subbing O for L. Continuing around the "R" at the center and this time using the L as L, the Latin word "ALIA" is produced, meaning "other, another; different, changed," as well as "by another/different way/route." All of these words imply that this Key reveals his other Rosicrucian names, however another important meaning becomes clear after the message is complete. This key transposition is the "Key" to understanding his alternative route to his birthright.

And so with a build up like that, let's take a look at Lines 1 – 7:

1	K	**Y**	A	*L*	R	*M*	Y	1
2	**E**	**R**	**I**	*T⊣*	*I*	*B*	T	N
3	T⊣	**L**	A	V	*V*	K	Y	B
4	A	T	I	E	*O*	O	G	W
5	A	A	H	T	V	E	A	V
6	**V**	**M**	**L**	*V*	<u>2</u>	<u>E</u>	<u>S</u>	<u>T</u>
7	I	**A**	**S**	*D*	5	R	H	T

Having learned from Key 32 after revisiting it (those findings are in the next chapter), I learned that the acrostics are more than hints and context. Not only are they a part of the message itself, but they also point to the location of the specific information in the cipher text. Those letters also can be reused when identifying the specifics. So in the location of the acrostic "ME AN ALIAS" in Lines 6 – 8, I easily picked out the word "BEST" from the underlined letters with B in place of 2, and then the name "SAMVEL" in bold on Lines 6 and 7 after subbing E for V. I would later identify the italic characters on Lines 6 and 7 as "DE." At first the 5 was used as an E, but then noting how many of the letters were being reused in overlapping anagrams (especially names), the V above the D was reused. However, the last name failed to appear.

Moving back to the top of the column I looked around the first "ALIA" acrostic for a name. Spotting a name on a hunch, an internet search of the name as a Renaissance artist paid off. (As you'll remember, artists figure prominently among Bacon's aliases). In a cross-shaped acrostic centered on Line 2 on its side, the bold letters spell "TIBERIO" after subbing B for Y and O for L as the arms of the cross. I found the last name crossing the first cross in a Y-shaped acrostic anagram. The italic letters spell a phonetic form of "TINELLI" by substituting E for V and L for O in Lines 3 and 4, respectively. Both use the double Tau (T⊣) as a single T, echoing his initials, Tiberio Tinelli. Also, an indication of the phonetic substitution of Y for I in the last name is indicated by the "I" at the center of the Y-shaped acrostic anagram, beside the B that became Y. Interestingly, many of Tinelli's paintings found their way into the private collection of King Louis XIII. As you'll see in the explanations to come, the artist aliases connect many of the royals of both the English and French courts. Speculation regarding the reasons for this appear at a later time.

Looking at the center of Lines 1 – 7, I noted more overlapping words and acrostic anagrams.

1	K	Y	A	L	R	M	Y	1
2	E	R	I	T⁻	I	B	T	N
3	T⁻	L	A	V	V	K	Y	B
4	A	*T*	I	E	**O**	**O**	**G**	*W*
5	A	*A*	*H*	*T*	V	E	*A*	V
6	V	M	L	V	*2*	E	*S*	T
7	*I*	A	S	D	*5*	*R*	*H*	*T*

The bold characters on Line 4 are an obvious anagram for the word "GOOD." The same italic letters of G, W, and the A directly below, with one substitution of S for G spells "WAS." The underlined letters in Lines 4 and 5 form "THAT." At this point, I thought about restarting the bottom portion as the last name hadn't presented itself.

Assuming the last name would appear in the next block of letters in the cipher, I continued to the next section. Having completed the first column of 19 rows and without noting an answer, I moved on to the next column. In Lines 20 – 26, the answer finally appeared as an obvious acrostic with the name directly below it. Of course, it seemed odd that the name was appearing here as opposed to closer to the first name. It stands to reason that because of the complexity of the plaque itself that it's extremely difficult to fit all of the layers of information into the same areas of the cipher texts. But then the hint I had missed of how to solve the problem appeared back in Lines 6 and 7.

The hints in this area were obvious only after seeing them in retrospect. After mentally removing the A, S, and D from the last row 7 and the name identified earlier, the letters on the bottom row suggested the word "RIGHT" with one substitution of G for S above on Line 6. Beside this is the number 25. Looking at the "right column," directly across from Line 6 was Line 25, where the last name was found. So, having missed the clues pointing to the letters that would complete the message of Bacon's "BEST" alias whose first name was Samuel, the last name appears in Line 25:

20	T	A	W	D	N	S	E	Me
21	T	L	C	3	W	T	O	S
22	R	I	*I*	3	E	A	P	T⊣
23	R	*C*	*T*	*A*	N	A	Æ	C
24	L	G	*P*	C	R	B	I	M
25	A̲Ǝ̲	L̲	A̲	N̲	M̲	S	A	I
26	V	E	O	I̲	C̲	H̲	O	E

You can see the word that immediately jumped out as an acrostic anagram in the shape of another cross on its side, spelling "CAPTAIN." Centered around Line 25 appeared the letters P, Æ, L, A, N, M, C, and H. In what appears to be the rudimentary shape of a ship with a rudder extending below and behind, the last name of "CHAMPLAIN" appears without substitutions. Bacon's message here states that Samuel de Champlain was his "best alias."

This idea runs so contrary to orthodox history as it's currently accepted and written, that it's a simple matter to just dismiss it. Following the clues where they led throughout this process presented something far more problematic than could have been imagined when this project began. The problem is, the name appears again in the next chapter in a more complete treatment of Key 32. Realizing far more evidence was necessary to confirm or dismiss this idea, I took a break from deciphering the keys and deeply dug into the names appearing in them to see if any evidence existed. As you will again see in a later chapter, I such evidence does exist, as crazy as all of this seems. Continuing to follow the messages where they led also provided more evidence.

Moving on to the remaining letters from Lines 1 – 7 in Table 7-2, the message can be continued with three new words in this section:

Table 7-2

K	*A*	*R*	*Y*	A
T	**N**			
T⊣	**A**	V	K	Y	B
A	**I**	E		
A	**V**	E̲	V̲	
I	5	R̲	H̲	T̲

On the first two rows, after a substitution of P for K the italic letters spell "PARTY." Below this, the bold letters spell "NATIVE" with no substitutions, and the underlined letters spell "THERE" after subbing E for V. This brings our tally in the Word Bank so far, to ALIAI, TIBERIO TINELLY, GOOD, WAS, THAT, BUT, ALIAS, BEST, SAMVEL DE, CHAMPLAIN (from the right column), PARTY, NATIVE and THERE. The message can so far be read as, "Tiberio Tinelli was good, but best alias was Samuel de Champlain…"

The leftover characters are also interesting, as they not only confirm the interpretation through cipher signatures, but they also contain a message in anagram form. The leftover characters and their values appear here in Table 7-3:

Table 7-3

Simple	1	1	1	9	5	20	10	23	2	72
	A	A	A	I	5	V	K	Y	B	SUM
Reverse	24	24	24	16	20	5	15	2	23	153
Kaye	27	27	27	35	31	20	10	23	28	228

The number 72 is the cipher signature for both "King Bacon" and King F. III in Simple. Number 153 is now very familiar to us as a signature, as "I Sir Francis Bacon" and "Francis Verulam" in Simple Cipher. Delving more deeply into the use of Bacon's "Four-Fold" Cipher system, we discover that the value of "Francis Bacon" is 153 in that system as well. The value of these characters in Kaye Cipher is 228, "King F. III" in Kaye and "King Francois III" in Reverse.

As previously mentioned, the characters also form two intelligible anagrams related to the message that seems to be appearing here. One such message could be read as "I BE A KEY AA." Friend and Oak Island researcher Erin Helton at one point had been researching Manuel De Moura y Corte Real and his father, Cristobol de Moura. Both were depicted in portraits holding a "chest" key whose bit and wards were in the shape of the number 25, the value of AA in Bacon's Four-fold Cipher, as well as the "B-E" in the beginning of the phrase. She also noted a relationship to sites dedicated St. Nicholas, the patron saint of sailors. As that area of research is still a work in progress, we're unsure of how two Portuguese noblemen are connected to all of this, if at all. However, I couldn't help finding the correlation interesting between the word "key" and the number 25 here.

Another interpretation of these letters which I believe is more to the point here, can be read as "KEE I BA BAA" with a substitution of B for Y. This message plays on the meaning of the name "Champlain" itself as *field of wool*, and therefore one "kee" to understanding Bacon as this alias. The popular rhyme "Baa Baa Black Sheep" originated in the 13th century in response to a wool tax, according to the BBC, and would be well-known to Bacon. And of course, the ending of the rhyme of "none for the boy down the lane," or also "none for the boy crying in the lane" would apply to Bacon as he never received his due. "Lane" in the rhyme can also be a pun on the French "lain" meaning wool. The message "I ba baa" can also be read as the "bleat" of the sheep. Both references relate to Bacon's sadness of not receiving his due, as well as the pun on the French "l'ain," meaning "eldest boy." Incidentally, the value of "KEE I BA BAA" in Bacon's Four-fold Cipher is 123, the cipher signature for James in Kaye, and BA BAA total 7, or G in Simple.

The message continues in Lines 8 – 13, where he names where "THERE" is, from the previous block of text:

8	I	A	N	S	E	E	F	6
9	I	O	N	T⊣	O	A	V	O
10	O	M	S	E	E	O	E	T
11	W	P	L	I	L	E	W	T
12	P	G	W	O	C	ME	E	S
13	R	H	N	P	O	Y	E	O

Centered on Line 9. The bold-underlined letters spell "TONGOIS" after substituting G for S. The obvious construction of the italic letters beginning Line 8 spell "I AM." Here, also note the "ST⊣" used in "TONGOIS" can provide "ST." To the right, the bold-italic letters spell "AV," and the underlined-italic letters in Line 8 and the O at the end of Line 9, spell "FLEET" with a substitution of T for 6 and L for O. The bold-italic letters on Line 11 produce "I LED" with a substitution of D for W. Using the same W and the other bold letters at the end of Lines 11 and 12, we use the acrostic earlier noted counterclockwise as "WEST." Lastly, in the center of Lines 12 and 13 another nautical word appears as "DOCK" after subbing D for W and K for P. Next, we'll create the first remainders table for clarity's sake by removing the previous words.

Looking at Table 9-4, the message is completed with special substitutions in the bold characters in Lines 12 and 13:

10	O	M	E	E	O		
11	W	P	L				
12	P	G			ME		S
13	R	H	N	O	Y	E	O

The first special substitution is with an A for an O as we've seen before. It wasn't until late in the process that I learned that the ligatured letters can either serve as both letters, or either of the individual letters including their substitutions. For the first time during the process, I realized I needed to use the ligatured "ME" as a single E, and substitute a V for the other E. Also, as other anagrams have "overlapped" in the previous words, the "S" in West is reused here as a G. In this way, this acrostic anagram forms the word "VOYAGE."

There are thirteen letters leftover to use as the checking system whose values' sums appear in Table 9-4:

Table 7-4

Simple	14	12	5	5	14	21	15	11	15	7	17	8	13	1 5 0
	O	M	E	E	O	W	P	L	P	G	R	H	N	SUM
Reverse	11	13	20	20	11	4	10	14	10	18	8	17	12	1 5 0
K a y e	14	12	31	31	14	21	15	11	15	33	17	34	13	2 2 8

As you can see, both Simple and Reverse Ciphers produced a total of 150, which is the cipher signature for "Rex Francois" in Reverse. The sum in Kaye Cipher is the same sum as the Kaye value in the previous block of text of 228, which is again the signature for "King Francois III" in Reverse, and "King F. III" in Kaye. The words appearing in this block of text are ST.

TONGOIS, I AM, AV, FLEET, WEST, I LED, VOYAGE and DOCK. Putting all of the words that we've deciphered so far in Lines 1 – 13 into the following word bank, allows a message to appear. ALIAI, TIBERIO TINELLY, GOOD, WAS, THAT, BUT, ALIAS, BEST, SAMVEL DE, CHAMPLAIN, PARTY, NATIVE, THERE, along with the latest words and the message becomes clear: "Tiberio Tinelli that good, but best alias was Samuel de Champlain. I am native party there au (at) St. Tongois dock. I led fleet voyage west." It bears mentioning again that as impossible as this message sounds, corroborating evidence appears in a later chapter.

The next block of text in Lines 14 – 19 provides equally impressive results.

14	N	H	T⊣	I	I	E	G	N
15	E	S	E	*I*	*T*	*V*	*B*	<u>T</u>
16	M	R	A	A	O	S	6	<u>O</u>
17	**E**	**V**	**H**	**O**	E	T⊣	*O*	W
18	**V**	**V**	**S**	M	Ys	G	I	*R*
19	P	T	N	P	T⊣	E	I	*K*

Multiple obvious anagrams appeared the first of which was the group of letters in bold on Lines 17 and 18. First, "SEE" appears backwards after subbing E for both V's on Line 18, and above it the word "OVER" appears with a substitution of R for H, producing "OVERSEE." Directly to the right, the italic letters spell "WORK," while the underlined letters directly above spell "TO." To the left of this on Line 15 we see a backwards "BVT I" in bold-italics. Removing these letters and words will clear up the space to provide two more words.

14	N	H	<u>**T⊣**</u>	I	I	E	G	N
15	*E*	<u>**S**</u>	<u>**E**</u>					
16	*M*	R	A	A	O	S	6	
17					E	T⊣		
18				*M*	*Ys*	G	I	
19	P	T	N	P	T⊣	E	I	

While deciphering this section, it became obvious that a technique I had used once or twice before was necessary. This technique requires looking at the column as a whole, and not only one "arbitrary section" at a time. Doing so made it obvious that one of the leftover letters from Line 13 above the double Tau in Line 14, "N," was needed in this part of the message. With it, the bold-underlined letters of Lines 14 and 15 form the acrostic anagram of "SENT." The italic letters directly to the left spell "ME," producing the phrase, "SENT ME TO OVERSEE WORK. BVT I..." One more obvious word to point out here (it removes an extra step of adding another remainders table) is the word "MY" on Line 18, using the Ys character as Y.

166

Removing these letters and words, and removing the empty spaces provides the remainders in Table 7 – 5:

One word had been suggesting itself in this section on Line 14 with "IEGN," and here we see the letter "R" just below and to the left to give us "REIGN." Removing these letters provides a new remainders table to see if any new anagrams appear in Table 7 – 6:

N	H	I	**I**	**E**	**G**	**N**
M	**R**	A	A	O	S	6
G	I					
P	T	N	P	T⊣	E	I

Table 7-5

Table 7-6

N	H	I			
M	A	A	O	S	6
G	**I**				
P	T	N	P	T⊣	E	I

In this arrangement we finally see *who* "SENT ME TO OVERSEE WORK," in the bold letters on the left. With two substitutions of K for P and N for M, the word "KING" appears. Originally the word THE on the last line was used, but I soon learned that these letters serve a different purpose. Again, removing these words gives yet one more remainders table:

Table 7-5

N	H	**I**			
A	A	**O**	S	6	
T	**N**	P	T⊣	E	I

Here we see the message completed with the bold letters spelling, "NATION." The message of this block of text appears as "KING SENT ME TO OVERSEE WORK. BVT I REIGN MY NATION."

Suddenly, the tragic story of Esau and Jacob, the Lost Dauphin, or in fictional form *The Tragedy of Hamlet, Prince of Denmark,* may have had a happy ending after all. Placing the values of the leftover characters in Table 7 – 8 produced the following results:

Table 7 - 6

Simple	8	1	18	6	15	19	5	9	81
	H	A	S	6 (F)	P	T⊣	E	I	Sum
Reverse	17	24	7	19	10	6	20	16	119
Kaye	34	27	18	32	15	19	31	35	211

The Simple and Reverse Ciphers produce their values of the signature of Francois in both Simple and Reverse, respectively. The Kaye value while puzzling at first, it doesn't take long to realize that 211 is the cipher signature of "King Stuart" in Kaye Cipher itself. So each cipher produces its own signature that coincides with the message of this section. As an added bonus, the remaining characters contain another similar message.

The letters in Table 7 – 8 are an anagram. Substituting R for H, G for S, and F for 6, provides the letters R A G F P T⊣ E I, an anagram for "FRA. T⊣E PIG." Incidentally, the value of "PIG" in Simple Cipher is 31, the same as "REX" in Reverse. It's value in Reverse is 44, the value of "REX" in Simple. After this discovery, the word "impossible" was permanently removed from my vocabulary.

When looking at the messages of the first column, the 19 rows of characters in this transposition, several questions come to mind. Could a famous historical personage like Samuel de Champlain, let alone Tiberio Tinelli, be an alias of yet another famous historical person, named Sir Francis Bacon? Who will ever believe such a thing? Why would he create aliases that would become some of the greatest names in history, William Shakespeare and Samuel de Champlain, instead of having history record his real name, Sir Francis Bacon? The answer I think lies in the cipher signatures in the "checking system" in this block of characters and the question itself.

Francis Bacon was never his "real name." His real name was actually Francois Stuart, or any of the other variations thereof, Francis Stewart, Fr. III, etc. Therefore, what difference to him would it have made if the name "Francis Bacon" appeared on the First Folio? (It just occurred to me that technically it actually does appear in the initials "FF" as they can be read as TT, 33). The more I pondered these questions, the clearer he became in my mind, and there were still 19 more lines of cipher text to decode.

The next set of acrostic anagrams appear in Lines 20 – 25. Please also note, another form of the same word appears as found in the previous column, "ALII" Latin meaning "others:"

20	T	A	W	*D*	N	*S*	*E*	*Me*
21	T	L	C	3	W	T	O	S
22	R	I	**I**	3	E	A	P	T⊣
23	R	**C**	**T**	A	N	A	_Æ_	_C_
24	L	G	**P**	_C_	_R_	_B_	_I_	_M_
25	Æ	L	**A**	N	M	S	_A_	I

As mentioned earlier, the first notable thing appears as an acrostic anagram in the shape of a cross on its side, spelling another word in the nautical theme, "CAPTAIN." The next obvious words appear on Line 20 in italic-bold as "SEND Me." The next two words "crossover" one another as we have seen in other sections, and therefore share two letters. The first is the word suggested by the letters below and to the right of the captain acrostic. The underlined-italic letters spell a phonetic "CARIBÆN" for "Caribbean." The bold letters on Line 25, along with the C and A used above, including the P from the captain acrostic, with one substitution of G for the S spells "CAMPAIGN." Removing these words allows us to see any other missed constructions. In particular, which Caribbean campaign Champlain had participated?

The answer would be in the form of the name of the "Captain" whose title so prominently appears:

20	*T*	*A*	*W*				
21	T	*L*	C	3	W	**T**	**O**	S
22	<u>R</u>	<u>*I*</u>		3	E	A	**P**	T⊣
23	<u>R</u>							
24	L	<u>*G*</u>						
25	<u>Æ</u>	L	<u>**A**</u>					

The underlined letters on the left side, seemingly wrapped around the space where the word "CAPTAIN" appeared, is the acrostic anagram for the name "RALÆIGH" with one substitution of an H for R in the underlined italic letters. Directly above this, the italic letters spell "WALT." On the right, note the word created by the bold letters as "STOP." Removing these words, we proceed to the remaining letters with the spaces removed in Table 7–9:

Table 7 - 9

T	C	3	W
3	E	A	T⊣
L			

The anticipated message at this point needed the word "TO" provided by the bold T and L.

While calculating the signatures of the leftover letters, one of them was puzzling. The Reverse total was 120, which is "King Francois" in Simple, and the Kaye sum was 185, "Francois" in Kaye. The Simple Cipher values however totaled 55, a number that introduced me to the Elizabethan Short Cipher. In this cipher, the value of "Francis Bacon" is 55. The leftover letters also produce an anagram.

Subbing D for W, the anagram states "33 C death," or perhaps in other words, "Bacon see Walt R. death?" This seemed to be a reference to Bacon's presence at Raleigh's execution. Or it at least appeared so.

The message here can be read a few different ways. Collecting our word bank gives a list of, CAPTAIN, SEND Me, CARIBÆN, CAMPAIGN, WALT, RALEIGH, STOP, and TO. Since there is a reference to Raleigh's execution, we can assume this is a reference to the attack on a Spanish outpost on the Orinoco River, violating the treaty with Spain and the terms of Raleigh's own pardon. This can be read as "Send me to stop Captain Walt Raleigh Caribbean campaign." Confused as to *who* "SEND Me," I looked back at Line 20 to see if an answer could be at the beginning of the line that provided "SEND Me." Adding the first four letters of the line totals 45 in Simple, the signature for James in Simple. Could that be the answer? Did James send Bacon to try to stop Raleigh?[Author's note: In the first version of this book, the author had failed to identify the name "IAMES" overlapping the letters comprising "CARIBEAN CAMPAIGN," so the name James was the correct answer].

However, the next name that appeared wasn't merely a captain, he was an Admiral, and the message was unrelated to Raleigh. Two words appeared to continue the nautical theme in Lines 26 – 32:

26	V	E	O	I	C	H	O	E
27	**I**	**R**	**M**	**I**	**D**	**N**	**S**	H
28	R	**E**	S	I	S	P	R	N
29	E	**A**	_O_	E	D	T	E	T⊣
30	M	T	_A_	_S_	_V_	_S_	V	W
31	M	*The*	_S_	_T_	_R_	_O_	1	V
32	T	I	A	S	F	_O_	D	H

In bold and in the shape of a carpenter's square, an acrostic anagram appears in Lines 27 – 29 and spells "MERIDIANS" with no substitutions. In Lines 29 – 32, the underlined-italic letters form an acrostic anagram spelling "ASTROLOGVS," after subbing a G for an S, and an L for O. This word is Latin for "astronomer, one who studies the heavens/predicts from the stars." The bold italic ligatured word "The" rounds out the initial pass in the search for words. Removing these constructions allows us to see what other words appear as well.

26	V	E	O	I	**C**	**H**	**O**	**E**
27							**S**	H
28	R		_S_	_I_	_S_	P	R	N
29	*E*			_E_	_D_	_T_	E	T⊣
30	*M*	T					V	W
31	M						1	V
32	T	I	_A_	_S_	F		D	H

The bold letters in the top-right are easily recognizable as "CHOSE." On the left, the bold-italic letters in Lines 29 and 30 spell "ME." In the center after a substitution of W for D, the bold-underlined letters spell "WISEST" which made contextual sense in relation to the word "ASTROLOGVS." At the bottom on Line 32, the italic letters spell "AS." At this point, it sounded as if someone "CHOSE ME AS WISEST ASTROLOGVS," in reference to Francis Bacon.

Removing these final constructions and the empty spaces, produces the first remainders table in this section, Table 7 – 10:

Table 7-10

V	_E_	_I_	O	
H				
R	P	R	N	
E	_T⊣_			
T	V	W		
M	1	V		
T	**I**	F	D	H

With the mention of meridians, the word expectedly formed by the bold letters in the remainders table, appears as "TIME." The underlined letters of T⊣ E, and the bold-underlined "I" finish the phrase "I TIME T⊣E MERIDIANS."

The last step was to find the name of the Captain who "CHOSE" Bacon as the astronomer. That name appears in Table 7 – 11:

Table 7 - 11

V	O		
H			
R	*P*	R	N
T	V	W	
1	*V*		
F	*D*	*H*	

Here we see the bold italic letters that require some substitutions to produce the rest of the message. Subbing a K for the P in the center, and A for 1, E for V, and R for H, produces the name "F. DRAKE."

Putting the message together, we arrive at "I TIME THE MERIDIANS. F. DRAKE CHOSE ME AS The WISEST ASTROLOGVS."

As a mathematician and astronomer Bacon would have been perfectly suited for navigation, and the implications here are enormous. As you'll see, the timeline fits. But first, we need to calculate the values of the leftover characters in Table 7 – 12:

Table 7 - 7

Simple	20	14	8	17	17	13	19	20	21	149
	V	O	H	R	R	N	T	V	W	Sum
Reverse	5	11	17	8	8	12	6	5	4	76
Kaye	20	14	34	17	17	13	19	20	21	175

First seeing the totals, I double checked the work. But then on a hunch, a quick calculation found that 149 is the Simple Cipher signature of "Samuel de Champlain!" While doing so, I realized that the value of Samuel was 67 in Simple, the same as Francis. So therefore 76 is the value of "Samuel de" in Simple, the same as "I Francis." However, it's also the Reverse Cipher value of "Walter." I believe that was the purpose of this value. Lastly, the Kaye value of 175 is the signature for "Francois Stuart" in both Simple and Reverse ciphers.

The last (next) section was puzzling for quite some time and though a few meaningful constructions could be picked out, it was incomplete. So, looking back at the previous section, since many of the messages appeared to be "layered" over one another, some of the lines needed to be reused. The message required the addition of Lines 30 – 32 to 33 – 38 for completion.

This section required more "remainders tables" due to the greater length. It also provides the unexpected "happy ending" to adventurous life of the man we call "Sir Francis Bacon." [Author's note: So many messages appeared as the decryption method was refined, that it was necessary to begin not only this second edition, but another book in the series. Many more shocking discoveries are to come].

30	M	T	A	S	*V*	*S*	*V*	*W*
31	M	The	S	T	**R**	**O**	**1**	**V**
32	T	I	A	S	F	**O**	D	H
33	S	E	D	G	T	O	I	E

The first words to appear were at the bottom in Lines 35 – 38, one of which hinted at a name that led to the addition of Lines 30 – 32. This word appears in the bold-underlined letters on the right of the column in Lines 35 and 36.

Subbing G for S and R for H, we form "GRANtS." In the lower left, the word "TO" appears in italics, while

30	M	T	A	S	*V*	*S̲*	*V*	*W*
31	M	The	S	T	**R**	**O̲**	**1̲**	V̲
32	T	I	A	S	F	O̲	D	H
33	S	E	D	G	T	O	I	E
34	O	T	V	Y	D	R	T	S
35	E	T⊣	H	I	A	**S̲**	**H̲**	**N̲t̲**
36	E	Yt	A	A	H	**A̲**	**S̲**	M
37	O	E	F	D	D	*B̲*	*A̲*	*I̲*
38	*T*	*O*	R	T	A	**P**	T	*T*

to its right in bold the word "TRAP" appears. Just above and to its right in the underlined-italic letters, the word "BAIT" appears. The word *grant* must be a reference to land, and only one person would have had that power. In Line 31 the word "ROI" is seen after subbing I for 1 as a Roman numeral appearing here in bold underline. As demonstrated in other areas of the key, a series of words being used in conjunction with each other appear here in an overlapping fashion. The underlined letters in lines 30 – 32 form the king's name "LOVIS"

by subbing L for O and again I for the same 1. Above this in Line 30, the italic letters spell "VSED" after substituting E for V and D for W. Removing these words allows us to pick out others.

30	M	T	A	S				
31	M	**The**	S̲	T				
32	T	I	A̲	S̲	F		D	H
33	S̲	E	D	G	*T*	*O*	I	E
34	O̲	T	V	Y	D	R	T	S
35	*E*	*T⊣*	H	I	A			
36	E	**Yt**	A	A	H			M
37	O	E	F	D	D			
38							T	

The complete words are used as they appear, the ligatured "The" in bold on Line 31, and "THAT" as the bold Yt symbol on Line 36. Removing some smaller words now (since they would be needed) will simplify things in terms of understanding, and the remainders tables to come. These include the underlined "SO" beginning Lines 33 and 34, the italic "THE" below on Line 35, as well as the bold-italic "TO" on Line 33. Lastly, Bacon uses the underlined-bold letters on Lines 31 and 32 to spell "ASS." Apparently Bacon felt disdainful toward the French King Louis XIII.

The first remainders table of this section appears here as Table 7-11:

Table 7-8

M	T	A	S			
M	T					
T	*I*	**F**	**D**	**H**		
E	***D***	**G**	**I**	**E**		
T	V	Y	D	R	T	S
H	I	A				
E	A	A	H	M		
O	**E**	**F**	**D**	D		
T						

In this remainders table only three constructions were chosen and used in the middle, and are delineated with bold, italics and underlining, as once again, Bacon used a group of overlapping acrostic anagrams for two of the words. The italic letters produce "TIED," while the bold letters spell "I FIGURED" with substitutions of R for H and V for E. The italic-underlined "I" provides another first person pronoun. Below these words we see the underlined letters. After substituting E for V and B for Y we can spell "DEBT." Below, we see the bold-underlined letters spell "FED."

The word bank accrued so far is GRANtS, TO, TRAP, BAIT, ROI LOUIS, USED, The, THAT, SO, THE, TO, ASS, TIED, I FIGURED, I, DEBT, and FED.

Removing these words and left justifying the remainders, allows one more important word to emerge.

Two words in Table 7 – 12 appear in the center and bottom line, and one has been prevalent as a theme in this key, in the bold-italic letters. Substituting an L for the O we have "ALIAS."

Table 7 - 9

M	T	**A**	**S**	
M	T			
R	T	*S*		
H	*I*	*A*		

Last of all, we can also spell a needed "AS" from the top row. For space purposes instead of yet another remainders table, the remaining letters are T M T R T H E A H M D T. While there were other constructions that can be made with these letters, none contextually seemed to make sense. Curious to see if any anagrams appeared in this set of leftover letters as had happened in other sections, I wasn't disappointed.

E	*A*	A	H	M
O	D			
T				

If we set aside the TTTT, the other letters can be arranged to spell "HE MR. W HAM" with a substitution W for D, or also "HE MR. de HAM." If we look at the quadruple Tau as a signature of Anthony Bacon, the sentence tells us that "Anthony, he Mr. de (of) Ham," meaning he was truly a Bacon. If we arrange the letters so that the repeating letters are together such as, TTTTMMHH, the remaining letters spell "READ." This becomes appropriate when checking values for cipher signatures.

Simple	19	19	19	19	12	12	8	8	17	5	1	4	143
	T	T	T	T	M	M	H	H	R	E	A	D	Sum
Reverse	6	6	6	6	13	13	17	17	8	20	24	21	157
Kaye	19	19	19	19	12	12	34	34	17	31	27	30	273

The Simple Cipher value of 143 is "Frater" and "Anthony" in Kaye Cipher. The Reverse sum of 157 is the value of "Fra. Rosi Crosse" in Simple. The Kaye Cipher total of 273 is the cipher signature for "William Shakespeare" and "King Francis Stuart III" in Reverse Cipher. The message of the signatures of the leftover letters becomes "Fra. Rosi Crosse Frater Anthony (and) William Shakespeare (and/or King Francis Stuart III)."

The message in this section tells an amazing story when combined with the previous section. The words in this last block of text states, "That alias fed bait to trap ass Roi Louis. I used the grants as I figured he tied to the debt."

Overall Message of E MASKER TT

It's appropriate to call this key the "Masker" as it seems to be about some of the "masks" Bacon wore as disguises. At the risk of revealing my own ignorance, I had never heard of Renaissance artist Tiberio Tinelli until finding his name in the cipher. Additionally, the idea that one of the greatest explorers in the history of the world, Samuel de Champlain, could have been an alias of Sir Francis Bacon would never have crossed anyone's mind because it seems impossible. I didn't believe it myself until I had found the corroborating evidence included in a later chapter, and it's still difficult. As stated earlier, I've since removed the word "impossible" from my vocabulary.

This section of Bacon's message claims to reveal not only some of Bacon's aliases, but an impressive role as a navigator and artist. The messages as they appeared are as follows:

- Tiberio Tinelli was good, but best alias was Samuel de Champlain.
- I am native party there au St. Tongois dock. I led fleet west.
- King sent me to oversee work, but I reign my nation.
- James send me to stop Captain Walt Raleigh Caribbean campaign.
- I time the meridians. F. Drake chose me as the wisest astronomer.
- That alias fed bait to trap ass Roi Louis. I used the grants as I figured he tied to the debt.

Placing these messages in a proper chronological order, an interesting story emerges. It would seem that in his early years, assuming soon after the death of Sir Nicholas Bacon, a young Francis returns from France where he had been learning to paint. Without a full inheritance, as implied in one of the acrostics, he had to go to work, and what better job for a young man of his time and station to take than as a navigator for the greatest sailor in England at the time, Sir Francis Drake?

174

The time he and Anthony Bacon spent together in Gray's Inn, was spent creating many of their aliases to conduct their intelligence work. As an artist, he would have direct access to the courts of royalty around Europe. He would have been able then and later, to create paintings and engravings of his aliases as authentication of a real person. Only a man of means would have the ability to contract such works, creating credibility of the identities as true personages. As a sailor with known privateer Sir Francis Drake, a man in Bacon's position would have been able to live a life of adventure, and even dupe King Louis XIII into not only funding his exploration of the New World but providing him his own nation to govern.

While the added cipher signature system also repeated many of these messages, only after finding corroborating evidence, did I accept these messages as being valid. You'll be able to decide for yourself after it is presented in the following chapters.

Chapter 8 – Another Impossibility – Key 32 Revisited

As previously mentioned at the end of Chapter 3, I discovered messages that completely had been over-looked within the transposition cipher produced by Key 32. I had missed these ciphers for a few significant reasons – I had incorrectly assumed that such a simple solution wouldn't produce any notable messages without using more algorithms to transpose the characters a second or third time; and I had no real idea what I was doing in those initial stages. This series of ciphers teaches the reader how to unravel them the deeper one goes into them. At the time, I counted myself lucky to have found the few phonetic messages and signposts noted in Chapter 3. So while preparing this text for publishing and editing that chapter, I spotted a clue. As the ciphers of Key 32 corroborate the information in Chapter 9, I offer the following as an additional message here. It began with an RC signpost.

The acrostic in the first three columns of rows 24 – 26 spelled out "ROSY MAP MAKER" as seen here in Table 8-1:

Table 8 - 1

24	E	R	O
25	P	*R*	S
26	A	M	Y

As you can once again see, starting at the "12 o'clock" position with R, proceeding clockwise reads "ROSY MAP." By reusing three letters and substituting the K for P, beginning at 6 o'clock, we see "MAKER." Since so much information in Key 38 that seemed to appear in and around its acrostics, it seemed logical the same idea would be at work here, which precipitated the decision to take a closer look in this area of Key 32.

In the lines of characters on rows 22 – 29, I saw a now familiar name in the form of an acrostic anagram.

22	*A̲*	T	S	N	S	E	O
23	*L̲*	A	A	A	A	O	K
24	*E̲*	R	O	M	ME	I	N
25	*P̲*	*R̲*	S	R	P	W	E
26	*A̲*	*M̲*	Y	H	*N̲*	E	E
27	*I̲*	T	*E̲*	*S*	*A*	I	T⊣
28	*C̲*	V	*W̲*	T	*M*	*V*	*O*
29	I	E	A	F	H	*E*	D

The underlined-italics letters along the left, after substituting an H for the R, spell "CHAMPLAI." Below and to the right we can see "DE" with a substitution of D for W. To the right of this, the italic-bold letters spell "SAMVEL" after subbing L for O," and juxtaposed above is the italic-underlined "N" needed to complete the last name, "CHAMPLAIN." So, in the exact section of the "ROSY MAP MAKER" acrostic, we see the name of the famous explorer and cartographer, Samuel de Champlain just as it had appeared in the previous chapter.

   While noting this in the original inspection of this key, the obvious notion was Champlain belonged to the Fra. Rosi Crosse. However, considering the previous chapter, a much closer reading of Key 32 seemed necessary. And delving into his background to try to flesh-out a small part of the story of the mysterious RC brotherhood, much of Champlain remained in those shadows.

   Living in Northern New York in the St. Lawrence River Valley, a short drive from southern Canada, the cities Montreal, Quebec City, and Burlington, Vermont on Lake Champlain, are favored weekend destinations. The influence of Samuel de Champlain is everywhere we look. And yet, I was surprised by how little is known about the childhood and early adult life of this giant. However, this was beginning to make sense. From what I have gleaned from my current research, it seems Bacon followed a pattern with his aliases. They were often based upon a real person whose name may have been similar to the name he used. The obvious example would be the actor Willam Shaksper (also Shaxper), and the name on the plays, William Shakespeare.

   In a real sense, an extreme modern-day version of this would be identity theft. This is hardly a new phenomenon. In fact, our modern intelligence agencies such as the Central Intelligence Agency often have followed Bacon's playbook when it comes to aliases and secret identities. For example, one method a field agent would use would be to go to a county clerk's office, and rummage through the copies of birth certificates of children who died as babies. While this would be more difficult today, the method remains the same. They would select one whose birth date closely matched their own, and use the birth certificate as a basis of a new identity in a completely different part of the country. This is just the modern day equivalent of Francis and Anthony were doing as part of their spy-craft. But back to the messages.

The acrostics draw our attention to a specific area to provide some context, and then the messages within that area provided still more context. Again using the techniques on Key 32 used on the later keys produced the following results.

After digging into Lines 22 – 29 and finding the name of the explorer and cartographer, I decided to look for any acrostics that might appear in the first section. In the very first row, one instantly stood out that was missed in the initial analysis, beginning with the "Y" below the "T" in the second column of the second row. It appears in bold:

1	**A**	**P**	**B**	**S**	**P**	**E**	**E**	V	6	
2	**E**	T	S	O	T⊣	I	**B**	T	S	3
3	**E**	**Y**	O	*O*	*K*	*O*	*S*	*T*	*I*	
4	M	G	∧	F	W	Q	O	I	*H*	E

Subbing B for Y in Row 3, and conversely a Y for B in Row 1 with K for P, the bold letters spell "BEE APYS KEE." The underlined letters also spell BEES, and subbing an R for H below the I and an L for an O, we have KLOSTRI, a phonetic spelling of a Latin word for "key." Enclosed by these words, the letters "I T⊣ O" can be interpreted as "I 33," but also adding the "T S" gives a sum of 70. The number 70 is the Kaye Cipher value of "Rex."

Another obvious message that reinforced the messages of the other transposition ciphers, appeared on the right side of the table of characters in the transposition of Key 32, in Lines 3 – 6 (which can be read as C – F, or "SEE F):

Table 8 - 2

S	**T**	**I**	
O	**I**	H	E
S	**A**	**D**	
Ys	**W**	V	D

Appropriately enough, the bold letters actually form the shape of the lowercase letter "f," and can be read as follows. By subbing F for T, the juxtaposed letters spell "F II" as in "Francis II." Starting with the W at the bottom and reading up and to the left we see "WAS." Again from the same starting position, by subbing D for W, and reading upward and to the right, we read "DAD." The word "dad" comes from Middle English, so it would have been in usage in Bacon's time, and even its obsolete spelling of "Dadde" can be constructed with the juxtaposed letters. So in the shape of a lower case "f" in Lines 3 – 6 (or C – F) we read the message, "F. II WAS DAD" or Francis II was dad. The message continues, however.

In looking at the other letters around this acrostic we can complete the message by substituting E for the underlined V. The Ys symbol spells "THIS" and the letters in the upper left spell "SO." Beneath this we clearly see "SAD" and on the right the word "HE." Starting in the lower right corner with the D and our substituted E, with the D A above it we have an acrostic anagram for "DEAD." The message then reads THIS SO SAD HE DEAD. If we are inclined to reuse the I's and S's we can even write out the complete thought, "Francis II was Dad. This is so sad he is dead."

Line by Line Acrostic Anagrams

Time for the section-by-section analysis. Here are Lines 1 – 5:

1	A	P	B	S	**P**	**E**	**E**	V	6	
2	**E**	T	S	O	T⊣	I	***B̲***	**T**	**S**	3
3	E	*Y̲*	*O*	***O̲***	***K̲***	***O̲***	***S̲***	T	I	
4	*M̲*	**G**	A	*F*	W	Q	O	I	**H**	E
5	R	O	T	V	H	W	S	A	D	

The bold-italic-underlined characters in Lines 2 and 3 are the first obvious acrostic anagram, spelling "BOOKS" without substitutions. The very first character in Line 1 appropriately is "A." I took this clue as a symbol of light shining downward to something we should "see."

Sure enough, two words appear together directly below, the bold letters spell "SEE" by subbing S for G, and the underlined-italic letters spell "MY." Between these words and the "BOOKS" the italic letters spell "OF." Using this as more context, we're then able to pick out the plain bold letters at the top and right – "P E E T S 3 I H." Subbing a V for an E, C for 3 and R for H, the word "PICTURES" comes into focus. After removing these characters, we move on to the next round of selections in Table 8 - 3.

Table 8 - 3

A	P	B	S	V	6		
T	S	O	T⊣	I			
T							
A	**W̲**	Q	O	I	*E̲*		
R̲	**O**	**T**	**V̲**	H	W	*S̲*	*A̲*

In the lower left, the underlined-bold characters spell "WROTE" by substituting E for V. By picturing the removal of this word, we can see an acrostic anagram appear to the right in context with Champlain, with the underlined-italic letters, "SEA." To the far left is the obvious word in italics which seems to match the meaning of sea, "AT."

Removing these characters, we can form the remainders table:

Table 8 - 4

A	**P**	**B**	S	V	*6̲*
T	**S**	*O̲*	T⊣	I	
Q	O	*I*			
H	W				

With references to Champlain and the sea, the bold characters on the left side of the table were obvious as "SHIP BOATS" with one substitution of I for the Q. The word makes sense because these small utility boats would be used with sailing ships during the age of exploration. The italicized letter "I" provides the subject for the previously found action word "WROTE." With the removal of ship-boats, a left justification places the 6 over O. The underlined-italic letters provide a needed "OF" with F in place of 6. The

180

leftover letters of V – T⊣ - I – W spell a known variant of the time, "WIT⊣E" with a substitution of E for V.

All of the words in this section appear as BOOKS, SEE, MY, PICTURES, WROTE, SEA, AT, SHIP BOATS, I, OF and WIT⊣E. At this point, the best grammatical constructions begin to make sense considering what we now know about Francis Bacon due to the previous cipher texts. Also as the rest of the messages are revealed, things will become clearer still. The sentence states, "I WROTE BOOKS AT SEA. SEE MY PICTURES OF SHIP BOATS."

If it hadn't been for the previous chapter, this would have been confusing, and I would have scanned Key 32 for any other acrostics that could help answer how or why Bacon could have "written books at sea."

6	I	T	Y	D	S	M	Ys	W	V	D
7	M	E	E	E	NT	D	C	N	N	
8	Y	R	T	E	L	H	C	A	E	5
9	T	Æ	G	O	V	D	The	V	T	
10	O	E	T	T	T⊣	T⊣	D	E	O	I
11	R	S	H	W	O	R	R	L	I	
12	C	**M**	**B**	**A**	**H**	W	O	Yt	E	1

First of all, note the complete words this section contains such as "THE," "THIS" as Ys, and "THAT" as Yt.

At first I noted that the letters in Line 12 with the usual substitutions for Y for B and R for H spell "MARY." After some deciphering, I was able to identify a message that repeated the usual message appearing in the other keys. In this instance, he states that Mary worried his true great identity would change the world. It also "tied out" using the leftover letters as a signature, one of which was 133, which is the Simple Cipher signature of both, "Baron Verulam" and "KING FRANCIS III." However, the message regarding books he had written at sea provided a different context that needed to be pursued.

Knowing individual keys produced multiple messages, following the evidence already deciphered provided that context. In the previous section, he stated he wrote a book at sea, and in the section below, the message named Samuel de Champlain as a "ROSY MAP MAKER." Using these messages as the context for Lines 6 – 12, they should provide more information about Bacon as the enigmatic explorer.

Starting fresh with the same set of characters and using this information as context, we begin with the obvious choices of "THIS, THAT and THE" as whole word constructions. With Yt, Ys and THE removed, I looked for obvious constructions that fit this new context:

6	I	T	Y	D	**<u>S</u>**	M	***W***	***V***	D	
7	*<u>M</u>*	*<u>E</u>*	E	**<u>E</u>**	**<u>Nt</u>**	D	C	***N***	N	
8	Y	R	T	E	L	H	***<u>C</u>***	***<u>A</u>***	E	5
9	T	*<u>Æ</u>*	***<u>G</u>***	*<u>O</u>*	*<u>V</u>*	***<u>D</u>***	V	***<u>T</u>***		
10	O	E	T	T	T⊣	T⊣	**D**	E	O	I
11	R	S	H	W	O	R	**R**	**L**	I	
12	C	M	B	A	H	**W**	**O**	E	A	

Shocked but encouraged, at the center of the arrangement in Lines 8 and 9, the bold-underlined-italic letters with substitutions S for G spell "TADOUSAC," an accepted variant spelling of "Tadoussac," France's fur trading outpost in Quebec, Canada at the time. In Lines 6 and 7, the bold-underlined letters spell "SENT." To the left in Line 7, the underlined letters spell "ME," while to the right in Lines 6 and 7 the bold-italic letters spell "NEW" after subbing E for V. Lastly, we see the bold letters in the lower right spell "WORLD." There are other obvious words, but removing the letters forming the words "SENT ME TADOUSAC THE NEW WORLD," allows for easier descriptions. Considering the context of the fur-trading outpost allows us to see what other words would appear.

For reasons that will be obvious, it didn't take long to find obvious words fitting this context, especially since more than one acrostic anagram to spell "FUR." When a word is important to the context, he provides multiple opportunities to form it. Beginning with the bold letters in the first column, by subbing an F for the T we spell "FOR," and in the underlined-bold letters to the right, again with a substitution of an F for the T we see the word "FUR." The

I	T	Y	D	M	D			
E	D	C	N					
Y	**<u>R</u>**	**<u>T</u>**	E	L	H	E	5	
T	**<u>V</u>**							
O	***E***	***T***	T	T⊣	T⊣	E	O	I
R	S	***H***	***W***	O	R	I		
C	M	B	**A**	H	E	A		

italic-bold letters in the lower center left, with substitutions for R for H and D for W, spell "TRADE." This produces a partial sentence, "SENT ME TADOUSAC THE NEW WORLD FOR FUR TRADE." Next, consulting the remaining letters table allows the identification of any words appear that would complete this part of the message.

Table 8 - 7

I	T	Y	D	M	D
E	D	*C*	N		
Y	E	L	***H***	***E***	5
T	**T⊣**	T⊣	E	O	I
S	**O**	R	I		
C	<u>*M*</u>	<u>*B*</u>	H	E	A

Wondering "who" sent him, led to the bold-italic letters *CHE*, which after substitutions of X for C and R for H, spells "REX." The bold letters in the lower left provide the needed preposition, "TO." The underlined-italic letters in the bottom row spell "MY" after subbing Y for B. While one intriguing word kept appearing, it wasn't used until all other possibilities had been exhausted. Removing these last few characters provided this table of remaining letters:

Table 8 - 8

I	T	Y	D	M	D
E	D	**N**			
Y	E	L	5		
T	T⊣	E	O	**I**	
S	R	I			
C	H	E	A		

The italic letters from the bottom two rows spelled "I SEARCH." The D and E in the second column could also be a part of those words as well, to form the past-tense "SEARCHED," but they were better suited for a different purpose. Lastly, the one word that kept appearing in the upper left corner throughout the process appears in bold, "IDENTITY" with no substitutions. This could also be "IDENTIFY" by substitution of F for T. The last step would be to pick through the remaining letters to flesh out the message:

Table 8 - 9

Y	M	D
D		
E	L	5
T⊣	E	O

The remaining letters spell "DEEMED," with the leftover letters being (from the bottom upward) T⊣ O L Y. For the first time, the double Tau symbol was used as an H instead of a single T as we've seen multiple times, so the leftover letters spell "HOLY." However, using these letters to check the work so far, adding the letters in Simple Cipher are very interesting, as each step produces a Bacon cipher signature. T⊣ + O = 33. Adding L we have 44. Adding Y we arrive at 67. In Reverse Cipher, these letters equal 33. Since all of the values of these leftovers are above 10, the result of Kaye Cipher is the same as Simple Cipher, 33, 44 and 67. However, there is a possibility the word *could* be used.

Logically speaking, perhaps "Holy" is referring to the King of France as mentioned in the last chapter as an "ass." Since it was a Catholic nation, the message could read, "The Holy Rex sent me Taddousac New World for fur trade." At this point, the message so far seems to echo that of the previous chapter, along with the additional words DEEMED, IDENTIT(F)Y and SEARCH, with no leftover letters.

This was the point when I finally believed I had worked out the system Bacon used. As you probably have noticed from key to key, there were times when the decryption procedure evolved, though following the same standard operating procedure. In the last chapter, there were specific instances where it "made sense" to reuse letters. While that works as a valid method, I encourage you to do the following if you plan to do any work with these keys. After decrypting a block of text using the methods as outlined at the beginning, revisit the same section using the procedure a second time. Use the first message for the context for the second, looking for new acrostic anagrams. That procedure was used in the following section in this second look at Lines 7 – 13:

7	M	E	E	E	Nt	D	C	N	N	
8	Y	R	T	E	L	H	C	A	E	5
9	T	Æ	G	O	V	D	The	V	*T*	
10	O	E	T	T	T⊣	T⊣	D	E	*O*	I
11	R	S	H	W	O	R	R	L	I	
12	C	M	B	A	H	W	O	Yt	E	A
13	O	L	R	S	S	T	M	E	O	

Using Champlain and the maritime theme as context, it's reasonable that the name of his ship should appear somewhere. In this section, it's found in Lines 7-10. Beginning in Line 7, Using the conjoined Nt as N and subbing O for L, reveals "DON." Below this on Line 9, subbing E for V produces "DE."

After removing the underlined-italic "TO," gives us "DIEU." So, the name of Champlain's ship, "The Don de Deiu" or "Gift of God" appears around the ligatured "THE." The words so far become "THE DON DE DIEU" and "TO."

7	*M*	E	E	*E*			C	N	N	
8	*Y*	*R*	*T*	*E*		H	C	A	E	5
9	T	Æ	G	*O*						
10	O	*E*	*T*	T	T⊣	T⊣				
11	R	*S*	*H*	*W*	O	**R**	R	L	I	
12	C	M	*B*	*A*	H	**W**	**O**	*Yt*	E	A
13	O	L	R	S	**S**	**T**	**M**	**E**	O	

184

Knowing Champlain's exploration sought a passage to the Pacific ocean, it was easy to locate the next word in Lines 10 – 13 in bold characters. With one substitution of N for M, the acrostic anagram spells "NORTHWEST." To the right, we use the underlined "Yt" character as "THAT." The bold-italic letters in Lines 7 – 9 in the form of a Tau on its side, subbing one V for E spell "ROVTE." To the left of this appears the word "MY." Below in Lines 10 – 11 the bold-italic letters spell "SHUT" by subbing V for E. Lastly, in the attached underlined letters that wrap around the "H," we spell "WAY" by subbing Y for B.

At this point, the word bank contains the following: DEEMED, IDENTIFY, SEARCH, THE DON DE DIEU, TO, NORTHWEST, THAT, ROVTE, MY, SHUT and WAY. Removing all of these from this block and left justifying the characters produces the first remainders table. Looking at the word bank gives the context to find the rest of the words to flesh out this message about using the *Don de Dieu* to search for the fabled "Northwest Passage." They again appear here in the following acrostic anagrams in Table 8 - 10:

Table 8 - 10

E	E	**C**	**N**	N
H	**C**	**A**	**E**	5
T	Æ	G		
O	*T*	T⌐		
R	*O*	R	L	*I*
C	M	H	E	*A*
O	L	R	*S*	*O*

The first two words to stand out to me were the bold-underlined letters in the left column, and the bold-italic letters in the lower right corner. The letters in the left column after a substitution of F for T spells "FOR," which probably would follow the word "SEARCH." The lower right corner, after subbing L for O spells "SAIL." The bold letters in the first two rows spell "CHANCE" with no substitutions. Lastly, in the column beside "FOR" we see another useful preposition "TO." This table therefore adds the words - FOR, SEARCH, SAIL, CHANCE and TO, to our word bank.

Word Bank:
DEEMED, IDENTIFY, SEARCH, THE DON DE DIEU, TO, NORTHWEST, THAT, ROVTE, MY, SHUT, WAY, FOR, SEARCH, SAIL, CHANCE and TO.

As we still have multiple characters remaining, removing the above and constructing a few more remainders' tables should round out the word bank and the message:

Table 8 - 11

E	E	*N*	
5			
Æ	G		
T⊣			
R	L		
C	M	**H**	**E**
O	L	R	

Considering the context of the current word bank and the previous messages, two necessary words appear. Near the bottom of Table 10-11, the bold-underlined letters spell "REX" after subbing X for C and R for H. Above this is a word repeated in another cipher text. The italicized letters spell "GRÆNT⊣" or "GRANT," with no substitutions, adding the words REX and GRANT to our bank.

Organizing our remainders one last time in Table 8 – 12 will complete the message with no leftover letters:

E	E	
5		
M		
O	L	R

The bold letters in the left column spell "MEO" after replacing 5 with E, Latin for "my." The remaining letters, after a substitution of V for E spell "RULE."

For this section, the word bank expands to the following group of words, which will be used to form an intelligible message: DEEMED, IDENTIFY, SEARCH, THE DON DE DIEU, TO, NORTHWEST, THAT, ROVTE, MY, SHUT, WAY, FOR, SEARCH, SAIL, CHANCE, TO REX, GRANT, MEO, and RULE. The message can be rendered as the following:

"REX GRANT MY DON DE DIEV TO SEARCH The NORTHWEST SAIL ROVTE, THAT WAY SHVT. IDENTIFY CHANCE FOR MEO RULE."

This is yet another cipher text stating that Bacon viewed New France as his kingdom. This message also reinforces the idea that he in a sense, "tricked" King Louis XIII into "footing the bill" by using the alias of Samuel de Champlain. This is reinforced by naming Champlain's ship, the Don de Dieu, granted to him by the king, in order to search for the sailing route we know as the fabled "Northwest Passage," all of which are corroborated by the orthodox view of history. Of course, our orthodox history corroborates these messages with the exception Sir Francis Bacon used the alias of Samuel de Champlain to accomplish it.

Perhaps another clue appears in the first three columns of the last two rows of Key 32, Lines 31 and 32:

31	V	O	S
32	I	O	N

Here we see the name of Champlain's "Holy King," Louis XIII, by substituting L for an O and using the Simple Cipher value of the letter N, 13.

While working on Lines 14 – 25, I hit an impasse. Two different messages seem to surface in this area of the transpositions, but nothing "tied-out" using the checking system at first. This was particularly frustrating as it was the first time that a message couldn't completely be decrypted. While some messages appeared regarding "gathering evidence at the Isthmus of Panama" associated with the name "Walt R," fleshing out the message wasn't possible until much later. Another message specifically repeats a part of the cipher text found in Key 38 regarding the Oak Island mystery. With mentions of his "thesauri" and "worked stones" and "the knee of Herakles," it appears that Bacon truly wanted that message to get through. Using a technique that had provided break throughs in the other key permutations, the next step was to work backward to see if the last lines of Key 32 would provide context for what lay between. Another message did appear, again about Sir Francis Drake.

In this section in Lines 26 – 32, one more tantalizing message can be deciphered:

26	**A**	**M**	Y	H	N	E	<u>E</u>	*I*	I	
27	*I*	**T**	E	<u>S</u>	<u>A</u>	<u>I</u>	<u>T̚</u>	***H***	***T***	***T***
28	C	V	W	T	M	V	<u>O</u>	***S***	B	
29	I	**E**	A	F	H	E	<u>**D**</u>	L	G	T
30	**S**	**V**	**E**	**N**	I	A	<u>**R**</u>	V	T	
31	V	O	**S**	**S**	**E**	**A**	<u>**A**</u>	A	P	6
32	I	O	N	G	N	<u>**K**</u>	<u>**F**</u>	<u>**E**</u>	I	P

Beginning from left to right, the italic "I" on Line 27 provides the first-person pronoun. In bold letters at the beginning of 26 and 27 is the acrostic anagram "MATE." Next the underlined letters spell "SAILETH" with one substitution of L for O, in the shape of a sideways Tau. The bold italic letters to the right also in a sideways Tau, after subbing F for T and R for H, spells "FIRST." Below this in the underlined bold letters, we plainly see the name of his captain, "F. DRAKE." To the left, words often associated with him appear in bold letters: "SEVEN SEAS" with no substitutions.

Removing these constructions, we can clear the way for more acrostic anagrams in the remainders table:

Table 8 - 13

Y	H	N	E	**I**			
C	V	**W**	**T**	M	V	B	
I	*A*	F	**H**	**E**	L	G	T
I	*A*	V	T				
V	*O*	*A*	*P*	6			
I	*O*	*N*	<u>G</u>	<u>N</u>	<u>I</u>	<u>P</u>	

In this table two necessary words clearly appeared right away as indicated by the previous words as context. In bold at the top center of the table an intertwined "WITH THE" appears, sharing an H, meaning that the words would be used together. In the center of the bottom two rows, the italic letters N A P and the underlined G N I P spelled "MAPPING" after subbing M for N. This provided a context for the name associated with Drake and mapping, formed by the Italic letters along the left-hand side. Subbing B for Y and Z for A, the name of the famous mapper of the Cartegena campaign

187

"BOAZIO" is formed. Removing these words provides the next remainders table, 8 – 14:

Table 8 - 14

H	N	E		
C	V	M	**V**	**B**
F	**L**	G	T	
I	**V**			
V	6			
I				

The bold letters in the shape of a Y spell "CLUERE" after subbing the R for H, which is Latin for "becalled, said to be; be reckoned as existing." To the right, the bold underlined letters spell "BE" after a substitution of E for V. The last word in italics is the first-person pronoun "I."

In this section, the acrostic anagrams have produced the following Word Bank: I, MATE, SAILETh, FIRST, F. DRAKE, SEVEN SEAS, WITH THE, MAPPING, BOAZIO, CLUERE, BE and I. Working out the only logical sentence these words could form, a problem appears. Since "WITH THE" overlapped and shared letters, this indicated they would be used together, and the basic meaning of implied sentence was "I SAILETH WITH THE F. DRAKE." That's when I noted the mistake. Looking back at Table 8 – 13 on the previous page, you may have noted that while the letters that form the first part of "MAPPING," the N A P, are italic while the remainder are underlined. The actual rendering of these letters should have been "MAP" after the M for N substitution, and "KING" after subbing K for P. Therefore, the only logical message to be constructed here would be: I BE FIRST MATE SAILETH WITH THE SEVEN SEAS KING, F. DRAKE. I MAP CLUERE BOAZIO. Before examining other aspects of this decryption process and jumping into the significance of the message in the context of all the others, piecing together the narrative, let's tie out our left-over letters.

The unused letters of the main message, their values and sums appear in Table 8–15:

Table 8 - 15

Simple	13	12	6	7	19	9	20	6	92
	N	M	F	G	T	I	V	6 (F)	Sums
Reverse	12	13	19	18	6	16	5	19	108
Kaye	13	12	32	33	19	35	20	32	196

Simple and Reverse tied-out immediately as "Bacon" and "Francis" in Reverse Cipher. I saw 196 and knew that it equaled no signature of Bacon or his true identity. When this would happen at the beginning of the process the assumption was that a mistake had been made. However, the previous key had taught to check for signatures related to the message itself.

I initially tallied the values of the name Giovanni Battista Boazio, noting that all of combinations of sums would be far too high. So of course the focus shifted to the other name mentioned, the King of the Seven Seas, Sir Francis Drake. The sums of his name appear in Table 8–16:

	Simple	Reverse	Kaye
Francis	67	108	171
Drake	37	88	115
Sums	104	**196**	186

The values of 67, 108, and 171 are obvious as they share the name Francis. Here the last value produced by Kaye Cipher in Table 8–15 of left-over, unused characters also produce 196, the Reverse Cipher signature of "Francis Drake."

This message states that Bacon sailed with Francis Drake as First Mate, and that he also performed the role of Drake's mapper, Giovanni Battista Boazio. After digging into Bacon's aliases, a few patterns have emerged. The first appears when calculating the value of the last name in Simple Cipher. While adding the values of each letter a Bacon signature appears, and the very next letter is always one of our "symbolic characters" discussed in the Chapter 1. The letters A or O as symbols of light, the Tau of truth, or an "I" to see that truth, occur next. For example, when adding the values of "Champlain" in Simple Cipher, adding "L" to "C-H-A-M-P" produces a total of 50, the signature of "Fr. III" in Simple. The letter "A" as a symbol of light immediately follows. Second, the last name usually contains some sort of pun, such as the name "Champlain" not only meaning "field of wool" but contains the French word "l'ain" meaning "oldest boy." Also, looking at the initials produces 18 and 3 in Simple Cipher. The number 183 is the cipher signature of "Francis Stewart" in Reverse. The value in Kaye Cipher of Samuel Champlain is 322, which is the Simple Cipher signature of "Francis Stuart-Valois-Angouleme."

The values using the Fourfold Cipher has been the key to understanding the relationship between Bacon and his aliases. First, I look at the multiple letter combinations and their values in isolation before adding the values of the single letters. In Champlain's case, we begin with AAA (49) MM (36) and LL (35). These values total 120 which is the value of "Stuart" in Kaye, and "King Francois" in Simple Cipher. Adding in the values of each of the single letters (S V C H P I N), the total comes to 206, the value of "Rex Francis Bacon" in Fourfold Cipher itself. Considering this, it's no surprise the same pattern appears when looking at "Giovanni Battista Boazio."

The most obvious feature of the name is the presence of "Boaz" in the name. One of the two famous pillars from the porch of Solomon's Temple, Jachin and Boaz figure prominently in the Old Testament and in Freemasonry. Boaz is the pillar meaning "in him / it is strength." After this in the name appears the first-person pronoun "I" followed by "O" as a symbol of light. Adding the letters in Simple up to I equals 50, just before the symbol of light, "O." Just like the example above, the total of 50 represents "Fr. III" in Simple Cipher. The initials of G B B are very interesting as well. Letter G represents "Bacon" and the B's can represent "BEES," and likewise we can use BB as 22, the number of Tav in the

Hebrew alphabet. In number form, arranging them as 227 produces the Fourfold Cipher value of "Sir Francis Bacon." However, one of the main tools in understanding the aliases is the Fourfold Cipher.

In looking at "Battista Boazio" as he was also commonly known, an interesting pattern emerges. Identifying all of the duplicate letters and their values in this alias produces the following letters (in the order they appear) and values: BB (26) AAA (49) TTT (67) II (33) OO (38). First of all, every number directly can be associated with Francis Bacon in Simple Cipher. 26 is actually Bacon's initials backwards, B F. 49 is the value of an abbreviated version of his name he had used as "Franci." The Triple Tau is 67, the finished version "Francis." The pillars "II" are 33, Bacon. The OO is 38, the double Tau in Simple, reinforcing O as a symbol of Light and Truth. These numbers total 213, or "BAC" as the first three letters of Bacon. We had the single leftover "S" and we have 231, the signatures for "Francis Stuart, Sir Francis Bacon, Rex Francis Bacon, and Francis Stewart III," all in Reverse Cipher. Incidentally, it's also the Kaye Cipher value of "Mary Stewart." (Author's note: A full discussion of the aliases and pseudonyms used by Francis Bacon, and the "formula" for verifying them, appears in the next book in this series, *The Ghosts of Bacon*).

One last observation before closing out this chapter, the last of the decryptions of the plaque ciphers. The interpretations in each chapter are the essence of the cipher texts and as such are incomplete. Here at the end of my learning curve, one last discovery was made. Each basic message appears as they were revealed, and they tie out using the signature-checking procedure. However there *is* one additional step. After finding the basic message, I think the intention is to go back to the section of the transposition with all of the characters back in place, and then find more anagrams that flesh-out the message as a whole. For example, in this last block of characters in Lines 26 – 32 of Key 32, returning to it and finding more anagrams provided the following additions to the original message:
I live my dream. I saileth as First Mate under the King of the Seven Seas.
Also by scanning the remaining characters in Table 8 – 13 where "BOAZIO" appears, all of the letters are also present to spell out "GIOVANNI BATTISTA" as well.

Here is a summary of the findings of this deep reading of Key 32:

- I WROTE BOOKS AT SEA. SEE MY PICTURES OF SHIP BOATS.
- THE HOLY REX SENT ME TADDOUSAC NEW WORLD FOR FUR TRADE.
- REX GRANT MY DON DE DIEV TO SEARCH The NORTHWEST SAIL ROVTE, THAT WAY SHVT. IDENTIFY CHANCE FOR MEO RULE.

- (The specific message of Lines 14 – 25 appears in the second book of this series, *The Ghosts of Bacon*).
- I BE FIRST MATE SAILETH WITH THE SEVEN SEAS KING, F. DRAKE. I MAP CLUERE BOAZIO

Though I now understand that the acrostic message of "SEE HAT" and the message regarding "SHIP BOATS" (plural) applies to more than one example, here is the one intended for Giovanni Battista Boazio. Taken from Boazio's famous map depicting the raid on Cartagena:

Figure 8 - 1

Though the original image contains vibrant colors, some important details can still be detected in this black and white image. As you will see in Champlain's 1612 map of New France, the cannons and waves have certain characteristics indicating they were created by the same artist. Also, the style of the scrollwork in the legends of both maps also indicate this (see Plate 13). Additionally, the large flag at the rear of the ship is the flag of Mary, Queen of Scots, as it combines the standard of England with the fleur des lis of Francis II (also later used in England). However, the most telling detail in my opinion appears as a lone figure in the ship boat, trailing behind (close-up Figure 8 – 2):

In this image, the striking detail to note is the hat as indicated by the acrostic. In most of the portraits of Bacon, he wears the characteristic brown hat. There also appears to be Hebrew letters on the side of the boat to the left of the figure. Lastly, note the 33 formed by the waves at the boat's prow.

As for the more detailed, fleshed-out messages, they are not necessary to understand the story that Bacon has told in the plaque ciphers. While many of these messages have been "fleshed out" at this point, some are too controversial to include at this time. I leave it to you the reader, to enjoy the thrill of discovery that made this project so fulfilling for me. Happy hunting.

Chapter 9 – The Plaque Character Counts and New Cipher Signatures

Though Chapter 1 presented the reader with multiple examples of the ways that numbering each character produces amazing correlations between symbolically significant letters and cipher signatures related to Bacon, that discussion had to remain incomplete at that time. As the messages of the cipher texts produce secret names of Francis Bacon, they later can be used to produce cipher signatures. As you have seen throughout these chapters, their signatures have appeared within the counts of the "leftover letters" of the ciphers. This inspired the question, what would happen if I created a list of the most likely names that Bacon could have used if Francis II had lived? The following table contains those possibilities. There were several others left out of the following table as they are the same as many of his known signatures, such as King Stuart (133) and Fr. Stuart III (144). However, the following were included as complete names to see what results they would yield.

These names and their values appear in Table 9 – 1 below. Signatures that correlated with the significant characters of A, F, G, H, I, T and the double Th symbol, in the regular count appear in **bold** font. Signatures that correlated with a significant character in the reverse or backwards count (not to be confused with Reverse Cipher) appear in *italics*:

	Simple	Reverse	Kaye
Francois	*81*	**119**	**185**
Francois Stuart	*175*	*175*	*305*
Francis Stewart	*167*	183	323
King Bacon	72	*153*	202
King Francis III	*133*	*181*	*289*
King Francois III	*147*	228	381

Roi Francois III	**148**	_202_	356
Francois III	_**108**_	_**167**_	**290**
Francis III	94	_121_	**198**

Table 9 - 1

Looking at the above table, a few features need to be pointed out. As mentioned above, some of the new signatures repeat previously known ones, such as 108, 133, 167 and of course 153. Out of all 27 signatures / numbers, only five do not match a symbolic or significant character, and three of those exceed the total number of characters on the plaque. So, out of the 25 possible "hits" this collection of numbers could produce, we have a total of 22 correlations. This is probably not statistically significant, considering a total of _50_ hits actually exists, because the results include a search from both the forward and backward counts. However, 17 of them are "hits" in terms of correlating with significant characters in _both_ the forward and backward counts. The forward count produced 17 correlations as did the reverse count, and as you can construe from Table 9 – 1, many of these signatures produced a correlation in both counts as indicated by appearing in both bold and italics.

If you recall, an image of the forward count of the plaque appears as Plate 7. Also, for the sake of organization purposes, these correlations are presented by cipher – Simple, Reverse and then Kaye, as well as the section of the plaque where they appear. This allows the inclusion of appropriate illustrations. First we'll deal with the regular count, started at the beginning at "I" with 1 and ending at "P" with 305 (See Plate 7).

Here in Figure 9-1, we can see the locations of characters 72, 108, 147, 148, 175, 181 and 185 from the Simple Cipher column:

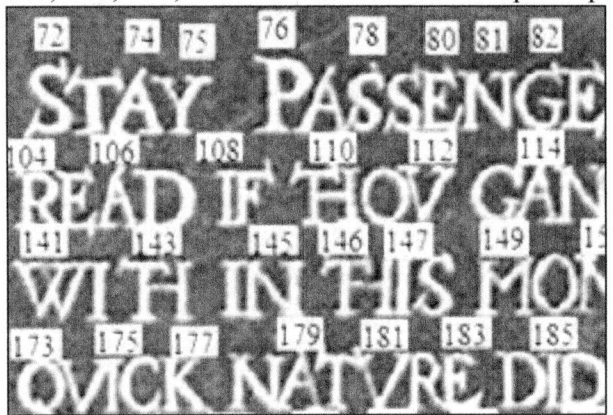

Figure 9-1

In the upper left, character 72 is the letter S, which can be the initial for Shakespeare, and knowing it can also be a G through the substitution system, we see the message that "King Bacon" is the secret behind Shakespeare. Next character number 108 (a common Bacon signature, but this time for "Francois III") we see the letter I for the message, "I, Francois III." Character number 147 again is the letter I telling us "I, King Francois III." Right beside it is 148, pointing out that the loss of the title "Roi Francois III" allowed Bacon to be Shakespeare as mentioned above.

194

Next, character 175 is Francois Stuart in both Simple and Reverse, and again is the letter I, stating "I, Francois Stuart." Character 181 is the letter V which stands for both Verulam and Valois-Angouleme (interestingly, opposite the 180 Tau is the A for the hyphenated name). Lastly in this section, character 185, "Francois" in Kaye Cipher, appears as the letter I, again telling us "I, Francois." Here in this area of the plaque we read "whom has been placed" in this "Tombe Shakespeare" five times, and we've only just begun.

Continuing in the regular count, we only will focus on characters numbered 119 and 153 at the heart of the plaque in Figure 9 – 2:

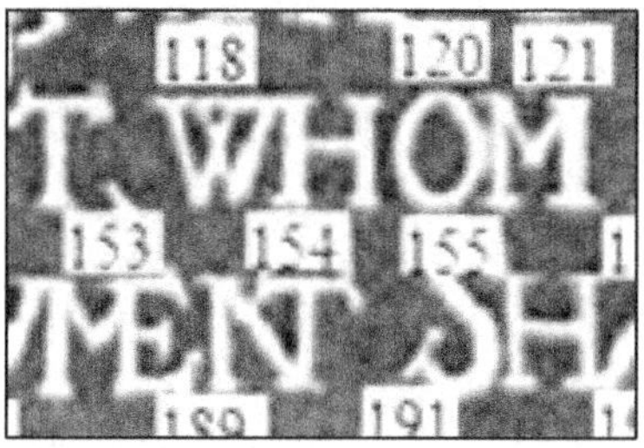

Figure 9-2

Here, character 119 as the signature for "Francois" in Reverse appears as the H in "WHOM," where the verse instructs to "read if you can whom death has placed in this tomb Shakespeare." The H of course the double Tau symbol. Juxtaposed with the word "WHOM" is character 153, the conjoined letters providing the answer by spelling "ME." And the answer appears in the number 153 the Simple Cipher signature for "Francis Verulam" and "I, Sir (or Rex) Francis Bacon." The next section contains three more correlations and two numbers are already familiar.

We recognize signatures of 133 and 167 as the Simple and Reverse Cipher signatures of Baron Verulam. However, when looking at Bacon's secret heritage, we see that 133 is "King Francis III" in Simple, and 167 is "Francis Stewart" *and* "Francois III" in Reverse. Lastly, 198 is "Rex Francois III" in Reverse Cipher. Using the regular count of the characters on the plaque we see in Figure 9 – 3, that 133 is the letter H, the double Tau.

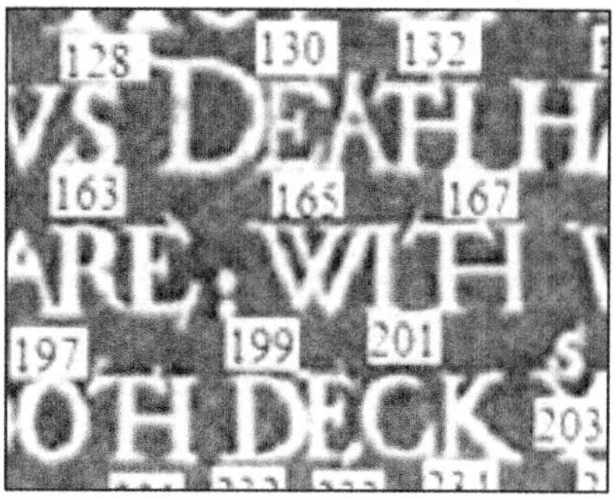

Character 133 is the letter H, a double Tau, just to the right of character 132 which is the TH double Tau symbol of Bacon. Directly below this juxtaposed with both, character 167 is another conjoined TH double Tau. While the double Tau is "TT," the juxtaposition represents the Triple Tau. As such, TT also represents the initials of Thirty-Three, all

Figure 9-3

of which represent "Bacon" in Simple. Character 198 is once again Bacon's conjoined TH symbol. An additional note about the number 198. This is a multiple of two Bacon signatures we have seen throughout this cipher. This number is the factor of 6 times 33, so in a sense it's the letter F (Francis) in Simple multiplied by the letter G (Bacon) in Kaye. Using the cipher signatures of 133, 167 and 198, all representing the names King Francis III, Francis Stewart, Francois III and Francis III, all therefore state that they are Thirty Three, or "Bacon." And still, we can read his name in other areas of the plaque.

The last three signature correlations appear in the lower right corner of the plaque in the area of the original keys of the transposition ciphers. They appear at characters numbered as 289, 290 and 305, which are the values of King Francis III, Francois III and Francois Stuart respectfully, all calculated in Kaye Cipher. Lastly, written as 2 (B), 8 (H), and 9 (I), with the double Tau symbol represented in H, can be read as an anagram of, "I be TT," which we know to be "I be Bacon." On to Figure 9 – 4:

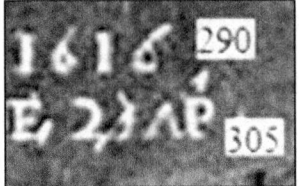

Figure 9-4

Rounding out this discussion of the regular or forward count, the first character we see in the 289th position is the second number 1 of the year 1616. This of course is the letter A in Simple, here the symbol sheds light and truth upon his noble birth as King Francis III. Right next to it we see character 290, the second number 6, which is F in Simple and T or Tau in Reverse. This points us to the Truth of F, or Francis, under his rightful name Francois III. Lastly, character number 305 is P, the last letter of the forward or regular count. While not considered to be an important or symbolic character, in this instance we have a unique case. First of all, it's extremely "coincidental" that the Kaye Cipher signature for the French version of his "real name," Francois Stuart, would be the exact number of characters on the plaque, 305. Additionally, as you'll see in the backward count of the characters, 305 is the letter "I." Also note the "misplaced comma" feature above it, as a slanted "7." Though speculation, this could mean to substitute the letter K from Reverse Cipher. Let's consider the nature of the messages of the cipher texts in the previous chapters and the nature of the Francis II's death. Then we can interpret the mark above it as a diadem or crown, and the K can represent the word "King," making the message, "Removing the P (Piss ear), I, King Francois Stuart."

A speculation, but once again an interesting one. Looking at the backwards count of the characters of the plaque, beginning with "P" at the lower right as 1 and the afore-mentioned "I" as 305 produces the same number of interesting correlations.

Again for convenience and clarity sake, Table 9-1 appears below. This time we'll focus on the signatures in italics as they represent the signatures matching significant letters in this backwards count:

Table 9 - 1	Simple	Reverse	Kaye
Francois	*81*	**119**	**185**
Francois Stuart	*175*	*175*	*305*

196

Francis Stewart	*167*	183	323
King Bacon	*72*	*153*	*202*
King Francis III	*133*	*181*	*289*
King Francois III	*147*	228	381
Roi Francois III	*148*	*202*	356
Francois III	*108*	*167*	*290*
Francis III	94	*121*	*198*

While planning how to arrange the following set of illustrations, an interesting geometric alignment presented itself.

In a large part of the left section of the plaque, 6 correlations appear. And by plotting them on the plaque, they form a right triangle with angles of 90 – 45 – 45, as you'll see in Figure 9 – 5:

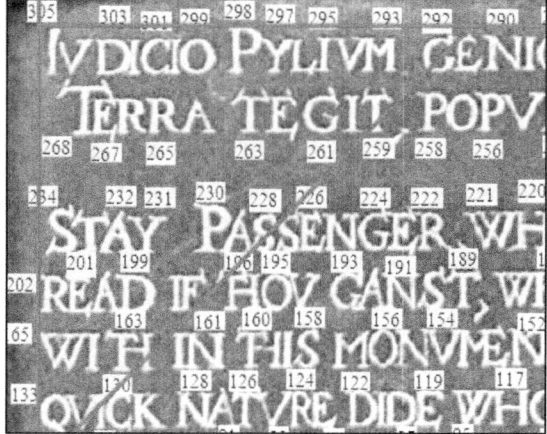

Figure 9 - 5

Going left to right, character 305 is obvious as the letter "I." 305 is the cipher signature of "Francois Stuart" in Kaye, so another answer of whose name appears on the plaque states, "I, Francois Stuart." Moving to the right, the next signature is 289, the Kaye Cipher signature for King Francis III. It appears on the far upper right as "I" in "GENIO," again answering the question of the name the plaque implores us to read.

Below this is character 228, the Reverse Cipher signature of "King Francois III" associated with the letter "S." At this point the reader will recognize that through the cipher substitution system, "G" serves as the Bacon signature in this example. Below this, we see 202 appearing as an "R" which becomes "H," the double Tau letter.

Character 202 represents two signatures, as "Roi Francois III" in Reverse, and "King Bacon" in Kaye. Next and to the right beside the hypotenuse of the triangle we see 198, the Kaye Cipher signature for "Francis III," appears as "I." Also, remember that 198 represents the Triple Tau in that 19 = T and 8 = H the double Tau, while it's also the

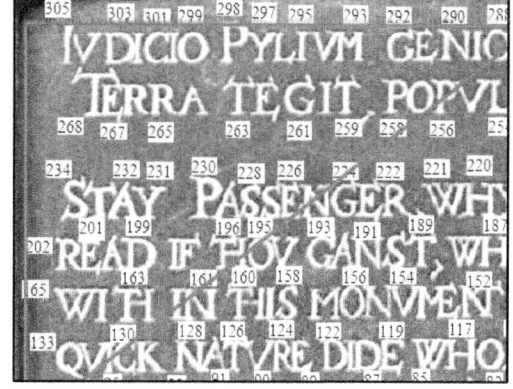

Figure 9 - 6

197

product of 6 times 33, or in a sense, F. Bacon. At the lowest angle of the triangle, we see character 133 of the backward count appearing as "Q," which is again the letter "I" after our substitution. The last character with a significant correlation in this image appears outside of the triangle. This is character number 121, the signature for "Francis III" in Reverse Cipher, appearing as "I" in the word "DIDE." Moving on to the center of the plaque, we can look at four more signature correlations. If we incorporate character 289, the "I" in "GENIO," into the triangle we form a perfect 3 – 4 – 5 Pythagorean right triangle with angles of 90 – 37 – 53.

In Figure 11-7, we'll see 153 (again), 81 **Figure 9 - 7** as "Francois" in Simple, 147 as "King Francois III" in Simple, and 181 As "King Francis III" in Reverse:

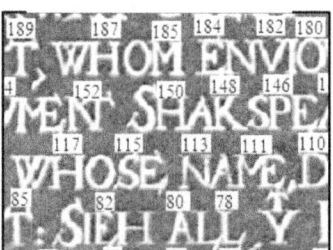

On the left we see the familiar character 153 as the ligatured "ME." Below this appears character 81(Francois in Simple) as the "H" in "SIEH," the double Tau, as if to say "SIEH Francois Bacon (TT)." Next, we move up and to the right to character 147, the "S" in the middle of "Shakespeare." Subbing G for S, we see the familiar Bacon signature. Lastly, above and to the right we see character 181 as "I" in "Envious," with yet another name to read in this monument Shakespeare, as "King Francis III" in Reverse Cipher Moving on to the last four signature correlations, we find them on the right side of the plaque.

In this last section, we'll see the correlations between characters 108 (Francois III in Simple), 175 (Francois Stuart in Simple *and* Reverse), 72 (King Bacon in Simple), and 167 (Francis Stewart in Simple, *and* Francois

Figure 9 - 8

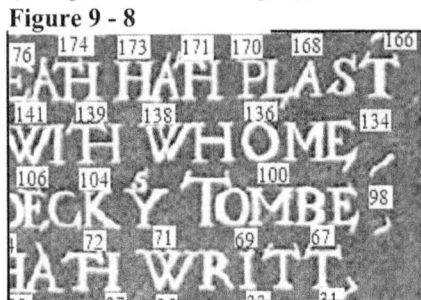

III and Baron Verulam in Reverse). Character 175 appears in the upper left of Figure 11-8 as the distinctive "A." Character number 72 appears in the lower left as the double Tau, T⊣, and lastly character number 167 appears as the "S" in "PLAST" in the upper right, which again can be read as "Bacon" (G) behind the mask of "S" (Shakespeare).

Looking at the above table, the same correlations as the forward count need to be pointed out. First of all, out of the 27 numbers, 17 of them are "hits" in terms of correlating with significant characters in *both* the forward and backward counts. When combined, only 5 signatures do not correlate to important characters, and 3 of those are higher than 305, the number of characters on the plaque. Speaking of which, as you can see in the above table, the Kaye Cipher signature of "Francois Stuart" is 305, which will become important again in a moment. The number 17 of course is the letter R for "Rosicrucian" and H in Reverse, the double Tau, and the value of "Rex" in Short Cipher. In both counts, there are 7 hits in Simple, 5 in Reverse and 5 in Kaye, spelling the letter "GEE" which we know is a Bacon signature. However, we also know we can substitute S for G, and spell the word "SEE" which has been *seen* multiple times in the cipher texts of the plaque. And ironically this was troubling.

Chris Donah had suggested using the number 17 as a possible key early on when I began sharing my information with him. It didn't seem feasible at the time as I hadn't seen any indication that 17 would be a key. However, as you will see in the next chapter in a cipher discovered in a copy of the coat of arms of family de Medici, the key to unlock its message appeared in the form of the number of Bacon signatures appearing in the words in the motto. I thought / feared that this could be a similar situation. However, this is purely speculation. A large possibility, or even a probability, exists in that I may have created too large or too small of a list of these hidden cipher signatures. If so, then such a notion of seeing intent or meaning in these numbers is erroneous, but it does make for interesting speculation.

Something new occurred to me as I finished the above table and typed the name "Francis III." I had always wondered how Kaye Cipher was created. Why did it include two, seemingly arbitrary characters, the ampersand and et., between Z and A? While I think we could learn important information by looking at Renaissance book covers and assigning 25 and 26 to these characters wherever they appear, I believed there was something more here. Originally, I reasoned that Bacon wanted to have G represent his name as the number 33, which is probably also true. However, the deeper answer of course was that Francis Bacon created it to reveal / conceal his secret. This was the only way he could make certain that the last name of his surrogate family "Bacon" would equal 111 in Kaye Cipher, so that we would eventually realize he was "FRANCIS 111," or "III," the third.

Chapter 10 – Summary of Key Messages

For the convenience of the reader, let's review the messages of the plaque as they appeared in each key permutation. In this chapter, first a summary of the findings within each key is presented in the order they have appeared in this book. Also for your convenience, each summary of each key is labeled in case you prefer to not read the summaries, so you can simply skip ahead.

The Biliteral Cipher Summary

While the presence of a Biliteral Cipher of the plaque should seem obvious because the number of characters is divisible by 5, the apparent complexity of the typeface makes such an interpretation appear to be impossible. However, when we rise above the "profane" assumption that the task is too difficult, a simplistic solution appears. The symmetry of the lines of each character suddenly reveals the "a" font and the "b" font necessary to solve the cipher.

Beginning with the letter "X" in the phonetic word "XPLAIN" was another ruse to discourage would-be cryptanalysts from continuing, but the message became "explain RC keys" and to "See Walter Ralegh let out of cage." Additionally we see the motto "LVX SI UMBRA" as a clue of how to proceed with the decryption, via inductive reasoning. Lastly and more importantly, Francis Bacon signs his work on the plaque with his cipher signatures and symbols.

While the possibility exists of other messages appearing within other biliteral ciphers, any other subtle differences between the characters eluded me. Satisfied with successfully finding a message using Bacon's biliteral cipher, I moved on to using the keys on the plaque to unlock the transposition ciphers.

Key 32 Summary

Aside from messages of how to proceed with the decryption, Key 32 produced the following preliminary messages:

- Pass my property to the RC (Ironic, considering he "died" in debt).
- C (see) Me Francis Bacon am Bard. Rawly no are me.
- Samuel de Champlain may be the "ROSY MAP MAKER"
- Clues on how to continue the deciphering – "TIE GOVD THE V TO E."
- APYS (BEES) KEES

While Bacon's statement of "being the bard," isn't new information in terms of the "Francis Bacon as Shakespeare" theories are concerned, the fact that the cipher texts explicitly confirm the idea *is* new. More surprising however, is the reference to Champlain as the "ROSY MAP MAKER," along with the strange reference to Bacon writing a book at sea, and the messages regarding his pictures of boats. These messages only became understandable in the context of " E Masker of TT," or the Key 5 transposition of Key 38.

Key 8 Summary

Using the number 8 as a key to transpose the arrangement created by Key 32, the algorithm generated the following messages:

- I KING of whichever of the two countries that I choose. I pass in leisure (on holiday).
- Although I'm the older brother, out of love for James, I surrender the throne, or perhaps, out of love I surrender the throne to James though I'm the older brother.
- Although I'm the Dauphin too, I swear obedience (allegiance) concerning the throne of France.
- Go endeavor it our growth from trying to coin money.
- My works are two alternatives. It is Shaks-speare.
- I attribute the fictitious name under the law from old Athena and Apollo (the spear-shakers) as figure head, not you (Not William Shaksper).
- We brag and I am the Brother William Shakespear.
- Mary made me Rex. Pay thy Mater the blame.
- We honor (nod to) bees, with hand placement to pattern that symbol (shape).

Key 8 of Key 32 was the first place I encountered the message regarding Bacon's true royal lineage more than once. It's fitting considering that these two keys together, 32 as "F" in Kaye Cipher, and 8 being "H" in Simple and therefore a double Tau, symbolically spell, F. Bacon.

Additionally, this key produced two explicit cipher texts where Francis Bacon takes credit for the works of William Shakespeare. He even states that he attributes the "fictitious name to ol' A A," and not the actor, and they "brag I am Frater William Shakespeare."

Lastly, I found a cipher text that explained what several of my friends and fellow researchers had been discussing over the last year – the meaning of the enigmatic "M" hand sign that we had noticed in so many Renaissance paintings. The letter "M" represents the body and wings of the bee they "honor." The letter M, 12 in Simple Cipher, and the word "BEE" totaling 12 in Simple Cipher, the symbolism was perfect. Providing answers while creating more mysteries, the Key 8 transposition of Key 32 gave me proof of concept of my original theory of how to decrypt this message. It also provided the clue that I needed to use Key 5 when the total number of characters was divisible by 5.

Key 5 Summary

The same theme appears within the messages throughout the Key 5 algorithm of characters of Key 8:

- I a whoresun too. James, my kid brother.
- O ME B, R CETE or, Oh, I Bacon am Dauphin.
- Now I the shunned Medici grandson.
- See, the Godly Queen Mary is our mother. Sic (thus) I'm Esau.
- Mum Mary overheard bad grandmother, threatened by our proximity, that I was sick from poison, but I lived.
- Felt hate as I saw this prostitute Mary deny me the throne.
- I felt hate as this prostitute Mary sire me with Francis then go to Scotland.
- I love seeing my brother on this throne. It was a trade. I'm not as fit for it - shocking (sarcasm) since my father was Francis II.
- Saved hate for punishment. Son saw a naked death. Freed of that one.
- Once I is 15, I stir them up. I bad leader. I'm not satisfied being a dressy helmsman.

This list of messages is compelling in that many of them in the list can be corroborated by history. The two most shocking explicit statements are that James was his younger brother, and that Francis was the Dauphin. The message can't be more explicit than that. It's also necessary to point out that the Biblical allusion to Jacob and Esau, appearing in this fashion and correctly applied to the context defies coincidence. Additionally, as son of Francis II, he would have been the Dauphin and Catherine de Medici's grandson, and she was rumored to have a strong penchant for the use of poison against her enemies. Francis II was indeed sickly and we also all know the famous story of Mary Stuart's "naked death." Lastly, we know that Francis Bacon was sent to France at the age of 16 "from the hand of the Queen," which makes sense if he "stirred them up" when he was 15.

In addition, it's important to point out the consistency of the theme of the messages, combined with confirmable historical references, indicates the veracity of these messages. Shocking as the messages are, they are seamlessly woven within known historical context and appropriate allusions.

So, on to Key 38.

Key 38 Summary

While the Key 38 algorithm produced many phonetic messages that repeated the messages of Keys 32, 8 and 5, it contained multiple Bacon cipher signatures in symbolic line numbers, particularly Lines 32 and 33. Multiple phonetic messages appeared throughout the lines of Key 38:

- I art F III ED (I art Francis the Third).
- I F. CVT AUT WAN BAMPS T IN THE TT.
- Bacon, though Eld Stew men, you second ova.
- House Stewirt. Fate needed a piss ear.
- Acrostics: MY RC A FOLIO and ROSY T CROS.

Aside from the acrostics and decryption clues, Key 38 also produced what I believe to be its main and most explicit cipher texts in the form of acrostic anagrams. Using the standard operating procedures outlined in the previous chapters produced the following series of messages:

- Pavo: From my cone stone Heracles a way to gold and tomes I wrote.
- Knights Baronet ratified.
- From Fr. II's death Dauphin was SCRVTI (rubbish, garbage).
- I made pit before room in cave in Acadia, on maps The Bay of Many Isles.
- HRM files well tell I'm Mary Stewart's son. Et thus the Nova Isles.
- By this garden of roses making use of this ground plan of these worked stones in this place, go to the duplicate knee - a hidden key stone.
- I shant dare enter my treasure chamber. Key is avoiding snares.

Needless to say, Key 38 produced a whole host of messages valuable to anyone interested in the Oak Island mystery in Nova Scotia. As stated earlier, this is detailed in Appendix A.

Key E Masker of TT

This transposition was one of the most surprising. While Bacon's biological heritage were shocking enough (and admittedly, somewhat disappointing), this key troubled me most. The assertions appearing here so greatly challenged known history, and my resolve to just "follow the process and clues" where they led. However, doing so led to the following messages:

- Tiberio Tinelli was good, but best alias was Samuel de Champlain.
- I am native party there au St. Tongois dock. I led fleet west.
- King sent me to oversee work, but I reign my nation.
- James send me to stop Captain Walt Raleigh Caribbean campaign.
- I time the meridians. F. Drake chose me as the wisest astronomer.
- That alias fed bait to trap ass Roi Louis. I used the grants as I figured he tied to the debt.

This key seems to confirm his "Philosophical Death," as he retired to New France to "rule his nation" and he left Louis XIII with the bill. We also learn that his nautical life and career began with the greatest Captain in English history and most notorious and successful privateer, Sir Francis Drake.

Key 32 Deep Dive

The deep reading of Key 32 yielded more information about Francis Bacon's secret life as an intrepid explorer and adventurer:

- I WROTE BOOKS AT SEA. SEE MY PICTURES OF SHIP BOATS.
- THE HOLY REX SENT ME TADDOUSAC NEW WORLD FOR FUR TRADE.
- REX GRANT MY DON DE DIEV TO SEARCH The NORTHWEST SAIL ROVTE, THAT WAY SHVT. IDENTIFY CHANCE FOR MEO RULE.
- (Specific message of Lines 14 – 25 appears in *The Ghosts of Bacon*).
- I LIVE DREAM. I BE FIRST MATE SAILETH WITH THE SEVEN SEAS KING, F. DRAKE. I MAP CLUERE BATTISTA BOAZIO

Francis Bacon used the identity known to all of us in history as Samuel de Champlain to trick King Louis XIII into giving him a nation to govern. While Louis sent him to oversee the fur trade and search for the fabled Northwest Passage, Bacon "identified" the opportunity to rule his nation. While repeating that Champlain was his alias, he also repeats he sailed with Sir Francis Drake. He then reveals that Drake's cartographer Giovanni Battista Boazio was yet another of his aliases. Many of the illustrative details on both his maps and those attributed to Champlain bear the mark of the same hand in the details of the ships, and particularly the execution of the waves and trees.

Confirmation

Due to the cipher signatures of the "character count system" echoing the messages of the cipher texts, all of the Rosi Crosse "keys," and the cipher signature checking system working with the acrostic anagrams, the validity of the cipher texts within these transpositions is overwhelming and convincing. The same messages and themes appear in transpositions produced by completely different keys and algorithms. In each of the previous chapters, I've produced twenty-seven tables that mathematically produce cipher signatures related to the messages themselves. And in every case, they produced correlating signatures and values in *all three of Bacon's ciphers – Simple, Reverse and Kaye.* This is a total of 81 specific values and signatures. (Again, 81 is the Simple Cipher value of the name "Francois"). The odds of this many signatures and correlating values, along with their "interaction" or echoing of the messages, all defy coincidence. However, *can the messages even be true?*

With each new "impossible" discovery in each section, I found myself writing the same phrase – "this will need to fully be investigated in a later chapter." Those chapters appear next exploring the plausibility of the messages in each of these transposition ciphers, and they identify corroborating evidence.

Chapter 11 - The Plausibility of the Messages and Orthodox History Pt. 1: Francois Stuart Valois-Angoulême

Challenges and Conclusions

The biggest challenge to the information communicated through the ciphers is cognitive bias, the powerful force also known as orthodox thinking. We have all learned a version of history that runs counter to these messages. These messages challenge strongly held belief systems, some held by individuals who have invested tuition, years, careers and lives in their chosen area. Academics and individual researchers have spent countless hours, even years, researching and writing books advocating the Prince Tudor Theory, that Francis Bacon was the unacknowledged son of the Virgin Queen Elizabeth I, a theory that I personally had always favored. Others have painstakingly scoured obscure, boring records throughout their entire careers, and pieced together every scrap of hard evidence they could muster, to prove that not only was William Shakespeare (with all of its spellings) a real living, breathing person, but that he and he alone was responsible for the writings bearing his name.

All that time, effort and solid academic work creates a vested interest that is completely understandable, and I can hardly expect to challenge with this book. As much as I would like (realizing the controversial nature of the messages), to just claim to "be the messenger," I can no longer do that. At first, I considered simply saying, "hey, *I'm not* the one making this claim. I'm simply reporting the messages I discovered encoded on the plaque with the cipher systems of Sir Francis Bacon." While that is technically true, that I'm reporting the messages and not "creating a theory," at this point I am stating plainly, all of these messages are not only real, but true.

At first I didn't think it could be possible. I didn't want to believe them. I had hoped for different messages. Some of the ones I hoped were there *did* appear, such as the question of Shakespeare's authorship, and the strange connection to the Oak Island mystery. Anything else other than confirmation of the Prince Tudor theory was unwelcome and problematic from my perspective.

However, after working through all of these ciphers, line by line, and character by character, it's easy to plainly state Sir Francis Bacon was responsible for writing the works of William Shakespeare. This is not a new claim by any means, about which much has been written, and now I add that I have read the message from the man himself. I personally had always believed that the plays were written in "the round," a collaborative process between the writers and actors, which accounted for the breadth and depth of experiences that would explain the content of the plays. While this could very well have been the process used (or one of many), the important message from the plaque is, Francis Bacon claims credit for their existence. He explicitly states that he used the name, that he was "the bard," and the name was inspired by Athena and Apollo and not the actor named Shakspere. As such, there remains nothing to add to that conversation here, other than the messages themselves as revealed in the previous chapters. That was the easy message to present.

People have been waiting ages for "a smoking gun document" written in the hand of Francis Bacon claiming authorship. The plaque of Shakespeare's Funerary Monument in Holy Trinity Church in Stratford-upon-Avon *is that document*. If it ended there, all of this information would probably accepted and even welcomed.

But the messages also explicitly, and troublingly, state that Sir Francis Bacon was the rightful heir to the thrones of both France and England, as he was the son of Francis II of France and Mary, Queen of Scots. I now believe this is true. This will be explored in its own section of this chapter, regarding not just its historical plausibility, but probability.

Yes, I firmly believe that Sir Francis Bacon was the older half-brother of James VI and I.

Lastly, a message points to the mystery on Oak Island, Nova Scotia. It's probable that the message has already been "used" so to speak. Though my initial investigation of the cipher was prompted by this very suspicion, after discovering the main thrust of the messages, I dismissed the Oak Island connection. Because of this dismissal, the bulk of Key 38 remained a mystery. Not until entertaining that possibility, did the cipher reveal its message. The full import of that interpretation is included in Appendix A. Whether anything can or will be found (at least what hasn't already been found unbeknownst to us) on Oak Island, remains a mystery as of this writing. However, the "Oak Island Team" or "Brotherhood of the Dig" as they are known, are well-aware of my discoveries.

Since the messages regarding Bacon's aliases and his time sailing with Sir Francis Drake, especially the Samuel de Champlain bombshell, are more "dis-believable" than his birth, its plausibility appears in its own chapter.

For me the most troubling aspect of these messages is this – by far the most believable message on the plaque (being supported by corroborating evidence by other independent researchers spanning centuries) is Francis Bacon wrote the works of Shakespeare. Messages produced by Bacon's own ciphers, explicitly state *I Francis Bacon wrote the works attributed to Shakespeare.* That's the message that we have all been waiting to see for centuries. That this smoking gun will be ignored due to its association with more extraordinary, credulity-straining messages, is my biggest fear. Being presented alongside far-more controversial and sensational claims makes the Bacon / Shakespeare information risk being dismissed without examination. I can only appeal to the readers' sensibilities to take the evidence of each statement on its own merit.

And now, to handle the historical aspect of these references to King Bacon, the Dauphin, and Francis III.

Turbulent Times and Intrigue

Though previously mentioned it bears repeating – When a friend posted this idea within a social media group to sort of "float the idea to see what others think," two comments really stood out. The first was a response from a well-respected Bacon scholar, whom I greatly admire, and appeared as the bare-assertion, "This easily can be dismissed." Another was from a historical researcher whose work I follow and also admire, who stated something to the effect, "that means that Catherine de Medici would have had a grandson and heir to the throne. Seems to me she would have been overjoyed about his arrival and protected him." The second of these demonstrates that even the best minds can be clouded by our biases, especially concerning familial bonds.

It's a common mistake to make - to judge what we would assume to be a natural familial bond in the past through the lens of our own modern experiences. However, doing so means overlooking or forgetting the reality of history.

We need to logically think about this and reason this through. While it's necessary to offer some speculation here, by piecing together the factual historical evidence that we know, we can make some logical inferences based upon the details provided by the cipher texts, and arrive at reasonable, logical conclusions.

To believe that Catherine de Medici would have been a doting grandmother ignore her sociopathic behaviors recorded by history. By all accounts, Catherine de Medici despised Mary as the wife of Francis II. Because of his death and she giving birth to Francis III, *Mary* would have been the Queen Regent of France for her son, instead of Catherine.

Catherine had been "Queen" of France for years at this point, and the Regent for Francis II. Considering Catherine de Medici's reputation, does anyone logically think that she would simply step down from power and walk away, to make way for someone she so strongly disliked? Would she have simply handed over the kingdom of France to Mary Queen of Scots?

Absolutely not.

Would she have welcomed a grandson into the family with open arms and kisses? A grandson born to a young and sickly King Francis II? Or would she have gone to one of her "secret cabinets" in the Chateau de Blois, where she reputedly kept her array of poisons?

That child became the primary threat to Catherine de Medici's power and influence over Francis II. Fortunately for her, Francis II died from what Bacon termed a *piss ear*. He also termed himself the *shunned Medici grandson.* Another message referenced Mary's fear, his illness, and the aforementioned poison.

If we consider the constant civil wars and religious conflicts in France during "the age of Catherine de Medici" when her sons were kings, if we consider her reputation as a "sinister Queen," and being an expert with poisons, the reason for Mary's fear makes perfect sense. So sordid was her reputation that one theory even claims that Catherine was the creator of the Black Mass! If "Francis III" became suddenly sick why wouldn't Mary flee from the danger and turbulence in France, to the danger and turbulence of Scotland?

And how would the Queen of England, Elizabeth I, receive the news of this challenger to her own throne, and one that already had an heir? Mary would seek her cousin's protection as she did later in life when she fled Scotland. What would be Elizabeth's terms regarding Mary's return to the islands? Would she demand that Mary give up Francis, or did Mary seek the help of Elizabeth to protect him? At any rate, what would have prompted Mary to give-up her first born son to be raised by Elizabeth's best friend and her Lord Keeper, Lady Ann and Nicholas Bacon?

Some speculation? Sure. Logical? Yes. But all interesting questions to be sure.

One individual who would have played a pivotal role in all of this would have been Sir Nicholas Throckmorton, Queen Elizabeth's lifelong friend. While he was ambassador to France, he also befriended Mary Stuart. He would have been the key person to negotiate Mary's return to Scotland as history records him as playing a "key role in the relationship between" the two queens. In fact, history states, "Throckmorton conducted the negotiations with the English court regarding her [Mary's] travel arrangements when she decided to return to Scotland from France." I think we can read the phrase "travel arrangements" as a Royal euphemism for negotiations. Again, it seems that if Mary were arriving with Francis, negotiations were necessary.

Another thought that can't be avoided - the nature of the illness and death Francis II. If Francis Bacon were his son, would he be later inspired to write a play about a prince whose father was murdered by his brother, who then took the throne in place of his brother and nephew? Would he then place a play called "The Murder of Gonzago" within the play we know as *Hamlet*, in which the murderous brother kills the sleeping king by pouring poison in his ear? Could we view the name as a word instead, meaning "slice of ham?"

Just speculation again, but more tantalizing thoughts.

Sir Francis Bacon was reputed to have suffered from poor health his whole life. Could this be a genetic inheritance of his father's weak constitution? Or was it a lie to cover his exploits, while also being a clue to his true father's identity? I suggest the latter.

When Bacon was 16 years old, he was sent away from England to of all places, France. England had been waging a proxy war by backing the Hugenots. And yet Francis travels to France where he is given a warm welcome at the French Court. Given the information provided by the ciphers, and how Elizabeth I treated Francis Bacon throughout her reign, I offer the following speculative explanation (see Timeline, Plate 1, and the timeline in Chapter 13).

In this scenario, Mary and the Dauphin Francis II were married on April 24th (the day of the year *after* the date on the plaque), in 1558. By simply doing the math using the known birth date of Francis Bacon, he would have been conceived on April 22nd (one day *before* the day of the year dated on the plaque), in 1560. Francis II dies on December 5, 1560, and his son arrives on January 22nd, 1561. On August 14th, 1561, Mary flees France with six-month-old baby Francis in tow and seeks refuge with Elizabeth I (as she would later do again when she fled Scotland in 1567 after being forced to abdicate the Scottish throne to her infant son James). Elizabeth I immediately sees the threat Mary and Francis pose to her own throne, but offers her protection with a stipulation - the people of England and Scotland cannot know about the Dauphin, Francis III. A queen with an heir returning to England would have reignited those who had challenged the reign of Elizabeth in the first place. Many in England saw Mary as the rightful heir, and Elizabeth I was born from an illegitimate marriage in the eyes of Catholics. Additionally, Elizabeth and Catherine de Medici were known to be in communication with one another, especially when they had shared interests. This situation certainly would qualify as such – it would have been a win–win for both Elizabeth I and Catherine de Medici. For the Queen's protection, Mary had to give up her son to be raised by Elizabeth's leading Lady in Waiting and the Keeper of the Seal, Lady Anne and Sir Nicholas Bacon. Francis Bacon became a state secret.

Francis intellectually thrived in that environment. It's possible that having learned of his true birthright, perhaps when he went to college, he could have, as teenagers are often known to do foolish things, presented himself to Queen Elizabeth I as knowing his true identity. Also, we need to remember one of the cipher messages where he states, *"ONCE I IS 15, I STIR THEM VP. I BAD LEADER."* So once when he was 15 years old, he "stirs them up?" Could one of the "them" be 13 or 14 year old Robert Devereux? And then he's sent to France. The positions of Sir Nicholas and Lady Anne, as well as the Queen's known affection for the boy, made the Queen exile him to France with Sir Amias Paulet for a time to teach him a lesson in humility. Interestingly, Sir Amias Paulet was the jailer for Mary Queen of Scots leading up to her execution and was asked by Sir Francis Walsingham to assassinate her to absolve Elizabeth of blame from her death. He refused.

While at the French court, as a member of what history books refer to as "a member of the English ambassador's suite," young Francis Bacon (aged 16 - 18) sees the work that the French Renaissance writers and intellectuals, the Pleiades, were doing - creating and consolidating the French language. He then decided he would do the same for England, because at the time, people in different parts of the country actually spoke different languages. Seeing how a national language unified the disparate parts of France, he realized it would do the same for England. He also apparently learned to paint.

He spent most of his career struggling to advance with Elizabeth I's court, and it wasn't until James VI of Scotland became James I of England, that he rose to his highest stations. James I knighted Bacon, named him Baron Verulam, and Viscount St. Albans. Looking at the cipher signatures of these titles, we see the cipher signatures of his "unknown identities," such as 181 as the Simple Cipher Signature of both Viscount St. Alban and Francois Stuart. He was "most proud" of his title "Baron Verulam" as the cipher signatures are 133 in Simple and 167 in Reverse Cipher. The value of 133 is also "King Stuart and King Francis III" in Simple Cipher. The value of 167 is also the signatures for "Francois III" in Reverse Cipher and "Francis Stewart" in Simple. King James I made him the most powerful politician in England until his fall from grace. At one point, Bacon was the Regent for a month. When Bacon was convicted of bribery, James I released him from the Tower granting clemency, and even paid his fine! Lastly, multiple historians have chronicled the stories of James allowing Francis to wear purple, a color only worn by royalty. Would King James have been this lenient to the bastard son of Elizabeth I, or to his older brother, the rightful heir to the throne?

Elizabeth's behavior appears to more like that of someone who was threatened by his presence, an someone useful that she needs to keep close enough, but not *too* close. Or perhaps she didn't wish to bestow *too much* attention on Bacon, as many in the Prince Tudor camp believe. James' behavior seems to be that of a loving brother helping his sibling. Bacon even states in one part of the cipher that he abdicated the throne to James "out of love."

Earlier I mentioned genetics. I find it interesting when comparing the portraits of all of these historical characters, that Bacon bears no resemblance to Sir Nicholas, Lady Anne, or Anthony (Plates 2 and 3). However, Francis and James I both have the red hair and light beards of the Stewart line, and note the resemblance to their grandfather, Mary's father James V of Scotland (see Plate 4). Francis also resembles his uncle on his father's side, Charles XI. When the miniature of the 18-year-old Francis Bacon is compared with the dual portrait of Francis II and Mary Stuart however, the family resemblance is obvious (plate 5). Note the eyes, mouth and hairline of Francis II and the young Bacon. He seemed to have Mary's chin and nose. After looking at the portraits side-by-side, in the words of a fellow researcher, "Once you see it, you can't *un-see* it."

An additional curious question - why did the young Sir Francis Bacon have a miniature painted of him by a Royal goldsmith and portrait artist "Nicholas Hilliard," who worked primarily for the likes of Queen Elizabeth I, Mary Queen of Scots, and Catherine de Medici? Where is the miniature of his older "brother" Anthony? Lady Anne and Sir Nicholas? Why is he in exactly the same angle and pose as Francis II at nearly the same age? The simple answer is they were not members of his true family, the Royal family. The deeper answer not only lies in Francis Bacon's true identity, but I suspect in his unknown aliases as well. It will suffice to say that all of these people who would secretly have been relatives of Francis, all had portraits painted by the same exact artist. You will see why in the next chapter.

While on the topic of the Bacons, Francis returned to England from France upon hearing of the death of Sir Nicholas Bacon. It's been recorded that "Sir Nicholas had intended to arrange for Francis' inheritance but died before he did so." None of his other children from his first marriage nor Anthony were left out of the will. He "had time" to include them, but not Francis. Though he owned several properties, Francis was left with none of them. Perhaps his inheritance wasn't overlooked at all, but Sir Nicholas decided to not provide for someone who was not his biological son. Proponents of the Prince Tudor Theory use the same reasoning. Speculation certainly, but logical. In fact, the same correlations used to support the "Elizabeth as mother" theories also support the case for Mary and Francis II.

Now that we have these explicit statements from the cipher texts, this "Stewart-Dauphin" hypothesis has the stronger claim.

However, another criticism of this idea of Mary Stuart being the mother of Francis Bacon, has been his hatred of her. One person with whom I shared the messages of the plaque claimed that she couldn't possibly have been his mother because Bacon vehemently advocated the execution of Mary. However, considering the cipher messages express that he "saved his hate" for her death, and refer to her as a "prostitute" and "whore," only seems to validate the veracity of these messages. The messages confirm his disposition toward her. He blamed her for the loss of his birthright. This is validating evidence of the messages' veracity and does not negate them. This is not the only evidence for Bacon as Dauphin.

One argument I've heard against the idea of Francis II and Mary having a child, was the statement that he was incapable of bearing children because it had been recorded that "his testicles had never dropped." Frankly, I see this more as a disparaging insult, regarding his youth and an insult of his masculinity, instead of a medical diagnosis. Frankly anyone needs to be suspicious of such a negative statement regarding a King's balls. It also seems to be a convenient way to revise history in favor of erasing the birth. History is indeed written by the victors, and Catherine de Medici and Elizabeth I were the victors. The "fact" that Mary and Francis never had a child is in the vested interests of both of these powerful women from history, and they were both in positions to make sure that his information would remain a closely guarded state secret. Lastly, I've been astounded by how much of the history of many of these key players is based on conjecture. Even some of the "primary sources" can give rise to questions regarding our accepted orthodox version of history. Luckily clues have been left behind in other forms, other than this old plaque with a cipher, which I argue is a "primary source."

One notable area that Bacon researchers always reference is the symbolism at work in the headpieces and frontispieces of his writings, as well as those of the Shakespeare Folios. Rawley's *Manes Verulamiani* is referenced in other areas of this text. While it contains 32 verses that are barely veiled references to Bacon's poetry and plays, it also begins with the following artwork as a headpiece noted here in Figure 11 – 1:

Figure 11 - 1.

First of all, the artwork contains all of the same elements other researchers have noted as typical of the Bacon and Shakespeare headpieces. The pair of cherubs (or putti) at each side holding spears pointing at the serpent or dragon. While some researchers have told me they believe the serpents or dragons to be sleeping, I disagree. A winged serpent is a symbol of the unification of opposites - wings join the air with the serpent that crawls upon the earth. As their eyes are closed, I think they symbolize the "death" of Francis Bacon, a man who had joined heaven with the earth through science, that above with that which is below. Note the face at the center growing from the stem of the flower. Additionally, this image also contains the AA and play between light and shadow of the Fra. Rosi Crosse. Lastly and most importantly, note the images below on either side of this face - two dolphins. The dolphins commemorate the man as Francis III, the lost Dauphin of France. This is not the only image related to Bacon that uses the dolphin symbolism.

The famous frontispiece of Bacon's *Novum Organum* depicts two ships sailing out beyond two pillars symbolic of the Pillars of Hercules. While many other researchers rightly have noted the image is emblematic of Bacon's role in England's colonization

Figure 11-2

scheme of America, there is also another message conveyed by the image when understood within the context of the cipher messages. Note Figure 11-1a:

On either side of the ship in the foreground are a pair of dolphins, one in light and the other shadow. In juxtaposition appear the anchors at the stern of the ship, completing the symbolism of the motto of the de Medici family, "festina lente." The banner flying at the bow has the letter "F" as a standard.

An Unexpected Twist

Pertaining to the specific messages regarding Catherine de Medici, I made one final discovery as I was finishing this chapter, needing to be include it here. It independently confirms the messages within the cipher text of the plaque, as well as the cipher method itself, from a completely different and unexpected source.

Chris Donah, friend and fellow researcher mentioned throughout this narrative, sent an interesting image of the de Medici family crest or coat of arms he had received from our mutual friend and researcher Christopher Morford. This example is different from the majority of the images that appear from a cursory internet search. While he had found this example on a post from a popular social media site, I was able to track down a high-resolution fair use image from Wikipedia Commons, called "Grand écu aux armes des Médicis," by Ateliers d'Alessandro Allori et de Francesco Curradi, meaning the Workshop of Alessandro Allori and of Francesco Curradi. It apparently dates from either 1590 or 1625, well within the time frame of Bacon's operations. Of the many odd things about this image are the names of the artists. While they held differing philosophies regarding their painting styles, Allori following mannerism and Curradi "counter-mannerism," (symbolizing light and shadow?) members of the Medici family commissioned work from both artists and at different times. Additionally, I could find nothing that indicated that these artists shared a "workshop," or ever collaborated, though it's possible. Given the image and its message, I suspect the naming of these artists was an assumption by scholars, or a ruse by Bacon. In fact, I believe he created it.

The immediate impression of the image (see Plate 5) is that it's a Baconian / Rosicrucian work, including the play between light and shadow. Note the familiar cherubs or putti in the upper corners crowning a child, and the child's face in the center, all echoing the positioning of the headpiece of *Manes Verulamiani*. Note his hairline in reference to the aforementioned hairlines of young Francis Bacon and Francis II:

Figure 11 - 2

One cherub looks down as the other has eyes uplifted toward the viewer presenting the esoteric principle of "as above, so below." While the exoteric meaning of the image is obviously religious considering the Papal history of the Medici family, the implications within the context of the message on the plaque become clear as we look at the "family motto" at the base of the image. The center of the shield contains the famous red "balls" of the Medici crest, along with the sixth upper most ball with three fleur-de-lis in a

216

field of blue, used with the permission of the French Royal family. But this is not the most important feature of this "family crest."

Note the close-up image of the characters comprising the family motto in the image in Figure 11–3:

Figure 11 - 3

After such a long and intense study of Shakespeare's Funerary Memorial plaque, the similarity of the image was striking. Aside from the same use of color of gold on brown, the ligatured NE and ME are a direct correlation to the characters on the plaque commemorating Shakespeare. Also, "NE" in Latin can be read as "not, lest" so at the center of the "motto" is the message "Not me." Noting that there were 9 characters in the first line and 6 in the second, the immediately thought is, "I, F" in Simple Cipher. In Reverse Cipher this becomes "QT." Though no known record exists of the phrase "on the QT" before the 1800's, the possibility exists that this phrase actually has an earlier usage among members of Fraternities utilizing secrecy, though it's not possible to substantiate such a speculation. The letters could be the initials of the Latin words "qui tacitus," but again this is speculation. However, there is no need to speculate regarding the Latin of the false "Motto."

The Latin phrase as it appears here can be translated as "From this source, all my glory." However, the motto of the Medici family is commonly known to be "festina lente," meaning "make haste slowly." As previously noted, the most common representation of this oxymoronic adage from Ancient Greece is the image of a dolphin wrapping itself around an anchor, alluded to earlier in the *Novum Organum* frontispiece. To make such a glaring "error," particularly using such familiar looking characters and iconography could only mean one thing –

There had to be a cipher message.

If this crest is the work of Francis Bacon, it seems he's sarcastically telling the world that "the source of all his *glory* is Catherine de Medici!" And as you'll see in the next few pages, this image is definitely the work of Francis Bacon.

Adding the Simple Cipher values of the first four letters, HINC, produced the sum of 33, the Simple Cipher signature for "Bacon." Doing the same with the next five, DECVS, totaled 50, what we now know is the Simple Cipher signature for "Fr. III." The Simple Cipher total of "OMNE" counting N and E as separate letters produces 44, the "secret" signature for Bacon. "MEVM" totaled 49, or without the ligatured E, 34, neither of which were signatures. However, translated into English, the word means, "my (personal possession); mine, of me, belonging to me; my own; to me." So, he states that these are his signatures.

It therefore appeared that Bacon may have signed more of his unknown work once again, in three signatures. So, I kept going.

In Reverse: HINC = 67, Simple for "Francis." DECVS = 75, Reverse for Fr. III. OMNE = 56, a "miss." MEVM = 51, another "miss."

In Kaye: HINC = 111, "Bacon" in Kaye. DECVS = 128, a "miss." OMNE = 70, a "miss." Lastly, MEVM = 75, "Fr. III" in Reverse.

Though there were a few "misses," five to be exact, there were seven explicit, positive signatures, the Simple Cipher numerical value of "G." The first word, "HINC" meaning "the source of," produced definitive and easily identifiable "Bacon signatures" in all three ciphers, meaning the source of this image is "Francis Bacon." Having noted the conjoined characters on the plaque as an indication of a transposition cipher, logically the same device should be at work on this counterfeit family crest. Due to this obvious purpose of the ligatured characters, "7" should be used as the key of the algorithm to see if it produced a cipher message. This made sense: 7 Bacon signatures, the key = G. Given the total of fifteen characters (counting conjoined characters as one), the transposition of the characters was placed in a table of three rows of five, the number of "misses." I then looked for acrostic anagrams using the same method as the plaque:

The bold letters can be rearranged to spell CENI, Latin for "mud, dirt; (or) scum, filth (in reference to persons)." The italic block of letters rearrange into "DOMENVM," Latin for "house of; house belonging to." From the leftover letters, a couple of possibilities exist. First of all in the

C	<u>V</u>	<u>E</u>	*Me*	D
Ne	C	M	*N*	*O*
I	<u>S</u>	H	*V*	M

Table 11 - 2

underlined letters, substituting an E for the V provides the word that appears in several the permutations of the Keys of the plaque, "SEE." A study of the remaining characters, CMH produce the number 75 in Kaye Cipher, which we now recognize as the signatures of "Stewart" and "Fr. III." However, by instead substituting a V for the E, and including the M beneath it, we can spell "SVVM" which is Latin for "their (own); theirs." The message then appears, referring to the name de Medici, "their own house of scum." With the remaining letters C and H, by subbing R for the H, we have the obvious signature of "RC," as well as the message "See TT."

All of the Bacon signatures, the use of symbols common to himself and the Rosicrucians, and the contexts of the exoteric and esoteric messages of the "motto," unequivocally demonstrate that Francis Bacon created this de Medici family crest to insult the House de Medici. The fact that my friends happened to pass this along the very morning I was writing this chapter, is amazing. It's difficult to be unfazed by this synchronicity. Especially when, just as I was finishing my final points regarding Francis Bacon and Catherine de Medici, the image appeared in my inbox. This image provides confirmation, from a source apparently unrelated to Shakespeare's Funerary Monument plaque, of the methods used in the cipher, as well as Bacon's feelings regarding House de Medici being the "source of all my glory." If only there were yet another source of similar information. As it happens, such a source does exist.

Figure 11 - 4

Another individual associated with Oak Island research, reached out to me to provide my take on the famous Rosicrucian image of the "Invisible College," the illustration of a work called *Speculum sophicum Rhodo-stauroticum* by Theophilus Schweighardt (Figure 11-4). The title translates to, "a reflection on the wisdom of the rose-cross." Because of the cipher texts of the plaque, I recognized that each figure of the man around the picture depicted Francis Bacon. The elements that are relevant to this discussion appear on the right side of the illustration, the figure falling from the cliff, and the figure with the anchor in the lower right.

Looking closely at the falling figure, (see Figure 11–5) three things immediately become obvious. First of all, his hands are overhead in a position familiar to Freemasonry, "begging mercy for a poor widow's son," which aside from Hiram Abiff, would apply all too well to Francis Bacon. Secondly, this is happening in the context of the figure "tripping over" the Latin phrase, "festina lente," the de Medici family motto!

Lastly, we can plainly see a hat and

Figure 11 - 5

sword falling from the figure as well. These represent the "Blessed Hat and Sword," a tradition for kings of Catholic countries whereby the Pope blesses a ceremonial hat and sword on Christmas and presents them to the

219

monarchs. This image shows the loss of this station and the political environment causing Mary to flee France with Francis.

Figure 11 - 6

There have been many images that express the motto of House de Medici, "make haste slowly." Two such images, and butterfly and crab, and a rabbit in a snail shell, embody the oxymoronic phrase. As stated earlier, the most famous show a dolphin wrapping itself around an anchor (Figure 11–6). This is the image being mimicked in the lower right of the illustration, here in Figure 11–7. Bacon wraps himself around the image of the anchor, as he uses it as a cross stave (minus the cross) to measure the elevation of the hand of God extending from the cloud overhead. This vignette is designed not to only exhibit the exoteric message of faith and the use of science to understand the works of God, but also Francis Bacon's true identity - the Dauphin (dolphin) of France, and the grandson of Catherine de Medici.

Figure 11-7

Not only does the cipher text of the plaque explicitly state Francis Bacon's true identity, but two separate highly symbolic images reinforce the Medici connection. These images reinforce the message that Sir Francis Bacon was the son of Mary Queen of Scots and Francis II. He was the rightful heir to two thrones as he states in the cipher texts. Though some researchers disagree with my contention of the figures around the outside depicting Bacon at different points of his life, they have been unable to offer an explanation that embodies all of the elements of the image in a context as coherent as this one. After reading the messages of the cipher texts of the plaque, all of the enigmatic images begin to "make sense" in light of Bacon's true identity.

Continuing to analyze this image, several clues of a steganographic nature in the form of "errors" in proportion on the right side of the image can be noted. By digging into the angle measurements suggested by the geometry of the image itself, an interesting story began to unfold, perfectly echoing the cipher messages of the plaque of Shakespeare's Funerary Monument. The angle measurements also reinforce the conclusion that the figures populating the outside of the image represent different stages of

220

Francis Bacon's life. It's also important to state that the utmost care and attention to detail was taken when making these measurements.

One of the prominent members of the Oak Island Team (known for his healthy skepticism) did bring up one concern when I presented the following information to them in my second "War Room" presentation. He stated how in order to analyze these angles and calculate the values I must have used an old-fashioned print out, ruler and protractor, which I readily acknowledged. He then asked an excellent question (as is his habit on the show), "well, couldn't it be possible for someone to sort of align the compass in such a way to massage the numbers to get the outcome they were looking for?"

While some readers might take that as an insult to my integrity, I didn't at all. The fact is, he was right. It was entirely possible, and I said so in my response. We need to remember how many theories these guys see each year. Many of the presenters could be motivated by trying to "get on television." However, my motivation was and remains, the sacred Tau, the truth. So, trying to fudge the numbers would be entirely counterproductive. Also, if more time leading up to that presentation had been available, I would have asked others to independently check my work, without foreknowledge of previous results or Bacon cipher signatures. Ultimately, everyone is free to check these angle values on their own and compare them to my results with one caveat.

I double and triple checked these angles. If I one of my lines seemed to deviate from the actual line as originally drawn, I started over with a fresh copy of the image. I didn't measure the angles until I was satisfied that the lines I had drawn were as accurate as they could be. And so if you choose to try the experiment, in all fairness you need to be just as willing to ensure the accuracy of each of your lines and measure them as precisely as you possibly can.

A full analysis of this image appears in the appendices. But for all intents and purposes here within this context, an overview analysis of the

geometrical relationships of the angles in the image appear here, as they seem to verify the messages of Key 38.

Figure 11 - 87

The Invisible College Illustration

After analyzing the angles and measurements of the "Emblematic image of the Rosicrucian College," I discovered multiple purposes and messages and this section deals with the geometry present in this illustration of the "Invisible College." As you will see, the angles and alignments produced on the left or northern portion reveal the latitude and longitude of a specific area of Nova Scotia. The angles framing the right-hand side of the image (the "southern" portion) reinforce the messages stating Francis Bacon was Dauphin of France.

First of all, a steganographic message appears on the left using the Ark on the mountain. While this might sound like fanciful thinking, the message is verified using the geometry of the lines on the left side of the illustration. The cryptograph of the juxtaposition of the Ark atop the mountain and the winged letter being sent to its right, "spell" "ArkadI, D C," or ARKADI, de Canada. Next to the Ark, the pair of birds represent the

222

crow and the dove from the Biblical story of Noah, repeating the symbolism of light and dark. Also, they appear in the shape of the number "4" or 44, which is of course the latitude of Nova Scotia. While this can be downplayed as conjecture, prominent lines in this area of the image produce angles that not only reinforce it by repetition, but they also provide something unusual - the longitude. As difficult as it is to believe, the angles in this area of the artwork produce the coordinates of 44°29' and 64°13', placing us in the center Mahone Bay, Nova Scotia, the location of Oak Island.

We begin by drawing two straight lines following along the paths of the winged letters being sent, ad I.D.C. on the left and Nostro T.S. on the right. These lines extend entirely across the illustration. This pair of lines meet exactly between the two windows of the building forming an X, and a perfect nexus with the line that separates the windows themselves. The left angle formed by these lines equals 81 (as does the opposite angle) and perfectly frames the travelling figure in the lower left and Noah's Ark on the mountain top.

The measurements of the angles of each quadrant are highly significant. The left and right angles (north and south, respectively) measure 81 and the top and bottom (east and west) measure 99 degrees (Figure 10-9). "Francois" is 81 in Simple (and Fourfold) Cipher, while 99 is the name "Stuart" in Fourfold Cipher. The

Figure 11 - 9

numbers 99 and 81 are important and symbolic for other reasons, not the least of which is the mathematical relationship. According to Mackey's Encyclopedia of Freemasonry 81 is "a sacred number in the advanced degrees because it is the square of 9, which is again the square of 3. The Pythagoreans however, considered the nine as a fatal number, and especially dreaded eighty-one, because it was produced by the multiplication of nine by itself." However this is not the only hint referring to Pythagorean geometry.

As previously noted, I began by looking within the quadrant containing the Ark on the mountain,

Figure 11- 10

believing the visual cryptography of the winged letter juxtaposed with the Ark spelled "ArkadI, DC," or "de Canada." As such, looking for opportunities where lines could be drawn in this direction to see if any interesting angles appeared. Drawing a horizontal baseline using the bottom of the windows as the guide, thereby creates a parallel from which angles can be measured.

The interior angle formed by this base-line of the bottom of the windows and the line of the left winged-letter measures 47 degrees. While this is a cipher signature using Bacon's cipher system related to this research, the number is significant here for different reasons. First of all, it is the number of Euclid's 47th Problem, the proposition explaining the Pythagorean Theorem. This of course indicates the need for the use of geometry. If we use a bit of Pythagorean math and subtract 47 from the 180 degrees of a triangle, the answer is 133 - the Simple Cipher signature for Baron Verulam, King Stuart and others. These lines also perfectly "frame-in" the image of the Ark on the mountaintop. All of these clues focus our attention on this area and any lines that might terminate here. In other words, we need to find the angles that will lead us to the place being depicted by the Ark, a symbol of the knowledge of the ancients that needs to be protected at all costs. So where is it?

The Ark itself provides a part of the answer. By drawing a line suggested by the angle of its roof down towards the building, the angle perfectly dissects the aforementioned nexus formed by the three other lines (four when including the line between the windows). The alignment of the roofline with the precise point where all of the other lines converge, creates an angle of 44 degrees with the horizontal baseline created by the bottom of the windows (Figure 11-11), as in the "secret" signature of Francis Bacon. (As mentioned earlier, the birds near the

Figure 11 - 11

Ark appear to be number fours with an open top). Additionally in this way, the illustration provides the general latitude of "ArkadI," but as you'll see this can be further refined.

In this image, "errors" in perspective and dimension are clues of where to focus our attention. One such area is the sword arm extending from the building - while intended to be symbolic in nature, its size is an instant call-sign. Drawing another line through the centerline of this sword, it passes directly through the aforementioned nexus produced by the first two lines and the line

Figure 11 - 12

between the windows, along the chain of the drawbridge and precisely through the corner of the drawbridge itself. Measuring the angle above the parallel formed by the bottom of the windows gives an angle of 18 degrees, the number of the letter G in Bacon's Reverse Cipher, a confirmation of heading in the right direction. The angle formed by the sword line with the original winged letter line measured 29 degrees.

The angle of the Ark's roof and the horizontal baseline, together with the angle provided by the centerline of the sword and the "ad IDC" letter, produce the numbers 44 and 29, which can be read as 44°29', the latitude of Mahone Bay, Nova Scotia. Amazing as this is, we can also find the longitude using the same technique.

Figure 11 - 13

To do so, I scanned over the image to find another "line suggestion." In other areas of this analysis, lines were "suggested" by various straight lines and edges - a walking stick, the base of the building, the drawbridge, etc. In this instance, if my theory was correct, the source of the line needed to appear in the same quadrant as the Ark, and / or terminate near it. Also, it wouldn't make sense if it was a horizontal line formed by the building, as they seemed to create the "base" from which the angles formed by the other lines are measured. The first candidate was the roofline of the cottage that appears to the left of the building, however the lines were imperfect, and lacked a straight edge. Yet the angle seemed promising and right beside it a parallel line is formed by the shaded pole supporting the pulley.

Figure 11 - 14

Following the exact line suggested by the shaded pole, and extending it, it terminated in the area near the Ark, right at the letter "T" in the word "SEPTENTRIO." As is always the case, the Tau must make its appearance. Using the foundation of the building as the base of the angle, the measure of the interior angle was exactly 64 degrees, the general longitude of Nova Scotia. To refine it still more, we need to look no further than the unshaded pole supporting the other pulley. Extending the line upward in the same direction but this time measuring the angle formed by the poles themselves, produces an angle of 13 degrees. The longitude of 64°13' is therefore represented by these "long" poles pointing upward in a vertical manner, like the meridians themselves and terminating by the Ark.

Taken all together, the observation of the possibility of the visual cipher of a phonetic pronunciation of Acadia in the presence of the Ark and

226

the characters on the winged letter, "ad I*D*C," representing "ArkadI, de Canada" seems to be confirmed by the geometry. Measuring the angles formed by the many straight edges with lines terminating in the same area, produces the latitude and longitude coordinates of 44°29' N, 64°13'W. These coordinates place us in the center of Mahone Bay, Nova Scotia, half-way between Big Tancock Island and Oak Island.

The Right Side of the Image

While the left side of the image provides directions in the form of map coordinates disguised within the geometry of the image itself, the right-side of the illustration of the Invisible College reinforces the main message revealed in the cipher-texts of the plaque of Shakespeare's Funerary Monument in Holy Trinity Church.

The bombshell information, aside from Bacon claiming responsibility for the Shakespeare project itself and membership in the Rosicrucian Brotherhood, was the revelation of his true parentage, that his biological parents were Mary Queen of Scots and Francis II of France. The iconography on the right side of the illustration verify and reveal the same truths in visual cryptography. However, the story does not end there.

The angles formed from the geometry of the right side of the image reinforce the message in the form of cipher signatures that appear in the cipher texts of Shakespeare's plaque, and echo the story as depicted in the illustration. The horizontal lines formed by the foundation of the building and the bottom of the battlement serve as bases for calculating the relevant angles. Each line that the image suggests reaches into this area of the image and terminates at the edge, near the images of the falling figure of Bacon, as well as the image of him with the anchor.

First of all, let's look at the letter exiting the structure with the words "Nostro T*S*." While an obvious connection with these initials point to the author of the book in which this image appears, Theophilus Schweighardt, I believe that the letters also serve multiple purposes in the illustration beyond the author being identified as "our own T.S." I suggest as an additional meaning "Our own F. (G)Bacon," after using the Reverse Cipher substitution system, by subbing the F for T and the G for S. The angle of the line attached to it when measured with the horizontal lines of the bottom of the battlement and foundation of the structure, measures 33 degrees which we know is the Simple Cipher signature for "Bacon." Additionally, the line created by the base of the top battlement and the distorted perspective of the line of the base of the right side of the battlement measures 7 degrees, the Simple Cipher value of "G" (see Figure 11-15):

Figure 11-15

These signatures act as indications that identify the falling figure as Francis Bacon.

Next, extending a line suggested by the edge of the drawbridge and creating a baseline from the foundation of the building, we have an angle measuring 50 degrees. The number 50 is the Simple Cipher signature for "Fr. III." The line crosses the falling figure at the knees therefore figuratively "cutting him off at the knees," which is what happened to his identity as Francis III of France. This is appropriate as the family de Medici caused his "fall" and appears in the form of the motto, "Festina Lente."

Taken together, 33 and 50 identify Bacon as Francis III. It's also incredibly important to note the position of the falling figure's arms, a signal for "who will help a poor widow's son?" in Freemasonry. Mackey's Encyclopedia of Freemasonry states, "The claim has often been made that the adherents of the exiled House of Stuart, seeking to organize a system of political Freemasonry by which they hoped to secure the restoration of the family to the throne of England, transferred to Charles II the tradition of Hiram Abif betrayed by his followers, and called him the Widow's Son, because he was the son of Henrietta Maria, the widow of Charles I. For the same reason they presumably subsequently applied the phrase to his brother, James II." I respectfully suggest that this tradition actually comes from Francis Bacon, whose younger brother was also James, James I of England. As Francis III, he was the widow Mary Queen of Scots' son.

The errors in perspective in this area of the structure indicate more messages. Note the length of the foundation on its right side seems too long or wide, and the wheel on the backside of the building is the same size as the closer wheels on the front. Likewise, the length of the bottom of the battlement above seems oversized, and the angle and length are somehow different from the foundation below when they should be parallel (Figure 11-16):

Figure 11 - 16

Accentuating the "error" in perspective, using the same procedure for the foundation on the right side, the angle produced by this line and the baseline produced by the front of the foundation is 17 degrees. 17 in Simple Cipher is the letter R, and is the value of "Rex" in Short Cipher. Juxtaposed within this angle is the kneeling figure "seeing" the hand of God. Therefore this number symbolically creates a signature of the Fra. Rosi Crosse as, R-See, or RC.

One final note regarding this area of the illustration. By creating a perfectly vertical line down from the center of the star at the top forms an angle with the kneeling figure's sightline to the hand of God of precisely 30 degrees. The angles formed by these lines are repeated in a geographical relationship between a key point on Oak Island, Nova Scotia, and the center of Temple Mount, Jerusalem. This is demonstrated in detail in the Appendix containing the theory submitted to the team on Oak Island.

In summation, the use of the emblem of a battlement riding upon the Wheels of Fortune is highly symbolic. The RC intended to create their "Republic of Letters" and make it highly mobile, in that they could be free thinkers within any country. By sharing their science and knowledge with one another, they realized they could affect the future (Fortune).

By placing the foundation of their brotherhood on the Wheels of Fortune, they were utilizing this symbol, the Wheel of Fortune, to signal that "she can make a King a pauper, and a pauper a king." Such was the life of Francis Bacon, the poor widow's son. And so if they utilized that power, they could bring down the monarchies, and raise the common man out of the well of his ignorance. One of the main tools they would use to achieve such an objective was the written word and *secret writing*, represented by the men with giant quills on the battlements and the winged letters.

My personal belief due to my work with the ciphered messages on Shakespeare's plaque? If Fortune determined Sir Francis Bacon would not be King of either country he had been born to lead, then he would take control of Fortune, and *there would be no kings.* The colonies in the Americas could be the means to that end.

Lastly, the kneeling figure of Bacon with his hands wrapped around the anchor mimics the symbolism of the emblems representing the de Medici family motto of "festina lente." As Dauphin, the French word for dolphin, having his hands wrapped around an anchor beneath those very words has obvious implications.

Therefore, this Illustration of The Invisible College contains confirmation of the messages of the cipher texts hidden in the plaque of Shakespeare's Funerary Monument in Holy Trinity Church in Stratford-upon-Avon. Most notably it reveals Bacon's true identity and the location of the Rosicrucian "Ark" where they preserved (at least at that time) their most important truths and knowledge – Mahone Bay, Nova Scotia.

Chris Donah's Confirmation Research

One last addition that needs mentioning. As I worked on the multiple cipher texts within the transposition ciphers, I had been keeping Chris Donah apprised of the progress. Meanwhile, he began to experiment with my character count and numbering system of the characters on the plaque. One of his methods was simply a straightforward approach of adding the count number of consecutive characters in areas he thought were significant to identify any correlations and signatures. And by independently using this different method, he found some extremely interesting results.

One excellent example he discovered by adding the values of the characters 1 through 259 as it is the cipher signature of Shakespeare in Kaye Cipher. According to his calculations, the sum of these numbers is 33670. If you've read this far then the significance is obvious. In the cipher systems 0's can be dropped, leaving 33 and 67, just one more way we can see "Francis Bacon" in "Shakespeare."

Conclusion

To conclude, when I began this process I was unprepared for the actual messages. I just thought it would be a fun project. It would be a distraction from the insanity happening outside my door. While I had hoped I might find an explicit message connecting Sir Francis Bacon with Shakespeare, or possibly a mention of Nova Scotia, I never expected bombshell information. Instead, explicit messages from Francis Bacon claimed authorship of the works of Shakespeare. One whole cipher text appeared to be dedicated to a message linking Bacon to the mystery of Oak Island, in Mahone Bay, Nova Scotia. Lastly and in my mind most

230

importantly, the messages reveal a Royal secret – the identities of Sir Francis Bacon's true birth parents.

I've always been an entertainer of the theory that Bacon could have written the works of Shakespeare. In addition, I had also suspected he could have been the secret son of Elizabeth I, though it seemed illogical in terms of her behavior toward him. Instead, the message not only calls that theory into doubt, but it directly refutes it. Francis Bacon was the secret son of Mary Queen of Scots. Such information would have upset the social order of France, a country already fraught with civil war and uprisings. The tumultuous rivalry of Mary Queen of Scots and Elizabeth I was one of the most complex political issues of the time period. The stability of two countries hung in the balance, making it necessary to keep Bacon's identity secret. This lends significance to his Shakespearian plays known as the "Henriad." Based upon the messages of the cipher texts, Bacon rather preferred to see his younger half-brother on the throne of England, and out of love abdicated it to him to "pass on holiday." Or as he put it, he shunned the responsibility of being a "well-dressed helmsman." However, one thing is obvious – he refused to allow the secret and the truth, his sacred *Tau*, to be lost to history.

He encoded a cipher in a plaque dedicated to his pseudonym (one of many), William Shakespeare, in Trinity Church in Stratford-upon-Avon, England, ensuring that one day the truth would be brought into the light. That he created the revered works as William Shakespeare is more than enough information to cement his place as one of the most important figures in history. But he knew that one day in the future, after enough time had passed and stability had been restored in Europe, that the truth could be told. The romantic notion of the lost Dauphin, of the Royal Prince being denied his birthright, and forced to live a "meager" existence, was true. And now it can be told and has been told at last. Francis Bacon should have been known as Francois III of France, and Francis Stewart I of England.

There is only one other message that begs credulity more than this chapter. That message involves what Bacon termed as his "best alias." Could he really have been Samuel de Champlain?

Color Plates

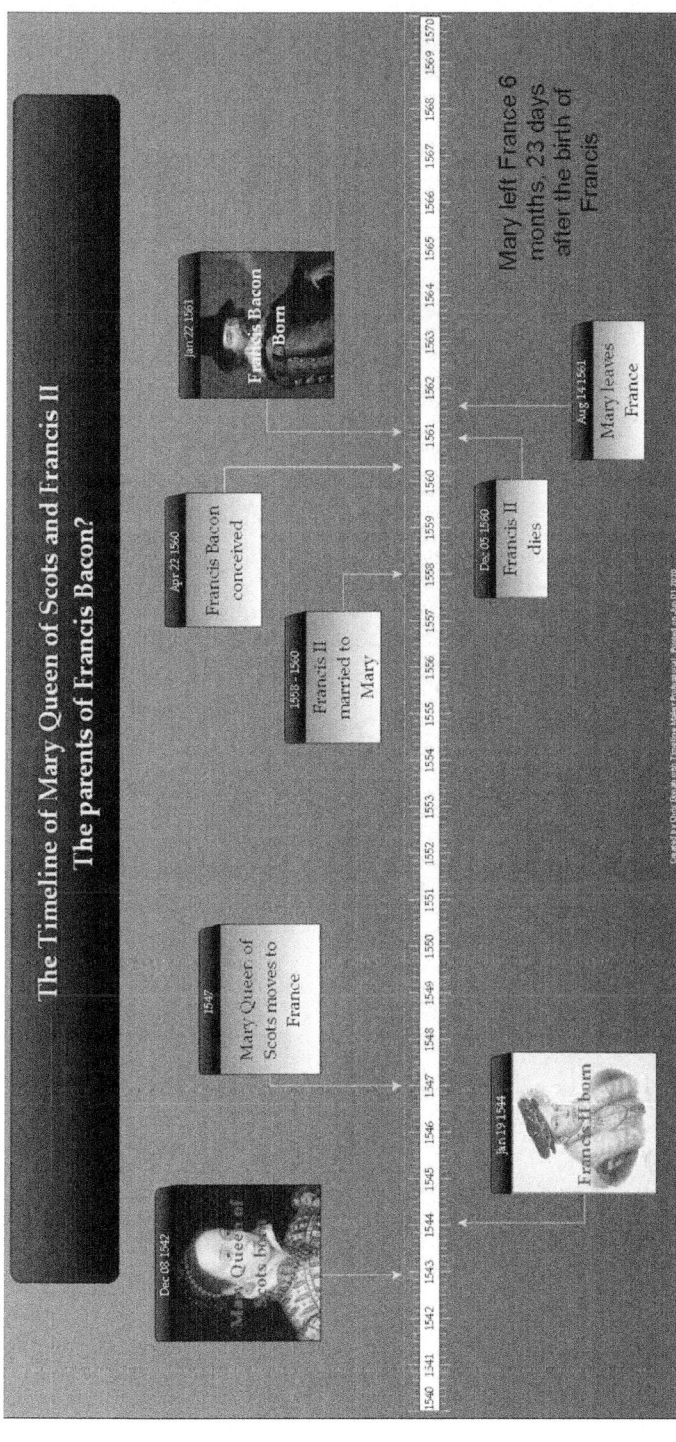

Plate 1: A timeline of the events from birth of Mary to her flight from France, 29 days after the birth of Francis Bacon. While orthodox history claims that Francis II was incapable of fathering an heir, I believe this is simply a ruse by the winners who wrote the history, namely Catherine de Medici and Elizabeth I of England. The birth of Francois III and Francis Stewart (Stuart) would be a threat to the power of both of the two most powerful women in Europe. Not only is the timeline a perfect fit with the messages of the cipher texts but it also follows a very logical premise. Mary's return would indeed have been negotiated, and I believe Bacon was the bargaining chip, resulting in his life-long hatred of his birth-mother. Image courtesy of Chris Donah. Used with permission.

233

Plate 2: Here we see a portrait Anthony Bacon, the brother of Sir Francis Bacon. Not only is there not any family resemblance, note the stark differences in hair color, eyebrows, and facial hair. Images courtesy of Wikipedia Commons under Fair Use.

234

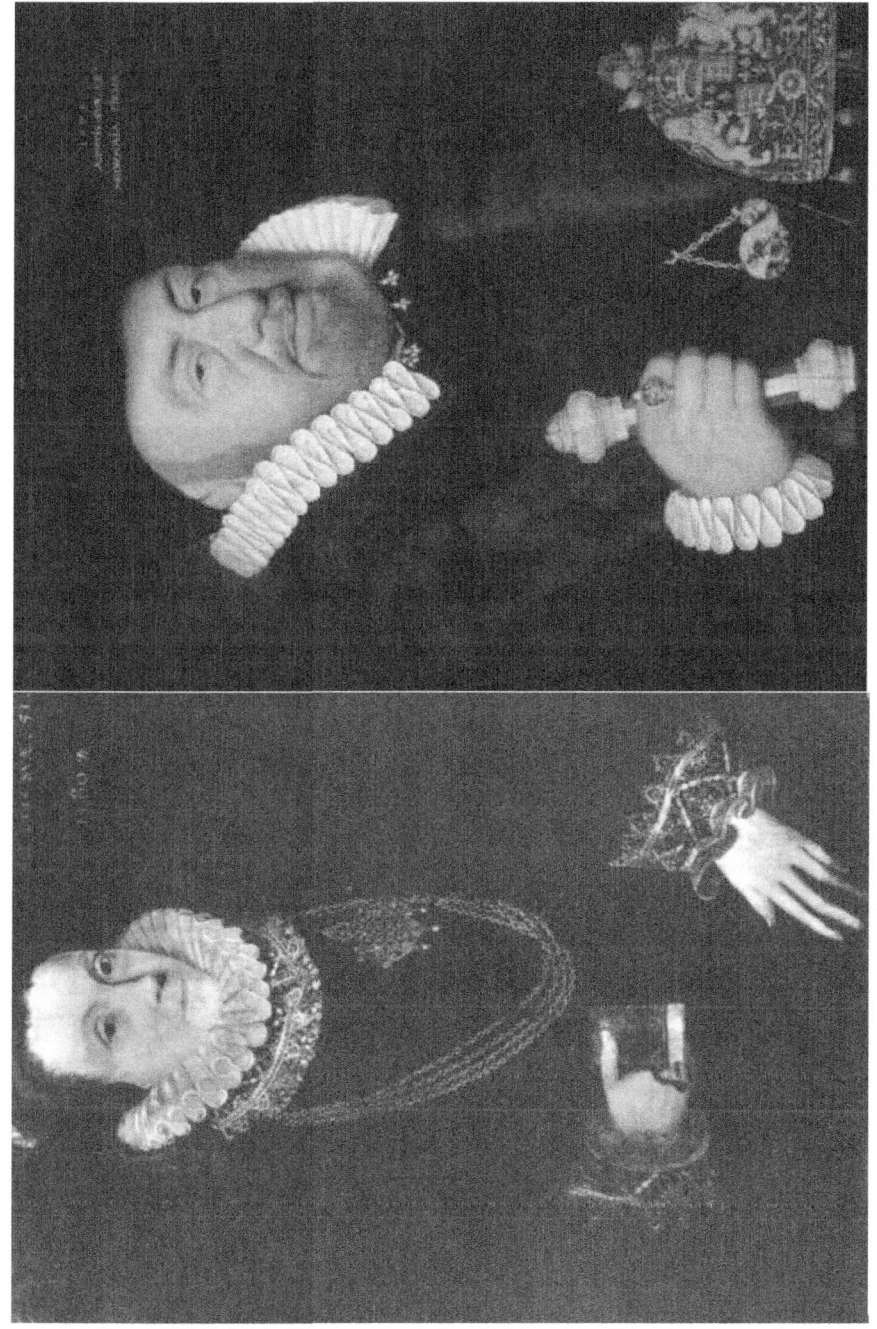

Plate 3: Lady Anne Bacon, second wife of Sir Nicholas Bacon, and his portrait as Keeper of the Great Seal. Images courtesy of Wikipedia Commons under Fair Use.

Plate 4: James VI and I, Sir Francis Bacon, and James V of Scotland, father of Mary Queen of Scots. When compared to the images of all three Bacons, this family resemblance between these three men is unmistakable. From facial structure, hair color, to the arch of their eyebrows, certain characteristics seem to run strong in the Stewart line. Images courtesy of Wikipedia Commons under Fair Use.

Plate 5: Francis II of France, Mary Queen of Scots at left, and miniature of Francis Bacon, all three at about the same age of 18. Even without the same level of detail, the miniature of Francis Bacon provides an unmistakable resemblance of his parents at about the same age. Note the eyes and hairlines of Francis II and III. Images courtesy of Wikipedia Commons under Fair Use.

Plate 6: The "faux" family de Medici Crest, I believe was created by Sir Francis Bacon. The characteristic cherubs at the top crown a child, and the dolphin (Dauphin) shapes apper in the filigree below the "motto." Note the characters in the false Latin motto, and how they exactly match the characters on the plaque of Shakespeare's Funerary Monument in Holy Trinity Church, Stratford-upon-Avon. Image courtesy of Wikipedia Commons under Fair Use.

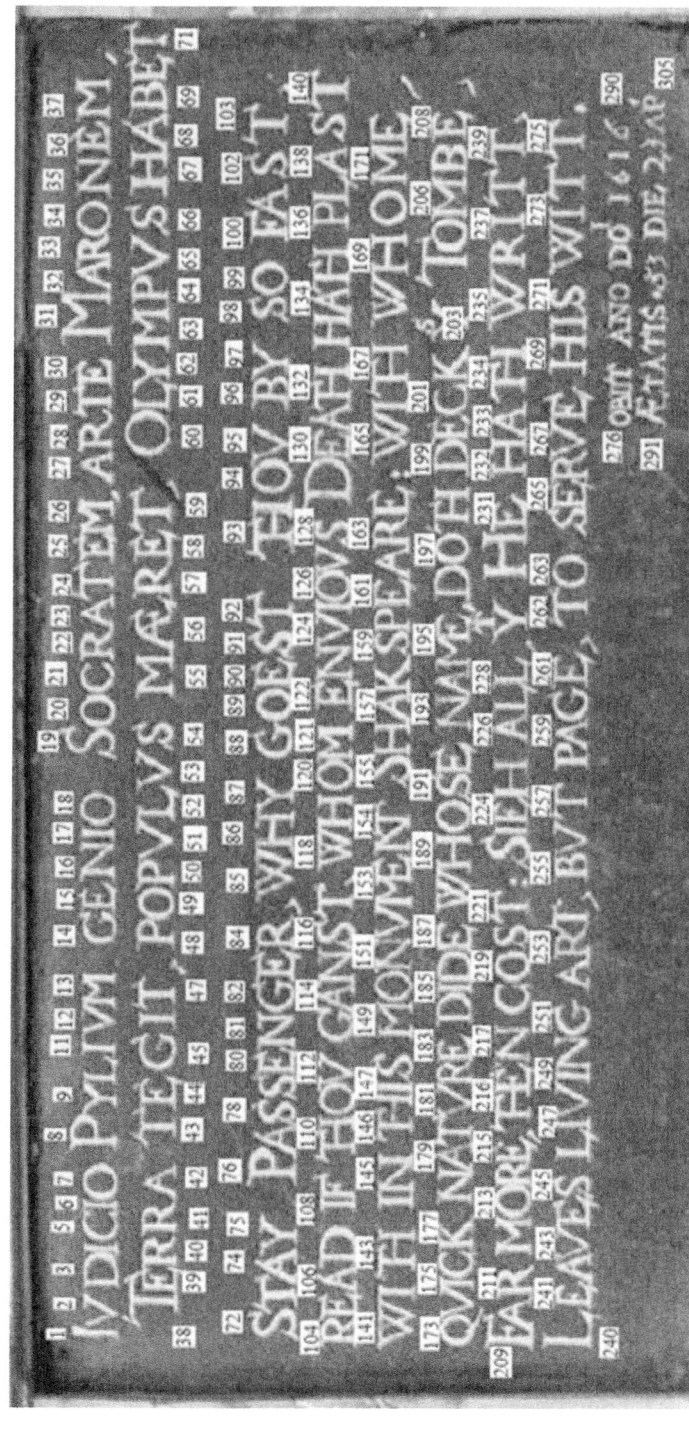

Plate 7: In this image, you can see the *forward count* of the characters as they appear on the plaque with I as 1 and ending with P in the lower right as 305. Assigning a number to each character allowed me to note the correlations between letters of symbolic significance and known (and later unknown) cipher signatures used by Sir Francis Bacon in his Simple, Reverse and Kaye Cipher system. As you can see, in this arrangement (and in its reverse, starting at P in the lower right as 1, and ending at I in the upper left as 305), the mathematical center is the number 153, *I Sir Francis Bacon* in Simple Cipher. The character at this number appears as the conjoined letters of ME. To *READ IF THOU CANST* whose name has been placed within the monument named SHAKSPEARE, just count the characters, and see who is at the center of the mystery. (*Image courtesy of Chris Donah*).

239

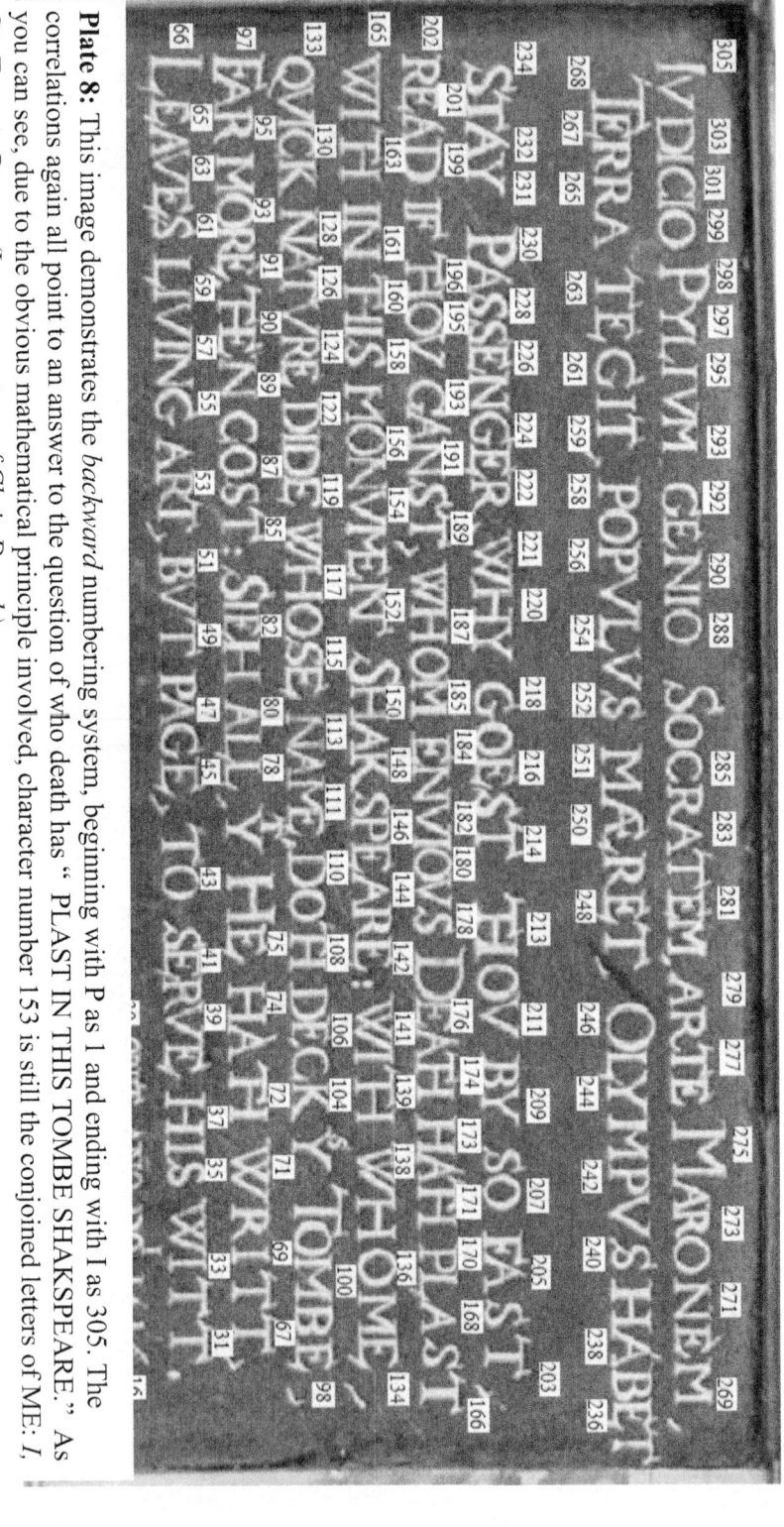

Plate 8: This image demonstrates the *backward* numbering system, beginning with P as 1 and ending with I as 305. The correlations again all point to an answer to the question of who death has " PLAST IN THIS TOMBE SHAKSPEARE." As you can see, due to the obvious mathematical principle involved, character number 153 is still the conjoined letters of ME: *I, Sir Francis Bacon. (Image courtesy of Chris Donah).*

240

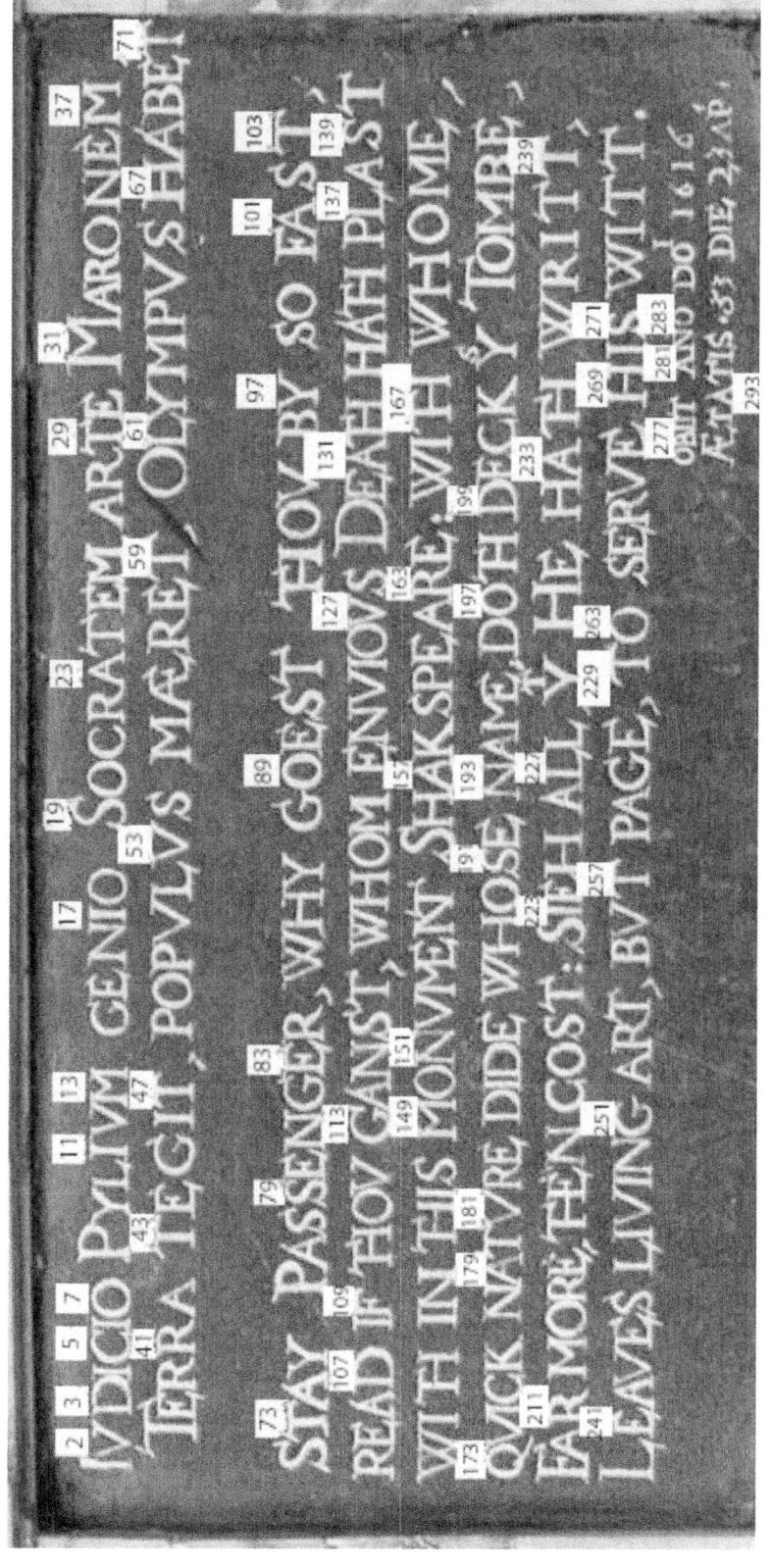

Plate 9: Here we can see all of the prime numbers of the forward or regular count labelling their corresponding characters. Note how all of them are either symbolically significant letters or their Atbash substitutes. For example, character 173 is the letter Q, which can be replaced by I, stating *I RC*. Only three characters do not meet this criteria and they are all the letter *D*. When added together in Simple, Reverse and Kaye Ciphers, the values are all the same as the word *BEE*, 12, 63, and 90, respectively.

241

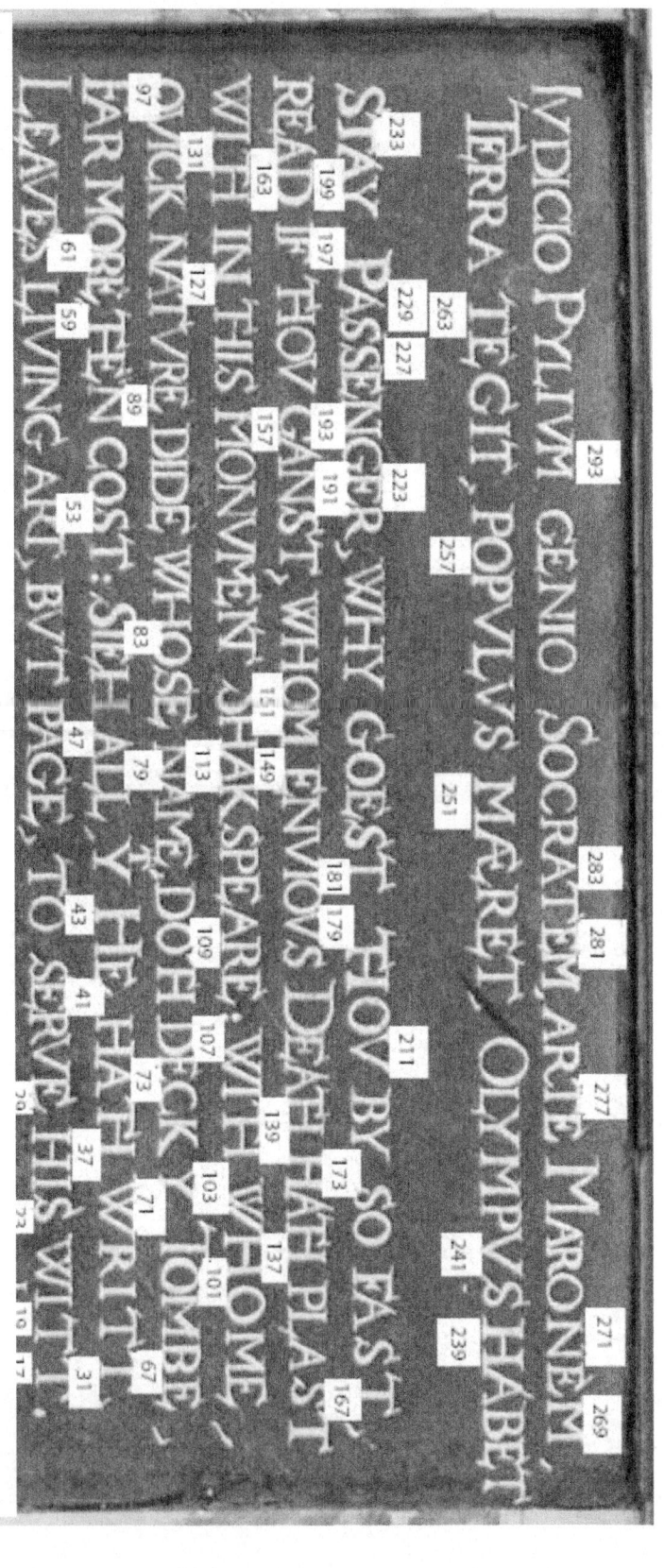

Plate 10: Depicted in this image of the plaque we see all of the prime numbers labeled according to the backward count, beginning in the lower right corner near the mistake the *age* of Shakespeare at the time of his death. In this count, every prime number correlates to a significant character or its Atbash substitute. The only letters here that do not match are again, two of the same D characters, another D and this time a W. The Simple, Reverse and Kaye totals of these letters respectfully are 33 (Bacon in Simple), 67 (Francis is Simple) and 111 (Bacon in Kaye).

242

Plate 11: The *self-portrait* of Nicholas Hilliard and its counter-part in the form of the miniature of Francis Bacon at age 18. I maintain they are both self-portraits, and that Nicholas Hilliard was Bacon's very first alias after his return from France where he studied art. Many of the sign-posts he left behind are very obvious, where he became more subtle with later aliases. Francis was the only member of the Bacon family to be painted by Hilliard, yet he mostly painted miniatures of Royalty, many of whom are connected with his secret identity as the son of Mary, Queen of Scots and Francis II of France.

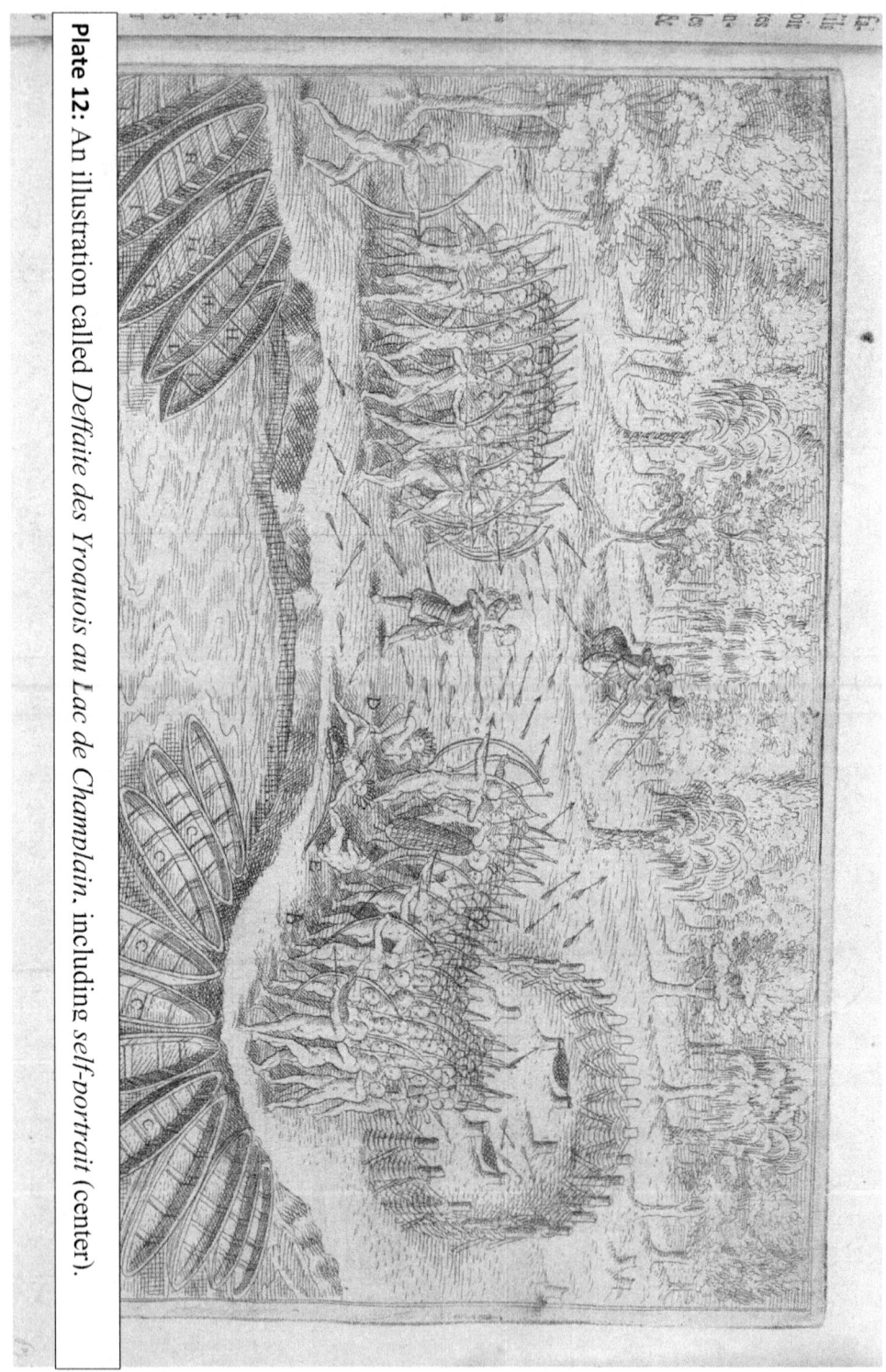

Plate 12: An illustration called *Deffaite des Yroquois au Lac de Champlain*, including *self-portrait* (center).

244

Chapter 12 – The Plausibility of the Messages: A Life of Aliases at Sea

"History is bunk."
-     Henry Ford

By far the most difficult message to accept is Champlain as one of Bacon's aliases. Though the cipher texts in Emasker of TT and Key 32 explicitly stated the case, more evidence is needed. It would never satisfy any self-respecting student of history. I needed to find corroborating evidence. Believe it or not, it exists, and it extended beyond the cipher signatures previously discussed in Chapter 8. Before delving into the Champlain evidence, one other alias needs exploration and explanation. Given the name of Tiberio Tinelli establishing Bacon as an artist, answered several questions.

Among all the connections in the hidden Francis Bacon story, with all of the people who would have known his true secret identity, one name kept appearing. This artist painted Francis, Elizabeth I and Robert Dudley, James' daughter Elizabeth, Amias Paulet, Sir Francis Drake, Henry the Duke of Anjou (uncle), Marguerite of Valois, Queen of Navarre (aunt), and even Mary, Queen of Scots (mother) during her captivity. This artist apparently also painted multiple portraits of Robert Devereux, 2nd Earl of Essex, leader of the failed "Essex Rebellion" against Queen Elizabeth I, Devereux's own mother.

Friends and fellow researchers Christopher Morford and Daniel Spino mentioned the speculation that Francis Bacon had been in love with Marguerite, to which I asked, "and if I'm right, and she was his aunt?"

One of them (remaining nameless) stated, "well, you know those Royals back then."

Fair enough.

But the example helps to illustrate the connection among all of these disparate historical figures from a common-born boy-turned respected Admiral of the Royal fleet, Drake, to a queen of the House Valois. What is the connection between all these people and others not mentioned? The secret birth of Francois Stuart-Valois-Angouleme.

Digging more deeply into the mystery of the aliases, as usual a pattern developed. When researching the network of names, when reading about the history of the individual, the phrases and ideas always cropped up: *While not much is known about Hamalota Barn's birth or early life... but Christening Records record his name as Meatonce Manger, which could be a local variation of the name at the time. Hamalota's name as we know it first appears in the public record..."* when the Bacon boys needed it to appear.

The point of course is that these "historical personages" often have very illusive early beginnings, and the names we know differ substantially from the records bearing their "original names." While the William Shakespeare example is the best known, and the similarity to Willom Shaxper / William Shaksper /William Shakspear the actor, allowed Bacon to wear the real man as a mask, the other original personages seem to be more illusive.

This is not meant to discount the impressive work that historians do, nor the accuracy with which they research the primary source documents they use to reconstruct these people and their histories. However when we consider this rationally, we need to recognize that the Bacon brothers created some of those documents. They were creating aliases, and even having those aliases "write letters to each other," sometimes "discussing other aliases to each other as if they are real people" to create the illusion that each of those personages were real people. Add to that the ability to "paint a self-portrait" or create an engraving of an "author" of a pamphlet in that time period, suddenly a powerful propaganda organ emerges.

I'm not the first person to point out the fragility of our understanding of the historical record.

While it was Henry Ford who famously stated, "History is bunk," as the cipher texts of the plaque revealed themselves, a passage from the book *1984* by George Orwell came to mind. The main character Winston Smith's job was to change history. In one instance, he invents a person named "Comrade Ogilvy." Winston then contemplates a truth about history – "Comrade Ogilvy, who had never existed in the present, now existed in the past, and once the forgery was forgotten, he would exist just as authentically, and upon the same evidence, as Charlemagne or Julius Caesar." He means that our understanding of all of our "real" historical figures that we think of as corporeal humans walking the physical earth at some point in the fluidity of time are based upon someone writing down their name. I respectively suggest that some of these historical personages with which we are so familiar, are forgeries perpetrated by one of the greatest minds of the last five-hundred years, Sir Francis Bacon.

248

Considering aliases, the first alias that I believe Francis Bacon created at the age of 18 is one of the keys to understanding all of this, the artist mentioned above connecting all of the Queen's Men (and Women) who were involved in the cover-up of Francis' birth.

The Artist Key

When I saw that one of Francis Bacon's aliases was a renowned artist, suddenly things began to make sense. If Bacon had created aliases and pseudonyms that were artists, this would give him access to the courts of monarchs around Europe, access that would have been valuable to a spy intent upon gathering intelligence. One of the biggest questions bothering me when I began this investigation surrounded one prevalent artist in the court of Queen Elizabeth I, Nicholas Hilliard.

Limner, miniature portrait artist, and jeweler, it had seemed very strange that the only member of the Bacon family he had ever painted was Francis. His Wikipedia page states, "His paintings still exemplify the visual image of Elizabethan England, very different from that of most of Europe in the late sixteenth century. Technically he was very conservative by European standards, but his paintings are superbly executed and have a freshness and charm that has ensured his continuing reputation as "the central artistic figure of the Elizabethan age, the only English painter whose work reflects, in its delicate microcosm, the world of Shakespeare's earlier plays."" No need to point out the irony of that statement.

Nicholas Hilliard was probably the very first alias of young Francis Bacon. While investigating Hilliard, an amazing pattern began to emerge which I have already pointed out – the very people of whom he was known to paint portraits would have been connected to his "secret" identity of Dauphin and prince. In reference to Sir Francis Drake, I suspect that falling-in with the adventurer and privateer as a young man would have provided him with a role model and income after the death of Sir Nicholas Bacon.

Understanding the clues Bacon left behind with Hilliard will allow us to see the clues he provides with Champlain. The first pieces of evidence that Bacon provides is the miniature that "Hilliard" paints of young Francis Bacon at the age of 18, juxtaposed with the "self-portrait" of Nicholas Hilliard (Plate 11). The second piece of evidence will appear in the portrait of his "wife." The third piece of evidence involves the cipher signatures of his aliases using his cipher systems. The final piece appears in the "artwork" of Samuel de Champlain, and his Map of 1612.

While some might speculate regarding the accuracy of paintings versus our modern photography, I always respond that this was the Renaissance. The artists of the time strove to perfect the capturing of the likenesses of their subjects. Ignatius Donnelly writes in *The Great Cryptogram*, "Bacon had returned from the higher civilization of France, (nearer geographically to the surviving Roman Culture), full of all the arts – music, poetry and painting. We see many references to the art of painting in the Shakespeare plays." And so as I began to look at the possibility of Bacon being a painter, I naturally had to look at Nicholas Hilliard. When looking at the portraits of Francis and Hilliard side-by-side, it's obvious that they are *both self-portraits* (again, see Plate 11).

While the Hilliard self-portrait purports to show him at 30 years of age in 1577, Bacon would have been 16 or 17, and the Bacon miniature depicts Francis at age 18, the resemblance is still uncanny. Though the hair color of Hilliard is black as opposed to the Stuart / Stewart red, it's obvious that he was in control of his color palette. It's an easy matter to change the hair color and add a beard that almost appears as if it were a theatrical costume or make-up in a Shakespearean play. The next piece of evidence appears as a signature of Hilliard in the portrait of his "wife," Alice (Bacon would later have a wife by the same name):

Figure 12–1 – Alice Hilliard

The important part of this portrait isn't the existence of this person in history. (This portrait is the evidence that she existed as a real living human being by the way. Bacon could have fabricated any documents and her much like Winston Smith did with Comrade Ogilvy from the *1984* example). Though there are elements of the portrait of a cryptic nature such as the collar and the knot of the black ribbon around her neck, near a rose, the important element here is the pair of signatures on the left and right. (The knot forms a backward R, or H in Reverse Cipher, and the right side forms a 6 as F for Francis). He signed his portrait of his wife with what is traditionally interpreted as his monogram, his initials N and H superimposed over one another on the left and right of the image. Upon closer examination of this signature, we'll see so much more than simply an N and an H.

The first question is, why would there be another backwards N?

While it provided visual symmetry to the image, it also created the double A (AA) symbol used by Bacon, with the pair of As leaning away from one another. This was enough of an indication to take an even closer look. Additionally, the AA also creates the quality of "mirroring" a reflection or shadow as two A's appear upside down as well. Due to the appearance of multiple double or quadruple letters, I decided to identify all of the letters that appear in this symbol, and calculate their value using Bacon's Fourfold Cipher.

This also created a bit of a problem as well. While the signature was created with two N's and an H, should I assume that the H represented the double Tau symbol as it had in the plaque cipher texts? And if I counted it as TT, should I also include the value of the H in addition? Or is it an "either/or" relationship? What about other letters appearing within the symbol itself? For example, if I included every letter I could see in the image, there were multiple letters that could go unnoticed, such as X, M, and W:

In the end I decided to just experiment with what I saw and see what resulted. So I began with the values of all of the double letter combinations that would have a unique value in the Fourfold Cipher: AAAA, NN, and TT (for H). With 73 = AAAA, 37 = NN and 43 for TT, the sum is 153, a number that I have demonstrated as a Bacon signature in a variety ways. It is the sum of "I Sir Francis Bacon" in Simple Cipher, however he didn't have that title at that time in his life, his true identity becomes the source of this signature. The values of "King Bacon" in Reverse, and the sum in the Fourfold Cipher of both "Roi Francois" and "Francois III" fulfill this purpose. The sum of M and W in Simple Cipher is 33, the Simple Cipher signature for "Bacon." Adding X and the sum is 55, the Short Cipher signature for "Francis Bacon," and which in Fourfold Cipher is the value of GGG. Also, one of the cipher texts we just read demonstrates 55 is the value of "Walt R" in Simple Cipher. If we take the "base" value of 153 and add X (22), we have 175, the cipher signature for "Francois Stuart" in both Simple and Reverse Ciphers. Adding the value of 33 for M and W to 175 produces a total of 208, the cipher signature for "Francois Stewart III" in Simple. Adding the additional and original H for "Hilliard" produces 216, the signature for "Francois Stuart" in the Fourfold Cipher. Considering TT had been used in place of the original H, if we only want to count these values once, we subtract 43 as the value of TT and the result is 173 – 17 3 or RC in Simple, as well as "Fama Fraternitatis."

Incidentally, the monogram can be said to be merely comprised of an H and X. In the substitution system these letters are, RC.

I then checked the values of this combination of letters in Simple, Reverse and Kaye Ciphers. The total in Simple was 123, the cipher signature for "James" in Kaye, and *Nicholas* in Reverse. The sum in Reverse Cipher was 152, the signature for "Rex Francois III" in Simple, "Stewart" in Kaye, and "William" in Kaye. The Kaye Cipher sum totaled 227, the cipher signature for Sir Francis Bacon in Fourfold, however Francis was not "Sir Francis" at the time of his creation of Hilliard. This number frequently appears in relation to Bacon, the plaque and his aliases. It's the 49th prime number and can therefore represent the idea of 7 x 7, or G x G. However, this number is the Simple Cipher signature for "King Francis Stuart III." The AAAA equals 108 in Kaye Cipher, which is the signature for "Francis" in Reverse and "Francois III" in Simple. The remaining letters, TTNNXMW total 119 in Kaye and Simple, which is the signature for "Francois" in Reverse. While this is an impressive list of results, the results for the name "Nicholas Hilliard" do not disappoint.

The best way to demonstrate the values of his name is Table 12 – 1:

Table 12 - 1

	S	R	K	4F
Nicholas	77	123	181	77
Hilliard	70	130	200	98
Sums	147	253	381	218

The Simple Cipher values yield very interesting numbers. "Nicholas" is 77 in Simple, which many people would point out is the value of "Rex Bacon" in Simple. While true, this signature better represents "Rex F. III." The value of 70 is the signature for "Dauphin" in Simple. The sum of 147 is the signature in Simple Cipher of "King Francois III" and of "Mary Stuart." The Reverse Cipher sums, aside 123 which is the signature for James, seem unremarkable. The sum of 253, much like the previous example could represent "I Rex Francis Bacon Stewart" in Simple. All three of the Kaye Cipher values are significant in relation to Bacon. The value of 181 is the Simple Cipher signature of "Francois Stewart," and the Reverse Cipher signature of "King Francis III." The Reverse sum for "Hilliard" of 200 is the Reverse Cipher signature of "Francis Bacon." The total of 381 is the cipher signature of "King Francois III" in Kaye Cipher.

252

When looking at this table, you might note that the Fourfold sum "doesn't add-up." Adding the values yields the signature of 175, "Francois Stuart" in both Simple and Reverse Ciphers. However, we need to remember that when considered as the whole name of "Nicholas Hilliard," the values of the double and triple letters change. Unless someone knew about Francis Bacon's true family heritage, the number of 218 would be meaningless. However, 218 is the Kaye Cipher value of "Francis V-A," the initials of his father's last name, House Valois-Angouleme.

The significance of Hilliard's "signature" on his painting, and the multiple significant cipher signatures in his name pointing to Francis Bacon, cannot be overstated. The juxtaposition of their portraits also provides significant visual evidence. The fact that so many of the cipher signatures overlap with Bacon's secret identity indicates to me that Nicholas Hilliard was one of Bacon's earliest aliases. I think that as he developed more identities that he began to become more subtle. Manly Palmer Hall writes in his *The Secret Teachings of All Ages* regarding Bacon, "He who understands the secret of the Seven-Rayed God will comprehend the method employed by Bacon to accomplish his monumental labor. Aliases were assumed by him in accordance with the attributes and order of the members of the planetary system." While using Bacon's cipher systems to test the names of his aliases can be a useful indicator, apparently a far more effective technique exists to identify his false names. Since Hilliard became increasingly obvious the closer I looked, I think he created the persona before he had honed his techniques for the creation of his later aliases as indicated by Hall. A full discussion and explanation of that system is covered in Book II of this series, *The Ghosts of Bacon*.

Conclusions

While Nicholas Hilliard is not directly connected to Champlain, it's important to establish Francis Bacon as a master artist. While the cipher text in Key 32 explicitly claims Tiberio Tinelli as a Bacon alias, one of the techniques used by Hilliard in his "signature" establishes the use of the Fourfold Cipher in its design, and this will be highly relevant in the Champlain connection.

Champlain and the Chain of Evidence

Following the clues from the cipher texts, in particular the statements of "I wrote books at sea," "See my pictures of ships / boats," and the acrostic "See hat" and the acrostic anagrams of "See hat / see trees," explicitly tell us where to look, and what to see. Though the cipher texts state that Champlain was Francis Bacon's best alias, finding more connections between these names would require more than matching cipher signatures. So, we begin with one of Bacon's best-known books, that had pictures of ships on the frontispiece, *Novum Organum*.

The ship in the foreground between the "Pillars of Hercules" is highly detailed and flanked by two dolphins. On the left of the ship, the dolphin appears near the anchor of the ship, as if as in an expression of the Family de Medici motto, "Festina Lente." The engraving is attributed to an engraving shop in Leiden, Holland called Wyngaerden and Moiardum. One of the interesting things about some of Bacon's creations is the names often have a hidden meaning that is sometimes comical. Wyngaerden means, "wine garden." Moiardum is a compound word created by combining the French "moi" meaning "I," and the Latin "ardum" meaning *thirsty or dry*. So the name of the "shop" where the engraving was created means "wine garden and I thirsty." Looking at the values of both words separately and added together yields multiple Bacon signatures. And so, it seemed logical to compare the images of the ship on *Novum Organum* with the ships that appear on Champlain's 1612 map of New France.

Figure 12-2 *Novum Organum*   Figure 12 – 3 1612 Map   Figure 12 – 4 1612 Map

Figure 12 - 5

Comparing the first image from *Novum Organum* with three of the ships appearing on Champlain's map of 1612, is compelling. The first thing that I noted was the way the cannons were depicted is the same in all four images. The same contour and shape of the sails and flags, as well as the anchors also indicated the same artist at work. I reached out to a friend who is an art professor at one of the local colleges. I didn't reveal the source of the images, and asked her if she could compare the first image with the other three and give an opinion regarding if they could have been done by the same artist. I did make her aware that they were Renaissance era, and the first image was from an engraving, while

254

the others were ink drawings. She replied that she was 87% sure that they were done by the same artist and for her, the most telling detail was the execution of the waves. Danielle indicated that it would be very rare for two different artists to take the same approach in their execution. The reason her certainty wasn't higher was her inability to examine the physical originals themselves. She also informed me that during that period, engraving and drawing were very similar processes. This only changed in the centuries after, so it would be natural for one artist to be capable of creating all of the images.

Before looking at Champlain's map of New France, we need to look at the only known "self-portrait" of Samuel de Champlain, since self-portraits seem to be a theme here. Additionally, this next example qualifies as a book Champlain "wrote at sea." The "self-portrait" such as it is, is an illustration called "Deffaite des Yroquois au Lac de Champlain," meaning "Defeat of the Iroquois at Lake Champlain." The image depicts Champlain standing firing a musket at the Iroquois amid a flurry of arrows. However, the cipher texts tell us what to look for – his hat, the trees, and the ship boats. The full image appears as Plate 12.

Remember the acrostic in Key 32, the key that stated Bacon had

Figure 12 - 6

written books at sea, and instructed us to look at his pictures of "ship boats?" Remember the acrostic "see hat / see trees, 33?" I've lived in Northern New York my entire life, and I have visited Lake Champlain on multiple occasions as an adult. I have yet to see a palm tree on the shore of Lake Champlain. Yet this picture appears to have 3! Look at Figure 12–6, and tell me what number you see repeated in the bark of the palm trees behind the battle?

The number 33 appears on the trees again and again, providing the impression of bark. If all of the trees in the whole image had the same appearance and the same bark, this could be coincidence. Also, there could be an inclination to attribute this to carelessness on the part of the artist ignorant of the details of the flora of the area. However, this isn't possible. One of the most compelling features of Champlain's map of 1612 is the detailed catalogue and drawings he includes of the plants of New France. If he drew palm trees with obscure bark on the shores of his eponymous lake, there must be a reason. As stated in previous chapters, when it comes to steganography and ciphers, "mistakes" are purposefully made to draw our attention to a message. The acrostic of Key 32 also instructed us to "See hat, see trees 33." Since we found "Bacon" in the trees, we need to take a closer look at the hat Champlain is wearing in his "self-portrait."

In this close-up in Figures 12–7 & 8, multiple Bacon "markers" can clearly be seen in the presumable "plumage" of Champlain's hat. Note how the arrows all seem to be pointing at the message, as if to repeat "See hat":

Before reading on, look at the hat to see if you can identify the markers just mentioned.

The hat itself could be constructed by a 6 on the left, joined by a 7 on the right. On the left, upside-down 3s can be seen one over the other, and between this 33 and the hat is a clear letter G. If

the circle in the hat forming the 6 is viewed with the brim as a 9, the numbers in the hat state, "I Francis Bacon" in Simple Cipher. The number 55, the signature for "Francis Bacon" in Short Cipher, seemingly floats above the hat, and in Fourfold Cipher this value also represents "GGG." Additionally, other than the G to the left of the hat, the flintlock is a G on its "face," and tilting our heads to the right, the outline of the hat incorporating the circle at the bottom is also G-shaped, echoing this triple G reference.

Figures 12 – 7 & 8

If we take a closer look at the face of the "only known self-portrait" of Samuel de Champlain, his eye and nose are in the shapes of T and S. Using the Athbash Cipher substitutions, these letters become F G, and with the Kaye Cipher value of G being 33, we see whose face is depicted in this self-portrait – F. Bacon. You may recall the role of these initials in the "Invisible College" illustration. As you'll also see, the letters "TS" will play a role later, appearing on Champlain's 1612 Map of New France in the form of the Hebrew letter "Tsade."

Conclusions

So far, in the illustration "Defeat of the Iroquois" drawn by Samuel de Champlain, stunning correlations appear between it and the cipher texts of Keys 32 and 5 of 38. The messages state that he (Bacon) wrote books at sea, and that his "best alias" was Captain Samuel de Champlain. He also uses acrostics instructing us to "See hat" and "see trees." Looking at pictures in a book Champlain wrote at sea, we *see* cipher signatures of "Francis Bacon" in the hat, and we see "Bacon" in the palm trees on the shore of Lake Champlain. The prevalence of the examples and the direct correlation between the image and the messages of the cipher are beyond coincidence. This in itself began to convince me that the outrageous claim could be true – Samuel de Champlain was an alias, albeit a very famous one, of Sir Francis Bacon. However, the clues do not end there. More correlations appear in this famous image of the Iroquois battle.

"Pictures of Ship Boats"

While Bacon directs us to look at his pictures of ships / boats, another reading of the messages can also be "see my pictures of ship boats." Ship boats of course are the smaller boats used to ferry sailors and goods between ships and shores. In this illustration of the battle however, I was struck by how much the "canoes" better resembled ship boats without the oars. In fact, there wasn't a paddle to be seen! This oversight of an important detail again draws attention to this area of the picture as a pictorial cipher.

An important detail to include as well is the source of the image being used as an illustration. This is an image of the actual document, a high-resolution picture of the original illustration as it appeared in Champlain's book *Voyages* in 1613. As such, it has his notations of key information to label and explain important parts of the picture. Later copies exist where the letters he used to label the canoes and shore have been removed. Since our attention is drawn to this area of the picture by Bacon's suggestion of seeing his pictures of ship boats, and the "mistake" missing paddles and oars, we'll take a closer look in Figure 12–9.

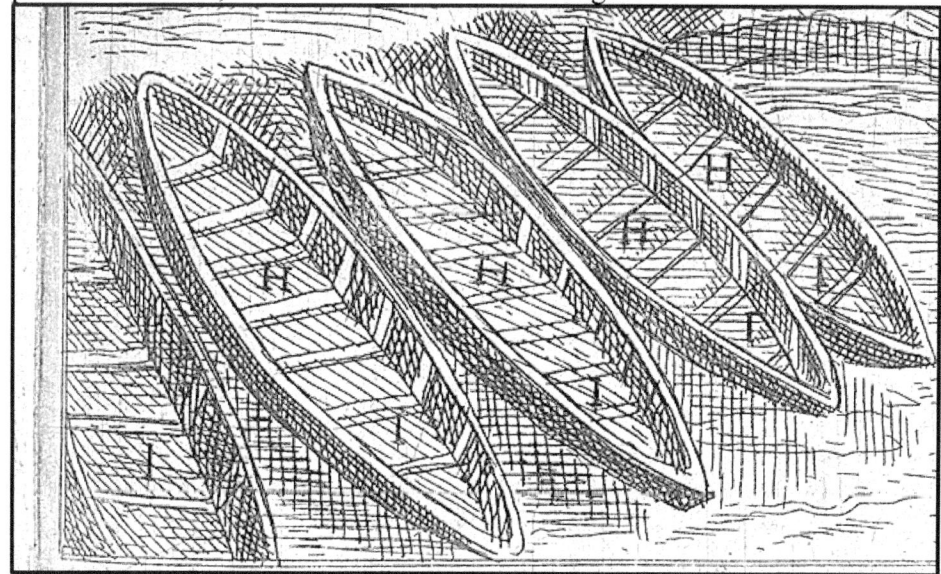

Figure 12 - 8

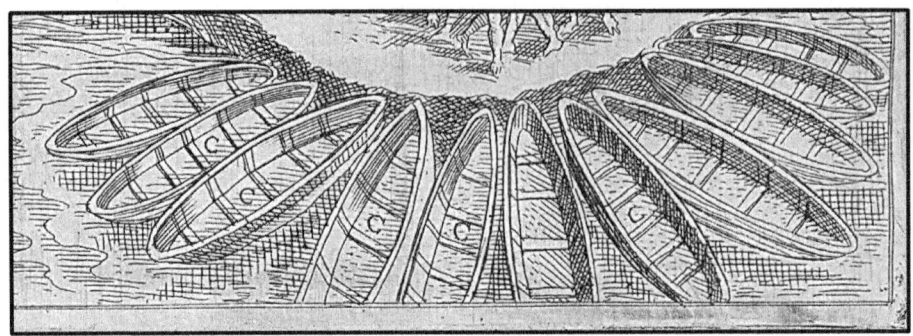

Figure 12 - 9

One thing that immediately that stood out was again, what was missing other than the paddles and oars. Looking at the two images, note that not all of the canoes are labeled with letters. Why go through the effort to label multiple canoes with H, I or C, but not all of them? If the labels were intended to provide information in the legend for all the canoes, why not just save time and effort, and label one on each side? First of all, "HIC" is Latin for "here, in this place." Subbing R for H the message can be read as an anagram for "HIC I RC." Also the only logical conclusion is the values of the letters were intended to be precise. Once again, Bacon uses his cipher system to sign his work, not just in terms of his illustration and his book, but also his role in the Beaver Wars and the defeat of the Iroquois.

The first image on the opposite page comes from the lower left portion of the illustration, and the second is its counterpart in the lower right. For our intents and purposes, the "meaning" of these letters as labels and their correlating meanings in the legend are irrelevant. What matters here are the values in Simple, Reverse and Kaye Ciphers.

In the left (first) image the Simple Cipher total of H H H H is 32, while I I I I I is 45. The Simple total from the right (second) image of C C C C C is 15. Adding the Simple Cipher values produces a sum of 92, the signature of "Bacon" in Reverse.

The sums in Reverse Cipher are H H H H with 68, I I I I I with 80, and C C C C C with 110. These values total 285 which is the signature in Reverse Cipher of "Roi Francois Stuart III."

The Kaye total rounds out our cipher signatures with the following values: H H H H = 136, I I I I I = 175, and C C C C C = 145. Added together these produce 456, a very confusing number at first. However, once again the answer lies within Bacon's secret history and his true identity. If we combine his Scottish and French heritage, viewing his name as it "should" have been, we see his name as "Francois Stewart-Valois-Angouleme III." The value of this name in Reverse Cipher is 456.

If any one of these cipher signatures appeared alone, whether they appeared in a tree, a hat or a canoe, it could be easily dismissed as nothing more than a coincidence or a meaningless anomaly. In and of themselves,

258

even though they all appear together in the same image and within the same context, they are not enough to conclude that Francis Bacon was the same person as Samuel de Champlain and drew this illustration.

However, when a hidden cipher text states where to specifically look in a picture and what to look for and we find it, the aspect of mere chance fades away. When we look at the continuing clues that also appear on Champlain's 1612 Map of New France, it dissipates completely.

The Map Evidence

Last year when I was working on the "Invisible College Illustration," I noted a hidden symbol beneath the movable castle in its shadow, appearing as an "Rx" or "Rc." This symbol is the equivalent our modern pharmacy symbol, and Francis Bacon was known to use it when notating manuscripts marking passages he wanted to remember. Noticing the same symbol appearing in multiple places on Champlain's map, it was an interesting correlation, along with the acrostic "ROSY MAP MAKER" from Key 32. However, making a closer study of the map, a series of discoveries corroborate the information presented so far.

Researchers have often commented on the accuracy of Champlain's more detailed maps versus the 1612 Map of New France, as it seemed to be a subjective map more concerned with general navigation as opposed to detailed accuracy of the coastlines. After studying the map in some detail, the map also served cryptographic purposes, the primary of which was communicating the identity of Sir Francis Bacon.

One feature of the map that begs attention is the royal emblem in the upper right of the map itself. The first thing noted was its similarity to the Dauphin Royal Coat of Arms:

**Figures 12 - 10 & 12 – 12 L – 1612 Map, R –
Coat of Arms of the Dauphin**

While one is encircled by laurel branches and the other is contained within the royal mantle, the real similarities appear in the inner concentric circles. The French fleur-de-lis appears at the heart of both images, encircled by a woven cord. While the Dauphin image contains seashells interspersed along the circular cord, the map image has what can be best described as beehives or a form of nut. Moving outward to the next concentric circle, the Dauphin Coat of Arms on the right contains the letter H, the fleur-de-lis, and heraldic helmet, interspersed with the fleur-de-lis appearing between each element. The medal and collar represent "The Order of the Holy Spirit" as created by Henry III of France, during the time Francis was there at court. The map has a strange series of interspersed and repeating symbols or emblems with the fleur-de-lis also appearing between each. I'll be focusing on these strange and repeating symbols, and this is where Nicholas Hilliard's "signature" symbol becomes relevant.

Each of these symbols can be read as a cipher signature in the same way as the Hilliard signature. At first glance there are three different symbols, however one contains a "mistake" drawing our attention to their construction. On closer inspection, we can see that these symbols are comprised of over lapping letters of the Elizabethan alphabet, and can be "read" using Bacon's cipher procedures. Let's look at each of them in turn:

Figure 12 - 13

The first example, Figure 12 – 13 is from the upper left beside the crown in the emblem, appeared at first glance to be a pair of X's in a frame, which added together in Simple Cipher equal 44, Bacon's "secret" signature. However, the X's are actually formed two V's, overlaid one another in a Masonic square and compass manner. The value of the pair of V's in the Fourfold Cipher is also 44. However, both of these values ignore the H or double Tau framing in both sets of letters. Since the shapes contain multiples of the same letter and the Fourfold Cipher yielded excellent results with the Hilliard signature, I applied it to the letters I saw at work in this symbol – VV XX TT, whose values in Fourfold Cipher are 44, 46 and 43. The sum of these values is 133 the Simple Cipher signature for "Baron Verulam," "King Stuart" and "King Francis III."

The second example in Figure 12 – 14 is the symbol with the "error," as it was missing a horizontal line across its middle, and therefore did not match any others, though it has a similar design. Identifying letters III, O and an upside-down V, I calculated their Fourfold values as 57, 14 and 20, respectively. Their sum totaled 91, the Kaye Cipher signature for the word "King." Then I noted that bottom of the

Figure 12 - 14

260

"O" provided curved lines creating not just one "A," but because of the center "I" created a composite AAA. Also, the upside-down "V" forms a "W" with the adjacent "I's." Adding the values of AA (49) and W (21) totals 161, the signature for "Francis Stuart" in Simple, and "Fraters" in Kaye Cipher. This symbol's counterpart with the horizontal line however, proves to be more complex.

This same basic symbol appears three more times in the emblem on

Figure 12 - 15

Champlain's 1612 Map, except a horizontal line cuts the middle of the symbol, making it the monogram of King Henry III (Figure 12 – 15). In the process, it creates an H or double Tau symbolizing the initials Thirty-Three, the Simple signature for "Bacon." This line also creates an obvious AA Bacon / RC symbol as it passes through the upside-down V. One line changes everything here in terms of the letters appearing in this third symbol. In addition to III and O, our collection of letters adds AAA, and the upside-down AA (left and right). The horizontal line also creates HH, and therefore the quadruple Tau of TTTT. All of these letter combinations in Fourfold Cipher respectively equal the values of 57 (III), 14 (O), 49 (AAA), 25 (AA), 32 (HH), 20 (V) and 91 (TTTT), totaling a sum of 288. This is the cipher signatures of "Roi Francois Stuart" and "Francois Stuart III" in Fourfold Cipher. The next symbol is visually the most complex in the emblem.

The most ornate symbol appears only twice as opposed to the four

Figure 12 - 16

times the others appear (allowing that the second symbol is a purposeful variation of the third). Again we see the incorporation of a stylized square and compass. Due to the incorporation of Y's, this shape produces multiple A's as well. As you can see, there are 3 upright A's and their reflections (or shadows) below, (as above so below?). So the initial analysis of the letter combinations appearing in this symbol with their values are 49 (AAA), 49 (AAA), 43 (TT), 47 (YY), 46 (XX), 8 (H), with a sum totaling 242. But then another "Y" also appears within the originals. This raised the question of what to include in the overall count. Though we used TT in the original count, H was also included, as it is visually present. So removing the value of YY and adding-in the YYYY value of 95, produces a sum of 290, the Kaye Cipher signature of "Francois III." Wondering what would happen if the value of 8 for H is removed, subtracting it gives 282, the Kaye Cipher signature of "Francis Bacon."

It appeared that Francis Bacon wanted to ensure that regardless which path one took, his name would appear in the decryption.

At the beginning of the interpretation of the emblem on the map, I skeptically asked myself, couldn't this emblem of "The Order of the Holy Spirit" just be a standard emblem of French maps of the time? Perhaps they all followed this style and used the same symbols, and I'm merely confirming my bias in my interpretation? In my search for the answer, I found only *two* such maps both published in 1609 in Paris by Marc Lescarbot. While two of the symbols are the same, the others seem to be simpler versions of the same idea, all containing Bacon signatures. In fact, I found that much of what we know of this historical personage comes from his own writings, and the name produces interesting cipher signatures. In Simple, the sum of the letters in "Marc" is 33, the signature of "Bacon" in Simple. The letters of Lescarbot total 123, the signature of "King Francis Valois-Angouleme" in Short Cipher. The total 156 is the Reverse Cipher signature of "Francis III." In Reverse Cipher, the value of the name "Marc" is 67, the value of "Francis" and "Samuel" in Simple Cipher. It's value in Kaye is 85, "Frater" in Reverse Cipher. The Fourfold Cipher of the entire name totals 169, the cipher signature for "King Francis" in Reverse. At this point with all of the work done using the cipher systems and calculating signatures, all of these correlations defy coincidence within this context.

One last aspect of Champlain's 1612 Map of New France needs mentioning and it involves *Baye de Toute Illes* as it's labeled on the map, or in English "The Bay of Many Isles." While local lore in Chester, Nova Scotia states that this was the original name of Mahone Bay, writer James McQuiston states he found documentary evidence maintaining the same. While some have disagreed with this assertion by claiming that "The Bay of Many Isles," is farther to the northeast, much of the basis of this claim is Champlain's Map of 1612, as the words appear on the map near the southeastern shore of Nova Scotia. In fact, later map makers placed that name on that region of their maps due to Champlain's map. This has been done despite historians of cartography knowing that this map is subjective and symbolic in nature as a chart, with a purpose of mapping between destinations, not one of detailed accuracy of coastlines. His maps of smaller areas show a detailed accuracy above and beyond the larger scale map and this also has been noted by historians. As such and given so many "cryptic clues" present on the map itself, I began to look at the map as a cryptogram. This meant that the discrepancy regarding the name of the bay is a part of a coded message. Due to evidence on the map itself, and due to the messages revealed by the cipher texts of the plaque of Shakespeare's

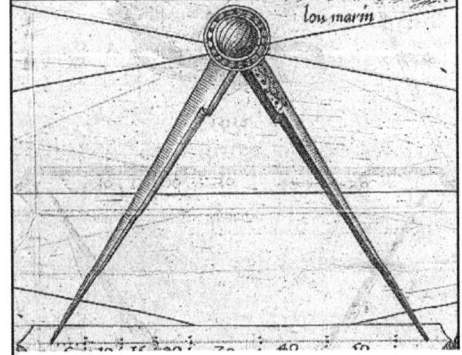

Figure 12 - 17

262

Funerary Monument, the map needed to be analyzed as a cryptogram. The evidence appeared as the cipher texts' specific references to Oak Island with its "cone stone Heracles," the statement that Captain Samuel de Champlain was his best alias, and the direct references to the pictures and map drawn by "Samuel de Champlain." Looking in these places, we find cipher signatures of Francis Bacon. Let's look at the clues on the actual map however and let them speak for themselves. (I suggest the reader go online to look at a high resolution version allowing you to "zoom-in" on a computer or tablet).

One of the map features that immediately draws the eye is the compass covering its center (Figure 12–17). Mentally extending the arms downward, the ruler within it creates a capital A, and the latitude line above it completes our AA symbolism.

The compass (divider caliper) was used in navigation to measure distances. Knowing a preset measurement on the map, setting the caliper to this measurement, and then counting how many times that measurement occurs between two points would provide the navigator with the true distance in miles. This example seems to be a premeasurement of distance for navigation purposes. As stated earlier, map historians refer to this map as a representational navigation map as opposed to some of Champlain's more detailed examples of cartography. However, like all of Bacon's other creations, it serves a dual purpose. This distance will prove to be important as we proceed.

The next step was to look for meaningful alignments and angles suggested by the evidence, in the same manner of the previous example of the Invisible College Illustration. Two navigational lines cross at a point near the center of the pivot point of the compass. Using this as a point aligned with the points of the compass itself, I looked to see if it created any significant alignments. It did.

Using the point where the map lines intersect as a starting point, creating lines downward following the angle created by the points of the compass itself, allows us to see if it pointed to any significant words or letters in the map legend below:

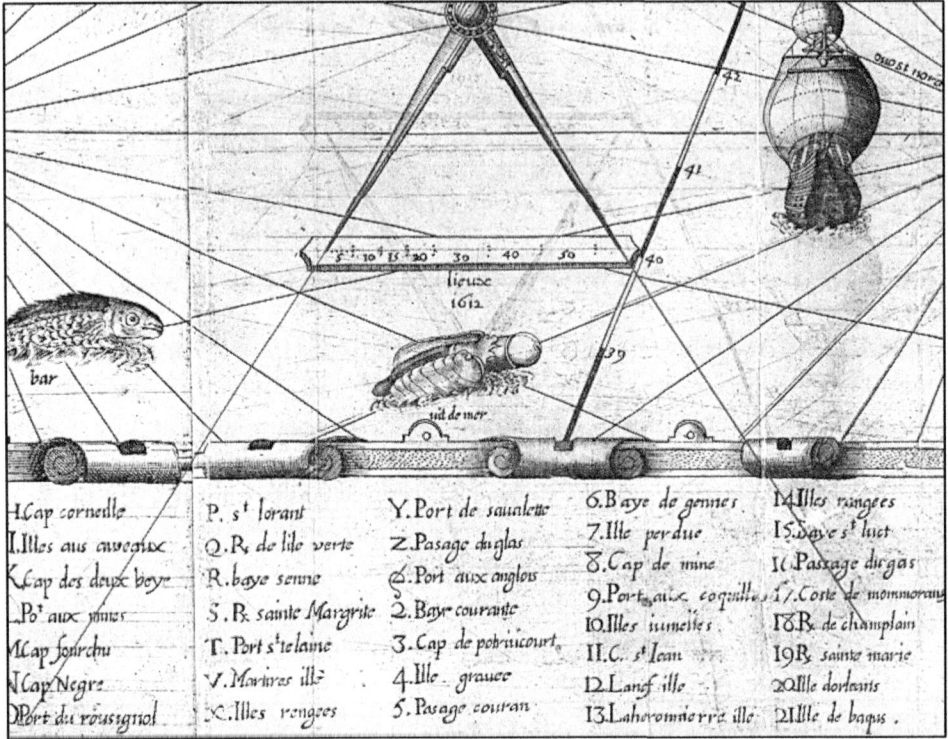

H.Cap corneille	P. s¹ lorant	Y.Port de saualette	6.Baye de gennes	14.Illes rangees
I.Illes aus aweaux	Q.R. de lile verte	Z.Pasage du glas	7.Ille perdue	15.Baye s¹ luct
K.Cap des deux beye	R.baye senne	6.Port aux anglois	8.Cap de mine	16.Passage dirgas
Po¹ aux pinnes	S. R. sainte Margrite	2.Baye courante	9.Port aux coquilles	17.Coste de monmoran
M.Cap fourchu	T.Port s¹telame	3.Cap de pobriucourt	10.Illes iumelles	18.R. de champlain
N.Cap Negre	V.Martires illr	4.Ille grauee	11.C. s¹ Iean	19.R. sainte marie
D.Port du rousignol	X.Illes rengees	5.Pasage couran	12.Lanef ille	20.Ille dorleans
			13.Laheromierre ille	21.Ille de baqus .

Figure 12 - 18

As can be clearly seen, the left line points directly to the letter "o" in Port du Rossignol, misspelled as "du rousignol." Again, another signpost of a cryptographic message, whose significance will become clear in a moment. The right line points directly to the "a" of the name, "Champlain" which is significant for obvious reasons (continuing the line downward at the same angle pierces the "a" in "marie", creating AA). These line points have been checked multiple times for accuracy in both physical and digital formats.

Champlin reportedly named Port du Rossignol after Captain Rossignol, an early founder of New France. However, Rossignol was also the name of France's premier cipher and code master. As just mentioned, please note the "misspelling" of the name as "rousignol" while remembering that "mistakes are signals" when decrypting ciphers. Given the trail of clues and data being followed, this was another significant indication of how to proceed. Obviously given everything reader has seen so far, this cannot be discounted as coincidence. An allusion to both Rossignol and Champlain from the Compass at the center of the map, points to a cipher at work regarding "a secret" about Champlain, a secret that we already know thanks to the cipher texts produced by "Shakespeare's" plaque. The logical next step was to look in the area on the map labeled "O. Port du Rossignol" and look for clues of the presence of a cipher. If you recall, the letter "O" is used by Bacon much like "A" as a symbol of "light" or "seeing."

The "O" label for Port du Rossignol appears on the southeastern shore of Nova Scotia. Visually when looking at a modern map such as Google Earth, the location is near Mahone Bay and Oak Island, modern day Liverpool, Nova Scotia. Looking at the features of the map itself as hinted by the letter O, didn't disappoint. First of all, at first glance at an island juxtaposed with the O label, it appeared to be shaped like a Mason's square. Zooming-in closer on the digital image however, I allowed myself some wishful or fanciful thinking for a moment, and wondered if I detected a "beak" and the outline of Oak Island:

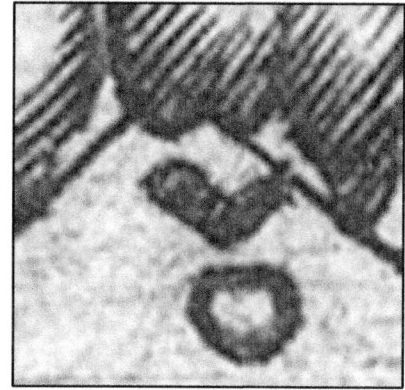

Figure 12 - 19

Again, this is speculation but it's interesting enough to include considering the other features and clues in this area of the map.

One more feature that needs to be addressed is the convergence of two navigation lines, extending from the two compass roses, one line from the Sun-shaped rose on the left, and one from the compass rose on the right. Before following this clue to identify the significance if any, the surrounding vicinity was studied to see what other clues appeared.

The first examples were in the other place labels on the southern coast of Nova Scotia on either side of the "O" representing Port du Rossignol. To the left, the letter "N" appears representing "Cap Negre" according to the legend, and "V" on the right representing "Martires Ille," or "Martyr's Isle" in English. Also, the nearby place names provide interesting clues.

Directly below this point and to the west, we see the name, "*Port au Mouton,*" meaning "Port of Sheep" in English:

Figure 12 - 20

One noteworthy detail appears right away – the letter "P" with the superscript "t" as an abbreviation of the word "port." First of all, the letter P is different than the others all over the map in that it doesn't "close" it's loop at the top. It's actually the Hebrew letter "Tsade," a precursor to the Greek Tau and Latin T. It represents the "TS" sound, which through the Athbash substitution system between Simple and Reverse, can be read as FG, which we have already

265

discussed as a Bacon signature. This is reinforced by every "ST" combination on the map in the texts in the upper corners, as they are "joined" above them with a curved notation. Note that to the right of this "fore-runner" of the Tau, the word "tau" itself actually appears beside it. This clearly is signaling to look at the "Truth" or Tau of this part of the map. This leaves us with the word "mouton" which is French for "sheep." This immediately struck a chord as a reference to Champlain, since the name itself can be translated literally into English as "field of wool." (As an interesting aside, the second half of the name is a pun on l'aine, French for "oldest boy"). Doing a quick calculation of the word "mouton" in Simple, Reverse and Kaye, reveals a sum of 92 in both Simple and Kaye, which is the Reverse Cipher signature for "Bacon." The Reverse Cipher total for "mouton" is 58 a number not normally noted as a cipher signature. However, it is the Simple Cipher value of "hang-hog" from the famous quote in Shakespeare's play, *The Merry Wives of Windsor,*" where a character states, "Hang-hog is Latin for Bacon, I warrant you."

The fact that this value is referenced by a word meaning sheep, from which we derive our word in English of "mutton" meaning the meat of sheep, appears to be a play on this idea. In this way, a play on words (and cipher values) connects Bacon and Champlain through "meat products."

One more discrepancy in a nearby place name draws our attention. To the left "Ille au leu marains" appears on the map near the place name for Cape Sable:

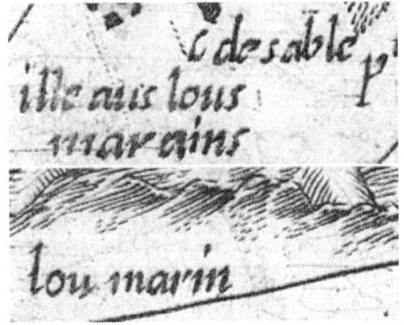

While this is traditionally translated as "Isle of the Sea Lions," note that the spelling differs from the actual sea lion depicted below the island, "lou marin." I consulted two of my colleagues in the French department where I work, and they both confirmed that despite the old spelling, "marains" was better translated as "sailors" or technically, "mariners."

Figure 12 - 20

The discrepancy made me wonder if the island in question harbored actual seals at all. After a little digging, I uncovered a reference that Bacon, if his life at sea is true, would have been well-aware. Also be forewarned, though many researchers might call the following an inference, a logical conclusion based upon details, I feel more comfortable calling it speculation. I believe that this reference to the "Isle of Sea Lions" actually refers to an island that would have been frequented by Dutch privateers.

In a publication called *Privateering in the Golden Age Netherlands* by Virginia Lunsford, there are multiple references to the phrase, "Lions of the Sea." The author writes, "While navy and privateer seamen alike are generally referred to as "pious Batavians" and "Lions of the Sea," whose "gallant deeds" help to protect "our Beloved and Dearly-Bought Fatherland," (90) the work goes on to recount and enumerate in chronological order the specific accomplishments of various privateers. This list is expressed in extremely vivid and fulsome language, referring to privateers as "brave Batavians," "valiant Netherlands Batavians," "our renowned Lions of the Sea," "upright Batavian[s] for the Fatherland," "Sea Roosters," "Zeelands Adventurer[s]," "Netherlands Adventurers," and the like" (Lunsford 195). Bacon would have been well-aware of this tradition from his mentor Sir Francis Drake. There were times during the Spanish domination of the seas that the English and Dutch joined forces against the Spanish. While all of this is historical fact, here comes the speculation.

What if the "Ille aus lous marains" with its spelling more akin to a translation of "mariners," actually refers to an island used by these "Lions of the Sea?" Why reference such an island associated with a tradition of privateering against the Spanish? Why vary the spelling of the French words for "sea lion" in such close juxtaposition unless trying to draw attention to it? The real speculation here is, could this map be pointing to this Isle of the Lions of the Sea? Time to get back to the clues on the map to see where they lead.

One of the earlier clues happened to be the converging lines in the Port du Rossignol. Tracing them back leads to the two wind roses or navigational compasses, the one on the left in the image of the sun, and the traditional-looking image on the right. It made sense to measure the angles of each of these lines as they left their sources (bold lines, Figure 12 – 21):

Figure 12 - 21

The line leaves the Sun wind rose at 45 degrees above the 90-degree parallel, which makes perfect sense in terms of dividing 180 degrees into quarters. It would be a standard in terms of navigational charts in 15-degree increments which seem to appear on the map.

Tracing the line back to the other wind rose however, produced interesting results (Figure 12 – 22):

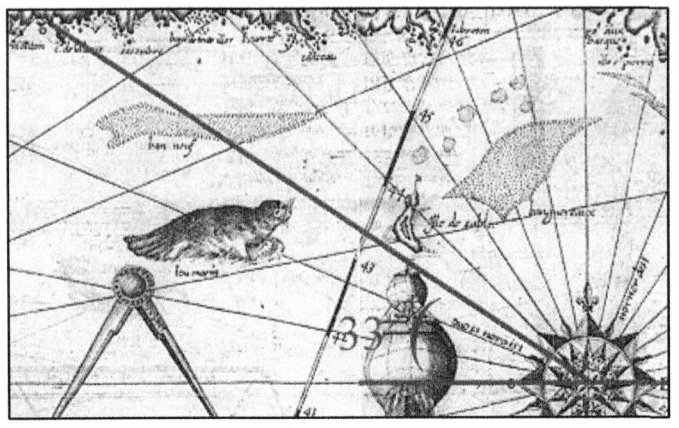

Figure 12 - 22

The line from the wind rose on the right to Port du Rossignol measures exactly 33 degrees above the 90-degree parallel, the signature of "Bacon" in Simple Cipher. (The accuracy was both physically and digitally corroborated multiple times). This measurement makes no sense as a standard division of 360 degrees. While interesting by itself, amid all of the other signposts it's highly significant. What would happen if the corresponding angles from both wind roses were measured? Would a pattern emerge? Not only did a pattern appear, but the results were also highly suggestive.

Measuring the angle above the 33 degree angle, coming from this wind rose produced another predictable 45 degree angle:

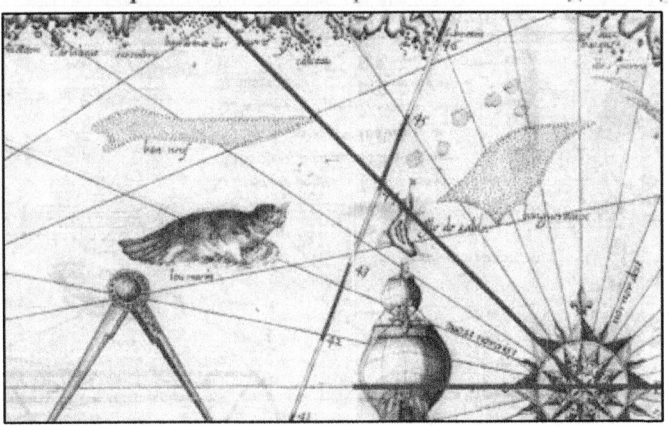

Figure 12 - 23

Following this line to its fruition at the coast of Nova Scotia, leads us directly to "Baye de la Toutes Illes," the Bay of Many Isles. Intrigued and curious as to what this might mean, I noted again another line terminating in the same place, cutting directly through the place name itself. This line led back to the Sun compass rose to measure the angle pointing to the Baye of Many Isles.

As you can see in Figure 12 – 24, the angle from the Sun wind rose is exactly 33 degrees, and points directly to the place name "Baye de la Toutes Illes." Again, the accuracy of these measurements needs to be stressed. All of the angles have been measured and remeasured, physically and digitally, as accurately as possible. Also, as a navigational chart, the angles were drawn with precision with the *intention of being measured by others*. The number 33 is purposefully encoded into two prominent angles in the heart of the map. This can only mean that the Simple Cipher signature for "Bacon" will figure as an important measurement. Before trying to reason out "what" is to be measured with this value, more data needed to be collected. But it appears that the 33 degree angles "join" Port du Rossignol

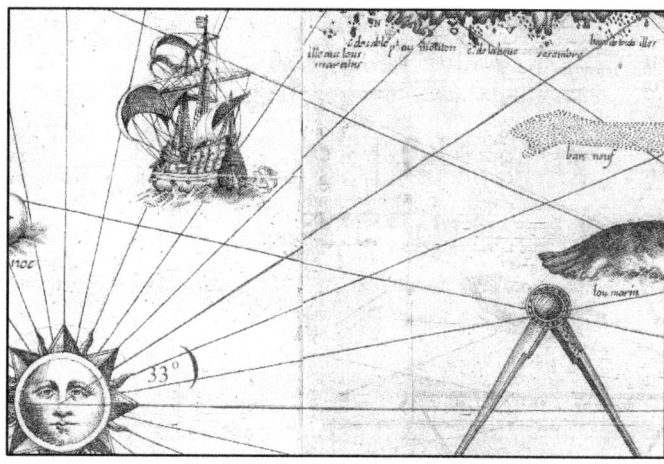

Figure 12 - 24

with the Baye de la Toutes Illes. So analyzing other prominent features of the map, the important signatures are not limited to only these angles coming from the wind roses. They continue in relation to the original alignments from the compass that started the whole process.

Investigating the lines beneath the wind roses, both the names the compass lines highlighted – "Rousignol" and Champlain in Figure 12 – 25 also have correlations:

Again by drawing the baseline at the 90 degree horizontal, extending the line down it ends at the last letter "L" of "rousignol." While L is a symbol of a carpenter's square and Light (and therefore knowledge), its substitution in the Athbash system is O, as previously explained. The angle created by this line and the 90 degree horizontal baseline is 67 degrees, and 67 is the Simple Cipher value of "Francis." It's important to remember that the line from the opposite wind rose at 33 degrees points directly to "Port du rousignol," while the line at 33 degrees to the northeast from the Sun wind rose points to "Baye de la toute illes."

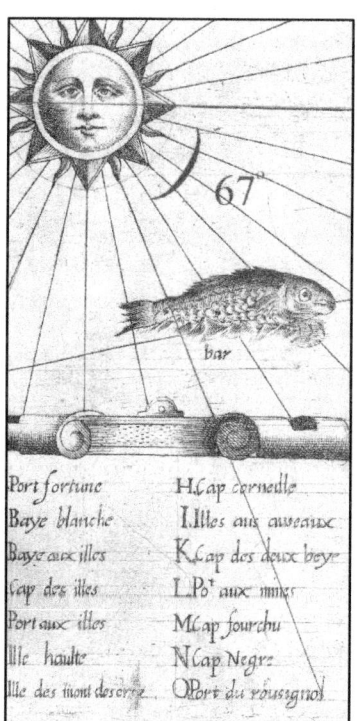

Figure 12 - 25

Applying these same principles to the wind rose symbol on the right allows other correlations to appear (Figure 12–26):

Sure enough, the line points at the letter C at the beginning of the name "Champlain" and measures exactly 67 degrees. The northwest line from this wind rose at 33 degrees points at the Port du rousignol. So, the significant numbers of 67 and 33, "Francis Bacon" in Simple Cipher, point from both wind roses to the names of Rossignol, Champlain, the Port of Rousignol and the Baye de la Toutes Illes. Both directional wind roses have lines leaving them at 67 degrees pointing at the very place names in the legend that were indicated by the lines extending from the arms of the compass. This interrelated series of ciphers and correlations of place names is obviously intentional, and significant. There is a message here. What conclusions can be drawn from these facts?

Figure 12 - 26

To answer this question, let's look at each of the things we now know:

- The cipher texts of the plaque explicitly names "Samuel de Champlain" as Francis Bacon's "best alias."
- The cipher texts instruct us to look at features of his pictures in his books (his hat and trees), and this message appears with the cipher signature 33 for "Bacon" in Simple Cipher, and 55 for "Francis Bacon" in Elizabethan Short Cipher.
- We find cipher signatures of "Francis Bacon" in those exact places in illustrations drawn by "Samuel de Champlain."
- We find an emblem resembling the Dauphin Coat of Arms on Champlain's famous Map of 1612.
- The emblem contains symbols encoded with cipher signatures of Francis Bacon and his true identity using his Fourfold Cipher and others.
- Clues and ciphers appear in the place names on the south coast of Nova Scotia, in particular "Ille au Lou Marains" and "Pt. au Mouton."
- Two alignments point to the name "Rossignol," the name of France's premier cryptographer, indicating the presence of a cipher.
- Following the clues of these alignments allows the discovery of two angles measuring 33 degrees, connecting Port du Rossignol with

270

"Baye de la Toutes Illes," and 67 degrees, connecting Champlain and Rousignol.

All of these things indicated that I was on the right path and that the map also contains what is called a pictorial and numerical cipher. It indicated the need to identify the connection between Port du Rossignol and Baye de la Toutes Illes, using the "language" encrypted into the map. As is the case with most pictorial ciphers the answer appears in the image itself, appearing in the form of the measurement system indicated by the compass or divider caliper dominating the center of the map.

I was able use this measuring tool by copying it directly from the image, adjusting the color for contrast purposes, and maintaining its exact size and proportions. Using it as an overlay on the southern coast of Nova Scotia to identify any relationship or correlation regarding this distance and the place names, was the next step.

In Figure 12–27, simply moving the exact copy straight above its original placement "joins" the T in "Pt." or "tau" with the S in "illes," exactly like the "curved notation" joining the S's and T's in the texts in the upper corners. Remember that through the cipher substitution system, these letters are also the initials "F G," a signature of "Francis Bacon." The

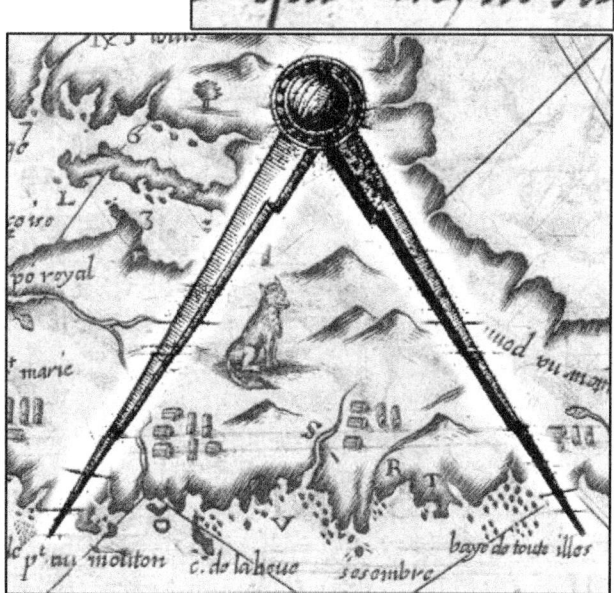

Figure 12 - 27

"Tsade tau mouton" message has now been linked to the "Bay of Many Isles." To test my theory regarding the Isle of the "Lions of the Sea," I decided to see what alignment appeared by moving the compass to point at that place name on the map. As an interesting sidenote, the "V" as the legend place marker provides a carpenter's square to complete the Square and Compass of Freemasonry.

Aligning the right point of the compass on the A in "baye," its counterpart points directly to the "a" in "aus" in the name of "ille aus lous marains," the Isle of the Sea Lions. If we are inclined to use the "joining" principle presented by the compass, we can join the "ba" in baye with the "C" in C de sable, providing the first three letters of "Bacon." Going further, we can complete the name with the "o" below C in "lous" and the "n" in marains below that. Or, the N from the legend label and the O labeling Port du Rossignol "encompassed" by the image itself. Also note the position of the island "shaped like a carpenter's square" in relation to the compass, in the

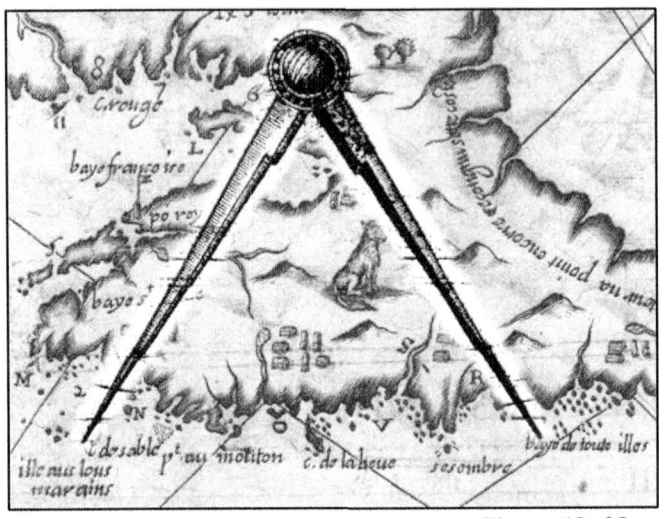

Figure 12 -28

same manner as the "V" in the previous placement.

All of these correlations indicate that Bacon is pointing to an island (speculatively) known to privateers as the island of the "Lions of the Sea," and it lay somewhere in "Baye de la Toutes Isles." If this is the case, then is it possible to use the map to locate it? As it turns out, that was the point.

Since this map has been called a navigational map as opposed to a detailed representational map, and since it contains the measurements necessary for successful navigation, the answer is yes. When the distances are applied, the intended locations are revealed. Another step was to place the ruler with the compass, to measure the distances between these areas in Figure 12–29 below. In this way, the true location of The Bay of Many Isles can be identified, and perhaps even the island that may have been known to privateers as the "Isle of the Lions of the Sea."

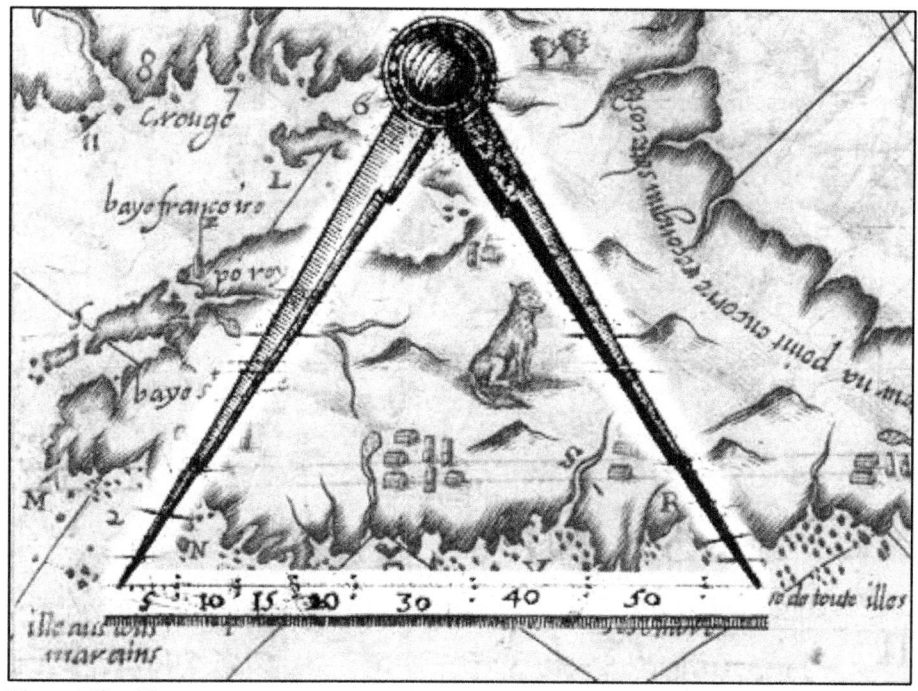

Figure 12 - 29

The distance from "Cape Sable" to "The Bay of Many Isles" appears as 60 miles, or 60 nautical miles, a much shorter distance than what is communicated visually on the map, as it covers most of the southern shore of Nova Scotia (Figure 12 – 30):

Figure 10 - 30

Also, note that the rule is graduated in the sense that the numbers become farther apart going from left to right. Looking at the ruler and map positioned by the compass, it appears that Port du Rossignol is at the 27-mile mark. Therefore, it appears that the Port du Rossignol is approximately 33 miles from the Bay of Many Isles.

So, the logical decision was to start where the clues began to point at the very beginning with the lines drawn from the compass at the heart of the map, and that place was Port du Rossignol, or modern-day Liverpool, Nova Scotia. As stated earlier, the distances and angles on this map were intended to lead navigators to exact locations. So in theory, we should be able to use the distances indicated by the tools of the map, geometry, and the angles indicated in the clues to find the way. With this idea in mind, I consulted Google maps. I wanted to see if the navigational chart created by the man called Samuel de Champlain, and the pictorial and numerical cipher it contained would lead to a place possibly known to privateers as the "Isle of the Lions of the Sea." The starting point lay in the bay in Liverpool, Nova Scotia, named by Champlain's 1612 Map as "Port du Rossignol."

As you can see in the accompanying image, the angles produced by the wind roses should connect Port du Rossignol with the Baye de la Toutes Illes, at 33 degrees:

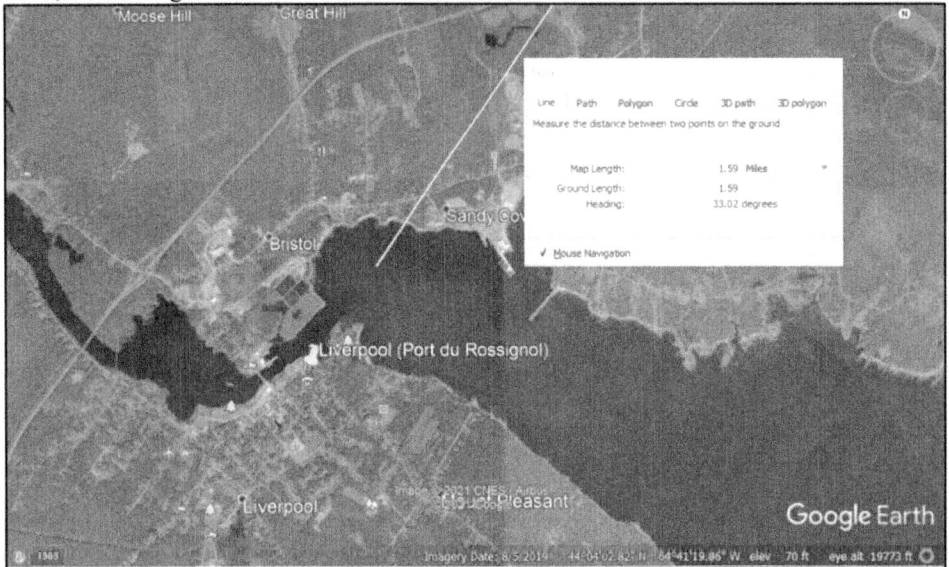

Figure 12 – 31 Source: Google Earth

I simply picked an arbitrary point in the bay, and drew the straight line at 33 degrees. Considering that the compass and rule indicated a distance of, not-so-surprisingly, 33 miles, I simply continued on the course of 33 degrees north to see where this course and distance would lead me. I arrived at the following point:

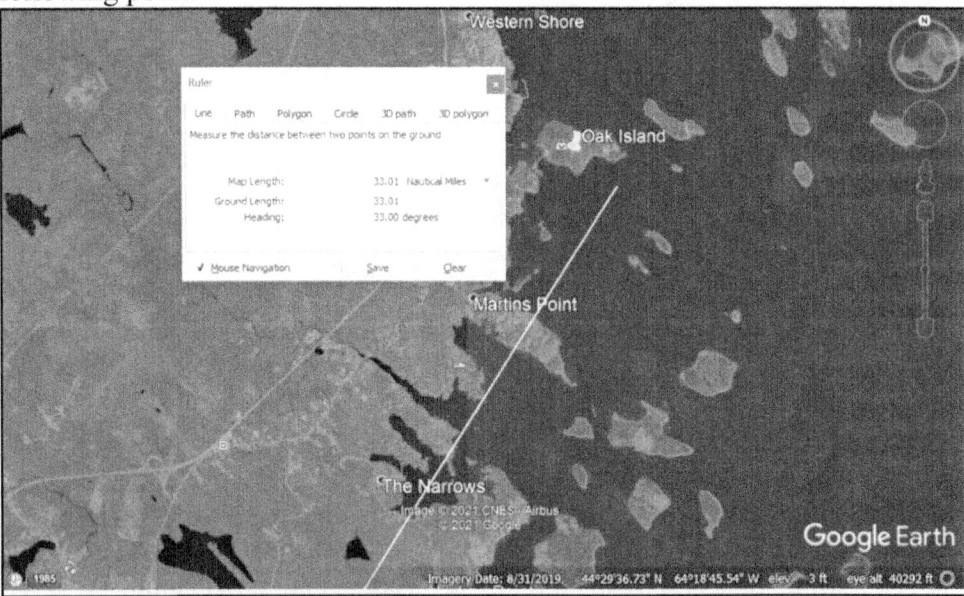

Figure 12 – 32 Source: Google Earth

274

As it turns out, beginning at an arbitrary point in the center of the bay near Liverpool, Nova Scotia, and following the course of 33 degrees that "joins" Port du Rossignol with the Baye de la Toutes Isles, at a distance 33 Nautical miles, leads directly to Oak Island in Mahone Bay. If we choose a starting point just at the shore east of the previous arbitrary starting point, that a parallel line would end closer to or even on Oak Island, and this was the result of that experiment:

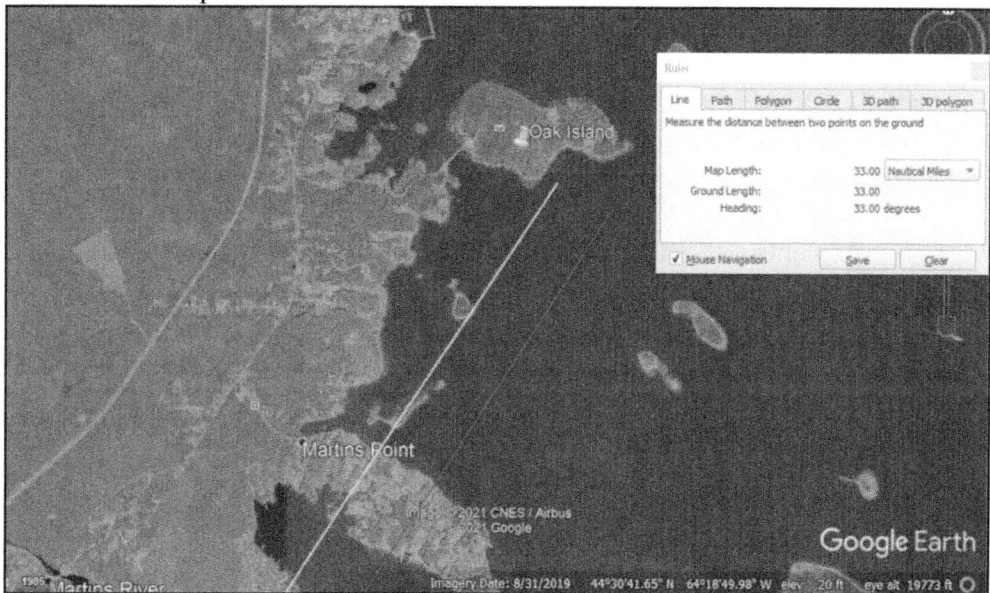

Figure 12 – 33   Source: Google Earth

Figure 12 – 33 shows the white line indicating the alternative shore-line starting point, once again leading directly to Oak Island, Nova Scotia. Curious regarding the distance in standard miles as opposed to the nautical mile measurement, the value can be noted in this image here:

As you can plainly, see, for all intents and purposes the distance is 38 nautical miles, the value of the double Tau (TT) in Bacon's Simple Cipher, and the symbol as it was used on the plaque of Shakespeare's Funerary Monument. Also, please remember that this symbol was the source of the "Key 38"

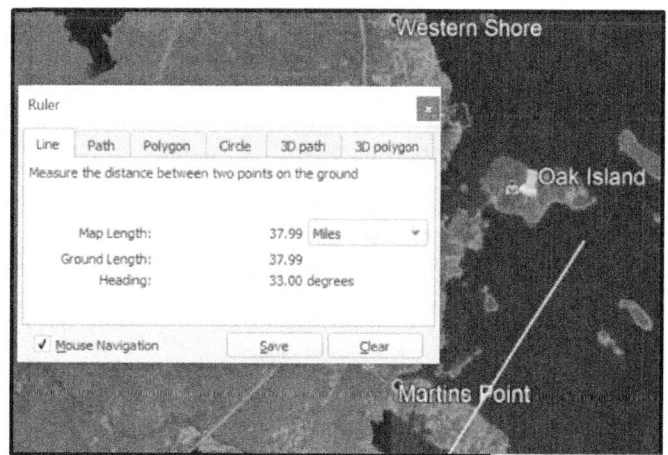

Figure 12 - 33

275

transposition cipher that explicitly states where to find Bacon's "thesauri" or treasure chamber.

Final Conclusions

As impossible as it sounds, this is where this quest for Francis Bacon's sacred Tau has led. One of the truths that Bacon wanted the world to eventually know, was his own truth. From the loss of two thrones, writing the world's most famous plays, the secret of his Royal lineage, to sailing "the Seven Seas" with Sir Francis Drake, the man known to history as Sir Francis Bacon led multiple lives simultaneously. In delving into the validity of his "best alias," as unbelievable as it sounds, the book, drawings and maps of Samuel de Champlain give all indications that the assertions of the cipher texts of "EMasker TT" and Key 32 are true.

A summary of these findings are as follows:

- As controversial as it is, the Key 32 transposition cipher names Samuel de Champlain as Francis Bacon's "best alias."
- The cipher texts explicitly state that the "ass Louis" sent Bacon to oversee the fur trade.
- It also states that Bacon, as Champlain, tricked Louis XIII into handing him his "nation to rule."
- The idea occurred to him when he realized that the "northwest sail route was closed."
- Studying "Champlain's" 1612 map reveals multiple cipher signatures, all pointing to Francis Bacon.
- I believe that the pictorial / numerical ciphers in the map are intended to point to an island Dutch privateers called the "Isle of the Lions of the Sea."
- Following the navigational directions provided by the relationships of the angles from the compass, and the two wind roses, reveals a relationship to this island, Port du Rossignol, and the Baye de la Toutes Illes.
- Following these navigational directions leads directly to Oak Island.
- Arriving there, one would only need to follow the directions in Key 38's transpositional cipher, and use the "cone stone Heracles" to create a map on the island.

When I first began working with the plaque ciphers from Shakespeare's Funerary Monument, while confident in the material and the procedures I used to attain them, one thing bothered me. Bacon couldn't be placed in Nova Scotia or New France. While the pictorial ciphers encrypted within the "Invisible College" illustration pointed to the center of present day Mahone Bay, "the dots could not be connected" in terms of placing

276

Bacon there. In this sense, Champlain's Map of 1612 is truly an encrypted treasure map.

Using that map to arrive at what is now Oak Island, Nova Scotia, there can only be one thing left to do. Follow the clues provided by the cipher texts of Key 38. Exactly how to do that appears in the Appendices.

Chapter 13 - Final Thoughts and the Timeline

When my work with the cipher texts of the plaque of Shakespeare's Funerary Monument first began to bear fruit one year ago, I immediately began to compile my notes into this book. When the initial messages about Francis Bacon and his birthright appeared, I became worried that his authorship of the works of Shakespeare would be lost in a sea of noise or dismissed as nonsense because of the context of the other controversial (read unbelievable) messages. However, following the clues and the ciphers where they led, continually produced (albeit shocking) results.

I didn't think they would lead here. While yes, my initial motivation for analyzing the plaque had been my friends looking for answers to the Oak Island mystery, after reading those initial clear messages, Oak Island disappeared into the mists of the North Atlantic. I no longer believed such a message existed. I focused instead on what I believed was the main context of the messages themselves, Bacon wrote the works of Shakespeare, and he was the son of Mary, Queen of Scots and Francis II. I wasn't writing "an Oak Island book." And I don't think I have done so. I think I have transcribed, to the best of my ability, the hidden autobiography of the man known as Sir Francis Bacon. And yes, it includes amazing information about the "Oak Island" mystery.

My next project involves the relationships between the fascinating men mentioned in the plaque cipher texts, namely Francis and Anthony Bacon, Robert Devereux, 2nd Earl of Essex, and Sir Walter Raleigh. One of the cipher keys revealed yet another bombshell, but one too involved to be revealed in this book. Stay tuned for that.

As far as the questions everyone asks, the ones you may be wondering now, I'll try to answer as best I can.
Q: Why would Francis Bacon create a plaque with an intricate cipher that no one could ever read?
A: This is the most asked question. Short answer – He didn't. I just read it over the last year. 😊 Long answer - it originally had been intended for his contemporaries back in his own time and the century that followed,

particularly a close circle of like-minded individuals. But also I am 100% certain others have decrypted it since that time. In fact, many ideas appearing in these cipher texts appear in the elements of classic fiction over the years in the works of Alexander Dumas, Edgar Allen Poe, Sir Walter Scott and Mark Twain. Others in intelligence circles are also "in the know."

Q: Why use ciphers? Is that even a thing?

A: Another top question. People today in the private sector pay top dollar for cyber encryption. In the Renaissance, nobles and royalty used ciphers on a regular basis to ensure the security of their communications. No difference exists between these two realities. The example used throughout this book to illustrate this concept is the intercepted cipher from Mary Queen of Scots that led to her execution. If you've read this far, you already know the implications of that scene.

Q: Why would Francis Bacon allow some other fake name appear on the greatest literary achievement in the English language instead of his own? Why would he allow his alias get credit for the discoveries and accomplishments of artists and Samuel de Champlain?

A: Short answer – because "Francis Bacon" was not his "real name" either. Long answer – To him, what difference did it make if the name Francis Bacon, William Shakespeare or Samuel de Champlain appeared on his accomplishments when in his mind, they were all equally not his true identities? Yet at the same time, he also had equal claim to all of those names? While they were not his true name, they were all equally his own identities. His true name *should* have been Francois Stuart-Valois-Angouleme, Francis Stewart, or any of the other variations I've identified within the ciphers, but that was not to be either.

Q: What about the evidence for the Prince Tudor Theory?

A: Every bit of that evidence is true, yet circumstantial. Every bit of that evidence also supports the idea that Francis Bacon was the son of Mary, Queen of Scots and Francis II of France. Now, we can add the evidence of the cipher texts concealed within the plaque of Shakespeare's Funerary Monument at Stratford-upon-Avon as evidence which unequivocally, explicitly states Francis Bacon's true biological parents are Mary Stuart and Francis Valois-Angouleme II. However, one cipher text in Key 38 explicitly names Edward deVere and Robert Devereux, 2nd Earl of Essex as the sons of Queen Elizabeth.

Q: How did Bacon have time to do all of these things when there is a historical record showing him to be a member of parliament or a judge, etc.

A: First of all it depends on the identity of the first person authoring the primary source document, and determining if he is an alias of Francis or Anthony. Second, we need to consider a famous letter of Voltaire who relates an anecdote. During his exile in England, he sought out the counsel of contemporaries regarding the wisest and most illustrious people in

England's recent history. Foreign emissaries often sought Bacon's wisdom. In the letter, Volataire recounts a visit to Bacon by the Marquis d'Effiat who escorted the princess to be married to King Charles. Because Bacon was "ill," he received the Marquis with a curtain between them. Marquis d'Effiat reportedly stated to Bacon, "you are like the angels. We hear much talk of them, and while everyone thinks them superior to men, we are never favored with a sight of them" (Baker). A great leap of logic is not required to picture William Ralley, Thomas Meauty, Ben Jonson or even Anthony Bacon scrambling to place themselves behind the curtain to receive the Marquis (and others). Meanwhile, Francis "passed on holiday" at sea or conducting his work around the continent, painting portraits of monarchs in their own courts and listening to state secrets.

The fact that the cipher texts state that he wrote books at sea provide another key part of this answer. As first mate and navigator to Sir Francis Drake, he would have spent months at sea, and much of that time would otherwise be idle. I easily could see him returning from privateering with Drake with a Quarto under his arm.

Also, we moderns have a very skewed view of life. We squander our time with work and distractions. Think of how much you could accomplish in your own life if you didn't spend your time in a 9 – 5 job, or watching entertainments, etc. Also, though he was a member of parliament, that was not what a regular job requiring his presence, punching-in and punching-out. Q: How did he accomplish all of these things when it was well-known he was a sickly man?
A: Short answer – See all of the above answers. Long answer – he perpetrated a libel against himself. His spy craft required subterfuge and deep cover. If Bacon publicly presented himself as strong and robust, if he publicly presented himself as a prolific writer and master artist, he would not have been able achieve his goals.

Many researchers of Francis Bacon and his life have commented on his goals of helping Elizabeth I and stay "hidden behind the scenes."

So the famous Voltaire comments that though the Marquis "spoke with Francis Bacon," it happened in Pythagoras fashion with a curtain between them. While this is not "proof" this was the situation, it is a qualitative anecdote proving that the Marquis believed many people had never seen the face of Francis Bacon, and he certainly didn't "see" him during his visit. "Seeing," light and shadow, are the RC keys. *Lux si umbra.* And curtains cause shade. This is definitely food for thought.

One of the final pieces of the "plausibility puzzle" lies within that question, "where did he find the time?" More clearly answering that question requires establishing a timeline. The following includes what would need to have happened according to the messages of the cipher texts. Additionally, information has been incorporated from other sources, such as the timeline available at "sirbacon.org" (though rudimentary in appearance it contains excellent information and supports the Prince Tudor theory), the timeline included in Markku Peltonen's *The Cambridge Companion to Bacon,* and the timeline Samuel de Champlain:

Timeline

1548 – Treaty of Haddington signed promising the marriage between Mary and Dauphin Francis

- August – Mary arrives in France

1558 – April 24th Mary and Francis marry (curiously date on Shakespeare's plaque is Apr. 23, necessary for Key 5)

1560 – December 5 – King Francis II dies. Some Catholics suspected poisoning by Protestants. Catherine de Medici becomes Regent for son Charles IX and covers-up Mary's pregnancy.

1561 – January 22nd – (Dauphin) Francis born 48 days after death of Francis II

January 25th – Bacon Baptized – "…registered at St. Martin's Church, London, and was described as "Mr. Franciscus Bacon." Why should the word "Mr. be used in the registering of an infant's baptism? No other infant had such a distinction" (Chronology).

Between Jan. 22nd and August 19, 1561 -

- Mary distrusts Catherine. Fears for her and her baby's life.

- Sir Nickolas Throckmorton negotiates with Elizabeth I for Mary's return to Scotland.

- Elizabeth threatened by Mary with heir. Declares Francis a state secret. Mary agrees to turn him over to the care of the Bacon's - Elizabeth's Lord Keeper Sir Nicholas and her close friend Lady Anne.

- Mary flees France with Dauphin Francis.

1561 – August 19 – Alone, Mary arrives in Leith, Scotland.

1563 – *The Schoolmaster* written. Prince Tudor theorists believe Elizabeth I contracted Ascham to write it for Francis because he was her son. He would have been 5 when it was published (Chronology).

- Penelope Devereux born. Could she be Elizabeth's first born? Is this why Robert Devereux proclaimed her to be his accomplice before his execution, to hurt Elizabeth? Is that the real reason she ignored the charge?

"**1565 – 78** Queen [Elizabeth I] pays numerous public and secret visits to Gorhambury (to keep an eye on Francis?) "You have made your house too little for your Lordship," the Queen says to Nicholas Bacon. "Your Majesty hath made me too big for my house," he replies" (Chronology). Prince Tudor theorists believe this is evidence for Francis to be Elizabeth's child. His statement that she has "made him too large for his house" implies the extra child. However, if she had made Francis a state secret and placed him in her Lord Keeper's charge, Sir Nicholas's statement still makes sense. All of the historical evidence suggests that she had a familial affection and interest in his upbringing.

1567 – November 10th – Robert Devereux Essex was born. He was the secret son of Elizabeth I and Robert Dudley. Was "Outwardly the son of Lettice Knollys, queen's cousin, married to Walter Hereford, Earl of Essex. There is no birth record of Robert being born at Herefordshire to his reputed mother, Lettice Knollys... In the Essex genealogical register of the 16th century Robert was not entered as the eldest son until after the earldom of Essex had been conferred on his reputed father, Lord Hereford. Then, and not till then, "was he put forward as the legitimate son of the Essex couple." (D. von Kunow, p. 17) Sir Henry Wotten records that "the Earl of Essex had but a poor conceit of him and preferred his second son, Walter"" (Chronology). As demonstrated by the second decryption of Key 38, the plaque repeats the idea that Robert Devereux, 2nd Earl of Essex, was Elizabeth and Dudley's son. The cipher references the "Essex Rebellion" in Key 38, stating Bacon obeyed the queen and prosecuted him, and doing so had been Bacon's "greatest folly."

1571 – Parliament passes a statute for the Queen not allowing anyone to speak of any successor to the throne other than her "natural issue" as opposed to "legal heirs." Prince Tudor theorists point at this as evidence she was leaving the possibility open for Bacon or Essex. However in light of the cipher texts, this would decidedly exclude Francis Bacon and James, in favor of Essex.

1573 – Francis Bacon attends Trinity College in Cambridge at age 12.

1574 – Samuel Chapeleau, son of Antoine Chapeleau and Marguerite Le Roy, baptized. Historians cite this as being Samuel de Champlain and the year of his birth. According to the plaque cipher texts, this is incorrect.

1576 – According to the cipher text in Key 8 of Key 32, Bacon states, "When I was 15, I stir them up. I'm a bad leader."

1576 – According to "Chronology Related to Francis Bacon's Life," on November 21st, "Francis and Anthony Bacon were admitted at Gray's Inn. But Francis appears to have spent a good deal of his time at the Court until September, when Francis was sent abroad, "Direct from Her Majesty's

Royal Hand," as a result of a Bolt from the Blue: Inciting Incident --
(According to Cipher[*not this author's discovery*]) The Queen reveals to
Francis that he is her son. Makes him swear never to write or speak, or print
secrets under his own name. Knowledge that he is unacknowledged "Prince
of Wales" catapults him into a premature adulthood."

Much of this runs counter to the cipher texts on the plaque included in this
book. While it's never disclosed "what cipher" to which it is according that
the Queen revealed the secret to Francis, I believe that if it stated that she
revealed his "Royal Birth," this would have been misinterpreted as meaning
he was her son instead of Mary's son.

- Queen Elizabeth sends Francis Bacon to Paris with trusted ambassador
Amyas Paulet. Studies with the Pleaides and travels Europe. I believe he
studied art under master artists.

1577 – 1580 – Sir Francis Drake circumnavigates the world.

1578 – Bacon paints self-portrait as Hilliard.

- "Hilliard" paints Mary, Queen of Scots in captivity

1579 – Nicholas Bacon dies. Francis left out of the will. Writes to the
Burleighs stating that the study of common law is beneath him.

1579 – 1580 – According to many researchers, Francis and Anthony create
secret societies. I believe this was when Francis began his work of creating
the English language as he had seen done in France. "A A" symbol first
appears. (Bacon would have been exposed to the symbol in France, as it had
been used by his grandfather, Francis I).

1580 – Francis writes four letters pressing his "suit" to the Queen, which
Prince Tudor theorists claim was a plea for recognition as the "Queen's
son." If so, which Queen? I also think that the letters include his plan for the
colonization efforts in the Americas, and his request for his own ship to sail
with Drake. Writes another letter asking his uncle Lord Burleigh to thank
the Queen for her "princely liberality" (Chronology). Prince Tudor theorists
count this as evidence of Francis as the son of Elizabeth, however the
implications are obvious considering the plaque's cipher texts.

1580 – 1582 – At 21, Francis traveled Europe in the custom associated with
Princes. I believe this allowed him to perform spy craft and set-up his
"network" of aliases.

1584 – Robert Devereux Essex at 14 lives at court. Has argument with
Queen about influence of Sir Walter Raleigh.

- Francis elected as an M.P.

1585 – Again from "Chronology," – "Francis writes to Walsingham his enigmatic letter to "put him in remembrance" of his "poor suit," which is really a request to the Queen, through her ministers, whether she intends formally to recognize him as her Heir and Successor to the Throne. Note: Leicester is out of favor with the Queen at this time, and Francis wonders whether this endangered his prospects of Recognition. Francis addresses a long letter of caution to the Queen with reference to the attempts to poison her. It begins with a curious note, which is a virtual statement that he is one of the Queen's natural children… "Care, one of the Natural and True-bred Children of Unfeigned Affection, awaked with these late wicked and barbarous attempts, would needs exercise my pen to your Sacred Majesty." (Chronology)

While this note shows Francis' devotion to Elizabeth I as his Queen, I disagree that it names him as her son. However, referring to himself as "one of the Natural and True-bred Children of Unfeigned Affection" is definitely telling. History records the Queen as thinking very highly of young Francis as well as visiting him. But the "True-bred Children" reference can just as easily be attributed to Mary and Francis II being his parents, and the pity and affection Elizabeth showed him.

- Francis as Hilliard, paints miniature of Sir Walter Raleigh

- Sails with Drake on Caribbean expedition?

1587 – Mary, Queen of Scots executed. Bacon "rid of that one."

- As Hilliard, paints Robert Devereux, 2nd Earl of Essex, "in tilting armor."

1588 – Defeat of the Spanish Armada. Leicester dies. Essex frequently fights with the Queen – openly acts like her son. Francis clerkship in Star Chamber.

- Francis as Hilliard paints Essex – "Melancholy youth."

1589 – Francis is an active participant in Parliament. Uncle Henry III assassinated.

- As Giovanni Baptista Boazio, creates engraving of Drake Cartagena map.

1590 – Queen furious at Essex for marrying "below his degree," meaning he was Prince.

1591 – Queen appoints Francis and Anthony Bacon to advise Essex.

1592 – Bacon "drops suit" to Queen regarding his position with her.

- Plays of Henry VI, I, II, and III appear.

1593 – 94 – Bacon falls out of favor at Court for opposing money bill.

1594 – Letters between Essex and Francis display affection for each other (Key 38 message refers to Essex as his "COZEN" and his regret in participating in his prosecution).

1596 – Sacking of Cadiz, under Robert Devereux, 2nd Earl of Essex and Sir Walter Raleigh. Essex commissions Bacon to memorialize the event as Giovanni Battista Boazio.

1597 – January – Francis speaks in Parliament.

1598 – Famous argument between Queen Elizabeth I and Essex – he turned his back on her, she boxed his ears, then he put his hand on his sword as if to draw it against her.

1599 – Begin of the downfall of Essex – failed Ireland campaign.

- Francis pleads to the Queen on behalf of Essex.

- Legend has it Queen gave Francis a ring to give to Essex – he is to give it to her if he ever needs help.

1600 – Disciplinary hearing for Essex who remained under house arrest.

- Queen takes away his monopoly on sweet wine.

1601 – Essex openly discusses with supporters his plan to storm the court to get rid of his "enemies" who have turned the Queen (his mother) against him, namely Sir Walter Raleigh.

- Essex Rebellion

- Arrested, arraigned, Queen orders Francis to help prosecute.

- Legend states he attempts to send Elizabeth I "the ring" but she never receives it.

- Essex executed in private part of the Tower of London reserved for royal prisoners.

- Anthony Bacon supposedly dies soon after.

- Francis writes to Cecil complaining of an argument he had with rival Sir Edward Coke.

1602 – Hamlet appears.

- Queen declines after death of Essex, apparently continually mourning her son. She allegedly states, "being aware of the impetuosity of his temper, she had warned him two years before… not to show such insolent contempt for her as he did on some occasions, but to take care not to touch her sceptre, lest she be compelled to punish him under the Laws of England and not according to her own… His neglect of this caution had caused his ruin" (Chronology).

286

1603 – Countess of Nottingham allegedly confesses to Queen Elizabeth her concealment of the fabled "ring" Essex had passed to her to give to his mother Elizabeth.

- Queen Elizabeth I dies. Younger half-brother of Francis, James VI of Scotland becomes James I of England.

- Within a year's time Francis Bacon loses Essex, Anthony and Elizabeth I.

- Much of what is known about Samuel de Champlain is "undefined," however this appears to be the year of his first trip at sea with Grave' du Pont.

- Bacon knighted by James VI of Scotland and I of England.

- Sir Walter Raleigh implicated in the Main Plot and convicted of plotting against James I. Spends next 12 years in the Tower of London. This incident will be more fully explained in *The Ghosts of Bacon*. Raleigh was intertwined with Francis Bacon, Essex and Sommerset, in a state secret that would lead to the deaths of both Essex (son to Queen Elizabeth) and Raleigh (whose relationship will later be revealed).

1604 – September – Champlain explores and maps Bay of Fundy.

1606 – May – At 46, Francis marries Alice Barnham (14 yo) for money. He wears purple, a color only allowed for Royalty.

- September - Samuel de Champlain Massachusetts expedition

1607 – Port Royal abandoned. Champlain sails home.

1608 – Francis becomes Solicitor General and clerk of Star Chamber.

- John Dee dies.

- Champlain leaves for third trip.

- Champlain establishes Montreal as fortified outpost to become center of the fur trade.

1609 – Battle against the Iroquois on Lake Champlain at Ticonderoga.

1610 – Henry IV of France assassinated.

- Lady Anne Bacon dies.

- Champlain returns to France. He marries a 12-year-old with a large dowry.

1612 – "Shakespeare" retires – no new plays.

- Champlain compiles his famous map of New France. Becomes Lieutenant Governor of New France.

1613 – Champlain's *Voyages* published.

1613 – 1615 – Champlain promotes New France.

1614 – *Fama Fraternitatis* anonymously published.

1615 – Champlain visits Huronia at south end of Georgian Bay, travels up Ottawa River, wounded by arrows in skirmishes in present day Central New York.

1616 – Actor Shakspere dies.

- Champlain returns with map of New France.

- Rosicrucian pamphlets published in Europe.

- Date inscribed on plaque adorning Shakespeare's Funerary Monument in Holy Trinity Church in Stratford-upon-Avon providing value of Key 32.

1617 – Francis Bacon becomes Keeper of the Seal at age 57. Regent while brother James is in Scotland.

- Raleigh released from Tower of London to search for Eldorado in South America.

- James sends Francis "to stop Raleigh's Caribbean Campaign."

1618   January   Francis made High Chancellor of England.

- Francis receives title Baron Verulam of which researchers say he was very proud. I believe this is due (at least in part) to the fact that its values in his Simple (133), Reverse (167) and Kaye (237) Ciphers were the same as versions of his true identity, including "King Francis III (133)," "Francois III (167)" and "I Francis Valois-Angouleme (237)."

- Sir Walter Raleigh beheaded.

- March – Louis XIII initiates the creation of colony – Champlain given the lead.

1619 – Champlain publishes *Voyages*.

1620 – Louis XIII makes Champlain Governor of New France – as the cipher texts state, Francis had his "nation" to rule.

- Height of Francis's career in England as High Chancellor until 1626.

- Publishes *Novum Organum* under the name Francis Bacon.

1621 – 60th birthday celebration.

- At large celebration, James I makes Francis "Viscount St. Albans." Francis allegedly wears royal purple and James allows it.

- Coke and Churchil, enemies of Francis, conspire to ruin his career. While appearing that he would defend himself from the charges of bribery, pleads guilty to every charge instead. "Too ill" to appear in person. Is fined but he

288

never pays, turns over the seals, and is sentenced to the Tower where he apparently only spends four days. Why tolerate such petty rivalries when he has a "nation to rule" on the other side of the Atlantic?

About 1622 – Shakespeare's Funerary Monument erected in Holy Trinity Church in Stratford-upon-Avon.

1623 – 24 – Ben Johnson lives and works in Bacon's house at Gorhambury, edits and compiles *Shakespeare's First Folio*.

- *De Augmentis Scientarium* published which includes a discussion of his use of ciphers.

1624 – With construction of Quebec started, Champlain leaves for France. (This is the only inconsistency in the timeline – it's assumed that as Champlain, from March of 1618 until 1624, he was overseeing the creation of Quebec in person. And yet, Francis Bacon appears advising James, in the Chancery, and at his birthday celebration in that interim. The only explanation if the cipher texts are true, would be that he frequently traveled back and forth between England and New France more often than is currently believed. This is quite probable considering that orthodox history records that Champlain made more than 25 crossings of the Atlantic without ever losing a ship).

1625 – Marquis d'Effiet brings Henry's daughter Mary to wed Charles, and visits the famous Francis Bacon while in London. "Bacon" was "ill" again, and receives the Marquis in his bed with the curtains drawn. Voltaire writes in his famous letter, the Marquis states to the veiled "Bacon," "You are like the angels. We hear much talk of them, and while everyone thinks them superior to men, we are never favored with a sight of them."

- March 27 – Brother King James I dies.

- Francis rewrites his will leaving his wife nothing.

1626 – April – Bacon "dies" on **Easter Sunday**.

1628 – April – Samuel de Champlain records that oxen were used to plow the ground in New France for the first time.

1629 – June – Champlain surrenders Quebec to the Kirke brothers. Is captured and taken to England.

1632 – Treaty of Saint-Germaine signed, returning Quebec to France.

1633 – Champlain again to take charge of the colony.

March   His final voyage back to the colony.

1635 – December 25 – Samuel de Champlain dies. Site of his remains still a mystery today. Sir Francis Bacon would have been one month away from his 75th birthday.

1649 – January 30 – Nephew Charles I of England executed. Engraving by "unknown German" depicts the beheading with an elderly gentleman crying in the foreground. Contains multiple Bacon cipher signatures and a biliteral cipher. Bacon would have been 88 years old.

Conclusions

One of the main points of concern in this timeline would be the appearance of Shakespeare's Funerary Monument, in relation to some of the events appearing in the cipher texts. The monument and plaque would need to appear after those events had taken place. Though the plaque contains the date of 1616 the year of the actor's death, most scholars agree that the monument appeared years later. It's first mention is in the First Folio when Leonard Digges refers to "the Stratford monument," which was in 1623, so historians state that year as the latest date of its appearance. Champlain being sent to New France to oversee the fur trade takes place before these dates, so the timeline fits what we know of history. The publication of Champlain's book, illustrations and maps also predate the erection of the monument.

Most importantly, one of the messages of the cipher texts references the "Knights Baronets ratified." King James I approved the plan of Sir William Alexander to create the order in 1621, granting him Nova Scotia. Only a few years later, the order was ratified.

One of the main questions people ask (myself included at the beginning of this process) is, how could Francis Bacon have accomplished all of these things? However, when looking at the timeline, we can see that events in his life appear on the timeline only once or twice per year. He appears and speaks in parliament for example in 1597. What did he do for the rest of the year?

Another important feature of this timeline is the timing of publications and other events. After Shakespeare "retires" and produces no new plays, Champlain publishes a book. After Bacon "dies," Champlain accomplishes the majority of his work in Montreal. Overall, the timeline fits quite nicely as evidence of the cipher texts being true. While it may difficult for we modern thinkers to believe, the timeline demonstrates the plausibility that Francis Bacon lived multiple lives simultaneously, with help from his friends and relatives, King James I, Anthony Bacon, Ben Jonson and Sir Walter Raleigh.

Appendices

In this section of the book you will find materials associated with the overall premise, yet added aside items of interest. Appendix A contains two theories submitted to the Oak Island Team which afforded me the opportunity to meet with them (virtually, unfortunately), and share my findings. As such, the first document deals specifically with the plaque of Shakespeare's Funerary Monument in Holy Trinity Church in Stratford-upon-Avon, and how to find Bacon's "vault" on Oak Island. Additionally, I have heavily revised the submission to include information contributed at an earlier time, that will more fully explain the theory to the lay reader.

The second document in Appendix A is another Oak Island theory sent to the Oak Island Team. This is the theory later presented in the "Virtual" War Room to the "Brotherhood of the Dig" via Zoom, along with my friends and fellow researchers Chris Donah and Erin Helton. Appendix B contains my analysis of the "Invisible College Illustration," or as it is specifically referenced, the "Emblematic image of a Rosicrucian College; illustration from *Speculum sophicum Rhodo-stauroticum,* a 1618 work by Theophilus Schweighardt."

The current document bears some resemblance to the original I created for Rick Lagina, however with corrections and a large amount of added material (some of which appeared in the previous chapter).

While I used facts and logic in deciphering the plaque of Shakespeare's Funerary Monument in Holy Trinity Church, since the appendices are theoretical in nature, some obvious speculation is involved, and I try to note such speculations at each point. However, instead of bare hypotheticals, I tried to only rely on reasonable inferences based upon the available details and data.

And so, though the following may seem to be a deviation from the main thrust of this book, the Funerary Monument plaque, it helps to "flesh-out" the bigger picture, and help the discerning reader to better understand why there could have been a connection between this plaque and the mystery on Oak Island, Nova Scotia. Many of those explicit connections appear in the following documents. I hope you enjoy reading them as much as I enjoyed discovering them.

Last of all, I have included in their own appendix each of the transposed algorithms produced by each key, for the reader to use and experiment upon if they so choose.

Appendix A:

What follows is the actual theory proposal I sent to the team of researchers on Oak Island. I've made minor revisions and edits for the sake of clarity.

Hello,

My name is Jake Roberts, and I'm a teacher, researcher and fan of the show *The Curse of Oak Island*. I submitted a theory regarding Nolan's Cross and the Swamp last summer, and since that time, I've made some discoveries I would like to share with you. The first discovery made was an error in my theory due to the cone positions of Nolan's Cross. However, I'm happy to say that in the effort to correct my mistake, I've discovered new information about the nature and function of the cones themselves. But more importantly, I've discovered a connection between this purpose, and Sir Francis Bacon.

In this theory, I will attempt to explain who, what, why and how, along with:

- the Sir Francis Bacon connection
- The Shakespeare Memorial plaque decoded - placing Bacon in France
- the "trap" of Nolan's Cross, that isn't a cross
- the dual purpose of the Cones of the cross, and how they actually produce a map utilizing the Tree of Life symbol
- the true role of archeoastronomy, and the constellation represented by the stones of Nolan's Cross

To summarize, most researchers (including myself) have fallen for a trick from a master treasure hunter in the form of what has become known as the legendary "Nolan's Cross." As other researchers have asserted, Oak Island was used as a location to cache away treasure to fund the Revolutionary War. The Rosicrucian Order and early Freemasons left their calling card with multiple examples of symbolism, such as the triangular Swamp and the nine platforms of the original Money Pit, representing the nine vaults beneath Solomon's Temple. The conical stones on the island serve more than one purpose, and they play a major role in Sir Francis Bacon's connection to the island. That connection appears in how those stones represent the sky. They truly are the key.

While this treatment of the material is unique and original as a result of my own research, I need to thank my friends and fellow researchers, Chris Donah, Christopher Morford and Daniel Spino. The quality, depth and breadth of detail in their work is astounding, intimidating, but ultimately inspiring. I owe them all a big debt of gratitude. In fact, I will encourage the reader to check out links to a couple of articles written by Chris Donah, in particular his work surrounding Jason and the Argonauts. In one of our many conversations about such topics, he intimated regarding the Argo, "it *has* to mean something." I think I may have found an answer to that question.

But before I jump ahead of myself to Bacon's role, I need to explain how I arrived there, and how my previous (current) theory propelled me forward. If you are already familiar with the Royal Arch degree of Freemasons, and the Legend of the Three Sojourners, feel free to skip ahead to page 3.

My Original Theory

It's only appropriate to quote *The Tempest* at this point by stating, "what's past is prologue." I've always contended that the story regarding the discovery of the Money Pit was a ruse. The reason being that it's a retelling of a legend from the apocryphal Book of Enoch, regarding the rediscovery of the original site of the Temple of Solomon. Just like McGinnis and friends, the "Legend of the Three Sojourners" tells the story of how three young men go to work for King Zerubabbel to uncover the lost Temple. They discover a keystone, and using a spade, pick and pry bar, they excavate nine vaults, each built directly over the other, exactly as described in the story regarding the original discovery of the Money Pit by McGinnis, Smith and Vaughan. The three Sojourners discover a precious tablet made of gold in the lowest, or ninth level beneath the original site of the Temple upon which was "inscribed the ineffable name of God." Of course on Oak Island, this story plays out with the discovery of the "90 foot stone" with its own enigmatic inscription.

This story signals an allusion to the Royal Arch degree of Freemasonry, in which the candidate acts out (in part) the above parable, however instead of a gold tablet inscribed with the ineffable name of God, the candidate discovers the Ark of the Covenant. (This is why many people try to claim that the Ark is on Oak Island, by misunderstanding symbolism, mistaking the "thing" for the "idea" or message). The Royal Arch degree and the Legend are the main reasons that I didn't believe the original discovery ever happened. However, when I watched all of the discoveries unfold in Smith's Cove, I decided that something *had* happened after all, and as you all have always believed, it was something highly significant.

To that end, I decided to apply what I knew about the Royal Arch degree and symbolism to the Oak Island mystery. In my initial zeal, I made several rookie mistakes. However, my original instincts were correct. All of these allusions to the Royal Arch degree were there to point us in the right direction. My original approach was to treat the island as a Bacon cipher or cryptogram, and use steganographic principles such as symbolism and geometry to see what they could reveal. I also looked at the triangle of the Swamp as a hint, urging us to complete the "Companion Jewel" of the Royal Arch, by providing the Swamp with its companion. In general terms, I used geometric and surveying principles to identify the "ideal corners" of the Swamp, as well as create its companion, as seen above in these accompanying photos.

As I said, my instincts were correct - Not only do the Royal Arch degree and the Companion Jewel play a role, along with the early days of the Freemasons, but there is also an irrefutable geometric relationship between "Nolan's Cross" and the Swamp. The "geometrical relationship" part of my theory will still come into play in a significant manner. I will delve more deeply into the Royal Arch degree, the Companion Jewel and the geometry of the island in a later section. In addition, the geometrical mapping scheme revealed that the dimensions of the island from due north to due south in the area of the Swamp remain constant at 2 furlongs, regardless of the change in coastline, revealing it to be completely contrived - just additional evidence that the Swamp is man-made, as if any more were needed. This is all information that Fred Nolan would have known, and a major reason he concluded it was man-made and what piqued his interest as the main area to investigate.

Speaking of Mr. Nolan, where did I go wrong in my above theory? I trusted the position of my starting point, Cone B.

Treasure Hunting 101

I had heard the rumors. The Cones of Nolan's Cross, as far as we know, are "as close to the original locations as we can get them." And so, instead of doing the extra work to create the most accurate map I possibly could, I took the easy way out and used the positions I had, just to see if my theory would work, and work it did. Now I understand why it worked so well. They were placed as a clever piece of bait in a highly effective ruse by professional surveyor, Fred Nolan.

In this entire section, I look closely at his behavior as a life-long treasure hunter on Oak Island. As I do so, please understand that I do it with the full recognition of him as a legend as large as Oak Island itself, and though I focus mostly on his obfuscations, I do so with the utmost respect. He was, after all, doing what treasure hunters do. Though the treasure I hunt is the truth, I certainly don't judge him for his behavior in trying to protect what he viewed as rightfully his own.

An excellent example of the "treasure hunter's code" appeared on the show. In Season 3 episode 7 of *The Curse of Oak Island* titled "The Missing Peace," Fred Nolan pointed at what he called, "a hot spot" on one of his maps. It was gratifying to hear Rick Lagina state what I had always believed, that in the history of Oak Island, Nolan possessed the unique skill set to find the treasure. I've always believed that a surveyor who owned that particular part of the island would most likely have found something by now. Watching that episode confirmed for me, that he may have done just that.

Again, I have the utmost respect for all of the men who have participated in the hunt for answers on the island. What follows is not intended to disrespect anyone. By this I mean, one of the most important points to be made – treasure hunters follow a certain code, and rarely do they deviate from it. To summarize the words of Karl von Mueller in his *Treasure Hunter's Manual #7*, the first and most important rule treasure hunters follow is, "when you're hot on the trail of something, you don't tell anyone." Likewise, "if you actually do find something, don't tell anyone." Additionally, another rule treasure hunters follow is, "when you find a cache, leave behind trash." That is, a piece of garbage, metal rubbish or junk that signals to anyone who follows that you "got there first." That is precisely what happened in Episode 7 of Season 3 of *The Curse of Oak Island*.

In that episode, Fred Nolan points to a specific point on the map at what he calls "a hot spot," and the framing shot of the next scene even includes a wooden tripod directly over the site. Rick and Marty show up with a drill team, and at the depth Fred Nolan indicated, they hit a piece of rusty metal. As the brothers use the heavy equipment to keep digging, the only other thing they find is a pointed bit of log, exactly like others Mr. Nolan had found in the Swamp. In terms of analysis, the team said nothing really, about Fred's "hot spot" not even being lukewarm. Though this is speculation, the only probable inference to be made here is, the team recognized that they had been "led-on" to "discover" what Fred had left behind for them - trash, and being the gracious folk they are, decided to let it slide. The old-timer had "put one over on them." There is also the story of an alleged discovery of an old iron wood stove found under one of the Cones of Nolan's Cross, which fits in with the tendency of treasure hunters leaving junk behind in a place where they may have found something and knew others would follow. That being said, the other inference to be made is, it may have been an actual cache site at one time.

I decided to use a screen shot of the graphic depicting the Nolan site from the show, to see how it lines up with the work I had done with the Oak Island ground plan I had at that time. By overlaying this graphic on my own map, I would see if this would confirm both the point on my map that was a high priority target for me, or indicate that this point on the map was an actual cache site. I felt if they overlapped, perhaps my mapping method could be used to identify other sites. Considering what I've already written above, and for reasons you are about to see, you'll understand why at the time, I thought I had been successful.

Here's an image of the screen shot from "The Missing Peace" episode depicting the Nolan Site, overlaid upon my own map of the first Tree of Life symbol I had created (my model creates four to be later explained):

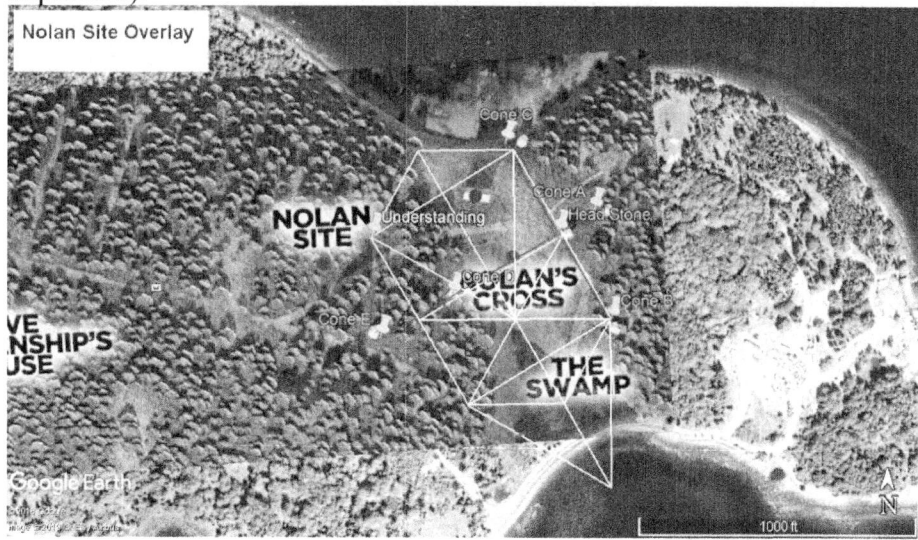

The image wasn't manipulated. I had tilted and resized maintaining proportion to match the cones of Nolan's Cross and the north and south coasts of the island. And as you can see, the site identified by Fred Nolan didn't match my preferred point of interest, the "Understanding" Sephiroth. At the time, I was disappointed. That was until I realized - I highly doubt that a treasure hunter would accurately portray a site on a graphic and then televise it... That's when I played with the opacity of the overlaying image and realized that Fred Nolan's house was in the wrong place in the graphic.

Assuming that Nolan's house would have been the starting point in judging the distance to the actual site, and again, I had recognized this was an assumption, I repositioned the overlay to place the point depicted as his house to where it actually is on the island. I kept the orientation of the graphic exactly the same, resulting in this alignment:

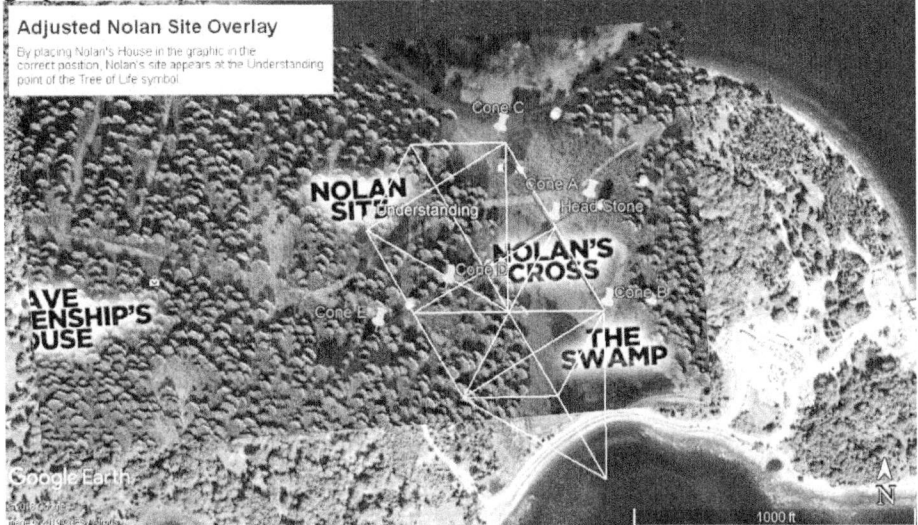

Suddenly the Nolan Site appeared at the Understanding point of the Tree of Life symbol. Of course, this could have been a coincidence and confirmation bias on my part, but I didn't think so.

If the graphic on the show was adjusted to hide the true site in this way, then this would have further confirmed the validity of the Tree of Life mapping system I still believe is at work on Oak Island. However, my method of creating the Tree of Life map was flawed from the beginning. I had used Cone B as my starting point, and in so doing I began the process in the wrong spot, because the cones have been moved.

As I stated earlier, out of everyone who has been a part of the search for answers on Oak Island, I had always believed that Fred Nolan, with his surveying expertise, was the best equipped person to solve the mystery. His behavior has also been "text-book treasure hunter." He surveyed every inch of ground, documenting every clue and significant stone with markings, and then he removed them (on the premise for safe-keeping). In reality, he was obscuring and hiding the clues from everyone else involved after he had recorded their locations and descriptions for his own use.

In the treasure hunting business, apparently misdirection is the name of the game. And that's exactly how I fell victim to the "Nolan's Cross" trap.

The whole concept of a "cross" on Oak Island was a fabrication from the start, intended to control the narrative. He moved the "Cones" into their current configuration, called it a cross and I used his construction to create a map. When my map seemed to align perfectly with the coastlines and other features of the island, I privately sang myself praises at my clever solution,

298

when it never occurred to me that all of my possible starting points had been "placed" by a surveyor, who had spent the greater part of his life studying the very island I had just begun to investigate. I don't blame Fred Nolan at all. I have no one to blame but myself, my own ego. I fell for his trap and forgive the pun, bore the cross as a result.

Obfuscation and misdirection is how an intelligent treasure hunter would handle his competitors, and that's exactly what Fred Nolan did with the large cone-shaped boulders. He moved them into the configuration where they sit today, calling it a cross. He even allegedly dug-up another large boulder at its center, affectionately referred to as "the Head Stone." The best way to hide what could have been an identifiable configuration, would be to replace it with a more readily identifiable configuration, and again, that's exactly what Fred Nolan did. In fact, I now know that Freemasons would have readily identified the shape of the original configuration. He replaced a familiar constellation (not the one you're thinking of) with an even more familiar symbol, one that would resonate with the public and researchers alike. If everyone saw a cross, and began looking for the Ark of the Covenant, or the Sepulcher of Jesus or Mary Magdalene, all the better. Meanwhile, Fred Nolan was free to continue the real search as he saw fit. He was a very shrewd treasure hunter, and a very intelligent man.

I fell for it. Looking back, as a teacher who teaches classes in critical thinking, well-versed in cognitive biases and logical fallacies, I shake my head at myself. I accepted his cross. But I take solace in the fact that I'm in very good company in those who have come before me. And, it seems that people associated with the search, knew something that he might not have known at the time - he was seen moving them.

I decided I needed a fresh start. I needed to approach the problem the way the original depositors of the treasure (and those who may have made a withdrawal) would approach it.

Just the Facts

I reverted to what would have been known before all of the clues were moved or destroyed, before the cones were moved and before the Dunfield crew conducted its devastating "scorched earth" search. In summary, we know the following as facts:

- Fred Nolan, as a tried and true treasure hunter, used obfuscation and misdirection.
- At least some of the conical stones of the so-called cross have been moved.
- My original theory, like so many others, was wrong as a result.
- Mr. Nolan placed the cones in a manner that created a *too* perfect map using my methodology.

- The Swamp could not be *moved* or affected in any meaningful way.
- Cone C has never been moved.
- The "Head" Stone, if the story is true, was actually underground out of view, and therefore should not enter into any "use" of what's referred to as "Nolan's Cross" in terms of archeoastronomy.
- Many researchers agree on the original location of another prominent feature on the island, the Welling Triangle.
- The common surveyor measurements of a rod, chain and furlong are at play on the island.
- *Someone* other than Mr. Nolan has an idea of the original locations of the stones.

So, I needed a fresh starting point, and I decided to begin with the one spot that everyone agrees hasn't been tampered with - Cone C.

I began the way I assumed a surveyor would - starting at Cone C as a known fixed point, I drew straight lines radiating out across the island in ten degree increments, making some interesting discoveries in the process. The original image appeared:

Several interesting alignments appeared from this arbitrary starting point. First of all, the first line drawn at 180 degrees due south passes directly through the round pool area at the southwest corner of the Swamp. Interestingly, another line at 130 degrees crossed directly through the Money Pit drilling can area:

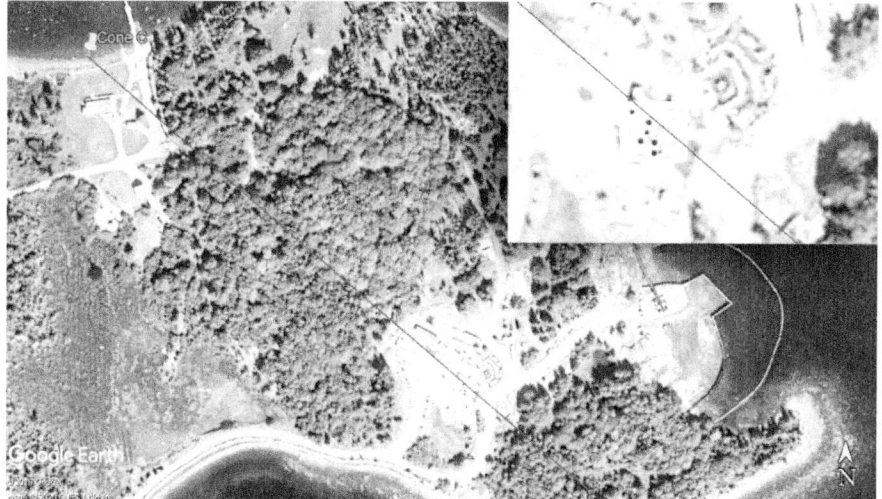

Another interesting correlation appeared from lines at 110 and 120 degrees from Cone C, perfectly framing in Smith's Cove. Line 110 actually points directly at what appears to be an ongoing excavation:

As an interesting coincidence, a line drawn at 111 degrees pointed directly at the slipway. 111 is the number the cipher signature for "Bacon" using the Kaye cipher system.

     Another very significant alignment that will become relevant, aligns with an area of the island that most researchers seem to agree on, which is the original location of the Welling Triangle. At an angle of 140 degrees from Cone C, on the way toward that very familiar feature of Oak Island that we all associate with the Welling Triangle, I noticed an interesting phenomenon as it passed through Fred Nolan's property. A correlation that would soon repeat:

The 140 degree line seems to align with the angle formed by the corners Fred Nolan's house and garage. But the real eye opener for me appeared with the line at 150 degrees from Cone C. At 150 degrees, the line precisely passes between the corners of the house and garage on the Nolan property, as if it were created as a form of sightline:

Note how the 150 degree line from Cone C bisects the teardrop-shaped patch of lawn in half with precision. The patch of lawn resembles a common two-dimensional representation of a field of vision, or perhaps even a primitive symbol of a theodolite that might be used by a surveyor. The line ends very near the corner of the triangular Swamp, which is an important point to identify when unraveling its secrets, as I hopefully will make clear very soon. Did Fred Nolan orient the buildings on his property to record important information, so that it wouldn't be lost? If one were to catalogue every man-made clue on the island, map them and their significance, and then remove them as Mr. Nolan is reputed to have done, wouldn't it be prudent to preserve certain important points if it were possible to do so? An intelligent person would incorporate such alignments into any construction under his supervision. And if that person happened to be a surveyor, wouldn't that make things easier to accomplish?

Only questions. But I suspect that with a little bit of time appropriately spent, features and alignments of Mr. Nolan's property hold some answers. I held one suspicion that this line of sight possibly could help place Cone B in it's original location.

The Spy

Though it's probably no secret on Oak Island, I was surprised to learn that Dan Blankenship had a few tricks up his sleeve as well. For some time, according to my source Dan allegedly had employed a former military man to keep tabs on what Fred Nolan was up to. Though I have this information second-hand, not only does it come from a very reliable source, but I actually have seen the communications between them. His name was Paul Wronclawski. Chances are, if anyone on the Oak Island team eventually reads this, they already know the story. But a part Paul's job allegedly was to follow Mr. Nolan and note his actions. Again, according to the messages I've seen, he watched Fred Nolan drive iron stakes into the ground around the cones of "Nolan's Cross" before he moved them, so as to have an accurate record of their true, or original, locations.

Being a resourceful individual and a reliable employee, Paul duly (again, allegedly) snuck around in full camouflage and recorded these locations.

As I have every reason to believe my source as a reliable person, and as I have no reason to trust or distrust the information he was provided, I decided that I had nothing to lose in experimenting with it, for two distinct purposes. First, to see if alignments or correlations exist that would have been otherwise over-looked because of the "cross" ruse, and second, to see if my original theory regarding the Royal Arch degree and the Companions Jewel could still hold true.

Though the new locations I have for Cones A and B (as they were obviously moved the farthest) could "be slightly off" in this digital age, they not only worked for both purposes as stated above, they worked exceedingly well. Please understand I didn't just simply accept this new information as gospel. For reasons already explained, I resolved to perform due diligence to see if these stone locations could be confirmed. I was operating under the "fool me once" dictum, but I saw no reason to avoid experimenting with the new positions. The corroborating evidence turned the tide on my reservations. Additionally, I would later learn from the highly detailed

LIDAR maps provided to me by fellow researcher Erin Helton, other data indicated that Paul's information was very accurate. I'll let you decide if it does the same for you.

"And put down Richard, that sweet lovely rose,"

Or in this case, that cross.

As I stated earlier, "Nolan's Cross" has been repeated and accepted so often, that it has become a truism, a beloved idea that creates a cognitive bias in *The Curse of Oak Island* fans, and researchers alike. Everyone, intent on seeing how the latest theory matches up with the "cones of Nolan's Cross," dismisses data or correlations that do not "seem to fit."

And like myself, they do it in spite of having heard the stories the boulders were moved. So, I know all too well that doing away with a time-honored trope of a highly popular television show won't beget me any fans. But, facts are facts, and if they truly have been moved, then this was my best chance to test my theory.

I entered Paul's overlay into Google Earth to see what would happen. The following picture includes the best current data regarding the locations of the stones known as "Nolan's Cross" and their adjoining lines researchers use. It also includes the overlay of Paul's locations. You will note the difference in the locations of Cones A and B:

Though no change seems to appear with cones D and E, the significant difference appears with A and B. The pushpins with the white lettering are my additions in the positions that Paul provided. The other changes I will be making in the paradigm that everyone has accepted of a "cross," will be the removal of the "Head Stone" introduced by Fred Nolan.

If the story is true regarding its discovery, including its shape and location, it was under the ground. For a stone to be relevant as a megalith marker, it needs to be on the surface or else it serves no practical purpose in terms of archeoastronomy. The stones on the surface do serve a purpose. The revised version according to this overlay, though slightly differing from my ideal model I created from alignments with Cone C, worked well for our purposes.

The new (or possibly original) model of the ground layout of the stones would appear in this fashion (please note the "Head Stone" is removed for reasons already explained). Though no updated data exists for Cones D and E, "Nolan's Cross" transforms from a cross into Nolan's "Rhomboid" with a dogleg:

So many researchers have tried to apply archeoastronomy to the previous stone locations with no true success. Yet no one, as far as I know, has ever tried to apply this configuration. So that's what I decided to do.

The Cipher Message from the Plaque

Since the reader is well acquainted with the cipher message, I'll simply insert how it fits in here without going into too much detail. The messages basically stated to "use the pattern of my cone stone Heracles as a way to" Bacon's "treasure vault," and that "on maps it's [La Baye de Toute Isles] The Bay of Many Isles in [Arcaty] Acadia." Another part of the cipher message states to "go to the dupli knee," or duplicate knee. And so, it wasn't until I had completed deciphering Key 38 that I had one form of confirmation of the use of Hercules as an astronomical map.

I wanted to be sure to fully test out that Hercules and the Keystone Asterism were the correct choice, and so I tried to find as much corroborating evidence as possible. As I gathered it, I tried to find ways to also corroborate the "knee of Hercules" as it appears as a treasure map on the island. Interestingly, this is possible to do. Plenty of evidence related Bacon to Hercules, and the conical boulders themselves provided their one surprise function.

The Northern Sky

When applying circumpolar constellations to the stones on Oak Island, Boötes and Cygnus receive the most attention for a few reasons. First of all, they easily can be applied to a cross shape, and the Cross narrative is so strong, it's never questioned. Secondly, the most popular theories on the show have involved these two constellations, and Petter Amundsen's work with Shakespeare's *First Folio* have become the stuff of legend in the online discussion groups. Both Cygnus and Boötes are referenced in many writings circulated among Enlightenment Era figures who have been linked to Rosicrucian ideas.

Since the popular constellations won't align to this tentatively "corrected" orientation, I needed to find a way to further narrow down the list of candidates. My first thought, because of the Temple of Solomon symbolism on the island, was Cepheus, whose central asterism is sometimes referred to as "Solomon's House" because of the house-like shape. And it's composed of five stars. However, I knew at first glance any hope of aligning the stars with the cones wouldn't work. The solution appeared from my original theory regarding the Royal Arch degree and the Companion Jewel.

I remembered the first Latin inscription on the front of the Companion Jewel around the circle surrounding the Star of Solomon: *"Nil nisi clavis deest"* meaning, "nothing but the key is wanting." I knew that the stones of Nolan's Cross were the key. And then it hit me - stone = key. Keystone, an extremely important symbol within Freemasonry, and in the Royal Arch degree. In the Legend of the Three Sojourners, one of the workers uncovers a keystone leading to the discovery of the vaults below Solomon's Temple. The answer had to be the keystone asterism at the center of Hercules, which would echo the cipher message I later discovered within Shakespeare's Funerary Monument plaque.

When I looked at the Keystone in Hercules, it seemed about right. It definitely had the right "feel," and one of the stars in his right thigh seemed a possible candidate for Cone E. The next step was to see if the constellation of Hercules actually-aligned with the original Cone placements.

This created a bit of a logistical problem, in creating an overlay that would actually be truly representative of the Hermetic dictum of as above, so below. I've seen researchers sometimes post sky-ground correlations online, and they simply place a screen shot of the constellation over

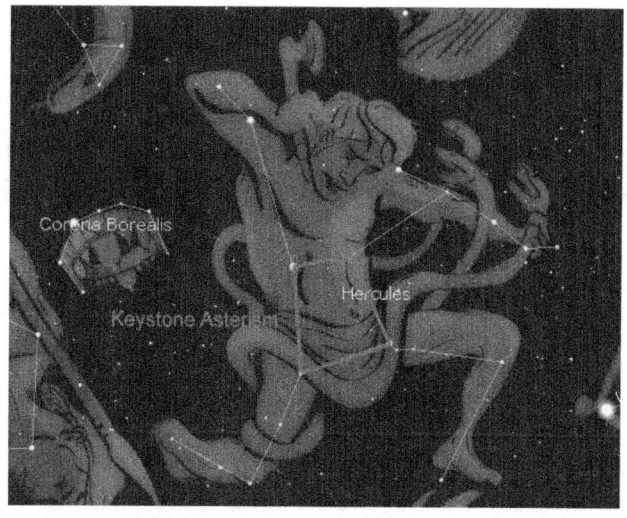

the ground image. This is actually incorrect. The original planners and depositors, if they intended to create a sky-ground connection, would use a mirror image so that the ground "reflected" the sky. They would be using an astrolabe to "see" the constellation from "above" it from the perspective of God, and project it down upon the ground from above. Here's an illustration of the concept:

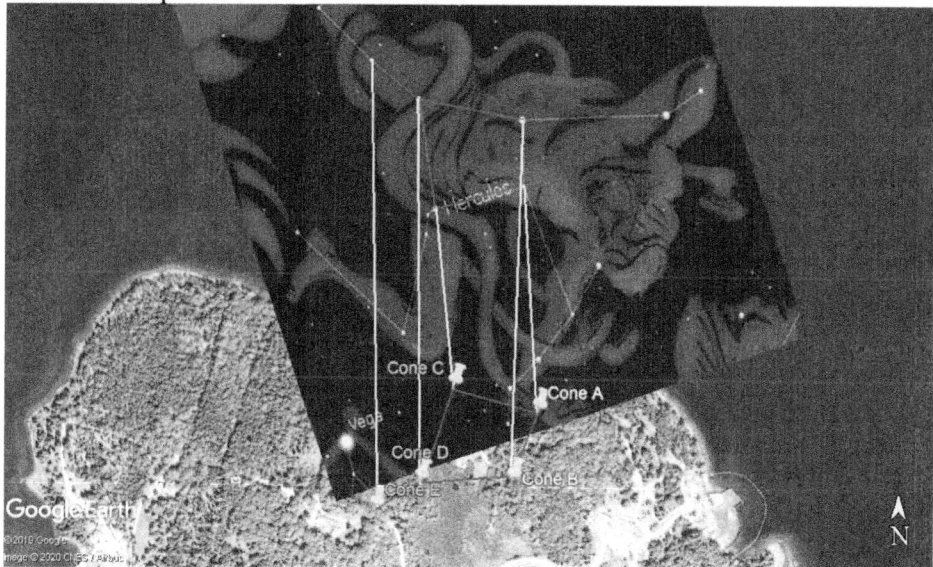

To that end, I was able to "flip" the constellation to create a mirror image, while maintaining the aspect ratio of the proportions, ensuring the integrity of any correlations as indicated above. If the stars of the Keystone matched the cones, then we would have proof of concept. Meanwhile I was encouraged by what seemed to be a close correlation as represented in the above image.

When I reversed and oriented the new image, resizing but maintaining the proportions, I arrived at the following result:

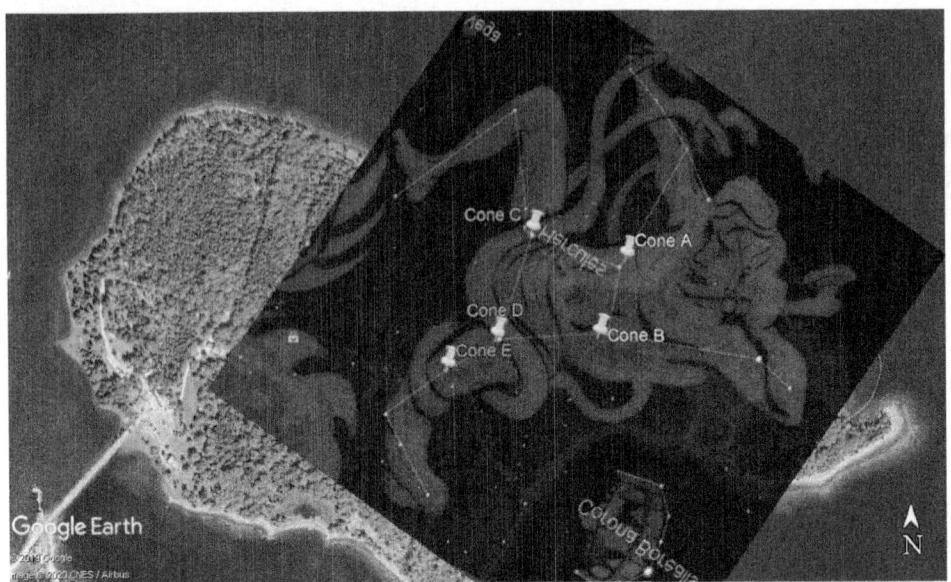

I was astounded. I still am. Considering that the cones had been moved, then placing them back as close to the original positions according to secondhand, albeit eye-witness, information, the correlation with the Keystone is about as "spot on" as I could ever have hoped. I decided to see if any of the other stars in Hercules seemed to correlate to any other known features. My shock continued. More interesting correlations appeared, and one is a highly significant point on the island.

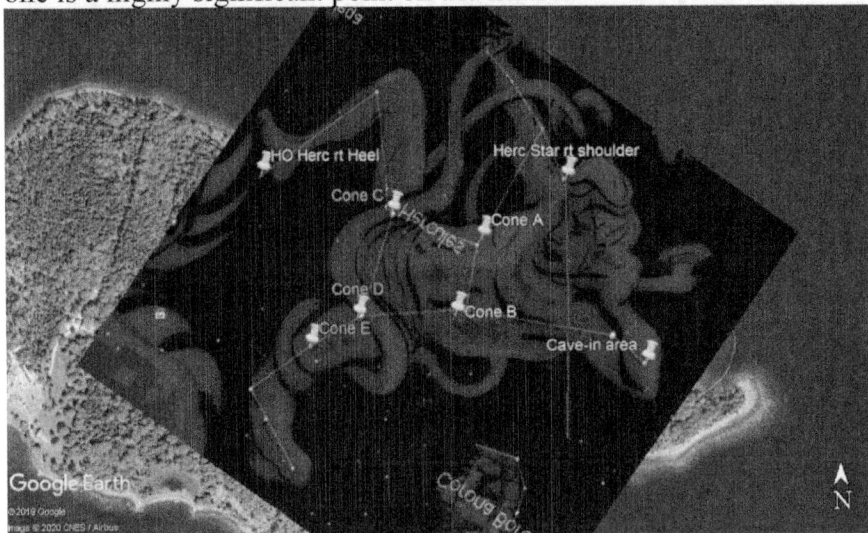

The star in Hercules' left elbow appeared directly over the Cave-in Pit. Two other interesting correlations were less concrete but interesting all the same.

The star representing his right shoulder appeared right on the edge of the north shore, nearly due north of the Welling Triangle area. After working with Erin Helton, she confirmed that not only did her theory involve the same point, but there was indeed a large boulder at that location, her "Anchor Stone." Speaking of, it was

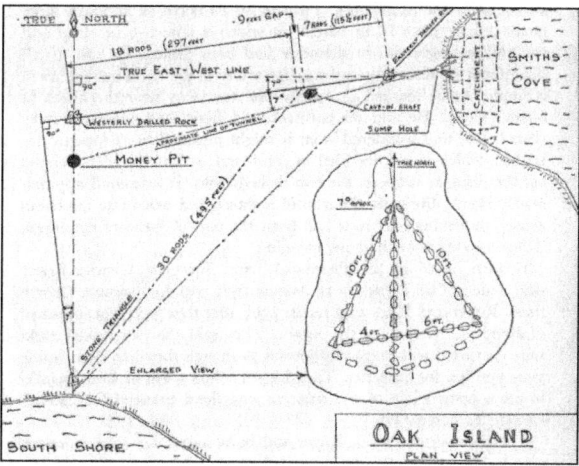

also very near an anomalous object or structure exactly 2 furlongs north of the Welling Triangle at a bearing of 353 degrees (7 degrees off true north, as indicated on the hand-drawn sketch of the Welling Triangle area):

Lastly, in the previous illustration, the star at his right heel is in an area previously identified by fellow researcher and friend Chris Donah as being the possible site of what has been labeled, the HO stone. In his own research, he had associated the HO stone with Hercules.

A Brief Summary

Up to this point, I was beginning to become what I would call "skeptically optimistic." Given the history of the island, and the men who have done everything they could to find answers, so many things have changed. Boulders covered in clues have been dynamited, the Dunfield crew all but devastated the Money Pit area, and Fred Nolan recorded and removed stones containing man-made clues. But there were now a few more items to add to my list of things that I knew:

- Cone C works well as a frame of reference to other areas of the island
- The cipher on the plaque of Shakespeare's Funerary Monument refer to Bacon's "cone stone Heracles" in "La Baye de Toute Isles," which many people believe was the original name of Mahone Bay
- The information regarding the "original location" of the Cones produces an excellent candidate for the astronomical alignment of the Keystone in Hercules
- The Keystone within the Hercules constellation contains the Perfect symbolic element for this moDel, pointing to early Freemasonry and the Royal Arch

- The other stars with*in* Hera*kles* seem to correla*te* or interact *w*ith oth*er* meaningf*v*l a*rea*s of the island, most notably the Cave-in Pit

The next steps in this puzzle would seem to be to answer the following questions:

- What date would provide such an alignment between the conical stones on Oak Island and the constellation of Hercules?
- What is the significance of the constellation Hercules, other than the importance of the Keystone?
- Are there any answers in previous theories that have been proposed, including my own?

And it's with the last of these questions, that I think I can answer the first two.

Cygnus, Boötes and the Argo

With researchers referencing the "Swan of Avon," and Boötes referenced in *The Tempest*, and the aforementioned ease with which both can be applied to the shape of a cross, there's little wonder in the interest of these two constellations in association with Oak Island. As I said, Petter Amundsen's work is always referenced in this area with very good reason. However, with so many researchers following clues to this area of the sky, I can't help but think that it reinforces the importance of the constellation Hercules, actually appearing right between Cygnus and Boötes in the northern sky. There are other important connections as well.

Hercules flanked by Bootes on the left, Cygnus on the right

In addition to the above constellations, the Argo Navis constellation also comes into play. Chris Donah has done extensive research of the Argo constellation, and the myth of Jason and the Argonauts, which can be read at - "The Constellation Argo Navis: Johannes Hevelius's Hidden Symbolism." The Argo and the myth of Jason was an important symbol to many of 16th and 17th century enlightenment thinkers. In fact in one tradition, Sir Francis Bacon reputedly referred to all "Rosicrucian-minded seekers of truth" as "Argonauts." The obvious connection to point out – Hercules was the strongest and most famous warrior of the Argonauts. This led me to look for a connection between Sir Francis Bacon and the mythic Greek hero.

12 Labors?

As I looked for a connection between the two, I did what all amateur researchers first do when looking for answers of an esoteric nature - I consulted Manly P. Hall's *The Secret Teachings of All Ages*. And there, I found this fascinating passage:

> In all probability, the keys to the Baconian riddle will be found in classical mythology. He who understands the Seven-Rayed God will comprehend   the method employed by Bacon to accomplish his ***monumental labor*** [author's emphasis]. Aliases were assumed by him in accordance with the attributes and order of the of the members of the planetary system. One of the least known--but most important--keys to the Baconian enigma is the Third, or 1637, Edition, published in Paris, of *Les Images ou Tableaux de platte peinture de deux Philostrates sophistes grecs et les statues de Callistrate*, by Blaise de Vigenere. The title page of this volume--which, as the name of the author when properly deciphered indicates, was written by or under the direction of Bacon or his secret society--is one mass of important Masonic or Rosicrucian symbols. On page 486 appears a plate entitled "Hercules Furieux," showing a gigantic figure shaking a spear, the ground before him strewn with curious emblems. In his curious work, *Das Bild des Speershüttlers die Lösung des Shakespeare-Rätsels*, Alfred Freund attempts to explain the Baconian symbolism in the *Philostrates*. Bacon he reveals as the philosophical Hercules, whom time will establish as the true "Spear-Shaker" (Shakespeare)." (551)

In the tradition of a Rosicrucian thinker, the author of the German work being referenced by Hall, named himself A. Freund, the German word for friend. The plate showing Hercules as a "spear-shaker" appears on the symbolically-numbered page 486. One interpretation using Bacon's Simple Cipher would be $4 + 8 + 6 = 18$, $1 + 8 = 9$. "Bacon" in the Simple Cipher = 33, and the relation to the number 9 is obvious.

I decided to check the Qabalistic numerical value of Hercules. Since the book referenced above appeared to be written by a Rosicrucian writer, I consulted the gematria table in Paul Foster Case's book, *The True and Invisible Rosicrucian Order*. The simple cipher used in this case does not use the letter "K." On Table 1 on page 34, under the heading "Number in Qabalah Simplex" and calculating the values of the letters "Hercules," I arrived at the following sequence - 8, 5, 16, 3, 19, 10, 5, and 17, totaling 83 (Case 34).

Qabalistically speaking, this could be an indication of Bacon. Subtracting Bacon's number of 33 from 83, we get 50. In Hebrew gematria, 50 is a number of letter Nun, and means, "everlasting, perpetuity and eternality." Did Bacon's group of brothers memorialize him as the Greek demi-god, Hercules, by adding the number of Argonauts of 50 to 33, and making him the "everlasting Bacon" in the northern sky? Additionally, 83 is the cipher signature of the word "Fraters," Latin for "brothers," in Simple Cipher. I began to think I may be on the right track.

Interesting question and observation to be sure. Obviously though, the big takeaways for our intents and purposes include the statements that the key to unraveling the "riddle of Bacon" involves Greek mythology, and a Rosicrucian writer referred to him "as the philosophical Hercules." This is very appropriate for the greatest of the "Argonauts."

Hall's mention of the "Seven-Rayed God" references the seven planets and the seven classical arts and sciences. This is relevant in light of Bacon's dedication to the natural sciences and pioneering the scientific method.

Next, I began looking for more clues regarding the ways that Sir Francis Bacon could be memorialized. So I read his eulogies in the form of the verses in *Manes Verulamiani*.

Shades of Verulam

The *Manes Verulamiani* is a collection of "eulogies" from academics and anonymous writers lamenting the loss of Sir Francis Bacon, published by his friend William Rawley. One cannot read them, with their countless references to Bacon's prolific works of literature, and poetry in particular, without being convinced that the writers of these eulogies knew he was behind the works of William Shakespeare. There were multiple references to his "royal nature," hinting at his possible true lineage as the bastard son of the Queen (AUTHOR'S NOTE: Having read the cipher messages, the reader will recognize that I had made the same assumption as so many other researchers at the time of writing this section of my theory for the Oak Island team). Additionally, they also made me believe that Bacon's "death," at least at the age of 65, is a fiction. I believe he embraced a "philosophical death." Frankly, the "eulogies" read like a modern celebrity roast! With puns, innuendos and other plays on words that would have drawn applause from Shakespeare himself, I could imagine Bacon sitting there listening to his friends say their final goodbyes, before he headed to a well-earned

312

retirement in the New World where he could personally oversee the Grand Experiment.

If he came to the New World as I believe, one of the favored colonies would need to be Nova Scotia.

Additionally, the phrasing and sentence structure indicated every eulogy contained steganographic codes. I decoded Roman numeral V, as it was short. And sure enough, even the hidden messages contained tongue-in-cheek quips such as "bihly he's a lilsad," referencing William Rawley as "Billy," I am sure.

Aside from the above, the eulogies in *Manes Verulamiani* also contain astronomical references, as well as referring to Bacon as their "demigod." Just as Manly P. Hall had stated, all of these references appear as allusions to characters in Greek mythology. Of particular note, most of the references refer to Bacon accompanying Astraea in the sky. Astraea, as the Greek goddess of law, judgment, and purity, was made into the constellation of Virgo. On the date that I finally settled upon to test my sky-ground theory between Hercules and Oak Island, an interesting alignment occurs between Hercules and Virgo. But more on that later.

I've included two of the eulogy verses in Appendix A, along with my annotations (AUTHOR'S NOTE: These materials have been removed from this edition). Here, I'll include a few of the references that caught my attention.

Eulogy IV., written by an individual with the initials R.P., provided several examples and in the first, we see an obvious reference to the astronomy in the northern sky in the form of Lyra. (ANOTHER AUTHOR'S NOTE: I now believe that the initials "R.P." are a Bacon signature. They total 32 in Simple Cipher, the number of verses in the publication, and is also the letter "F" for Francis in Kaye. In Reverse they equal 18 or G in Reverse, which can reduce to 9, the number of the "missing" I in "R.I.P." Also, the missing "I" in Kaye is 35. Added to the original 32, we have 67, "Francis" in Simple). The writer states, "As Eurydice wandering through the shades of Dis longed to caress Orpheus, so did Philosophy entangled in the subtleties of Schoolmen seek Bacon as a deliverer, with such winged hand as Orpheus lightly touched the lyre's strings..." In this reference to the constellation right beside Hercules, Lyra, we see the juxtaposition of Bacon with these characters of Greek mythology. In another telling line, we seem to be urged to "follow the stars to his funeral pyre."

This is one of the many veiled references to Hercules in the eulogies themselves. The writer alludes to Prometheus, the fire bringer. Fire is a universal symbol of knowledge, and it appears that the writer is comparing Bacon directly to Prometheus. He writes, "Let every star emit a spark into his pyre; be it sacrilege that the kingly pile should be kindled for

Prometheus from a kitchen fire." Not only is there a reference to Bacon's "kingly" status in reference to his "kingly pile," but by insisting that the stars should be used to "spark" his pyre, the writer speaks symbolically. The stars will be used "spark the memory of Bacon" in the form of a constellation. This also means that if "every star emits a spark into his pyre," that the sparks of these stars can be followed to find it. The stars will direct us to the pyre - lighting the way. But what direction will they lead?

The writer "R.P." tells us, only a few lines above the last quote. He states, "The Columbus of Apollo with his lordly crew passes beyond the Pillars of Hercules in order to bestow a new world and new arts," which refers to Bacon's Novum Organum, as explained below. But first, several references happen in this one sentence, and I will treat each in turn. [First of all, the use of Columbus contains multiple cipher signatures of Francis Bacon. The total sum of the letter values in Simple is 100, "Francis Bacon" in Simple. The sum of the values in Reverse Cipher is also 100. The total in Kaye is 152, which is the Kaye Cipher signature for "Stewart." Additionally, there is an added significance to this number. Using the forward and backward counting systems of the characters on the plaque, the 152nd characters appear on either side of the conjoined letters "ME" at the mathematical center of the characters, 153. To the right of "ME" are the conjoined letters "NT" which when we add their values in Simple, the total is 32, or "F" in Kaye. To the left if we follow the same method suggested by the right side, we have the pair of letters "NV," which when added together produce 33, the Simple Cipher signature for "Bacon"].

Columbus also can be read as an astronomical reference to Columba at the bow of the Argo, in the sky directly opposite of Hercules. As everyone knows, Bacon revered (and embodied) all of the things that Apollo represented, the arts and sciences. From healing to poetry, it makes sense to compare him to the famous explorer "of Apollo." Also, it's interesting to note that both Apollo (as Delphic Apollo) and Hercules were revered by sailors and seafarers. Additionally, as stated earlier, Bacon referred to his like-minded brethren and seekers of truth as "Argonauts." This explains his "lordly crew" as they all pass beyond "the Pillars of Hercules."

As mentioned above, the Pillars of Hercules figure prominently on the cover of Bacon's *Novum Organum,* with a ship placed directly between them. At the bottom of the image, in Latin a motto reads, *Multi pertransibunt et augebitur scientia,* which translates as, "Many will pass through and knowledge will be the greater." The remainder of the sentence quoted above, "in order to bestow a new world and new arts," implies that Bacon may have headed to the New World.

Another interesting reference from the same Eulogy manages to cleverly combine the ideas of Hercules, oak trees and the number 33, all in one allusion. "R.P." alludes to the famous wrestler of ancient Greece, the

314

historical figure Milo of Crotus, whom writers have compared to Hercules countless times. We see it when he writes, "What mighty Milo enrages the oaks, when gibbous old age weighs more heavily than the ox?" Again, the poetic writing requires a step by step analysis. First of all, Milo enraging the oaks would refer to the legend of Milo's death, where he attempted to rip apart the trunk of a tree with his hands, only to have them trapped by the tree in the process. He was then killed by wolves (or a lion, depending upon the source) as he had no escape. At the risk of invoking my own biases, I would also like to believe the "oaks" could be a reference to the eponymous "island in the North Atlantic." On the surface of things, "gibbous old age" refers to a waning moon, but in my opinion, it refers to Bacon's mid-section. Many of the eulogies make fun of his body in a similar manner, giving added weight (forgive the pun) to the punch-line of the ox reference. Incidentally, the Rosicrucian Qabalah Simplex cipher number of ox, is 33, the Simple Cipher value of Bacon.

In the next reference, he is not only referred to with the same status as Hercules, but R.P. states that Bacon had constructed his own tomb. He writes, "While our demi-god transmitted sciences to all ages to come, he is found to be the altogether too premature constructor of his own tomb." While the orthodox interpretation would have us believe that the speaker feels Bacon died too early and should have lived longer and died due to his experiment of freezing meat, that is not what is said at all. He states, "he is found to be *the altogether too premature constructor* of his own tomb." Considering the literal meaning of the word "altogether," the speaker means that Bacon was *in every way* premature in building his own tomb. In other words, *he wasn't dead yet.*

While we all resist the urge to quote Monte Python, perhaps the "demi-god" reference being repeated in several of the eulogies performs a dual purpose. The first, would be a tongue-in-cheek reference to Bacon's royal lineage, and his lack of status. It would be the perfect vehicle to make fun of a friend who happened to be the forgotten son of a queen, Divine Right or wrong.

The second purpose of course, would be to equate Bacon to a demigod of Greek mythology, the most famous of which arguably is Hercules. In addition, the author also clearly stated that Bacon had constructed his own tomb, another allusion that is repeated throughout the eulogies.

The last references from eulogy IV., allude to the "Tripod" of Law and a specific constellation in relation to Bacon. R.P writes, "From the tripod of Law go on uttering oracles disciples of Themis…." The tripod "of Law" is juxtaposed with the word oracle to compare Bacon and his legal contemporaries with the oracles of Ancient Greece and the goddess Themis. In particular, the tripod and oracle refer to the Delphic Tripod, Hercules' attempt to steal it, and the struggle that ensued with his half-brother Apollo. (AUTHOR'S NOTE: We can now recognize this also as an allusion to a throne and Bacon's half-brother). The constellation allusions continue, as the writer states, "....Thus, blessed inhabitants of heaven, let Astraea enjoy her champion of old, or with Bacon give back Astraea." By asking the "inhabitants of heaven" to let Bacon be with the virgin goddess of justice and innocence, the speaker is placing him in the sky as well. Further, he is having her enjoy his company, meaning he would be nearby in the sky. Astraea became the constellation Virgo, meaning that Bacon is meant to be nearby.

Such references are seemingly endless throughout the collection of eulogies, but I will include just one more, as it contains highly significant details. This next quote comes from an anonymous eulogy, yet the writer refers to himself within the text at its conclusion as "William Boswell." Obviously a pseudonym, the first name would seem a nod to another more famous nom de plume. Boswell is a word meaning, "a person who records in detail the life of a usually famous contemporary." Using the Kaye Cipher, the full name totals 286, 1 less than "Fra Rosi Crosse," possibly signifying the symbolic "loss" of Bacon from their ranks. He makes the following remarkable statement, "He hath left the living, whom alone it was wont to bear the laurel crown, for Verulam reigning in the citadel of the gods shines with a golden crown; and enthroned above the bounds of the sky he loves with face towards Earth to view the stars;" The "laurel crown" was originally given by Hercules to the winner of a race, honoring Zeus, and here Boswell places one on Bacon. However, in the sky he "shines with a golden crown," in the form of Corona Borealis which appears next to Hercules. And he is placed above the stars looking down upon them as he faces Earth, reinforcing the idea that the constellation and Keystone would appear on earth in mirror-image form.

Looking at the night sky on the winter solstice in 1626, the year of Bacon's "death," just before dawn on the longest night of the year, an interesting thing happens above Oak Island. Apollo draws the sun toward a group of constellations representing the collected contributions of Sir Francis Bacon. Chris Donah actually attributes them as a "mega" constellation representing Apollo, the god revered by Bacon. These constellations reflecting Bacon's life, interests and accomplishments line up on the horizon, including the "desired" position of Hercules to match the Cones of Nolan's "Rhomboid." Astraea, as Virgo, presides over the Scales of Justice of Libra. On one side of Hercules / Bacon, Lyra, representing his beloved Apollo, the Muses as referenced in each eulogy, and the arts. On the other side, the Crown, Corona Borealis, finally in reach of the rightful heir? Beneath, healer Ophiuchus, fulfilling the first charge in *Fama Fraternitatis*, to profess nothing other than healing the sick, the symbol of medicine

316

representing Bacon's *History of Life and Death*, his treatise on extending life. Above, Boötes the Plowman, representing his horticultural studies *The Advancement of Learning,* and *Valerius Terminus*. Last but not least, on the left Cygnus, representing the sweet Swan of Avon:

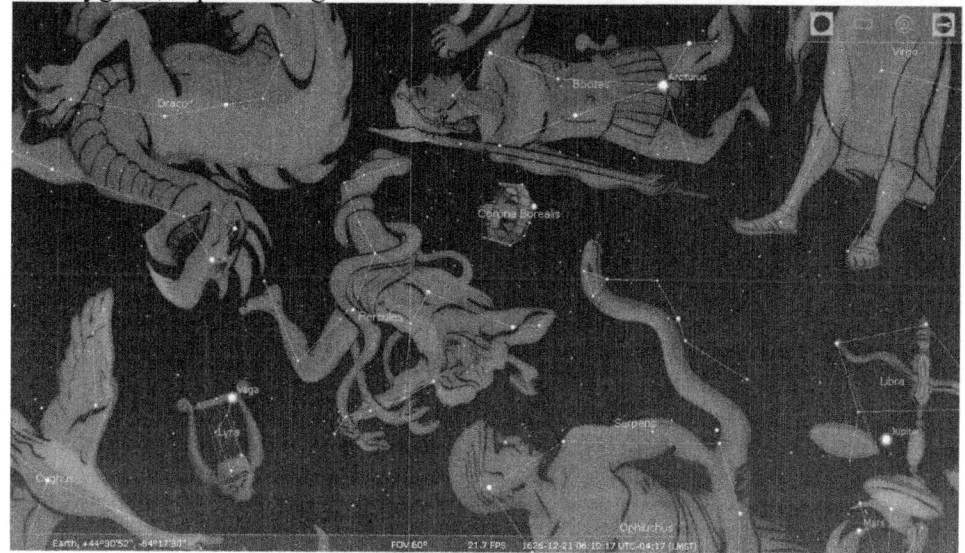

It just occurred to me that, while friends and fellow researchers Chris Donah, Christopher Morford and I had started an earlier project, discussing multiple constellations and their relation to Freemasonry, what we have here is a whole section of the sky dedicated not to a group or brotherhood, but to the one man who possibly started it all: Sir Francis Bacon.

I was only planning on identifying a date for my sky/ground alignment. But as I sit here writing this, I'm left with a profound sense of awe. A group of men, so inspired by Bacon honoring him in this way is truly mind blowing. Seven constellations. Could they be another manifestation of the Seven Rayed god, and the Seven Classical Liberal Arts and Sciences? However, there is one additional nearby constellation that also needs mentioning - Delphinus.

This small constellation is that of a Dolphin, and also associated with Apollo. With Rosicrucian wordplay in mind, it's not a large stretch to the French word for dolphin, "dauphin," a term meaning the eldest son of the King in France. I contend that this is yet another reference to Bacon himself as the secret son of Mary Queen of Scots and Francis II of France. And according to astronomical calculations provided by Chris Donah, Delphinus sets over Bacon's place of birth at 287 degrees, the number for Fra Rosi Crosse in Kaye Cipher. But back to the date and the task at hand.

The horizontal inversion or mirror of the Keystone asterism aligns with the original positions of the conical stones on the island. The orientation of the picture has been adjusted to the correct direction where it appears in the sky:

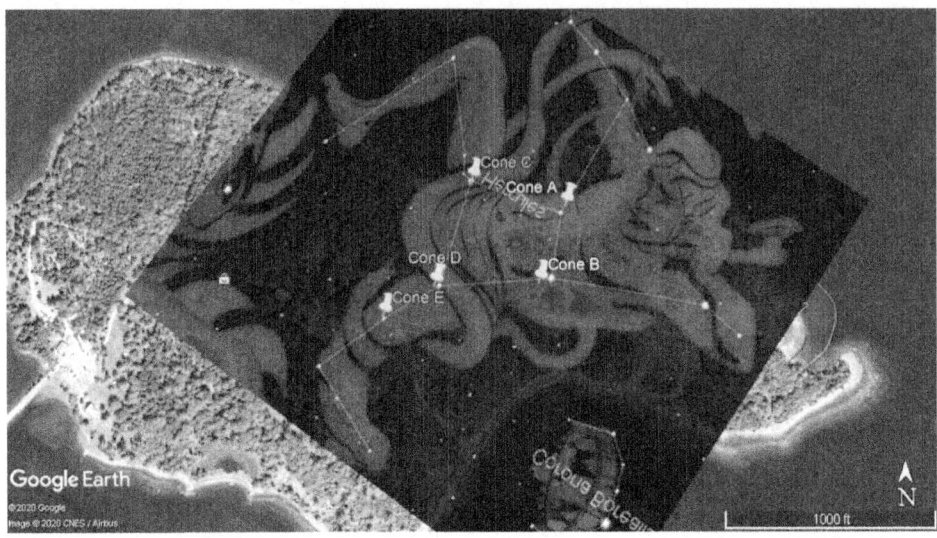

In summary of this section, I believe the following:

- There are several strong symbolic allusions relating Bacon to Hercules.
- Sir Francis Bacon's contemporaries, be they Rosicrucian brothers, early Freemasons, or both, commemorated him with not just one constellation, Hercules, but a whole section of the sky representing his great influence.
- The *Manes Verulamiani* contains references pointing the reader's attention to that area of the sky and Hercules
- Before dawn on the Winter Solstice in 1626, those constellations line up on the eastern and northeastern horizon on Oak Island.
- On that date, the Cones of Nolan's "Cross" align with the Keystone asterism at the heart of the Hercules constellation.
- Hercules Constellation confirms Paul's original Cone locations as accurate.

The last thing I thought I would find is such a strong symbolic connection between Bacon and Hercules, let alone an entire section of sky. This now leaves us with the big question - what do we do with all of this?

Finding the X On the Map

I suspect that if the many treasure seekers who have been to Oak Island actually had seen the Cones of Nolan's Cross in their original locations accurately displayed on a map, they may have recognized its significance. After all, many of those individuals were prominent Freemasons, well-versed in the rejected Keystone legend, and the Royal Arch degree. Applying the Hermetic dictum of "As above, so below" would

318

have been the next logical step. As stated previously, not only the cones aligned, but other areas of interest appeared as well:

- A point on the north coast of the island, nearly due north of the welling triangle (One of Erin Helton's anchor points as seen in Season 8)
- The site of the Cave-in Pit
- And a proposed location of the HO stone

When looking at the other possible targets offered by the remaining stars in the constellation, an area of interest presents itself:

The three stars in the lower leg of Hercules appeared to be possible interesting targets. I decided to check my 10 degree lines radiating from Cone C to see if any interesting alignments occurred that could narrow down the targets. However, I didn't get the expected result:

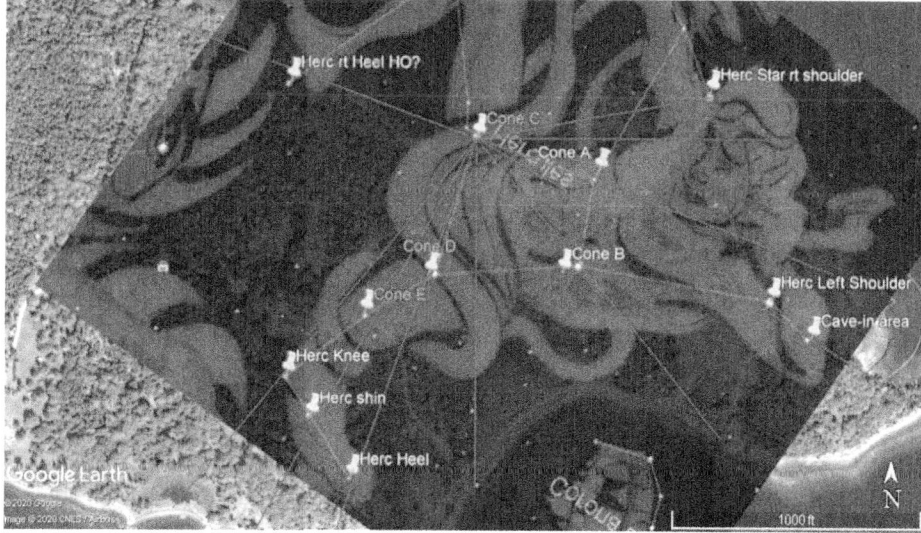

Starting from right going clockwise, the first line at 70 degrees from C terminates exactly at the star in the shoulder of Hercules. (As previously noted, I later learned of a large boulder in the same area). The line extending at a right angle from Cone C (which is in a highly significant area of Hercules for a variety of reasons) appears to precisely penetrate his "third eye." The next line down is my 110 degree line where I had originally placed my optimum location for Cone A, corresponding to the star at his solar plexus, and the line passes directly through it. The next line is the 120 degree line that passes directly through the Cave-in Pit area and its associated star in the elbow and left shoulder of Hercules. The next line clockwise is the 140 degree line, passing directly through the corner star in the Keystone, in my ideal location I had identified for Cone B, slightly off from Paul's location. After the vertical 180 degree line, the 200, 210 and 220 degree lines correlate with each of the heel, shin and knee stars respectively. Though the 220 degree line passes closer to the knee star than the other lines do to each of their correlating points, I think the correlations are too close to rule any of them out. However, the sacred Tav is the 22nd letter of the Hebrew alphabet. (NOTE: *This was prior to my complete deciphering of Key 38 which references the "duplicate knee"*). The line extending from C at 290 degrees passes very near the other heel of Hercules.

And so, even though my idea of checking the Cone C ten-degree lines didn't eliminate any targets, it actually had several "hits" in terms of correlating points. It aligned closely with all three target stars as well as the other significant areas of the sky/ground connection, which I feel is actually a good problem to have. There are more data points involving simple geometry that seem to confirm the correlations.

At this point there is one area that needs to be completed, and it can be used as a form confirmation, pointing us in the right area. (*Though we have the cipher text naming the "duplicate knee," the geometry confirms the cipher*).

The Companions Jewel and the Kabalistic Tree of Life

My original theory always has been based upon the Royal Arch degree. The story of the original discovery of the Money Pit, and the description of it, was an obvious representation of the nine vaults beneath Solomon's Temple. When I originally thought of an archeoastronomy connection, my first thought was Cepheus because the asterism is sometimes referred to as Solomon's House. I now realize that it's actually an allusion to Salomon's House and the College of the Six Days Work, as depicted in Bacon's work "The New Atlantis." In fact, Bacon's *Great Instauration* intended to restore the arts and sciences to the world, and "Bacon compared this work to rebuilding Solomon's Temple, or the Temple of Wisdom" (North 2).

320

The Companions Jewel is an extremely important symbol, not only containing the Star of Solomon, but also containing the Triple Tau. Some might argue against this hypothesis because they believe many of the artifacts pre-date Freemasonry and some of the symbols of The Royal Arch degree in its current form. However, a Francis Bacon scholar named James North asserts in his academic paper titled, "Francis Bacon's Alphabet of Nature and The Triple Tau," the fact that these symbols of the Royal Arch and The Triple Tau predate Freemasonry and The Royal Society, and were in existence at least by 1679 (2).

Freemasonry provides an excellent "definition" of the Triple Tau's symbolism in terms of what each individual tau represents. The first tau represents, "The Temple of Jerusalem," which was Solomon's Temple. On Oak Island, this is represented by the original Money Pit for the obvious reasons stated above. The second Tau is defined as, "the key to obtaining that which is precious." For reasons that I'll explain soon, on Oak Island in addition to the Keystone asterism, the Swamp still has its role to play. The third and last Tau, is defined as and represents, "the place which contains the precious thing" or "the precious thing itself." This either represents the very vault and contents that everyone has sought for two centuries or, the truth sought by all "Argonauts."

Upon completion of the initiation into The Royal Arch degree, the initiate receives a medal of a very specific collection of symbols, with a specific set of Latin inscriptions. On the front of the Jewel, two Latin phrases appear: "*Nil nisi clavis deest*" meaning, "nothing but the key is wanting," and "*Talia si jungere possis sit tibi scire satis*" meaning, "if thou comprehendest these things thou knowest enough."

At least, this is what the initiate is told. However once one is *initiate*d, this means he is meant to take *initia*tive. If one were to actually interpret the Latin inscription himself, he would discover that "comprehendest" or, understand, requires more than one word in Latin.

The two Latin words used to convey the word comprehend, are *Jungere*, meaning "bring together, or unite," and *Possis,* meaning "to be able, avail, have influence." This is why people express their understanding by saying, "I put it together that…" So, the phrase "if you understand these things," means that the successful candidate of the degree must be able to put these "things" together. What things? The shapes inside the circle, and the other symbols on the medal. If he can accomplish this, then he knows enough. The hexagram, or six pointed star, is composed of two equilateral triangles pointing in opposite directions, and are the most basic of common symbols.

In a curious example of fiction accurately depicting real scholarship, anyone who has watched the movie or read the book *The Da Vinci Code* by Dan Brown remembers Professor Robert Langdon explaining the "blade and chalice" shapes as representing the masculine and feminine principles. The upright triangle is the masculine shape, and the downward pointing triangle is the feminine. In the six-pointed star we have the unification of opposites the alchemists sought. It is the balanced life, and mind, that people desire. We also have the Hermetical dictum of "as above, so below." We also have a formula for making human beings, by bringing these two things together and keeping the species in existence. "Thou knowest enough" indeed.

The second Latin inscription reads, *"Nil nisi clavis deest,"* meaning "nothing but the key is wanting." I found this phrase to be curiously worded. Most interpret this as meaning that the only thing that is missing is the key, but there is another meaning. It means the key is *wanting*, i.e. - missing something. In this case, the triangular Swamp is missing its Companion - a triangle overlaid in the opposite direction. A unification of opposites.

This concept is repeated by overlaying the Hercules constellation on the conical stones of Oak Island, uniting that which is above with that which is below.

The group who left their mark on Oak Island understood and used this symbolic representation to communicate their message to future searchers, knowing or assuming that the future searchers also had access to this knowledge. They would then leave clues to these future searchers of what to do next. In my mind, those people were Francis Bacon and friends, and the future searchers were the Founding Fathers of America. We've already used those clues once to track down Francis Bacon in the sky above Oak Island. The second half of the key is to use the stones for their second purpose: geometrical alignments that will create the six-pointed star of the Companions Jewel over the Swamp. Once created, it can be used to generate the Kabalistic Tree of Life symbol as a map on the island, to see how it will interact with the constellation of Hercules.

Using the "corrected" positions of the stones of Nolan's Cross provided by Paul Wronclawski, the stones can be used to map out a six-pointed star on the Swamp. We begin with the markers and clues on the island that we can use to "frame" our shape. In this case, the Swamp. We start by creating a straight-line due south from Cone C (the only one that hasn't been moved), and another line due west from the Welling Triangle area. Knowing that the interior angle of both equilateral triangles in this construction should measure 60 degrees, we can draw two parallel lines at 120 degrees from Cones D and E, and let them terminate at the Welling Triangle line:

322

The next step will be to draw a line due south from Cones A, B and D:

Next I drew a line at 60 degrees from the corner of the vertical C line and the Welling 90 degree line, to the 120 degree line from Cone D, to create the base line for the triangle of the Swamp. I also drew an experimental line 90 degrees from Cone E, to the Cone B line, just to see if it would create a point to align one of the triangles:

The line at the base of the Swamp, from the corner to the Cone A vertical line measured exactly 545 feet according to Google Earth. As I stated earlier, traditional standardized surveying measurements were used, as they were approved by Queen Elizabeth in Bacon's time. 545 is significant in that it is 33 rods in length, the number of "Bacon" in Simple Cipher. And the Cone E line to the vertical C line is also 545 feet. Continued just past the vertical B line, where I placed my "ideal" B, measured 771 feet. This would be exactly 1 furlong plus 111 feet - the number of "Bacon" in the K cipher.

Using basic geometric principles, and what may be Bacon's signature measurement of 33 rods, the chalice portion is easily added by beginning at the point in the bay on the due south line from Cone B, and drawing it due north for 33 rods, or 544.5 feet (with Google Earth, it's easiest to round up or come as close as is possible). Creating a 60 degree angle and traveling across the Swamp, the "rim" of the "chalice" triangle is formed. The final line is formed from simply connecting the last two points of the triangle:

Leaving us with the only slightly malformed final product:

While not the perfect outcome, it's actually very productive. It proves that hidden within the locations of the Cones, they can be mapped and used to create a 6 pointed star over the Swamp. Even though it's imperfect, it's an accurate proof of concept. The other, more important point to make here is, if one of the intentions of the cones was to create the symbol on the Swamp, it reveals the original locations of the Cones with greater accuracy through the inaccuracies of the star itself. Based upon the areas of imprecision, it seems that the Cones that are still inaccurate would be Cones A, B and D, due to the discrepancies in these angles:

The white circle represents the discrepancy that can be explained by Cone B error, or inaccuracy of the Welling triangle area, or both. The yellow circle indicates the error in placement of Cone A, or Cone D, or both. The only points that can be used with any accuracy are Cones C, and (possibly) Cone E.

This logically can be reasoned out. Many of the 10 degree lines radiating out from Cone C have significant alignments, one of which aligns perfectly with the Welling Triangle area. If this was intentional, and I believe everything concerning these points was intentional, we can use this measurement to refine our Welling Triangle point. Additionally, by creating a second grid pattern using Cone E, we can cross reference significant points. The angles used in the Star of Solomon are a matter of geometry. Lastly, the cardinal points from the cones were used as lines in the creation of the star symbol, and if we accept that so many measurements seem to be Baconian numbers, then we should be able use such significant numbers as measurements.

Also, some might say, "well, if the stones represent the Hercules constellation, why not just use the stars on the map to find the locations?" A good question, but that would be far too convenient and self-serving. It's a form of circular reasoning - I'm trying to prove that the stones not only represent the constellation of Hercules on the ground, as well as demonstrate they produce a six-pointed star over the swamp. If I simply use the stars as points, or "back-engineer" using logic and geometry, the original placements of the cones, then I'm operating under the self-serving assumption that my theory is correct, and then moving the data points to support it. Though this would be an interesting exercise, I'm not going to taint the work already done by doing that here. Instead, I'll follow the leads as they currently have presented themselves.

Up until now, I've satisfied my own reservations not only about the Hercules alignment, but also that the Cones were strategically placed to create the Star of Solomon symbol in the swamp. As I sit writing this now, it just occurred to me that this particular symbol, especially its location, is a particularly Rosicrucian calling card. If we complete the star as it was produced by the Cones, we get the following if we take away all of the lines used to construct it:

We can then, using either the interior or exterior hexagon, manifest the three dimensional cube:

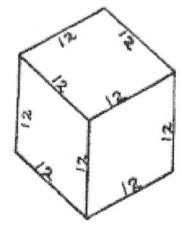

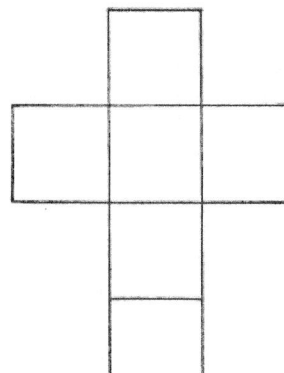

The cube is a Rosicrucian symbol. It represents the human body living in three-dimensional physical reality. By unfolding it, we get the Rosicrucian Cross, and inside is the Rose on the cross, representing the unfolding reality of the blooming human soul. Even in most modern representations of the Rosicrucian cross, the lines appear separating it into 6 equal squares, to represent the unfolding of the cube, with the rose at the center.

Given what I've seen of their sense of humor, I'm not surprised that the "rose" in this instance, is at the center of "the nasty, smelly swamp." This is not the only purpose of our six-pointed star, however.

As I stated earlier, one of the important mathematical qualities of the Star of Solomon is its ability to geometrically produce the Tree of Life symbol. So, I decided to see if the star produced by the cones would create a Tree of Life toward the western part of the island, possibly aligning with one of the three stars in the leg of the Hercules constellation. However,

327

before I created the Tree of Life symbol, I decided to use geometry to see if I could determine how "far-off" the other cones were.

First, I created lines from each cone toward the sunset on the winter solstice. I reasoned, if the cones were placed to represent Hercules on the winter solstice, then meaningful alignments could also be encoded into their positions:

As you can see, all of the lines have slight variations from one another, which seems odd. Since I knew the original triangle representing the Swamp was based upon the alignment with Cone C, and then created using known mathematic principles, that of the two shapes, I could trust its alignment and geometry the most. I bisected the eastern angle and drew a line west, with the following result:

The bisector line crosses the exact point where the vertical line dropped due south from Cone D crosses the line made from the sunset line drawn from my (Paul Wronclawski's) position of Cone B. The length of this line is exactly 1 furlong, or 660 feet.

In my mind, it seems that this point would be the ideal location, geometrically speaking, of the vertices of the "chalice" triangle that has been super-imposed by the other cones (that have been moved). Cone E obviously had been moved north of its original location. I decided to use this point to create the Tree of Life symbol for a variety of reasons. First and foremost, it is far less problematic. But most importantly, it's far more logical that the original designers or architects of this scheme would have used this point. Geometrically speaking, bisecting a known angle that creates a line due west would be the "correct" way to create the Tree of Life symbol.

I bisected the angles of the "trusted" triangle, and created a circle around it, in the fashion of the Companions Jewel, in order to obtain the correct measurement of the radius. The radius of the circle was exactly 314 feet, the number of pi, and the cipher signature of "Francis St. Alban" and "Walter Raleigh" in Kaye Cipher. The symbolism was encouraging.

Completing the Tree of Life symbol at this point was simply a geometric exercise, with the following result:

After the completion of the Tree of Life symbol pointing westward in the direction of the three stars in the leg of the constellation of Hercules, by placing the overlay of the constellation on the island once again, we can check to see if we have a correlation that would indicate which star represents a significant location.

Once again, the correlation is obvious:

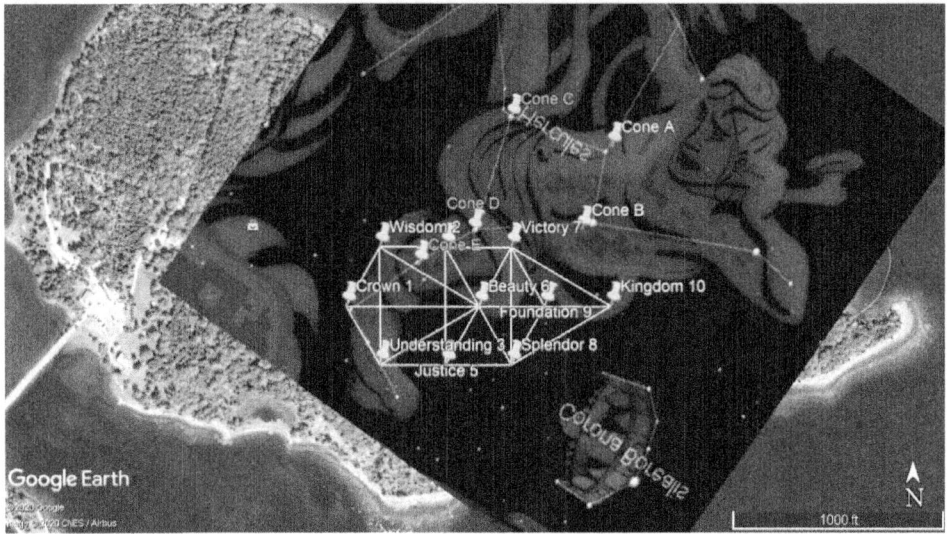

Crown Time.

The representation of the Tree of Life generated by the Swamp as its Foundation, ends with its Crown point at the knee of the constellation Hercules, who was also known under the appellation of "the kneeling one." The original placement of the stones as a representation of the Keystone asterism, their ability to locate points around the swamp that would generate the Tree of Life symbol with this particular star, along with all of the other correlations, cannot be happenstance. For these reasons and a variety of others, I have come to believe that Oak Island is a marker for the resting place of Sir Francis Bacon. The first Tau was the constellation, "the key" to the thing. The second Tau is the map created by the cones and Tree of Life. (The third Tau is the vault containing the precious thing, or the thing itself – the Crown / Knee point. I believe this to be the site of the "hidden keystone" referenced in the plaque cipher text).

Conclusions

After identifying Paul's placement of the cones on the map, it became obvious to me that the constellation being mirrored on Oak Island is that of Hercules (Heracles). Fred Nolan, in a stroke of genius, invented the concept of his cross, knowing that such a powerful symbol, being so easily recognizable, would hide the true meaning of the conical stones on his property. The mystery has attracted the notice of so many members of the Freemasons, that it only would have been a matter of time before one of them recognized the Keystone asterism being mirrored on a map of the island.

The obvious caveat is that the overlay of the image of Hercules is not what we would consider a *perfect* match. However, I would have been very concerned if it *had* been a perfect match. Firstly, Paul's image I used to place the conical stones in their positions in my model, was skewed in the

330

sense of not being corrected for its "tilt" within the Google Earth program. Therefore, there could be a possible error of my placement because of perspective within the image itself. Secondly, the possibility exists that Mr. Nolan was not the first treasure hunter to move the stones. (*Another late addition: Using Erin Helton's Lidar imaging, I have been able to further refine the cone positions with far more accurate results*). I believe that the answer lies in the use of the stones as a tool for creating the Companions Jewel over the Swamp. Using this symbol, I believe that true original positions can be "back-engineered," though I don't believe that any information generated by such an exercise would be useful. Be that as it may, let's not overlook the significance of this use of the Cones of Nolan's "Cross" in the first place.

The fact that very simple geometric principles, using the stones as starting points, create a nearly perfect six-pointed star, the Star of Solomon, over the Swamp is highly compelling. Being juxtaposed with the Money Pit on the island, as a symbol of the nine vaults beneath the original site of Solomon's Temple, is also very telling. I would like to point out, that both were found by discovering a "keystone."

Discovering a keystone led the Sojourners of the legend to discover the nine vaults beneath Solomon's Temple, and the golden triangular tablet engraved with the name of God. On the island, the Keystone asterism leads us to the triangle of the Swamp, the subsequent "Jewel," and the western emanation of the Tree of Life. The Crown point of the tree coincides with the knee star of the Hercules constellation, whose appellation was "the kneeling one." Why would this demigod be kneeling on Oak Island?

Given the multiple connections other researchers have found between Oak Island and Sir Francis Bacon, given the multiple references to Bacon as a "demigod" in his eulogies, and given all of the allusions to the constellations around Hercules, all of which pertain to his half-brother Apollo (venerated by Bacon), I can think of only one thing. Bacon knelt to his own half-brother James I King of England just like Hercules kneeling beside Corona Borealis.

It's also fitting that the point of the Tree of Life that coincides with the convergence was the Crown Sephiroth. Perhaps it's one more way that he "shines with a golden crown." Therefore, this point on Oak Island would be my primary area of interest for investigation.

In conclusion, I believe that Sir Francis Bacon, with the help of scholars and other enlightenment thinkers, planned to create an independent country here in the New World. The symbolism of Solomon's Temple is an allusion to his "unfinished" work, *The New Atlantis*. Oak Island was used as a cache site in the early days of Freemasonry, that would help eventually fund America's fight for independence. To that end, Bacon experienced a "philosophical death," as indicated by *Manes Verulamiani*, published by

Rawley, and came to the New World. Somewhere, his remains were interred.

As an interesting aside, I suspect Bacon ultimately of being behind the standard measurement system of the English mile, furlong, chain and rod, each being multiples of 33, the Simple Cipher of his last name. As another, many people mention the strange shape of the outline of Oak Island. I remember one woman said she thought that it looked like a baby elephant! To me, I thought it far more resembled a boar, similar to what is depicted on the Bacon family heraldry. However, I now can see it as the shape of a dolphin.

(Readers will note the following paragraph appeared pre-decryption): Many areas remain for further research. First and foremost, the plaque on Shakespeare's monument. Currently, Christopher Morford, Chris Donah and I have been working on the mystery surrounding the plaque, as we suspect there could be more clues or references to the Oak Island mystery. As of yet, I've found no references to Nova Scotia or Oak Island. However, I have discovered multiple numerical "signatures" of Francis Bacon. The most impressive of these appeared as the 33rd line of text, "IEGOKDT(t)W." Not only does he name himself with the word "I," it repeats as EGO, Latin for I, and the letters add up to 108 in Bacon's Simple Cipher. This number is the Reverse Cipher signature for "Francis." In Reverse Cipher, the total is 111, "Bacon" in Kaye Cipher. Kaye Cipher produces the sum of 212, the Reverse Cipher signature of "Francis Verulam." Additionally, I'm continuing my steganographic deciphering of *Manes Verulamiani*, as I believe the 32 eulogies contain more esoteric communications within that specific group of thinkers that are possibly also relevant.

Interactions Between Cone C and the Companions Jewel

By using the first triangle created from the starting point identified by Cone C and the Welling Triangle site, the "companion" triangle can be created in its corrected location and dimensions. By using lines that bisect the angles of it, the "chalice" triangle is added by joining lines to the points created by the circle around the triangle and the bisectors:

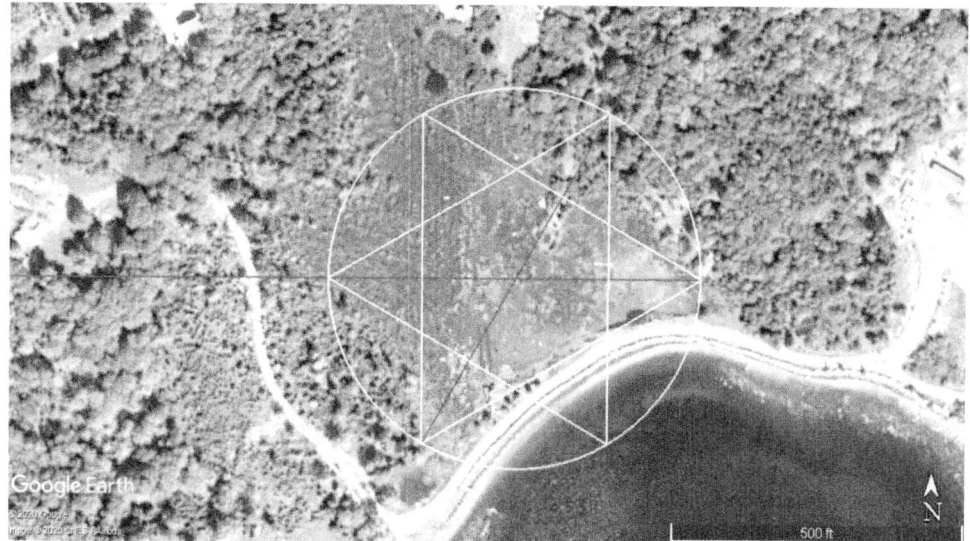

The next step is to add the lines from Cone C that intersect the Companions Jewel symbol and accompanying lines.

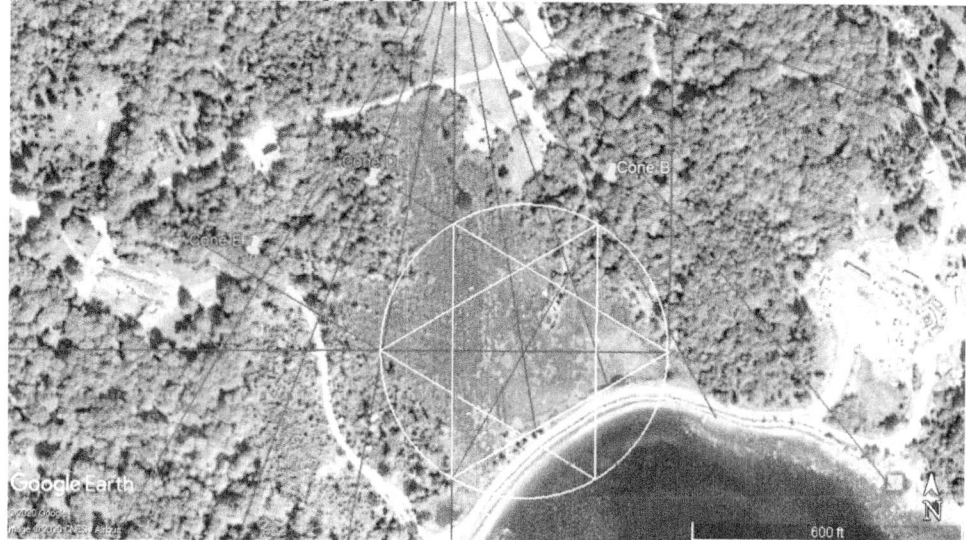

Aside from the points where the lines intersect near the current positions of the boulders, the lines in ten degree increments radiating out from Cone C interact with Jewel symbol in interesting ways. The 190 degree line intersected the western point of the "chalice" triangle on the left side of the Swamp. The 170 degree line passes through the center point of the Swamp identified by the bisector lines of the initial triangle. Lastly, the 160 degree line bisects the right side of the chalice triangle right at the point where the bisector line of the angle formed by the eastern most point of the star bisects it.

Other Areas of Interest

An interesting aspect of the Qabalistic Tree of Life is that it's said to have four manifestations. This is also true on Oak Island. The first, I've already discussed as it relates to and interacts with the Hercules constellation on the island. The four manifestations of the Tree of Life would appear emanating from one common Foundation point, ironically in the Swamp. As a builder would never create a foundation for any solid structure in a swamp, I find this to be another expression of the sense of humor of Rosicrucian thought that so often appears in their written, symbolic, and encoded messages.

Here is an image of the four manifestations of the Tree of Life symbol, emanating outward from the six pointed star on the Swamp:

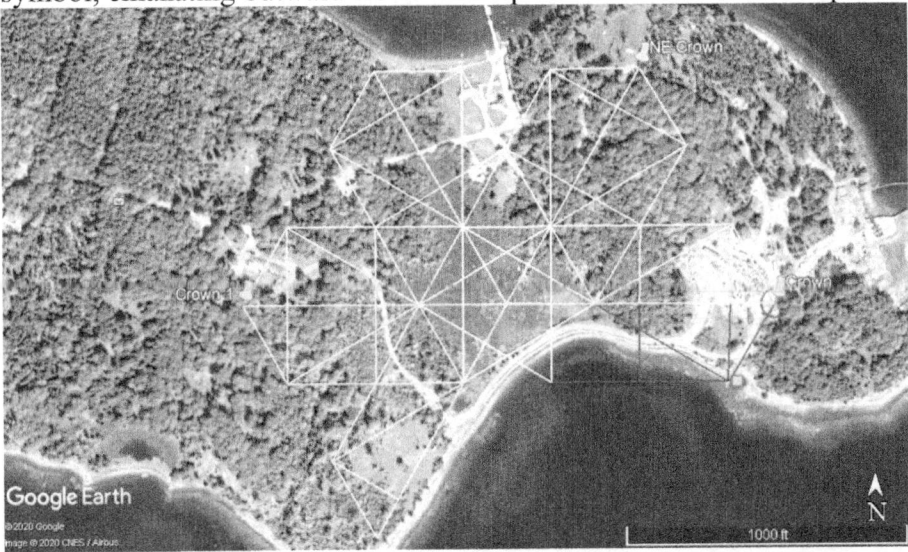

I counted southwestern-most and the eastern "halves" as one Tree of Life together, as only half of each actually appears on land. I included the southern section of the eastern ToL in red, to show how closely the Welling Triangle area matches up with the Wisdom Sephiroth. At the Crown point of the eastern branch, we have the Money Pit area. The Crown point of the northeastern branch appears at an interesting feature on the island.

One of the interesting features of this model of the ToL symbol radiating out of the Swamp, is what happens with the famed "Mercy" point. The Mercy Sephiroth has been forever placed into the Oak Island mythos by Amundsen's work. However, in this model, the Justice (Severity) and Mercy points overlap, as if in perfect balance with one another:

I can't think of any example of symbolism that would better represent Francis Bacon: a judge and Rosicrucian luminary, balancing justice with mercy.

One of the things I have noted since the beginning of my research on Oak Island, is the symbolism of the number 9. This number represents man's physical, lower nature. It's believed that through the initiation experience, man takes the three steps necessary to become complete, represented by the number 12. Solomon's Temple had 9 vaults beneath it, and the Money Pit had 9 platforms. The Swamp being a triangle, contains a total of 180 degrees, 1+8+0=9. The Welling Triangle reportedly contained a total of 27 stones, which again, reduces to 9.

When looking at the Tree of Life Symbolism on the island, it seems very fitting that Sephiroth 9, the Foundation, is at the center of the Swamp for all four of them. Justice and Mercy, are Sephirah 5 and 4 respectively, and since they overlap each other (in perfect balance), they total 9.

One last interesting correlation occurred when I placed the Cones of Nolan's Cross on the screen with the multiple Trees. Cones A, D, and E formed a perfect line with two of the Justice / Mercy points, and the Crown points of the northeast ToL and the original ToL to the west:

Is our attention being directed to these two points on the island? As one last experiment, I drew a line connecting these points and extending them southwestward. The line seemed to follow a ridgeline pattern formed by the trees, as if aligning with a topographical feature:

Here is a close up, highlighting the area. Note the direction of the tree / ridgeline in conjunction with the line created by Cones A, D, and E, and the Crown and Justice / Mercy points:

Appendix B

Symbology of the Illustration from *Speculum sophicum Rhodo-stauroticum* by Theophilus Schweighardt, 1618, much of which appeared in the final chapter.

Abstract

This paper includes my initial study of the "Emblematic Image of the Rosicrucian Society; illustration from *Speculum sophicum Rodo-stauroticum.*" While researchers have often puzzled over the enigmatic images in it, scant information is readily available to the average researcher concerning the symbolism, intent and composition of the image. Throughout my investigation of the image up to this point, I've been able to determine the following key points:

- the figures of the men around the image are intended to represent Francis Bacon at different times of his life
- the imagery is intended to outline / convey the overall philosophy of Fra. Rosi Crosse
- the imagery is intended to communicate that the ideas of The Invisible College, Fra. Rosi Crosse, Men of Letters and The Republic of Letters are all one and the same.
- much of the iconography is borrowed from the Tarot
- the angles of geometry in the image contain specific messages, including the latitude and longitude of Mahone Bay, Nova Scotia

General assessment

While people usually focus on the literal image, historical references, and the author of the publication in which it appears and its artist, I focus on the underlying or symbolic meanings of its iconography.

For example, Ben Johnson makes an obvious reference to this image in one of his works called "The Fortunate Isles and Their Union." The interchange between the two characters Merryfool and Johphiel describes the illustration:

> *Mere.:* Outis ! Who is he?
> *Johp.:* Know ye not Outis? Then ye know nobody :-
> The good old hermit, that was said to dwell
> Here in the forest without trees, that built
> The castle in the air, where all the brethren
> Rhodostauric live. It flies with wings,
> And runs on wheels; where Julian de Campis
> Holds out the brandished blade.

This interchange reveals an interesting truth about the Invisible Rosicrucian Order. The word "Outis" means "no one," setting up Johphiel's joke, of

"Know ye not Outis? Then ye know nobody." Stating that he's a hermit who lives in a forest without trees and built a castle in the air which is where the RC live reveals the truth – the Invisible Order is invisible because there is no real organization. While much has been written regarding the surface or superficial meaning of the image, in this treatment I present an interpretation of what I believe is beneath the surface. What follows is what I believe are the symbolic, esoteric or occult meanings within the images themselves.

The simplest way to treat the information as it appears in the image is by assessing the overall image as whole as it's presented, then focus on the separate elements in a clockwise manner beginning in the upper left hand corner.

The illustration presents the "fraternity" as a movable fortress, with writers manning the battlements, armed with quills and shielded with the name of God. There are four "guards" as one would be unseen on the opposite side of the edifice. Inside, a man sits at a desk while letters fly in and out of windows, and in the next room is what appears to be an alchemist's furnace and crucible. In Latin above these windows is "*I ESVS NOBIS OMNIA,*" which can be read in two ways. Firstly, it means "we go by reason that all things consume (destroy) / are consumed (destroyed)." Noting the space between the letters, and by separating "E" from "ESVS" and forming E and SVS, a pun is revealed as, "We all go by reason of Sus," meaning *a hog*. This indicates through this pun on the name "Bacon," that they all have come together because of Francis Bacon. Above the door is written "VENITE DIGNI" meaning "you coming is a worthy act," and the drawbridge to the right indicates that the occupants allow entry only to those they deem worthy. Appropriately on either side of the door appears a Rose and a Templar-style Cross.

Looking around the entire picture, we see the images of a man in various poses, and I contend that this man is intended to be Francis Bacon involved in different roles throughout his life. Also, at the top, right, bottom, and left edges appear ORIENS, MERIDIES, OCCIDENS and SEPTENTRIO respectively, which represent the four cardinal directions with "EAST" in the top position, giving this image the trappings of a Masonic tracing board.

340

Specific Elements

In the upper left hand corner we have a star amid clouds, shining through the image of the constellation Ophiuchus between the word VIDIAMINI and the date 1604. A star is a symbol of knowledge surrounded by darkness, an embodiment of the philosophy of the Rosicrucian Order, "Lux si umbra," meaning "light amid shadow." The clouds are a traditional symbol of (sometimes divine) revelation. "Vidi" means "to see, or to be seen," while "amini" means "undertake; endeavor; or as a result of." All of this taken together commemorates the scientific discovery of SN1604, Kepler's super nova.

Moving on to the right, we see the cloud "revealing" the ineffable name of God emblazoned with the wings of the divine. We see the hand of God reaching downward pulling a cord that is attached to top of the structure of the "COLLEGE FRATERNITATIS," indicating its divine purpose, as well as it being a work of God. It appears that this cord continues up through the hand of God and exits through the winged Name just beneath the third Hebrew character of the Tetragrammaton in what appears as a Tau

shape (This symbol was used by the Rosi Crosse to represent the light of divine TRUTH). The cord continues down to the anchor representing the stability provided by faith, which a Bacon figure is using as a quadrant or cross staff. I will explain this part of the image more in depth below. This symbol in conjunction with the anchor figure is very similar to the All Seeing Eye of Reason in effulgence. Both represent the Rosicrucian and Enlightenment thinkers' concept that through the use of reason and careful study of creation, one can come to know the mind of God.

Beneath the banner with "COLLEGIVM FRATERNITATIS," is a very interesting image, as it appears to be a "double Tau." This symbol was

instrumental in my work decoding the cipher hidden within the text of the plaque on Shakespeare's Funerary Monument in Trinity Church. First of all, double Tau represents the first letter in the two words of the number 33, TT, which of course is Simple Cipher signature of the name "Bacon." While researching it's meanings, I came across another interesting piece of information. As it appears in this illustration, it has taken on the form of what is called a "Legend" in heraldry, which appeared across the top of

341

the shield of the first born son of a king. Considering the hidden message on the plaque considering Bacon's true lineage, I found it interesting that this image was incorporated into this illustration. Beneath this, the letters "S S" appear as a Latin abbreviation that can mean, "sacred scripture" regarding early Church writings except for the Bible. However, another meaning can also be, "superscriptus," meaning "inscribed." As the image obviously has several meanings "inscribed" within its symbols, I suspect these *initials* are a signposts for *initiates* to look deeply into the image.

Next in the upper right corner, we see another cloud of revelation around another star shining through the constellation of the Swan. Once again the word "VIDIAMINI" appears, only this time upside-down, and in shadow, all of which represent the comets of 1618. I believe the shadow is present because of the Roman Inquisition's pronouncement against

heliocentrism, as well as representing the philosophy of the group, "Light Amid Shadow."

Next, I need to address the letters that are flying to and from the building of the Invisible College (believe it or not, that pun was accidental).

First of all, the fact that they have wings (as well as the building itself) indicates divine reverence. The letters themselves represent the "Republic of Letters" and the "Men of Letters" who wrote them. On the top one we see written, "FRATRI" meaning "brothers." Beneath this, is a

letter being "sent" from the man working inside the building that appears to say, "NOSTRO T * S*." While the word nostro most closely matches the word for "our," at first I was at a loss for the initials. The only interpretation I could find was after I applied one of the deciphering methods that appears within the cipher on Shakespeare's plaque. In Bacon's cipher system, he utilized the Simple and Reverse Ciphers as a form of *substitution cipher*, where by letters with the same values can be substituted for one another. Therefore, T*S* can be rendered as "F*G*." "F" is the abbreviation for "Francis," and "G" is a signature for "Bacon." (The Simple, Reverse and Kaye Ciphers each are used to produce cipher signatures in the others - G = 33 in Kaye Cipher, and 33 is "Bacon" in Simple). So it appears the Invisible College claims F Bacon as one of their own.

Next, below the letters we see a man falling from the cliff, and losing his hat and sword in the process. The hat and sword represent a loss of station or position of importance. The image is also reminiscent of the "Fool" trump in Tarot, as it is the logical result of the image on this particular card, that he's liable to tumble off the precipice. While some might think this represents Bacon's fall from grace when he was charged with receiving a bribe, and well it might, I have a different opinion. The main secret contained within the cipher of Shakespeare's plaque is nothing less than the secret of his birth - he was the son of Mary Queen of Scots and Francis II. Due to foolish political moves on her part, Bacon blamed Mary for his loss of station in life as Dauphin of France, after the death of Frances II.

 Please note the arm position of the falling man, as if he is asking, "who will help the poor widow's son?" Mackey's Encyclopedia of Freemasonry states, "The claim has often been made that the adherents of the exiled House of Stuart, seeking to organize a system of political Freemasonry by which they hoped to secure the restoration of the family to the throne of England,

transferred to Charles II the tradition of Hiram Abif betrayed by his followers, and called him the Widow's Son, because he was the son of Henrietta Maria, the widow of Charles I. For the same reason they presumably subsequently applied the phrase to his brother, James II." I respectfully suggest that this tradition actually comes from Francis Bacon, whose younger brother was also James, James I of England.

Secondly, this is happening in the context of the figure "tripping over" the Latin phrase, "festina lente," the de Medici family motto. Catherine de Medici would have been Francis Bacon's grandmother. As the Queen Regent, she always disliked Mary, and never would have abdicated her position so that Mary could replace her, overseeing the reign of her newborn son.

We can plainly see a hat and sword falling from the figure as well. These represent the "Blessed Hat and Sword," a tradition for kings of Catholic countries whereby the Pope blesses a ceremonial hat and sword and presents them to the monarchs. This image shows the loss of this station and the political environment causing Mary to flee France with Francis.

Additionally, the motto can also indicate though Bacon and his brethren are impatient to fulfill their plans, they proceeded slowly. Visually, this idea is reinforced by the winged letters, and the large stone building on wheels. The building itself embodies the four elements – air with its wings, earth with the wheels and the stone construction, fire with the alchemist crucible seen inside, and water with the image of Bacon being drawn from the well. It *is* the edifice of science.

Next, beneath the battlements we see the horn, symbolizing the announcement of the presence of the Fraternitatis Rosi Crosse. Beneath the horn we see the letters, "C*R*F," the initials of the fraternity reversed.

Interestingly, a church steeple appears just to the right of the trumpet blast representing the rejection of the Catholic Church's hegemony on truth.

Moving downward along the outside of the fortress, we see the drawbridge with its caption, "SI DIIS PLACET," meaning "if it pleases God." Bridges represent the idea of joining or bringing things together, so if it pleases God, one can join and enter. In the background we also see the plowed fields, representing the idea of "we reap what we sow." This works in conjunction with the de Medici family motto on the cliff to the right, "make haste slowly." The seeds they plant together will take time to bear fruit.

Next we see the next image of the man, presumably Bacon, using an anchor as a quadrant or cross staff used for astronomical observations with his hat, staff and backpack on the ground at his side. The "hooks" at the bottom of the anchor form the "AA" symbol. But as is often the case with Rosicrucian symbolism, sometimes what's most important to the meaning, is what is missing.

Anchors symbolize faith, and when associated with Christianity are depicted with a cross bar to represent the cross itself. However in this case, even though he's using the anchor to "see" the Creator, no cross bar exists. Taking note of this omission, I was able to solve this puzzle on the opposite side of the illustration. Continuing with the anchor, we see that this symbol is borrowed from Key 35 of the Tarot. The number 35 is the letter "I" in Kaye Cipher (also called "Key" Cipher). Also note in the accompanying picture of card 35, "The Anchor," it's associated with the 9 of Spades, and 9 is also "I" in Simple Cipher. The cord from the name of God goes directly to the "eye" of the figure with the anchor, indicating that through careful observation, the scientist can see and understand God. This pun of "I" and "eye" also tells the observant viewer of the illustration that there is more here to understand. One of the recurring themes of the ciphers on Shakespeare's plaque is the multiple spellings of the word "see," sometimes just the letter "C," and the use of the word "eye." As you will see, the multiple "I's" here will be important.

However, Bacon with the anchor carries a far more important message to him personally. There have been many images that express the motto of House de Medici, "make haste slowly." Two such images, and butterfly and crab, and a rabbit in a snail shell, embody the oxymoronic phrase. One of the most famous ones shows a dolphin wrapping itself around an anchor. This is the image being mimicked in the lower right of the illustration. Bacon wraps his hands (himself) around the image of the anchor, as he uses it as a cross stave (minus the cross) to measure the elevation of the hand of God extending from the cloud overhead. This vignette is designed not to only exhibit the exoteric message of faith and the Rosicrucian philosophy of using science to observe God's works. It also reveals Francis Bacon's true identity - the Dauphin (dolphin) of France, and the grandson of Catherine de Medici. This idea is reinforced in a later section regarding the symbolic meanings of the angles that appear in this area.

The Latin inscription along the cord extending from the eye of the observer to the name of God, reads "IGNORANTUM MEAM (MI?) AGNOSCO IVVA PATER." The space between "meam" and "agnosco" is difficult to make out in the image, but I've rendered it as "mi" meaning "my, mine; I, me; myself" as it completes the thought of, "I take responsibility for my ignorance to serve the Father."

Just to the left we see what appears to be an actor carrying a spear over his shoulder. Next we see the figure on horseback, preparing to cross the bridge to the image of the same man being drawn out of a well. As we know, a bridge represents a connection being made, and it can also mean a connection between the sky and earth (often as a rainbow). Also, the supports beneath the bridge form letters, M V and A in the shadow to the right (a commonly used symbol by Bacon). The total of these letters using Simple Cipher is 33, the signature for Bacon in Simple. The rider can be seen as the Knight of Pentacles of the Tarot. Representing the idea of being hardworking and methodical, this behavior can lead to being drawn out of the "well of ignorance." Before jumping too deeply into that subject, the

Latin words between the two eight-spoke Wheels of Fortune or Fate need to be read.

The letters spell "MOVE AMVR." While the word "move" is obvious, "amvr" has no meaning beyond "am" meaning "around; having two." Though this "college" structure is obviously intended to "move around," it wasn't until I began to look for a steganographic message that it appeared. The line in his hat provides an "I," his collar is a "C" and his arm with the lines of his pantaloons and horse

blanket form an "A." Using the substitution system between Simple and Reverse Ciphers, V becomes E and the phrase appears as "MOVE AMERICA," indicating the future plans of the RC to relocate to the colonies.

Again, all three of the visible wheels with eight spokes of this movable college are the Wheel of Fortune Key from the Tarot. Looking at the man on horseback, his head is next to the spoke that would represent the Hebrew letter Waw, in that rendering of YHWH. Being the sixth letter of the Hebrew alphabet, it would correspond with the letter "F" in English, representing the name "Francis." This letter is also known as "the hook," which gains significance in context of the Fama of the RC. While this symbol of Fortune represents the ever-changing nature of chance, it also has an instructive side advising the knowledgeable not to trust in Fortune, but instead take control of their own future. One way to do so, involves another image in the illustration to be discussed soon, which means planning and preparation. In this way, the meaning of the image of the battlement of the Invisible College riding on four Wheels of Fortune takes on a new meaning, particularly juxtaposed with the message regarding the move to America. Appropriately, these images appear closest to the word "OCCIDENS" and face west.

Next we see the figure of the man being pulled from the well, between the Latin words "PUTEVS" meaning "well," and "OPINIO NVM" possibly meaning "not opinion," just as was noted by the caption on the line between the anchor and the name of God. This caption indicates that facts and reality will raise the individual from the ignorant well of opinion. The Latin caption next to the cord and pulley states, "Per multa ria discrimi ria

revum," meaning "by means of intense study and thinking." This indicates the symbolic meaning of the rope pulling the man from the darkness of the well. Additionally, please note the two poles and pulleys, as one is in light and the other in shadow. Likewise, the man's right side is in light, and his left is in shadow, in keeping with the Hermetic dictum regarding the left and the right. It is also symbolic of Francis Bacon's championing of inductive reasoning as

a keystone of his scientific method – we need to use what we know (the light) to delve into the unknown to make it known (the shadow) – Lux Si Umbra. This knowledge of the unification of opposites again allows him to be raised from the ignorant darkness of the well, a place where "light" only shines once per day. The word "well" is phonetically the same as "whale" reminding us of the descent of Jonah, and the lesson of that allegory. Only when one descends into the darkness can it be joined with the light of the midday sun. The image is reminiscent of the Hanging Man card from the Tarot. While the Tarot Card depicts the man suspended upside down from a Tau cross, the symbolic meaning of these images is the same. The Tarot card represents a life in suspension, and some claim the self-sacrifice of Odin in order to attain wisdom. Just as the hand of God pulls the cord that raises the Collegium Fraternitatis, so too the fraternity raises the individual from the well, completing the symbolism of the unification of opposites and the connection between the microcosm of man and the macrocosm of God. As the hand of God raises the Collegium, its members raise him from the well.

Next, the image of the man is walking with his staff, a symbol of stability, direction and purpose, appears beneath the word "NOTA," meaning "note; learn; find out." In other words, by studying this area there is something to be learned. He seems to be walking on the path leading to the cottage that has what appears to be a quadrant staff, Jacob's staff or back staff used for astronomical observations protruding from the window. If you recall, on the opposite side the figure is depicted using an anchor without a cross bar as a quadrant. Here we have an explicit depiction of the actual instrument. As I mentioned earlier, the absence of an element is often just as telling as the elements themselves. If we provide the missing element, we may be able to "learn and find out" an important piece of information.

By creating the "mirror" image line from the figure's head through the cross bar of the quadrant staff, the line leads directly to the hand of God

above. This actually is highly significant, and I will fully explain later on in this paper. Meanwhile, the quadrant staff line aligns with the hilt of the sword held by the hand protruding from the side of the building, the angle of the face of the left battlement "guard," and the exact angle of the V in the word "COLLEGIVM." This provides 5 points of alignment confirming this piece of steganography. The rays shining down from the stars hint of the square and compass of Freemasonry, and sure enough a square *is* present within the geometry of the illustration. By continuing the line from the lower winged letter on the left, we see the point where it meets the corner of the drawbridge. Extending a line along the edge of the drawbridge and upward completes the image, though imperfect:

The descending line from the winged-letter bisects the corner of the battlement, passes trough the head of the man seated at the desk and highlights the pyramid shape of the desk itself as it bisects the upper left and lower right corners of the window. The line continues the alignments as it passes the corners of two arms of the Templar cross, to then end at the drawbridge. (As an interesting aside and an area of future interest, extending the line beyond the drawbridge it aligns perfectly with the back of the striding figure's head, back and leg). The drawbridge line also has a significant role which will be explained later in the section regarding the significant angles.

Along with the edge of the drawbridge, the second line follows the exact angle formed by the letter "A" in "AGNOSCO" and the knees of the falling man.

Moving on to the next element we see the arm protruding from the building holding a sword. An arm is a symbol of strength and force, coupled with the sword indicates forceful action. The caption beneath the hand is one of the few parts of the illustration that I don't have an adequate explanation. Here is written, "IUL: de Campi." This means, "July:" and "de" means "down/away from, off; about; according to." Campi is Latin for "plain; level field / surface; open space for battle / games; sea, scope; campus. If we read it as the name "Julian de Campi" however, we have a direct reference to an allusion Ben Johnson makes in a play to the Rosicrucian Order, and this image itself. Also the word "CAVETE!" especially appearing under the image of Noah's Ark on the mountain is understandable. Another possibility could include possible anagrams.

"Cavete" is Latin meaning "beware, avoid; take precautions / defensive action; give / get surety." By the juxtaposition of this symbol of strength with the symbol of Noah's Ark, the Invisible College is demonstrating the importance of taking strong action in taking precautions by preserving "that which is precious," knowledge. This is also another demonstration of the lesson Bacon learned from the de Medici family motto, *festina lente.*

The image of Noah's Ark is extremely important for Rosicrucians, as it represents the preservation of all knowledge that needs to be protected at all costs. The image of the Ark with two birds is also symbolic in terms of the philosophy of the Fra. Rosi Crosse. While most people know that Noah released a dove to find out if the waters had receded, few remember that he also released a raven. The two birds beside the Ark represent the raven and dove, the dark and the light, the opposites, the light and shadow. Additionally and more importantly, all of the animals in it represent the preservation of the ancient truths and philosophies by the Fra. Rosi Crosse as a sacred charge and pledge.

Lastly for the individual elements of the overall image, the two winged letters on the left side. The incoming letter contains the words "ad Fratres" meaning "according to Brothers."

The letter below this appears to have written on it, "ad I*D*C*." If we assume that the "C" beneath the I*D* is intended to come between these two characters, I can only hypothesize one explanation. It could simply be using the letter D as a pictogram of a sunrise. Then the message becomes "I C D (the light)." I only offer this explanation because I have identified this message repeatedly in the ciphers encoded on Shakespeare's Funerary Monument plaque.

One area that I mentioned but have not analyzed are the writers on the battlements. While Bulwer-Lytton popularized the phrase "the pen is mightier than the sword," in a play in 1839, the idea itself is much older. It's expressed in "Shakespeare's" *Hamlet*, as Rosenkrantz states, "...many wearing rapiers are afraid of goose-quills and dare scarce come thither." The shield with the name of God though a defensive weapon, also indicates secrecy. Taken as a whole, these four writers are sending their thoughts via hidden / secret / esoteric writing to the four directions to cover the globe. The name of God on the shields indicates that much of their scientific knowledge was hidden steganographically and in cipher form in writings that on the surface appeared in line with the Church. In this way they passed unnoticed by Inquisitors but could be seen by those with eyes to see. They appear on the battlements prepared to defend the "faith" of the Invisible College, Invisible Republic and the men of letters that comprised it.

One element of the illustration that I found odd was the error in perspective in the right foundation of the building. The angle used at the bottom is different than that of the battlement at the top, making the base of the building longer at the bottom than the top. To me this indicated a message, and so measuring the angle of the bottom of the foundation produces an angle of 161 degrees. 161 is the Kaye Cipher signature of "Fraters." This message tells us that the "Brothers" are the foundation of the Invisible College. This error in perspective was also a clue which unlocked other secrets revealed by the geometry, again to be treated in a later section.

A Line to God

As I mentioned earlier, the line drawn from the hand of God downward to the left through the quadrant staff and to the walking figure's head is highly significant. I was not only surprised but shocked at the results of working with this line and its apparent implications. I believe that studying this line was what we should "NOTA."

When Chris Donah passed along this task to me, he related to me the notion of another researcher's work with the illustration. He mentioned the idea of associating the image of the name of God and His hand with Temple Mount, Jerusalem, and there could be a connection to Oak Island and the anchor line. Here are my findings.

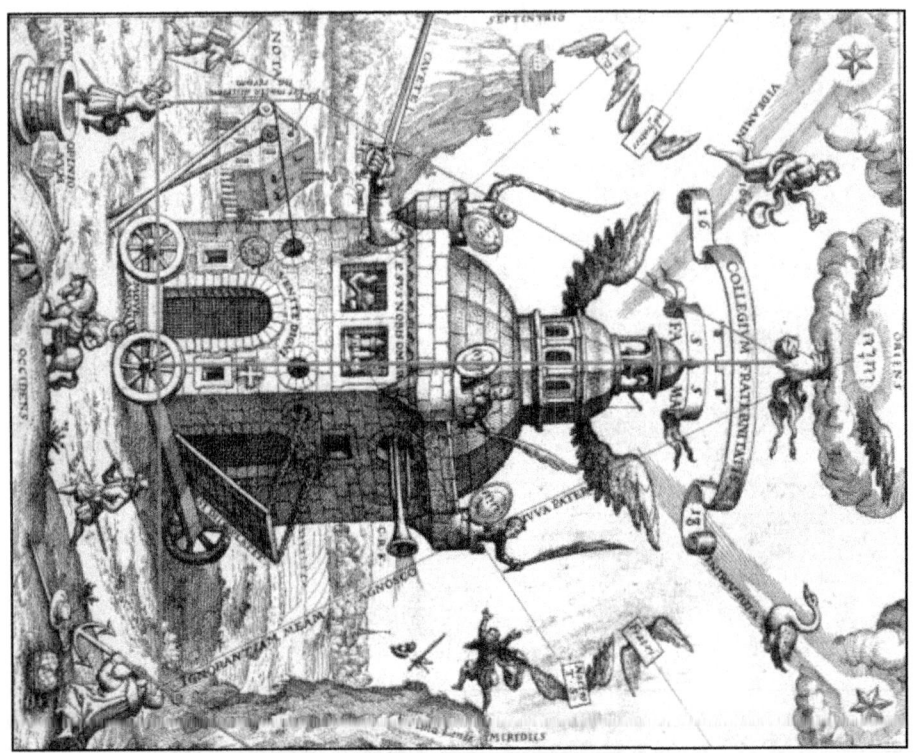

To better gain a perspective, I completed a triangulation scheme I had noticed earlier in the analysis. Due to the symbolism of eyes and the philosophy of the RC, I had noted an interesting correlation between the figure at the anchor, and the figure drawn from the well. A line drawn 90 degrees from the eye of the figure at the anchor connects directly to the eye of the figure drawn from the well, passing along the line of the foundation of the building, just above the axles of the wheels. Additionally, along the line of sight of our well figure, following the cord upward, a line connects directly to the center of the quadrant extending from the building. In this way, the well figure becomes a "plum bob," allowing us to measure the angle from the top of the walking figure's head, to the hand of God.

Continuing the line downward from the hand of God to the base of the triangle where it meets the foundation of the building actually creates a 30, 60 90 right triangle, with the 60 degree corner ending at the walking figure's heel. The angle at the point of the anchor figure's eye measures 65 degrees from the perpendicular line to our well-figure. This means that the angle deviating from due east would be 25 degrees north of due east. However if we measure the angle from the staff of the anchor, we have an exact 60 degree angle to the Godhead. As you will see, this 60 / 30 degree relationship seems to be inverted. In order to test out any possible correlation between these lines and a connection between Temple Mount Jerusalem as represented by the cloud revealing God, and one of the two points represented by the figures in the illustration, I decided to orient the illustration to the cardinal directions in the way we do today (as seen above).

We can see that using the anchor as a staff produces a 60 degree angle between the upright of the anchor and the line to God. The fact that it's missing the cross member, makes me believe that we should be looking at the angles expressed in the opposite side of the image where we see a real quadrant - 30 degrees. To be honest and candid, I wasn't sure of the next course of action here. However, when I drew a straight line downward 90 degrees from the star on the upper-right corner down to the head of kneeling figure, the angle formed by these lines was also 90 degrees. Instead of just blindly accepting this, I used a bit of inductive reasoning and logic.

I decided to use Google Earth and chart a line from Temple Mount to Oak Island, and note the angles involved. I reasoned that instead of attempting to contrive a line at the "correct" angle from Oak Island, I would plot the opposite line from Jerusalem to Nova Scotia, and *then* check the angles involved to see if any correlations appear. The image from Temple mount is as follows:

The red line leaves the Temple on a northwest bearing at 47 degrees above the parallel east-west line. (As an interesting aside, 47 plus the 90 degree right angle equals 137, the 33rd prime number. This number is used in the Shakespeare Funerary Monument plaque to refer to Bacon). However, we do not have a match for any of the geometry that appears in the illustration. When we look at our "landing point" on Oak Island however, our fortune seems to change:

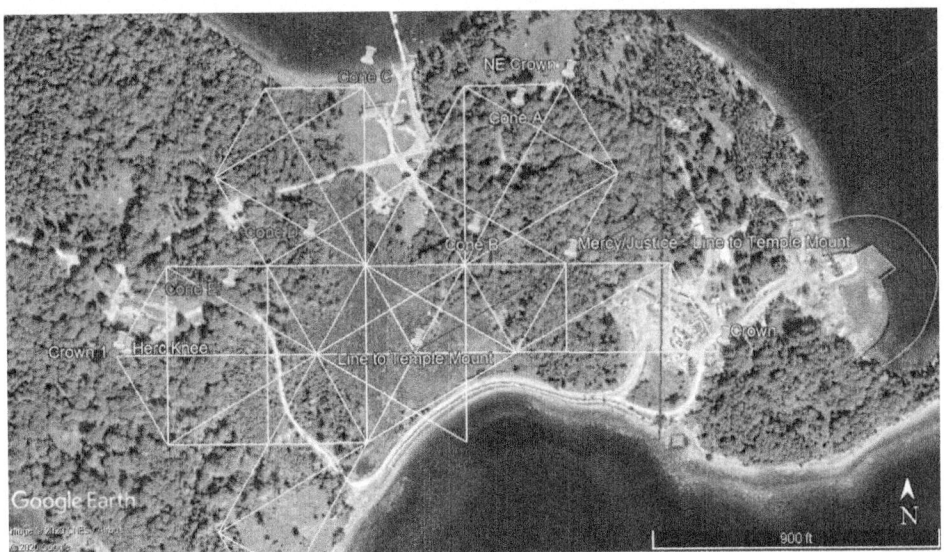

When I first plotted the line between Temple Mount and Oak Island, I had forgotten that the manifestation of the Tree of Life symbols from the six pointed star over the Swamp was still being displayed from my Oak Island theory. I was glad it was, otherwise I would have missed some of the significance of this line from the Temple Mount.

The line appears on Oak Island at 30 degrees above the parallel. It passes directly through a Mercy / Justice point and the exact geometric center of the Swamp produced by the cones of Nolan's Cross that I have identified in my theory. This is just an observation, not a proposal of confirmation of my theory.

Though not conclusive for neither my own theory nor the angles on the Invisible College Illustration, the fact that we have a 30 degree correlation on the island connecting it to the Temple Mount, with all of the island's symbolic elements that reference Solomon's Temple, along with specific points I've identified using the geometry of the features of the island, should be noted as being significant. Therefore I delved more deeply in to the geometry of the Invisible College Illustration.

Angle Cryptanalysis of Invisible College Illustration

After analyzing the angles and measurements of the "Emblematic image of the Rosicrucian College," as usual I discovered multiple purposes and messages and this last section deals with the geometry present in this illustration of the "Invisible College." As you will see, the angles and alignments produced on the left or northern portion reveal the latitude and longitude of a specific area of Nova Scotia. The angles framing the right-hand side of the image (the "southern" portion) reinforce the message I discovered of Francis Bacon as Dauphin of France.

Previously, I've mentioned the cryptograph of the juxtaposition of the Ark atop the mountain, and the winged letter being sent, "spell" ARKADI, de Canada. The pair of birds represent the crow and the dove, however they appear in the shape of the number "4" or 44, which is of course the latitude of Nova Scotia. While this can be downplayed as conjecture, prominent lines in this area of the image produce angles that not only reinforce it by repetition, but they also provide something unusual - the longitude. As difficult as it is to believe, the angles in this area of the artwork produce the coordinates of 44°29' and 64°13', placing us in Mahone Bay, Nova Scotia.

We begin by drawing two straight lines following along the paths of the winged letters being sent, ad I.D.C. on the left and Nostro T.S. on the right. These lines extend entirely across the illustration. This pair of lines meet exactly between the two windows of the building forming an X, and a perfect nexus with the line that separates the windows themselves. The left angle formed by these lines equals 81 (as does the opposite angle) and perfectly frames the travelling figure in the lower left and Noah's Ark on the mountain top.

The measurements of the angles of each quadrant are highly significant. The left and right angles (north and south, respectively) measure 81 and the top and bottom (east and west) measure 99 degrees. The numbers 99 and 81 are highly significant and symbolic for a variety of reasons, not the least of which is the number of 33's they produce. According to Mackey's Encyclopedia of Freemasonry 81 is "a sacred number in the advanced degrees because it is the square of 9, which is again the square of 3. The Pythagoreans however, considered the nine as a fatal number, and especially dreaded eighty-one, because it was produced by the multiplication of nine by itself." However this is not the only hint referring to Pythagorean geometry.

I began by looking within the quadrant containing the Ark on the mountain, as I believed the visual cryptography of the winged letter juxtaposed with the Ark spelled "ArkadI, DC," or "de Canada." As such, I looked for opportunities where lines could be drawn in this direction to see

if any interesting angles appeared. As such, I drew a horizontal baseline using the bottom of the windows as the guide, thereby creating a parallel from which angles could be measured.

The interior angle formed by this base-line created by the bottom of the windows and the line of the left winged-letter measures 47 degrees. While this is a cipher signature using Bacon's cipher system related to my research, the number is significant here for different reasons. First of all, it is the number of Euclid's 47th Problem, the proposition explaining the Pythagorean Theorem. This of course indicates the need for the use of geometry. If we use a bit of Pythagorean math and subtract 47 from the 180 degrees of a triangle, the answer is 133 - the Simple Cipher signature for Baron Verulam. These lines also perfectly "frame-in" the image of the Ark on the mountaintop. All of these clues focus our attention on this area and any lines that might terminate here. In other words, we need to find the angles that will lead us to the place being depicted by the Ark - where is the knowledge of the ancients that needs to be protected at all costs?

The Ark itself provides a part of the answer. By drawing a line suggested by the angle of its roof down towards the building, the angle

perfectly dissects the aforementioned nexus formed by the three other lines (four when including the line between the windows). The alignment of the roofline with the precise point where all of the other lines converge, creates an angle of 44 degrees with the horizontal baseline created by the bottom of the windows. The number 44 is known as a "secret" signature of Francis Bacon. (As I mentioned earlier, the birds near the Ark appear to be number fours with an open top). Additionally in this way, the illustration provides the general latitude of "ArkadI," but as you'll see this can be further refined.

In this image, "errors" in perspective and dimension are clues of where to focus our attention. One such area is the sword arm extending from the building - while intended to be symbolic in nature, its size is an instant

call-sign. Drawing another line through the centerline of this sword, it passes directly through the aforementioned nexus produced by the first two lines and the line between the windows, along the chain of the drawbridge and precisely through the corner of the drawbridge itself. Measuring the angle above the parallel formed by the bottom of the windows gives an angle of 18 degrees, the number of the letter G in Bacon's Reverse Cipher. To me, this is a confirmation of heading in the right direction. The angle formed by the sword line with the original winged letter line measured 29 degrees:

The angle of the Ark's roof and the horizontal baseline, together with the angle provided by the centerline of the sword and the "ad IDC" letter, produce the numbers 44 and 29, which can be read as 44°29'. The latitude of Mahone Bay, Nova Scotia. Amazing as this is, we can also find the longitude using the same technique.

To do so, I scanned over the image to find another "line suggestion." In other areas of my analysis, lines were "suggested" by various straight lines and edges - a walking stick, the base of the building, the drawbridge,

etc. In this instance, if my theory was correct, the source of the line needed to appear in the same quadrant as the Ark, and / or terminate near it. Also, it wouldn't make sense if it was a horizontal line formed by the building, as they seemed to create the "base" from which the angles formed by the other lines are measured. My first candidate was the roofline of the cottage that appears to the left of the building, however the lines were imperfect, and lacked a straight edge.

Yet the angle seemed promising - right beside it I then saw the parallel line formed by the shaded pole supporting the pulley.

Following the exact line suggested by the shaded pole, I extended a line that terminated in the area near the Ark, right at the letter "T" in the word "SEPTENTRIO." As is always the case, the Tau must make its appearance. Using the foundation of the building as the base of the angle, the measure of the interior angle was exactly 64 degrees, the general longitude of Nova Scotia. To refine it still more, I looked no further than the

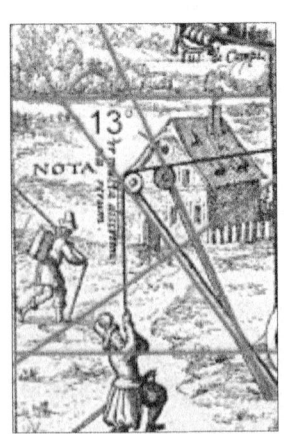

unshaded pole supporting the other pulley. Extending the line upward in the same direction but this time measuring the angle formed by the poles themselves, produces an angle of 13 degrees. The longitude of 64°13' is therefore represented by these "long" poles pointing upward in a vertical manner, like the meridians themselves.

Taken all together, I first observed the possibility of the visual cipher of a phonetic pronunciation of Acadia in the presence of the Ark and the characters on the winged letter, "ad I*D*C," representing "ArkadI, de Canada." By measuring the angles formed by the many straight edges with lines terminating in the same area, we can arrive at the numbers that produce the latitude and longitude coordinates of 44°29' N, 64°13'W. These coordinates place us in the center of Mahone Bay, Nova Scotia, half-way between Big Tancock Island and Oak Island.

The Right Side of the Image

While the left side of the image provides directions in the form of map coordinates disguised within the geometry of the image itself, the right-side of the illustration of the Invisible College reinforces the main message revealed in the cipher-text encoded within the plaque of Shakespeare's Funerary Monument in Trinity Church.

The bombshell information, aside from Bacon claiming responsibility for the Shakespeare project itself and membership in the Rosicrucian Brotherhood, was the revelation of his true parentage. He reveals that his biological parents were Mary Queen of Scots and Francis II of France. As I've already discussed, the iconography on the right side of the illustration verify and reveal the same truths in visual cryptography. However, the story does not end there.

The angles formed from the geometry of the right side of the image reinforce the message in the form of cipher signatures that appear within the cipher texts of Shakespeare's plaque, and echo the story as depicted in the illustration. To simplify the process, due to overlapping lines and confined space, for this section I decided to provide one image containing all of the pertinent lines angles in one image, with the degrees labeling the lines that form the angle. The horizontal lines formed by the foundation of the building and the bottom of the battlement serve as bases for calculating the relevant angles. Each line that the image suggests reaches into this area of the image and terminates at the edge, near the images of the falling figure of Bacon, as well as the image of him with the anchor.

First of all, let's look at the letter exiting the structure with the words "Nostro T*S*." While these are the initials of Theophilus Schweighardt, I have already interpreted them as alsoas meaning "Our own F. (G)Bacon," after using the Reverse Cipher substitution system. The angle of the line attached to it when measured with the horizontal lines of the bottom of the battlement and foundation of the structure, measures 33 which we know is the Simple Cipher signature for "Bacon."

Next, extending a line suggested by the edge of the drawbridge and creating a baseline from the foundation of the building, we have an angle measuring 50 degrees. The number 50 is the Simple Cipher signature for "Fr. III." The line crosses the falling figure at the knees therefore figuratively "cutting him off at the knees," which is what happened to his identity as Francis III of France. This is appropriate as the family de Medici caused his "fall." Taken together, 33 and 50 identify Francis Bacon as Francis III.

The errors in proportion in this area of the structure indicate more messages. Note the length of the foundation on its right side seems to long or wide, and the wheel on the backside of the building is the same size as the closer wheels on the front. Likewise, the length of the bottom of the battlement above seems oversized, and the angle and length are somehow different from the foundation below.

Extending the line of the bottom of the battlement and measuring the angle from the horizontal line formed from the battlement in the front produces an angle of 7 degrees. The number 7 is the letter G in Simple Cipher which is the number 33 in Kaye Cipher, an obvious Bacon signature.

Accentuating the "error" in perspective, using the same procedure for the foundation on the right side, the angle produced by this line and the baseline produced by the front of the foundation is 17 degrees. 17 in Simple Cipher is the letter R. Being next to the kneeling figure.

In summation, I believe that the use of the emblem of a battlement riding upon the Wheels of Fortune is highly symbolic. The RC intended to create their "Republic of Letters" and make it highly mobile, in that they could be free thinkers within any country. By sharing their science and knowledge with one another, they realized they could affect the future (Fortune).

By placing the foundation of their brotherhood on the Wheels of Fortune, I believe they were signaling that they were utilizing this symbol, the Wheel of Fortune - she can make a King a pauper, and a pauper a king. Such was the life of Francis Bacon, the poor widow's son. And so if they utilized that power, they could bring down the monarchies, and raise the common man out of the well of his ignorance. One of the main tools they would use to achieve such an objective was the written word and *secret writing*.

My personal belief due to my work with the ciphered messages on Shakespeare's plaque? If Fortune determined Sir Francis Bacon would not be King of either country he had been born to lead, then he would take control of Fortune, and *there would be no kings.*

This Illustration of The Invisible College contains confirmation of the messages of the cipher texts hidden in the plaque of Shakespeare's Funerary Monument in Holy Trinity Church in Stratford-upon-Avon, most notably Bacon's true identity and the location of the Rosicrucian "Ark" where they preserved their most important truths and knowledge – Mahone Bay, Nova Scotia.

Appendix C – The Cipher Signatures

Given all of the messages and the new information about Sir Francis Bacon they contain, I thought it would be appropriate to add significant numbers to my original list of cipher signatures. In light of Bacon's revelations regarding his royal parents, the following names should be considered for calculations of cipher signatures: Fr. III, Francis III, Francois, Francois III, Francois Stuart, King Francis III and King Francois III or Roi Francois.

Cipher Signatures used in the Cipher Encoded within Shakespeare's Memorial Plaque - Trinity Church Stratford upon Avon

Name	Simple Cipher	Reverse Cipher	Kaye Cipher
William	74	101	152
Shakespeare	103	172	259
Francois	81	119	185
Francois Stuart	175	175	305
Francis	67	108	171
Bacon	33	92	111
Francis Bacon	100	200	282
Baron Verulam	133	167	237
Fra Rosi Crosse	157	168	287
King Bacon	72	153	202
King Francis III	133	181	289
King Francois III	147	228	381
Francois III	**108**	**167**	290

Fr. III	50	75	137
Iames	45	80	123
Stewart	100	75	152
Iames Stewart	145	155	275
Mary	53	47	79
Mary Stewart	153	112	231
Queen of Scots	151	149	255
Frater(s)	65(83)	85(92)	143(161)

Adding the values of the titles Rex, King and Roi also produce significant numbers.

Prime Numbers appearing as signatures: 47, 53, 67 (19th = Tau), 79, 83, 101, 103, 137 (33rd = Bacon), 157 (37th), 167 (39th = C I), 181 (42nd),

Significant Correlations

137 = 33rd prime number. Also Simple Cipher signature of "Dauphin Francis" (70 + 67 = 137).
Stuart = 94, Simple signature of "Mary Stuart" = 147, same as "King Francois III."
193 = 44th and Tau "C," or See Truth.

Illustrations and Images

All images used fall under fair use doctrine under Wikimedia Commons, as two dimensional images created in the 17th century.

All Google Earth / Stellarium images used fall under the user guidelines for both companies. By using their software and displaying the images, I make no proprietary claims regarding their use.

Works Cited

Case, Paul Foster. *The True and Invisible Rosicrucian Order*. Boston: Red Wheel / Weiser, LLC, 1989. Print.

"Chronology Related To Francis Bacon's Life". *Sirbacon.Org*, 2021, http://www.sirbacon.org/links/chronos.html. Accessed 27 Mar 2021.

Dawkins, Peter. *http://www.fbrt.org.uk/wp-content/uploads/2020/06/The_Secret_Signature.pdf*. June 2020. Web. 1 July 2020.

Friedman, William. *Sources in Cryptologic History Number 3: The Friedman Legacy*. Washington DC: National Security Agency, 2006. Electronic.

Hall, Manly Palmer. "Francis Bacon and his Secret Empire." *Horizon: Journal of the Philosophic Research Society*. Summer, 1946. Volume 6, No. 1. Manlyhall.Org, 2021, http://www.manlyhall.org/prsjournals/horizon/horizon-0701-summer-1947.pdf. Accessed 14 Aug 2021

Hall, Manly Palmer. *The Secret Teachings of All Ages*. New York: Penguine, 2003. Print.

Lunsford, Virginia. *Piracy and Privateering in the Golden Age Netherlands*. Palgrave Macmillan, New York: 2005.

"Mackey's Encyclopedia Of Freemasonry - E". Phoenixmasonry.Org, 2021, http://www.phoenixmasonry.org/mackeys_encyclopedia/e.htm. Accessed 19 Jan 2021.

Peters, Gregory H. "The Stone which the Builders Refused." n.d. *Peitre Stones Review of Freemasonry*. Web. 21 May 2020. <http://www.freemasons-freemasonry.com/stone_refused.html>.

"Samuel De Champlain | The Canadian Encyclopedia". *Thecanadianencyclopedia.Ca*, 2021, https://www.thecanadianencyclopedia.ca/en/timeline/samuel-de-champlain. Accessed 27 Mar 2021.

"Universal Freemasonry." n.d.

"Voltaire's Essay On Francis Bacon". *Www-Personal.K-State.Edu*, 2021, http://www-personal.k-state.edu/~lyman/english233/Voltaire-Bacon.htm. Accessed 27 Mar 2021.

Printed in Great Britain
by Amazon

48995786R00209